Crafts, Cookery, and Country Living

MW00632741

Kathleen
from Ed 1977

Crafts, Cookery, and Country Living

Kim Victoria Abeles

VNR VAN NOSTRAND REINHOLD COMPANY
NEW YORK CINCINNATI TORONTO LONDON MELBOURNE

Copyright (c) 1976 by Litton Educational Publishing, Inc.

Library of Congress Catalog Card Number 76-6914

ISBN 0-442-20236-9

All rights reserved. No part of this work covered by the copyright hereon may be reproduced or used in any form or by any means -- graphic, electronic, or mechanical, including photocopying, recording, taping, or information storage and retrieval systems -- without written permission of the publisher.

Printed in the United States of America.

Published in 1976 by Van Nostrand Reinhold Company
A division of Litton Educational Publishing, Inc.
450 West 33rd Street, New York, NY 10001

Van Nostrand Reinhold Limited
1410 Birchmount Road, Scarborough, Ontario M1P 2E7, Canada

Van Nostrand Reinhold Australia Pty. Limited
17 Queen Street, Mitcham, Victoria 3132, Australia

Van Nostrand Reinhold Company Limited
Molly Millars Lane, Wokingham, Berkshire, England

16 15 14 13 12 11 10 9 8 7 6 5 4 3 2 1

Library of Congress Cataloging in Publication Data

Abeles, Kim Victoria, 1952–
Crafts, cookery and country living.

Bibliography: p.
Includes index.
1. Handicraft. 2. Cookery. I. Title.
TT157.A2 745.5 76-6914
ISBN 0-442-20236-9

The dedication is a reflection after writing a book...
to Ken and the unbelievable artwork called life & perception;
to Ken because his goodness & patience help me through the oddities of thought.
A special thanks to Rich Hunter, who guided me past the winter '74-5;
to Bill & Judy Morgan for enabling us to live in the silo, therefore to enjoy the earth;
& to a number of good people finding wisdom in their own unique direction.

Contents

Introduction

CRAFTS, COOKERY, AND COUNTRY LIVING is a collection of processes involving arts, crafts, and natural or manufactured materials. It is an introduction to activities of the senses and new experiences to stimulate further involvement in artistic and living endeavors.

Nature and the bountiful countryside are woven throughout these pages, directly or indirectly; indirectly because the arts we enjoy are an arrangement of the movements and correlations surrounding us; directly when one makes tangible use of the treasures outdoors. There can be no exaggerations about Nature's beauty of design, function, and delightful details. Absorbing the open air, earth, and life is enriching and full of thoughtful intrigue.

PATCHWORK
PATCHWORK
PATCHWORK
PATCHWORK
PatchWork
Patchwork
Patchwork

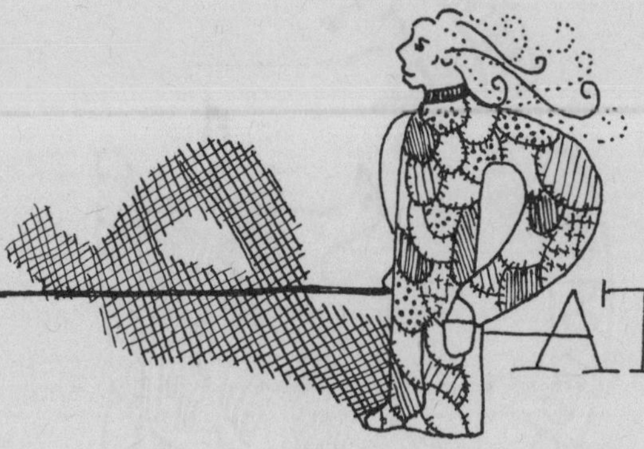

PATCHWORK

The versatility of patchwork and the potential economy excites the imagination. Specifically, any thing that can be sewn can become a pattern of varied colors, textures, and shapes. Use of a sewing machine hastens completion and beautifully old pump machines of grandmother's age can be purchased reasonably and run without electricity. However, hand-sewing is also possible and has its own "earthy" characteristics. Ask friends for scraps of fabric and take a peek in granny's basement ~ old, fantastic fabrics can usually be found disguised as old clothing. Batik, woodcut printing, and natural dyeing can also be used to transform white or solid color material (techniques found in later sections of book.) Embroidery and appliqué are possible additions amid or upon the patches. Generally, embroidery is used to decorate small areas and lines, while appliqué depicts larger areas of color. Used together, the possibilities are limitless ~ anything from naturalism to abstraction. For men, women, and children, hand sewing offers a creative outlet and tranquil pastime.

Embroidery

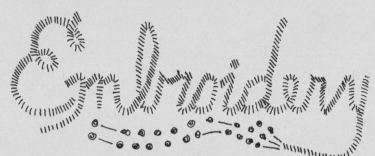

Embroidery thread (which comes in NUMEROUS colors), a needle, and a pair of scissors or a pocket knife are the essential tools for embroidery. A hoop is also useful and inexpensive, but not always necessary. To use the hoop:

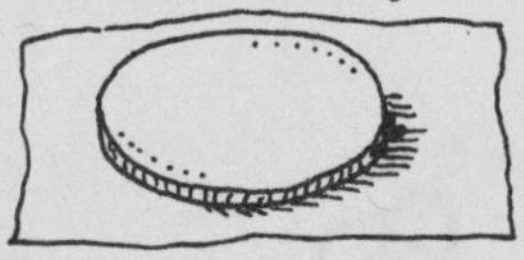

LAY THE INSIDE HOOP ON A TABLE; PLACE THE FABRIC ATOP*; PUSH THE OUTER HOOP ONTO THE FIRST.
*TO KEEP SMUDGE OFF LIGHT COLOR FABRIC, PLACE TISSUE PAPER OVER FABRIC THEN PUSH OUTER HOOP OVER BOTH. CUT OUT PAPER OVER AREA TO BE STITCHED.

Embroidery thread comes in small packages containing a length of 6 strands. Use 2 OR 3 strands, cut to a comfortable length for sewing (about 2½ feet). Here is an easy method of separating the 6 strands, that my mother taught me years ago:

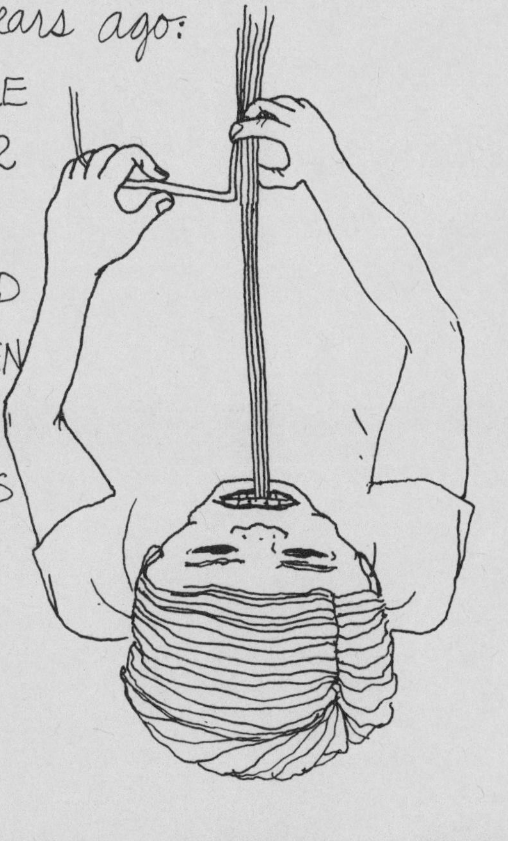

CUT THE 6 STRANDS TO A COMFORTABLE LENGTH ... AT ONE END, SEPARATE 2 STRANDS (OR 3) FROM THE REST.... HOLD THE 2 STRANDS IN LEFT HAND AND PUT THE OTHER FOUR BETWEEN YOUR TEETH .... PULL THE 2 STRANDS STEADILY, SLIDING RIGHT FINGERS DOWN TO THE END;
THE 4 STRANDS WILL TWIRL AS YOU PULL TO THE END.

Embroidery Stitches

STRAIGHT STITCH

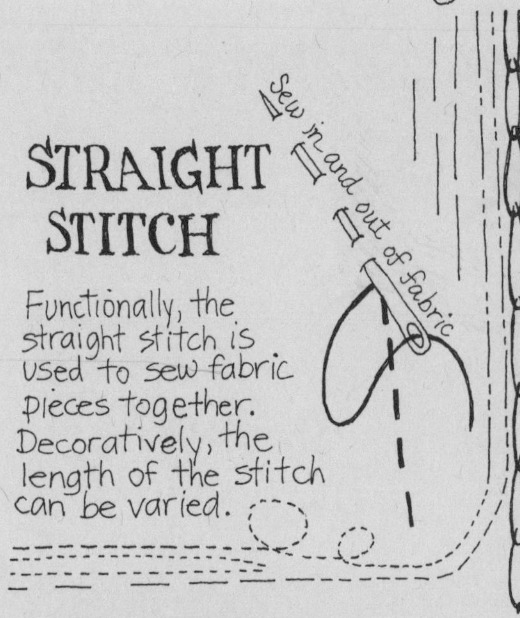
Sew in and out of fabric

Functionally, the straight stitch is used to sew fabric pieces together. Decoratively, the length of the stitch can be varied.

CHAIN STITCH

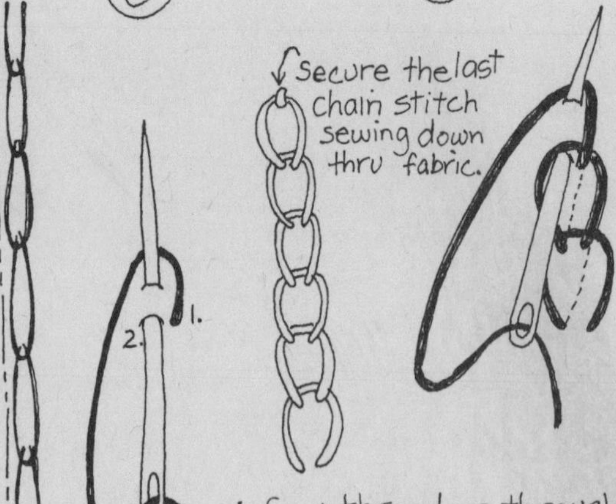
Secure the last chain stitch sewing down thru fabric.
1.
2.

Secure twice for wide chain stitches

1. Sew thread up through fabric
2. To the left of 1., sew in and out of fabric, looping thread behind needle. Pull thru and begin next chain stitch.

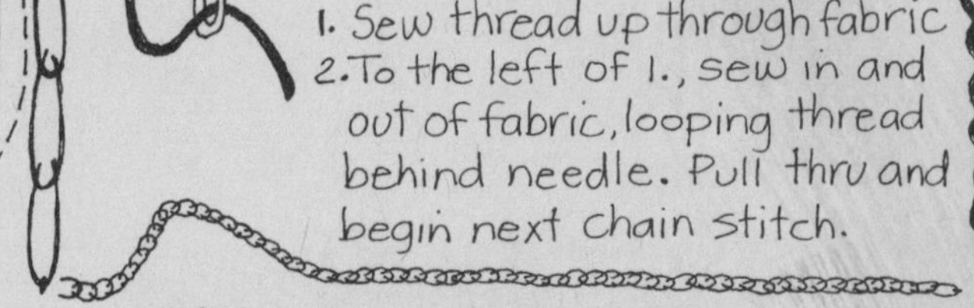

FRENCH KNOT

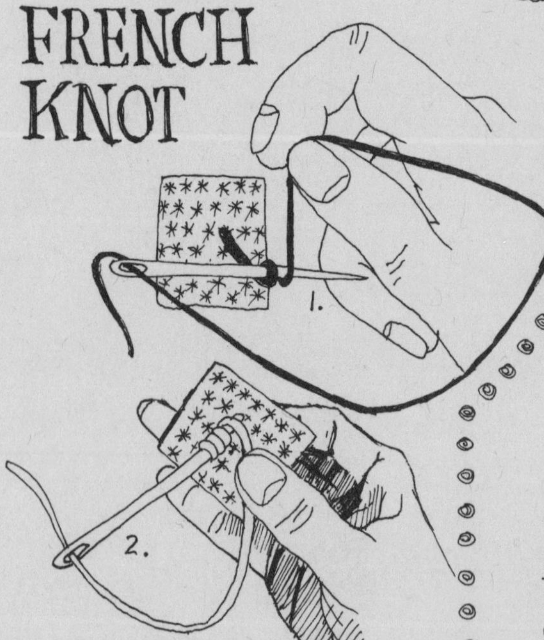
1.
2.

1. Pull needle and thread up through fabric. Wind the thread around needle 3-5 times.
2. Pull thread to slightly tighten the wrapped thread closer to the fabric. Insert needle close to thread entrance point of 1. Pull thru and move under the fabric to the next french knot.

SATIN STITCH

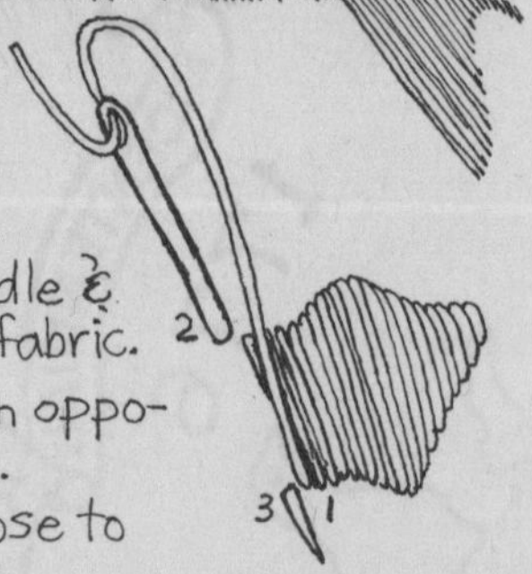
2
3
1

1. Begin by pulling needle & thread up through fabric.
2. Push needle through opposite edge of design.
3. then, up through close to the thread from 1.

wide satin stitch

Space exit and entry points of needle as wide as desired.

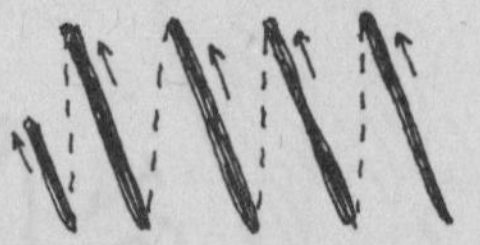

The satin stitch is used to fill in small areas of design or monograms. (Lettering at the back of this book can be used.) Mark the design or letters onto the fabric; free-hand with tailor's chalk;

OR
1. trace the design onto paper
2. Lay out fabric, with dressmaker's tracing paper over the area of the design.
3. Align the traced design on the tracing paper.
4. Mark with the tracing wheel.

Tracing Wheel

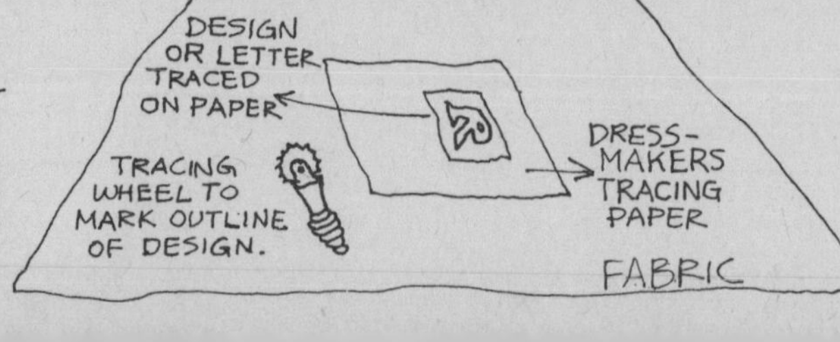
DESIGN OR LETTER TRACED ON PAPER
DRESS-MAKERS TRACING PAPER
TRACING WHEEL TO MARK OUTLINE OF DESIGN.
FABRIC

BACKSTITCH

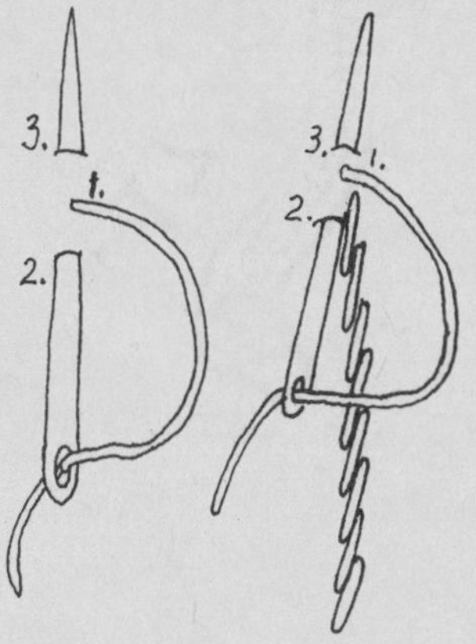
3.
1.
2.
3.
1.
2.

1. Bring thread up through fabric.
2. Bring the needle back and insert through fabric. Push needle forward and past 1. and,
3. move needle up through fabric. Pull thread thru and begin next backstitch.

COUCHING

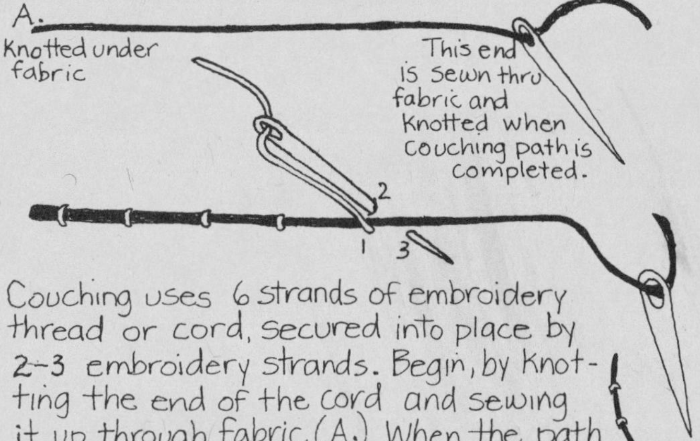
A.
Knotted under fabric
This end is sewn thru fabric and knotted when couching path is completed.
2
1
3

Couching uses 6 strands of embroidery thread or cord, secured into place by 2-3 embroidery strands. Begin, by knotting the end of the cord and sewing it up through fabric (A.) When the path of the couching is completed, sew the cording through the fabric and knot.

1. Bring 2-3 strands of thread up through fabric next to the cord.
2. Insert the needle through fabric on the other side of the cord, and
3. Push needle forward and exit from other side of cord. Pull through and continue couching.

CROSS-STITCH

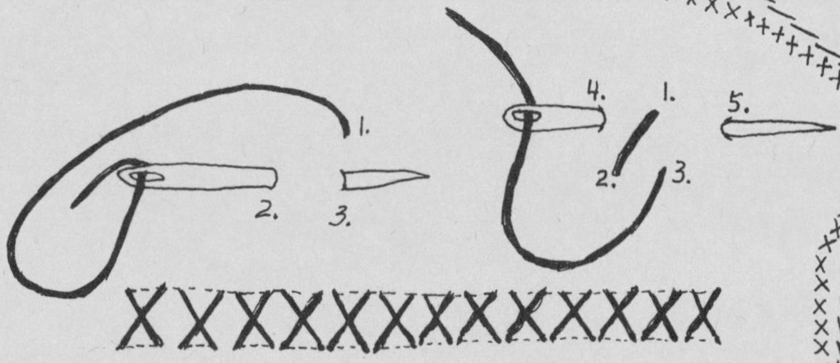
1.
2.
3.
4.
1.
5.
2.
3.

1. Bring thread up through fabric.
2. Insert needle at a point to the lower left of 1., and
3. Push needle under fabric and up through, below 1. Pull through.
4. Insert needle above 2. and,
5. Push needle under fabric, past 1. and up through—(5. will be point 1. for the next cross-stitch.) Pull through and begin next cross stitch.

SLIP STITCH

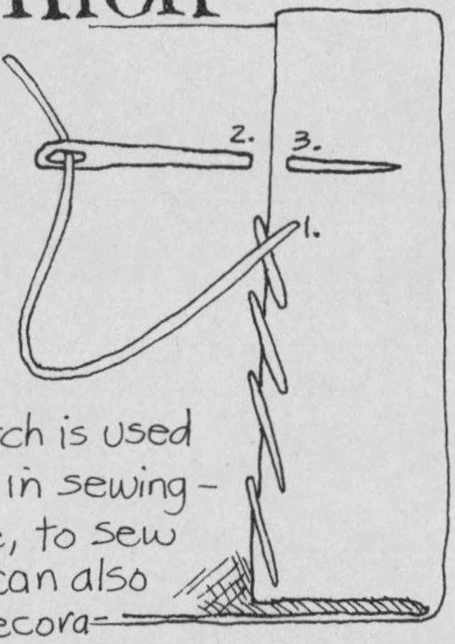
2.
3.
1.

The slip stitch is used functionally in sewing—for example, to sew hems, but can also be used decoratively.

1. Bring thread up through fabric.
2. Insert needle to the upper left of 1. and,
3. Push needle under fabric and up through, above 1. (For hems, the distance between 2. and 3. should be as short as possible). Pull thru and begin next slip stitch.

Books for more ideas and embroidery:

CREWEL EMBROIDERY by Erica Wilson; New York: Charles Scribner's Sons, 1962.

STITCHERY - FREE EXPRESSION by Ann Woelders; New York: Van Nostrand Reinhold Co., 1973.

APPLIQUÉ

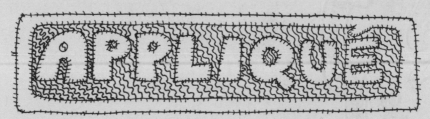

Appliqué is a fairly fast and flexible method of stitchery, depending on the simplicity or intricacy of the design. Technically:

1. CUT OUT THE DESIRED SHAPE(S) AND COLOR(S), LEAVING ¼" SEAM ALLOWANCE.

2. PIN THE SHAPE TO THE FABRIC TO BE APPLIQUÉD.

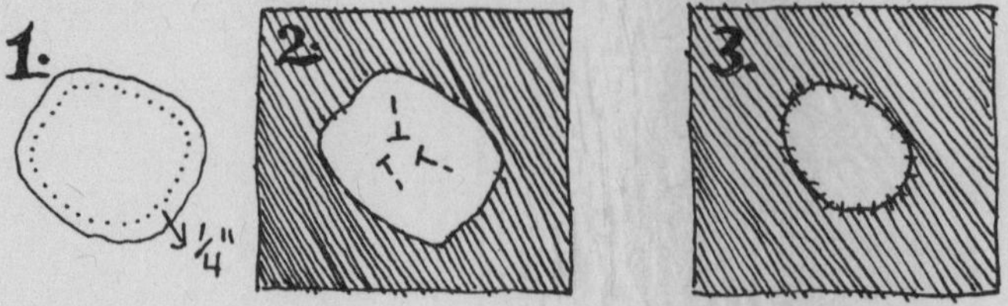
1.
¼"
2.
3.

3. TURN UNDER SEAM ALLOWANCE AND SEW EDGES DOWN WITH A **BLIND STITCH**

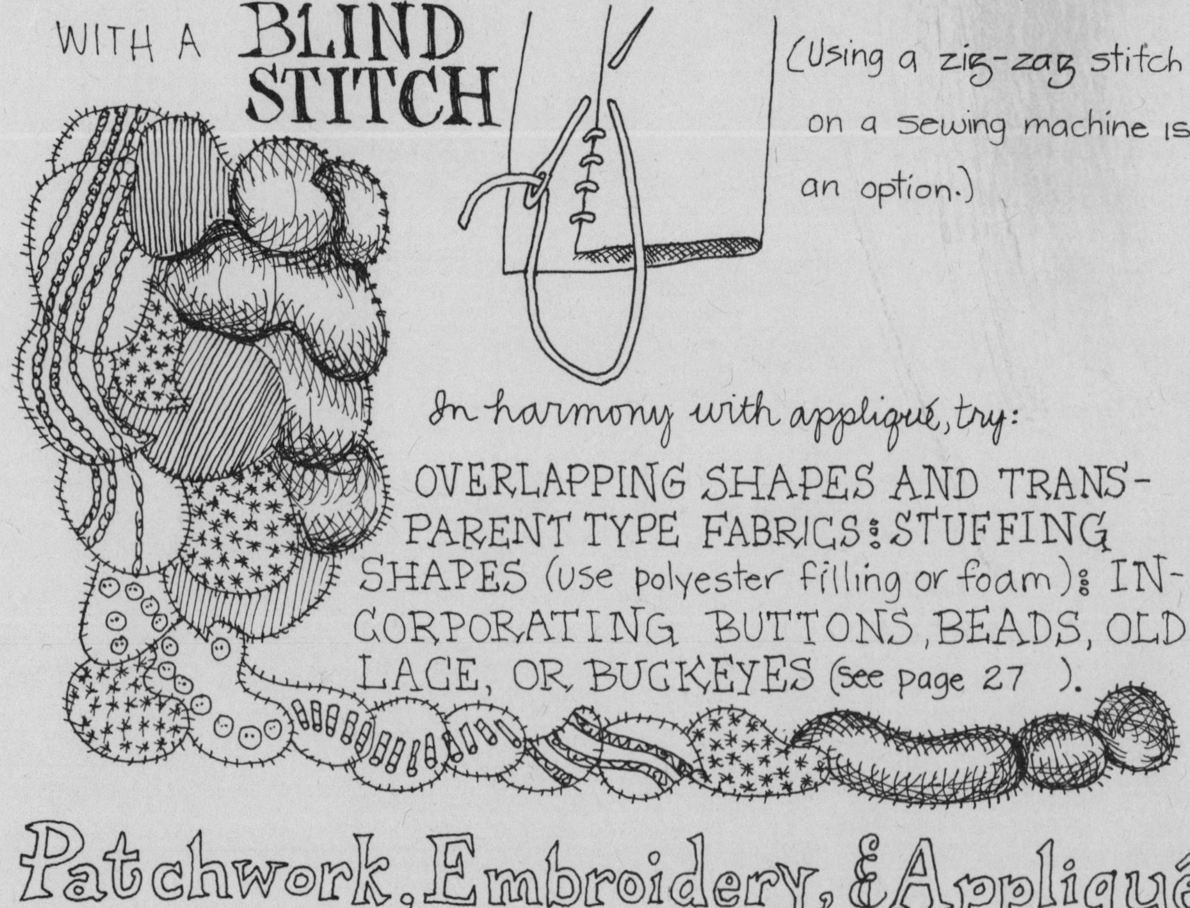

(Using a zig-zag stitch on a sewing machine is an option.)

In harmony with appliqué, try:

OVERLAPPING SHAPES AND TRANSPARENT TYPE FABRICS: STUFFING SHAPES (use polyester filling or foam): INCORPORATING BUTTONS, BEADS, OLD LACE, OR BUCKEYES (see page 27).

Patchwork, Embroidery, & Appliqué

CAN BE USED TOGETHER OR SEPARATELY ON ANYTHING THAT CAN BE SEWN:

tablecloths ... skirts ... shirts ... sweaters ... pants ... hats potholders ... upholstery ... quilts ... purses ... placemats coats ... belts ... wall hangings ... pillows ...

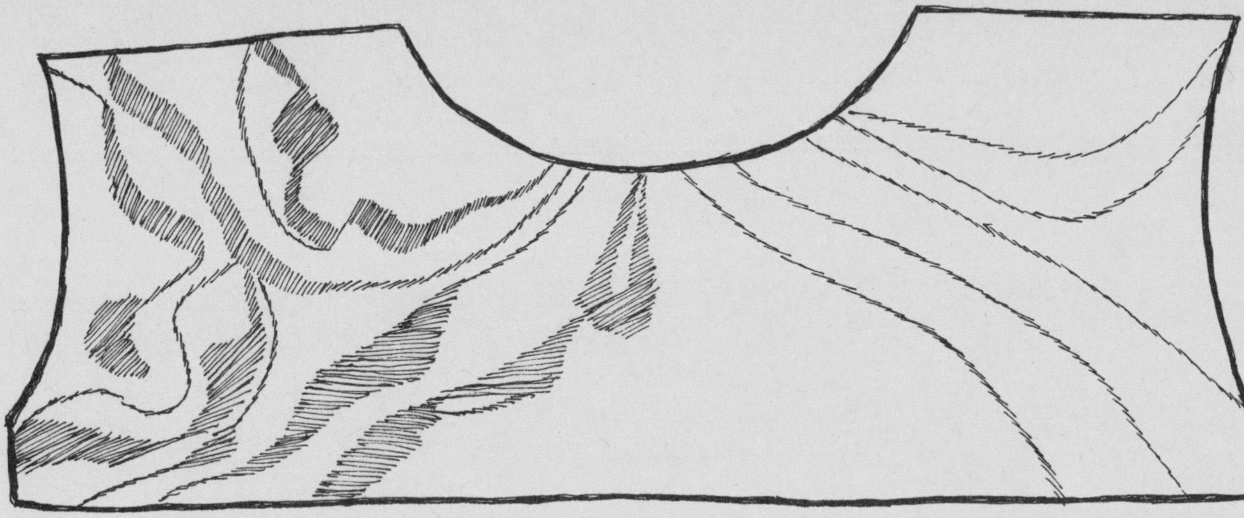

Satin Stitch　　Backstitch

Yokes

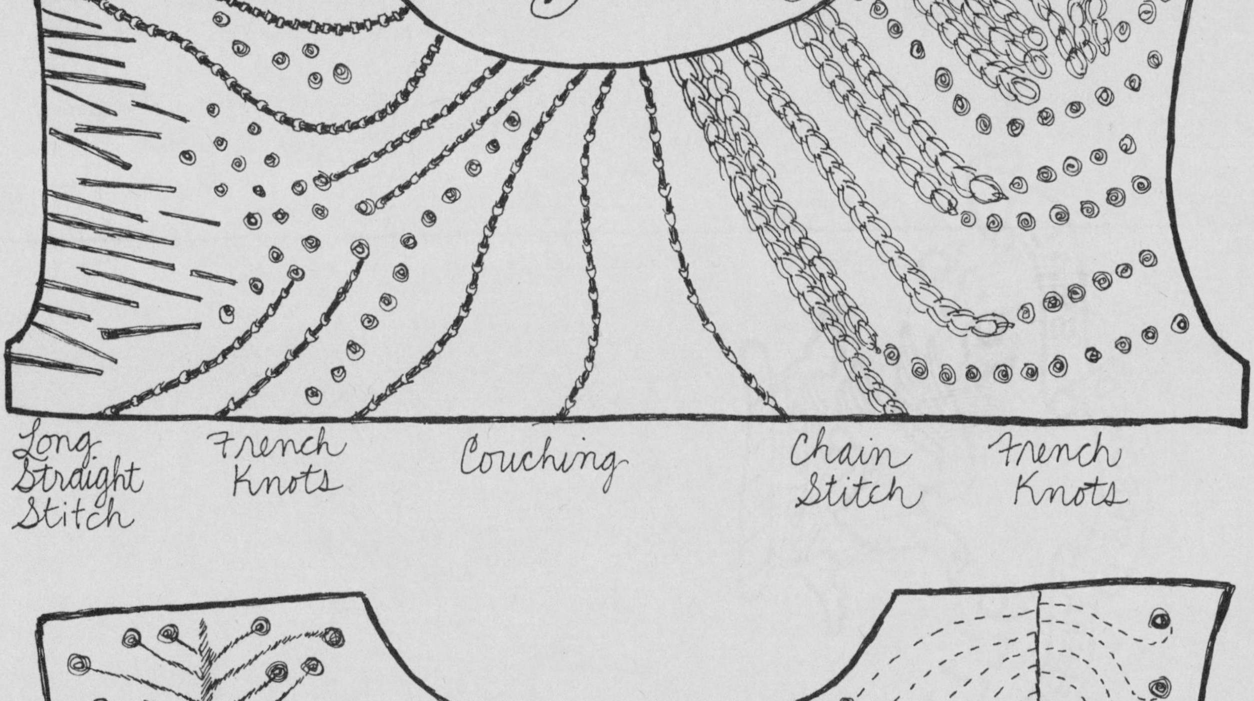

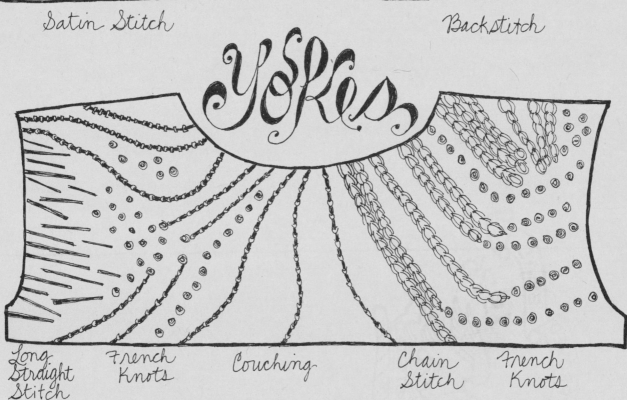

Long Straight Stitch　　French Knots　　Couching　　Chain Stitch　　French Knots

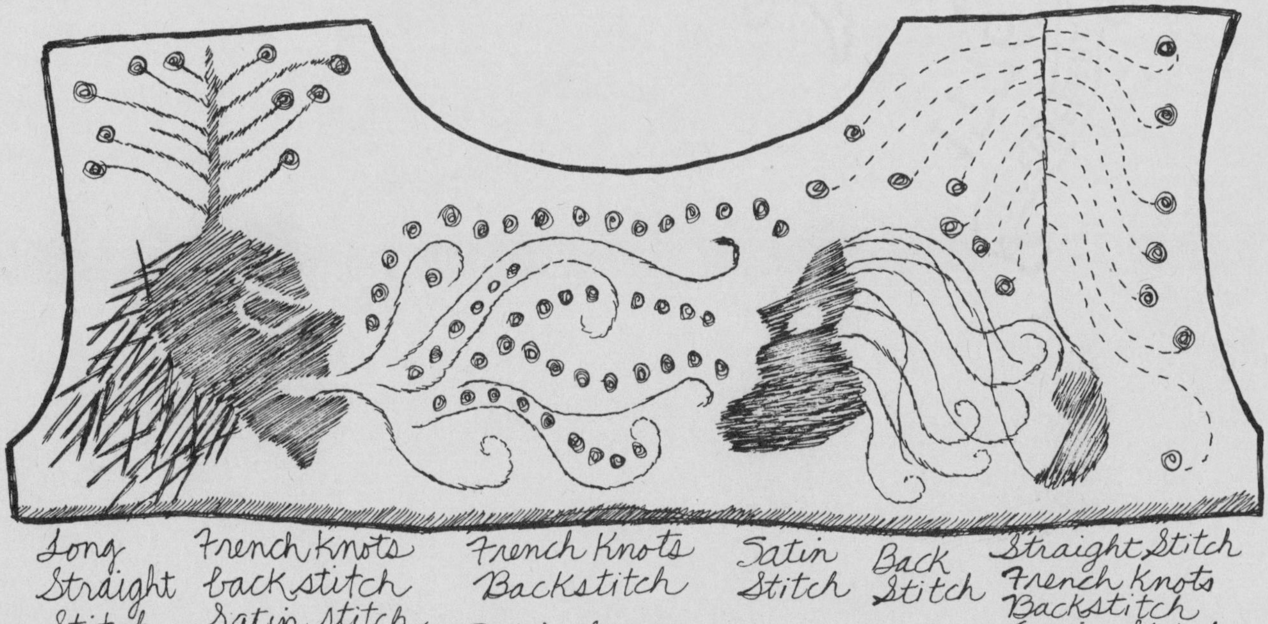

Long Straight Stitch　　French Knots back stitch Satin Stitch　　French Knots Backstitch　　Satin Stitch　　Back Stitch　　Straight Stitch French Knots Backstitch Satin Stitch

Satin Stitch along base

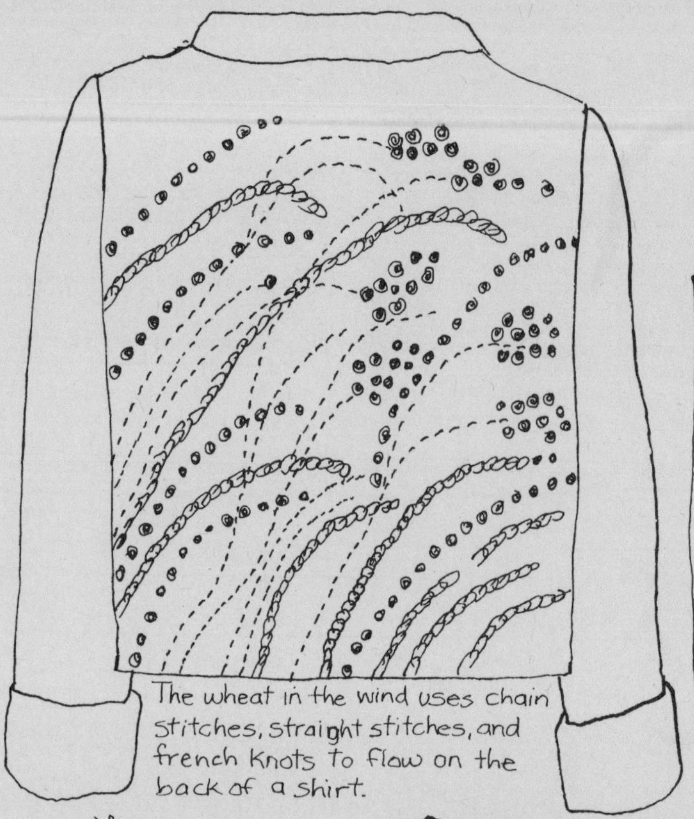

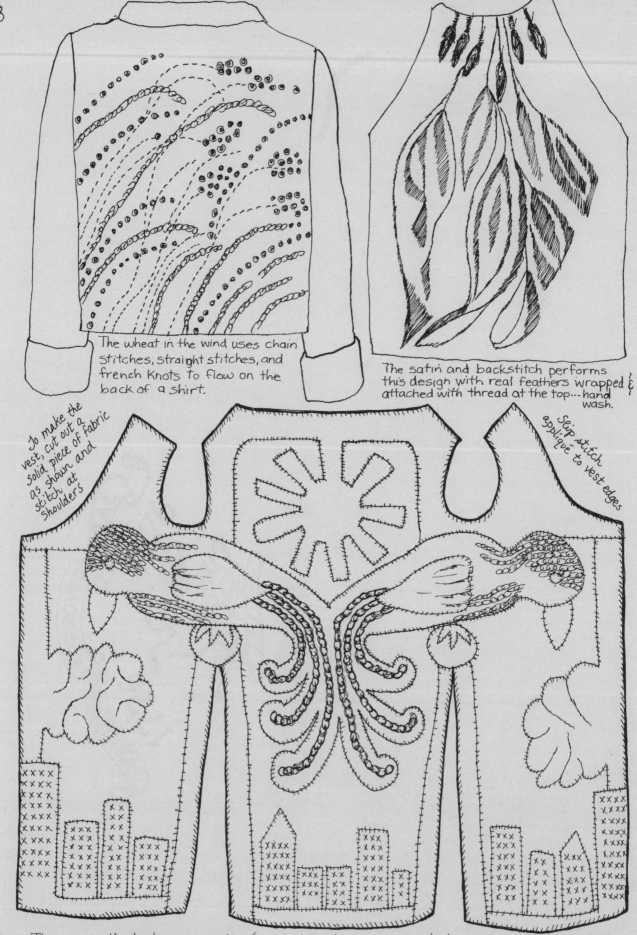

The wheat in the wind uses chain stitches, straight stitches, and french knots to flow on the back of a shirt.

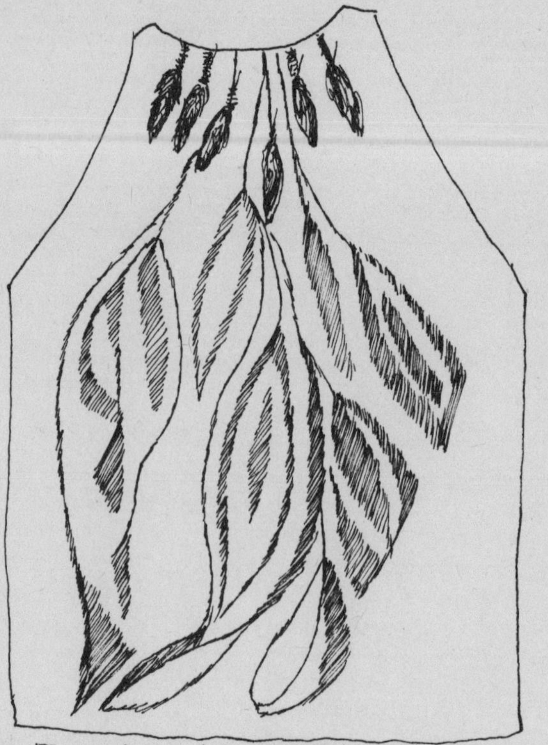

The satin and backstitch performs this design with real feathers wrapped & attached with thread at the top... hand wash.

To make the vest, cut out a solid piece of fabric as shown and stitch at shoulders
Slip stitch appliqué to vest edges

This vest illustrates an appliqué suited to the garment. Windows are cross-stitched before appliqué is blind-stitched onto the vest; whereas, bird pieces are appliquéd first and then secured and decorated with the chain stitch. The wing of each bird is gathered to create a slight puffy effect. Clouds are backstitched after appliqué.

The Quilt

The making of a quilt can be done quickly and simply or can become the season's project..... hopefully before winter summons the fire. Whatever method or style of quilt, the result is a cozy, personal, and unique comfort.

Quilt 1 one one one

SUPPLIES:

Fabric: generally cut into squares although interlocking shapes can be used.
Thread: quilting thread, embroidery thread, and regular sewing thread for any appliqué.
Scissors
Needles and pins
Cardboard
Tailor chalk = a good marker to have for all sewing projects.
Batting (found in fabric stores)
Top sheet in the size you wish your quilt **PLUS** 4 inches around; sheeting by the yard is also available.
Quilting frame is quite optional, but makes the quilting of the 3 layers easier. The frame is rather inexpensive new or used.

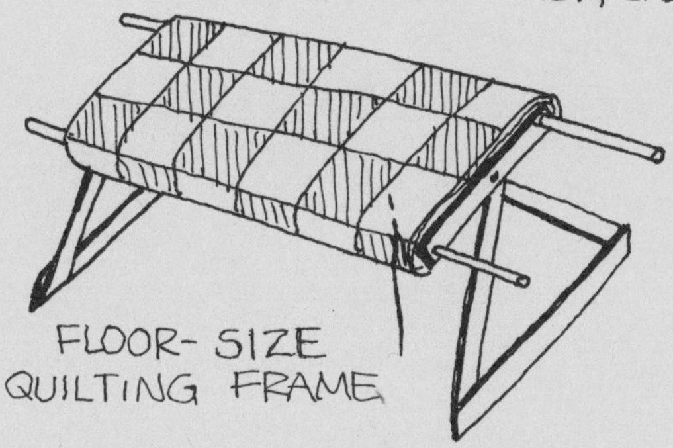

FLOOR-SIZE QUILTING FRAME

THIS QUILT INCLUDES 3 LAYERS OF WARMTH

QUILT
BATTING
SHEETING

instructions:

1. Cut sheeting to size of desired quilt PLUS 4 inches around. Lay out and use to check number of squares needed.
2. Cut a piece of cardboard into a square, triangle, or other geometric shape— BE SURE TO ADD A ½" SEAM ALLOWANCE.
3. Place the cardboard pattern on fabric and trace around with tailor chalk. Cut out squares.
4. Lay the squares on sheeting, overlapping seam allowances; rearranging squares as you like.

5. If you've planned embroidery or appliqué on individual squares, now is the best time.

6. Sew squares together, one row at a time, then rows sewn together. By hand, use a straight stitch by putting right sides of fabric together and sewing up seam. Or, fold under one seam allowance, lapping it over the allowance of the second square, and attach with a blind stitch.

WRONG SIDE
WRONG SIDE
RIGHT SIDES

WITH STRAIGHT STITCH

WITH BLIND STITCH

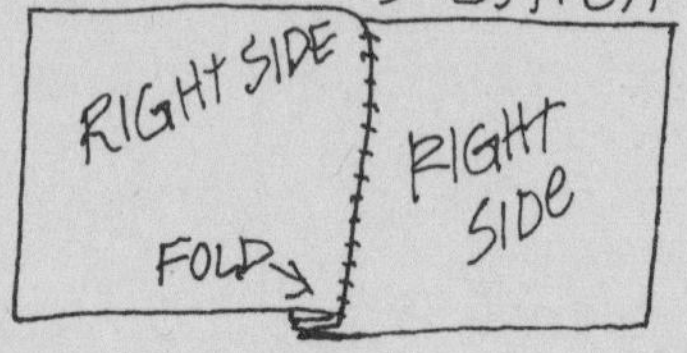
RIGHT SIDE
RIGHT SIDE
FOLD

7. Lay out sheeting; unroll batting on top to the same size as sheeting... there may be excess batting which is cut off and arranged on the batting for extra thickness. Place the patchwork as the 3rd layer. Pin layers together on edges and within. If using a quilting frame, roll onto bars.

8. Here are 2 ways to quilt the 3 layers together.

Quilting

Use tailor chalk or a line of pins to mark straight or curved lines on the patchwork quilt. Follow the lines with a straight stitch through all 3 layers.

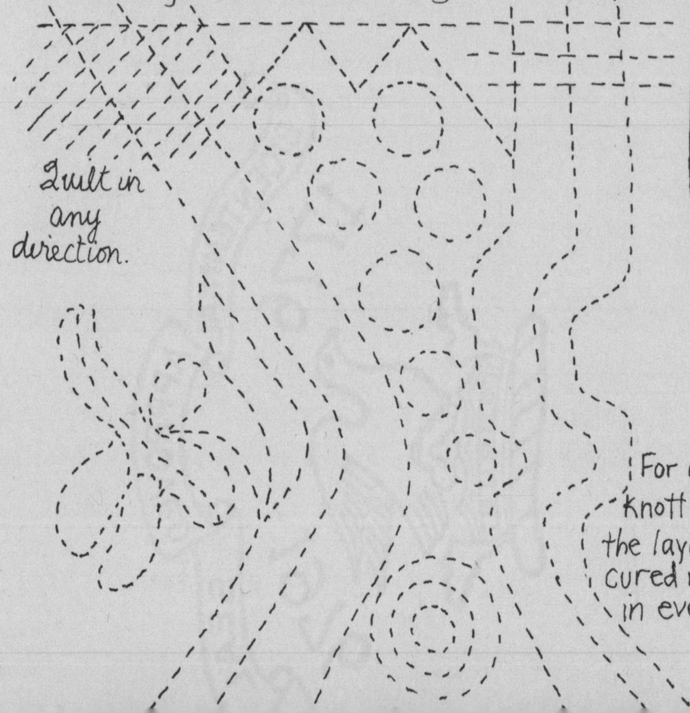
Quilt in any direction.

Knotting

Using a needle and thin yarn or carpet thread, knot the layers together. Knot each square or in a direction-just making sure that there is a knot 3 inches in every direction. (If knots are farther apart than 3 inches - the batting will scatter into a few large wads when washing the quilt.)

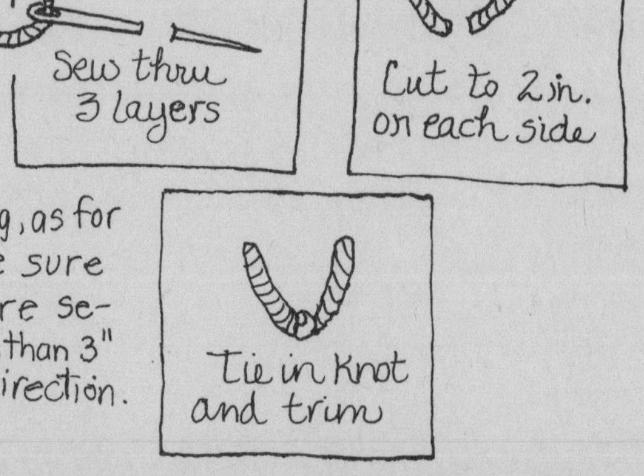
Sew thru 3 layers
Pull thru
Cut to 2 in. on each side
Tie in knot and trim

For quilting, as for knotting, be sure the layers are secured no less than 3" in every direction.

9. A cost-free way to finish the quilt uses the extra 4 inches of sheeting and batting. Fold over both onto the patchwork, also folding under ½" of the sheeting edge. Pin, over ½" of the patchwork edge and sew together with a blind stitch.

SHEETING
½" of patchwork edge; & sheeting folded under
PATCHWORK
Fold and blind stitch corners.

(OPTIONAL: Blanket binding can be added over edge; sew the binding on front and back with a blind stitch.)

Quilt 2 Two Two Two

Quilt 2 is a pillowy, reversible style with colorful patches on both sides; or muslin patches on one side. Patches can be geometric shapes or interlocking forms.

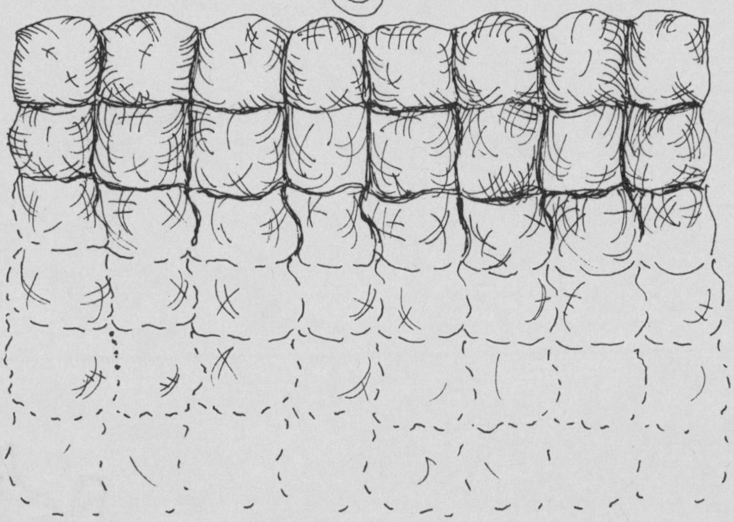

SUPPLIES:

Thread- quilting thread or polyester sewing thread, embroidery thread if desired
Scissors
Needles and pins
Fabric for patches and any appliqué
Tailor chalk
Card board
Polyester filling

instructions:

1. Cut out a cardboard pattern and use to trace on fabric as for *Quilt 1*, Steps 2 & 3. (The pattern should be at least 5" x 5"). Cut out the necessary number of patches for the desired quilt size, keep in mind that patches are needed for the **FRONT & BACK**.
2. Add embroidery and appliqué now, if desired.

3. Rearrange patches for front and back as you like. Then, place a front and back patch with right sides together. Sew along all but 1 side with a straight stitch (½" seam allowance) Turn inside out and press open seam edges in. Repeat for all patches.

wrong side
CLIP ANGLE
wrong side
OPEN SEAM FOLDED IN
Right Side

4. Fill each 'pillow' with polyester filling so that it is puffy but **not** packed tight.

5. Begin sewing rows of pillows, by sewing an open seam end of a pillow with the closed end of the next, using a slip stitch or straight stitch. Continue sewing pillows together in the same way; then sew the rows together.

Slip Stitch
Straight Stitch

• *Quilt 2 can be constructed from any interlocking shapes. In the following designs, dimensions for the cardboard pattern are given— use as many shapes as needed for the desired size of quilt.*

After sewing, clip curves and corners as needed.

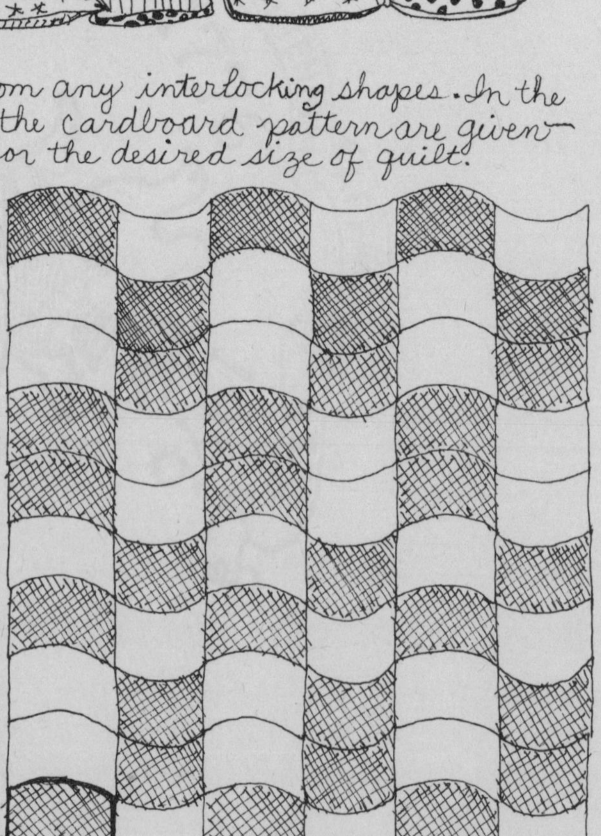

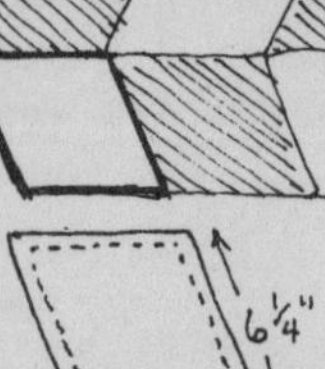
6¼"
6"

Pattern dimensions include ½" seam allowance.

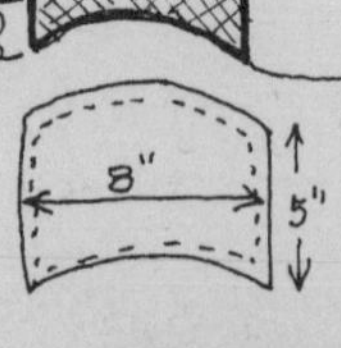
8"
5"

Pattern dimensions include ½" seam allowance

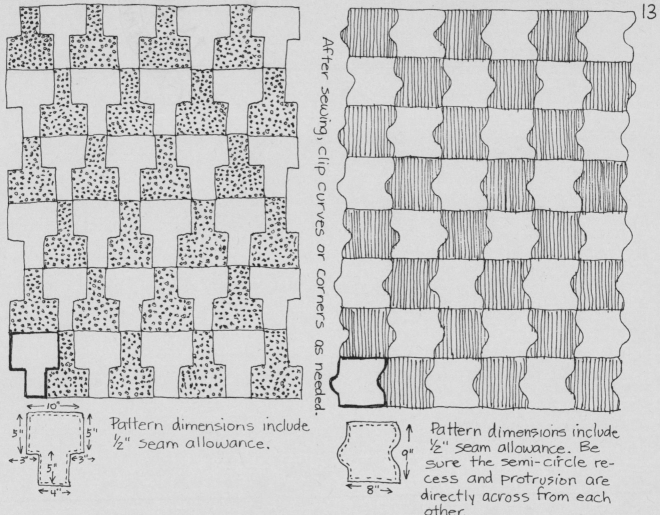

After sewing, clip curves or corners as needed.

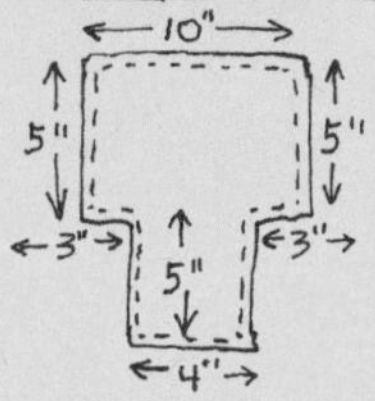
10"
5"
5"
3"
3"
5"
4"

Pattern dimensions include ½" seam allowance.

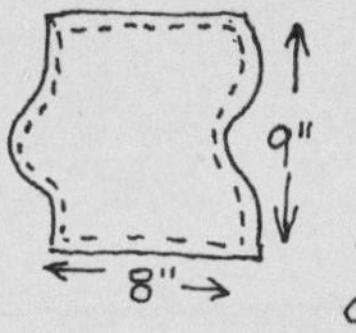
9"
8"

Pattern dimensions include ½" seam allowance. Be sure the semi-circle recess and protrusion are directly across from each other.

The following pages include quilt designs with the dimensions and basic instructions written below. Quilting lines are not shown when they would interfere with the clarity of visual description. Size can be altered by increasing or decreasing, 1. the number of squares, 2. the size of the squares, 3. the dimensions of border pieces. The designs have been constructed according to Quilt 1, but can easily be modified for Quilt 2 by dividing any solid fabric areas into smaller pillows (no more than 1'×1'—including ½" seam allowance).

Books for more ideas about quiltmaking:

COMPLETE GUIDE TO QUILTING by Aubrey Heard and Beverly Pryor; Des Moines, Iowa: Better Homes and Gardens Books, 1974.

AMERICA'S QUILTS AND COVERLETS by Carleton L. Safford and Robert Bishop; New York: E. P. Dutton & Co., Inc., 1974.

Quilt size: 63½" x 93½" Size of squares: 8½" x 8½" (allows for ½" seam allowance around) - 84 squares
Size of center fabric: 16" x 46" (allows for ½" seam allowance around)

The appliquéd birds are felt pieces, and because felt is not a woven fabric, it does not need a ¼" seam allowance folded under. Appliqué onto center fabric before constructing the quilt.

Sew together, patchwork to left and right of center section and center fabric; then sew top 3 and bottom three rows of patchwork to the middle patchwork and solid fabric. The outer patchwork is quilted diagonally and the center is knotted 3 inches in each direction.

Quilt size: 63½" x 87½" Size of squares: 4" x 4" (allows for ½" seam allowance.)

Size of center fabric: 73" x 19" (allows for ½" seam allowance)

Use three solid colors or prints for the squares and opening circles.

88 squares 92 squares 236 squares

Center fabric is a 4th fabric choice.

Knot or quilt. Circles, appliquéd.

Quilt size: 71½" x 83½"   Size of larger triangles: (9¾", 9¾", 13¾"), 40 triangles.
First, Sew 2 together, forming squares 9" x 9" (allows for ½" seam allowance)

Size of smaller triangles: (5¾", 5¾", 8⅛") 88 triangles
Sew 2 together forming squares 5" x 5", (allows for ½" seam allowance.)

Size of center fabric: 17" x 17" (allows for ½" seam allowance.)
Size of top and bottom fabric: 69" x 13"; Size of sides: 15" x 57" (allows for ½" seam allowance around.) Quilt intended for solid color fabric – basically, maintain light and dark relationship. Quilt with color quilting thread, as shown and also on patchwork (or knot patchwork.)

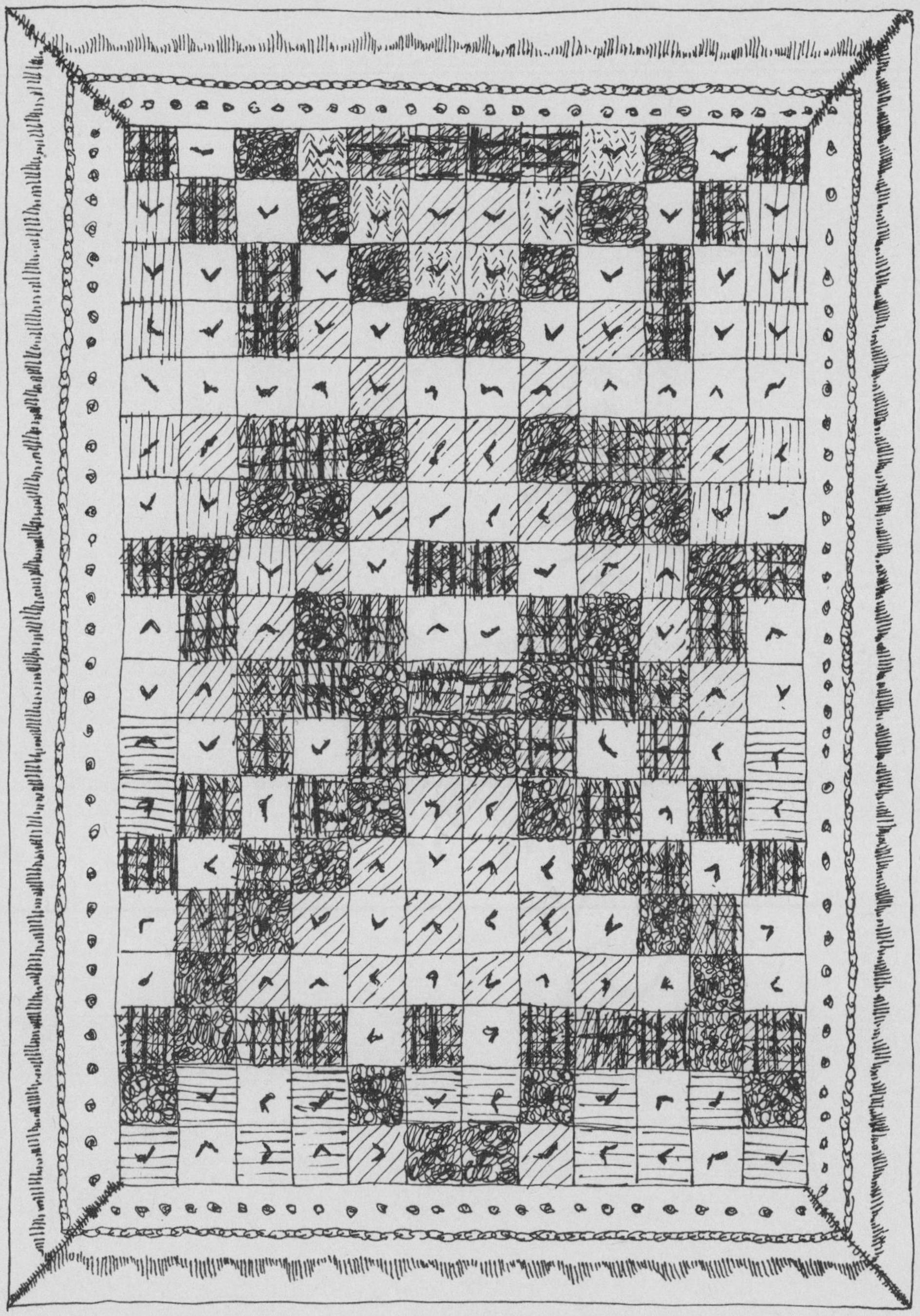

Quilt size: 54" x 75"   Size of squares: 4½" x 4½" (allows for ½" seam allowance)
Sheeting size: 67" x 88"

This quilt design is of wool plaids and fake furs. Retain the light and dark composition using a variety of colors. There are 90 dark squares and 126 light. To construct the quilt, the patchwork is sewn together as normal; but when laying out the sheeting and batting, place the patchwork in center, with 12½" of excess sheeting around. Then, 6½" (allows for ½" seam allowance) of sheeting is folded forward; with seam allowance folded under and sewn to patchwork. Corners can be trimmed and sewn at an angle, or squared. Add embroidery rows on edge; at least 3 rows. Knot each square. Blanket binding is unnecessary but could be added.

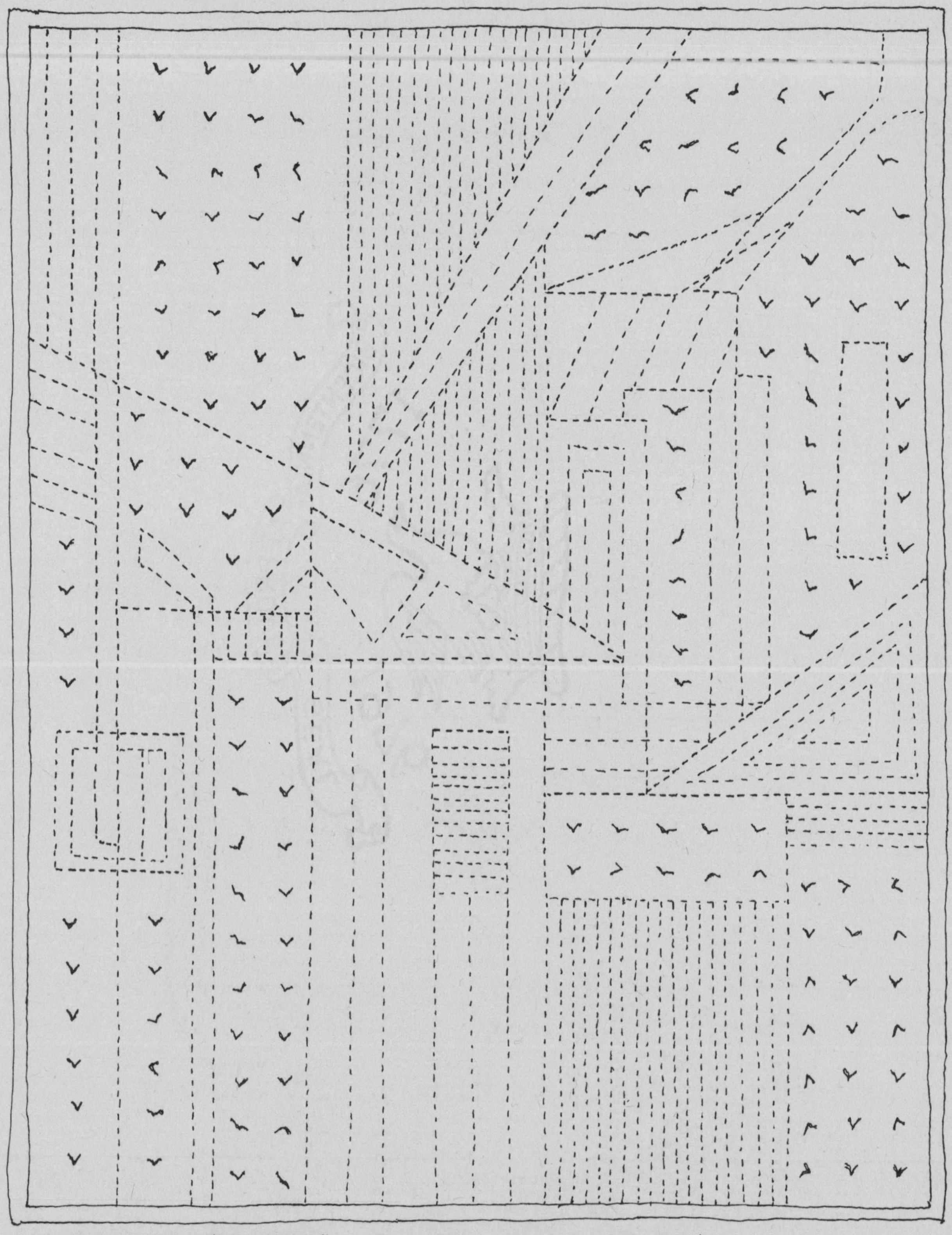

Quilt size: 78½" x 99½"   Size of top fabric: 75" x 96"

This quilt involves a solid piece of fabric with design incorporated by decorative quilting (thru 3 layers of quilt) and knotting. Technically, remember that at least every 3 inches must be quilted or knotted. Trace design onto fabric with tailor chalk and be certain the 3 layers of quilt are pinned together securely and without creases. (A quilt frame makes this easier.) Stitching knots can be started at the edge, although some ends of quilting will have to be knotted on back. Traditionally this method of quilt making is done white thread on white; but sheeting for top could be dyed; or use color lengths of fabric sewn together; or use color thread.

ABC QUILT

The ABC quilt is a more elaborate presentation using appliqué and embroidery. Of course, pictorial representations may be altered to suit a more personal scheme. All letters are cut out of fabric with a 1/4" seam allowance and appliquéd with the blind stitch. On the following pages, information concerning appliqué shapes and embroidery stitches is found beneath each enlarged square. The quilt incorporates squares of 12"x12", in checkerboard design of 24 lettered and 24 solid squares. It can be constructed by the methods of either Quilt 1 or 2.

JUICYFRU

ADD 1/4"-SEAM ALLOWANCE TO ALL APPLIQUÉ SHAPES.
(SEAM ALLOWANCE OF SQUARES NOT SHOWN)

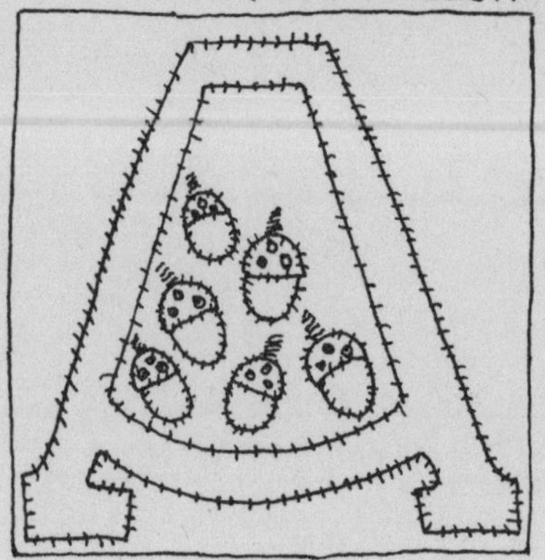

Acorns: appliqué shapes

Stems: satin stitch
Caps: Add French knots

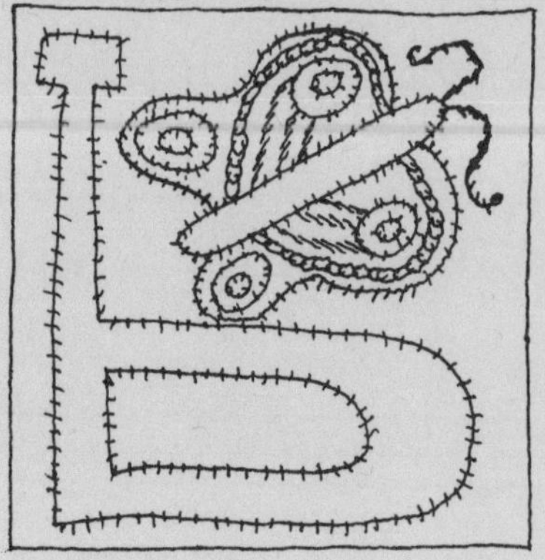

Butterfly appliqué shapes:

Antennas: backstitch
Wing designs: Satin stitch and chain stitch

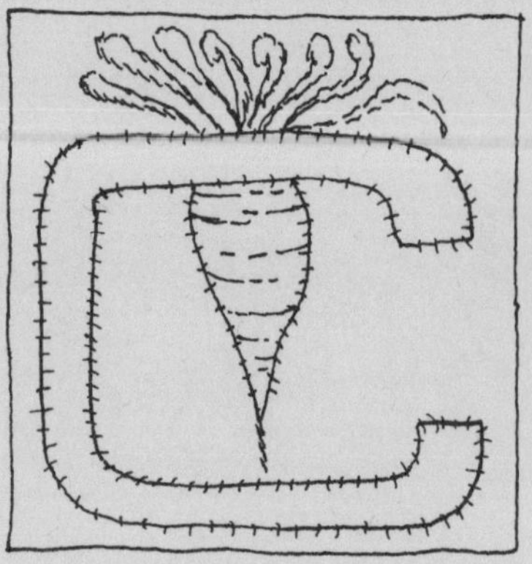

Carrot appliqué shape:

Root, leaves, and carrot ridges: backstitch

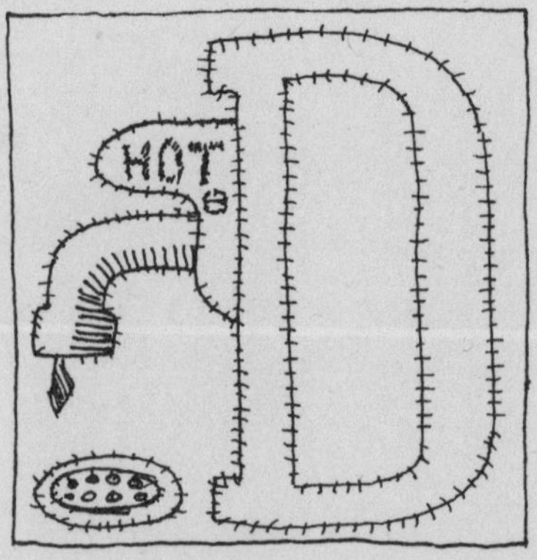
HOT

Faucet and drain appliqué shapes:

Shadow and Drip and "HOT": Satin stitch
Screw and drain ring: backstitch
Drain holes - french knots

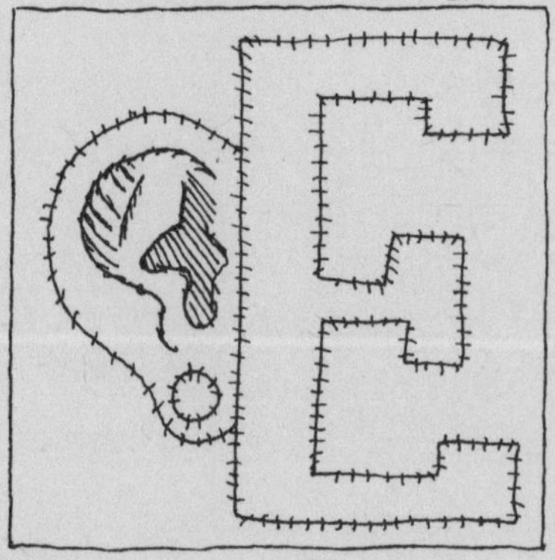

Ear and Earring appliqué shapes:

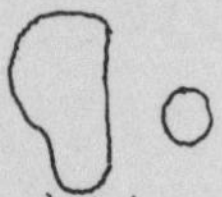

Ear curves: backstitch
Ear shadows: wide Satin Stitch.

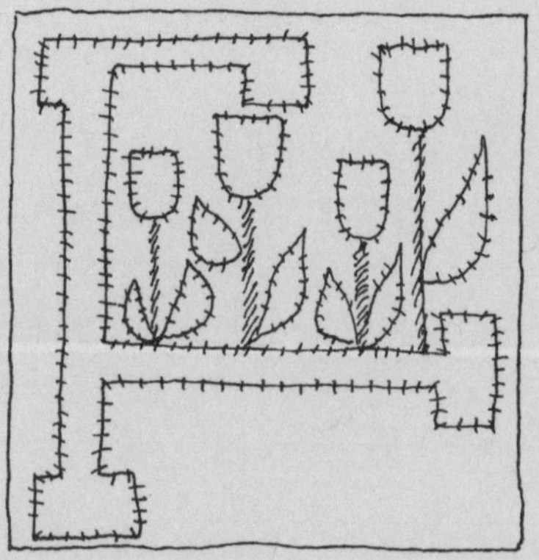

Flower appliqué shapes:

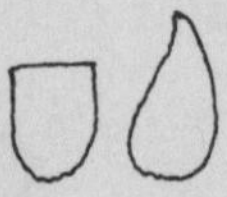

Stems: Back Stitch or Satin Stitch

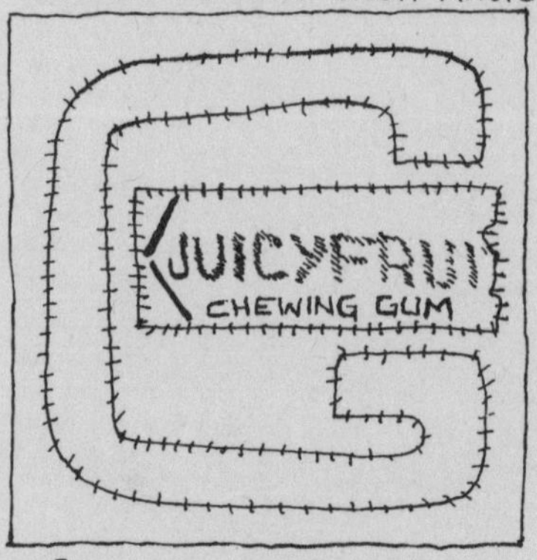
JUICYFRUI
CHEWING GUM

Gum wrapper appliqué shape:

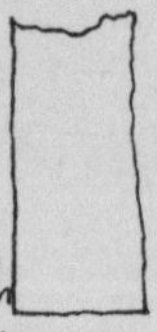

Arrow and lettering: backstitch or satin stitch

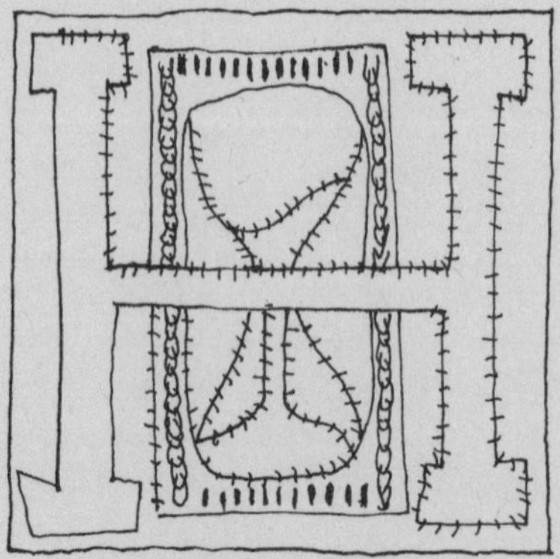

Hour glass and Sand appliqué shapes:

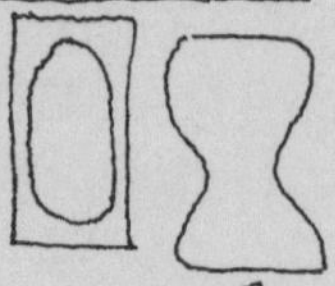

Hourglass Embroidery designs

Top & Bottom: wide Satin Stitch
Sides: Chain stitch

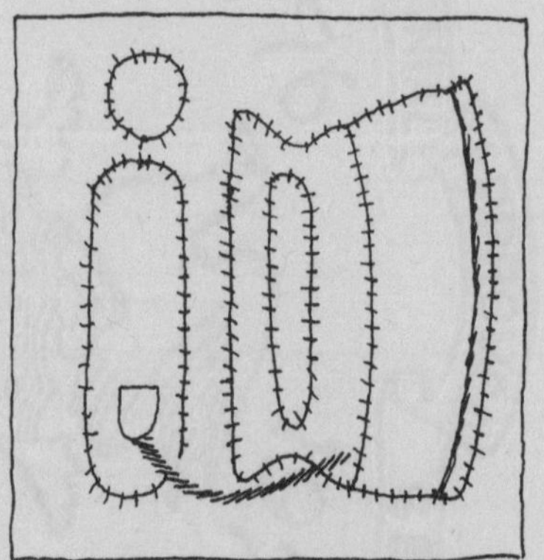

Iron and plug appliqué shapes:

Cord: Satin stitch
Iron rim: Backstitch

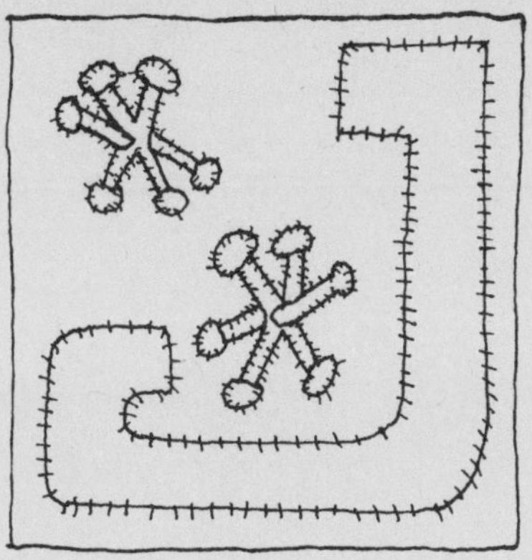

Jacks appliqué shapes:

Outlining in jacks: Backstitch

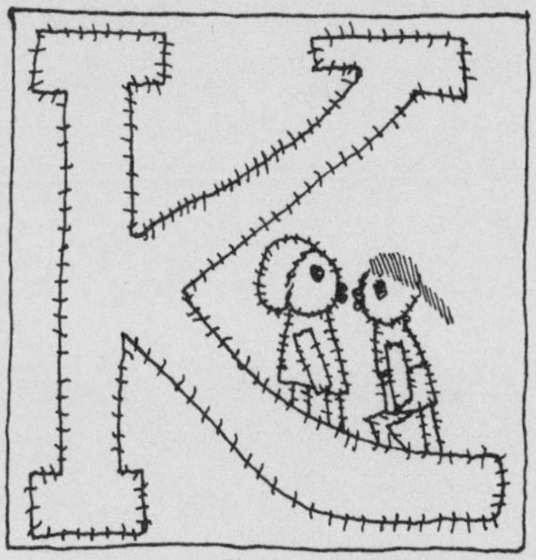

Girl appliqué shapes: head & hair, legs, arm, dress

Outline hair: backstitch

Boy appliqué shapes: head, arm, legs, shirt, pants

Hat: satin stitch

Lips and Eyes: French Knot

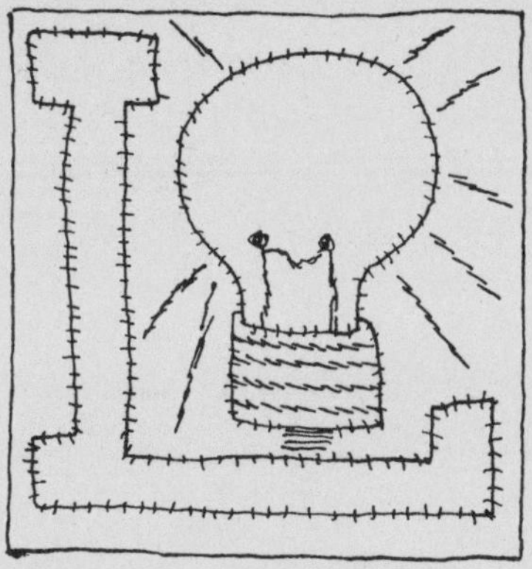

Lightbulb appliqué shapes:

Filament – backstitch and 2 french knots

Threads of base: back and light rays: stitch

Below base: satin stitch

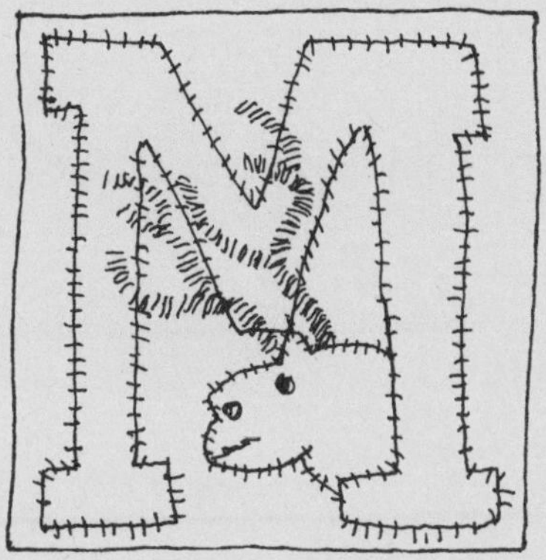

Moose appliqué shape:

Mouth: backstitch

Antlers: satin stitch

Nose and Eye: french knot

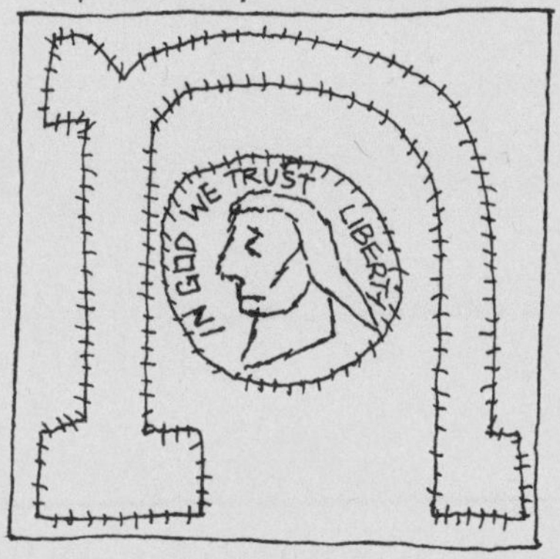
IN GOD WE TRUST
LIBERTY

Nickel appliqué shape:

Jefferson's head and lettering: Backstitch

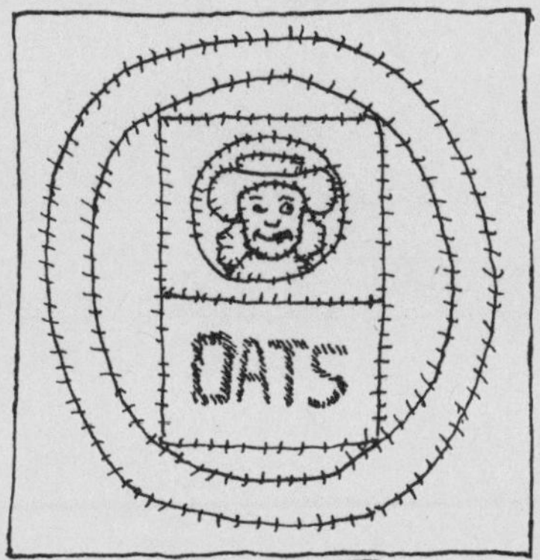
OATS

Box appliqué shapes:

Quaker's appliqué shapes: HAT, HEAD, NECK, HAIR

Face details: backstitch with Eyes: french knots

"OATS": Satin Stitch

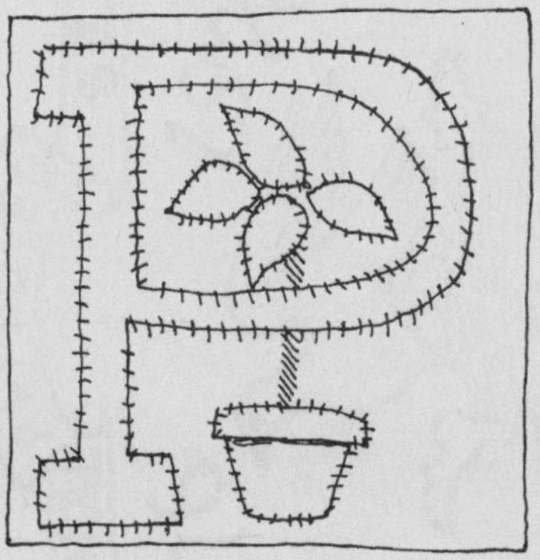

Plant appliqué shape

Pot appliqué shape

Stem: satin stitch

Pot rim outline: backstitch

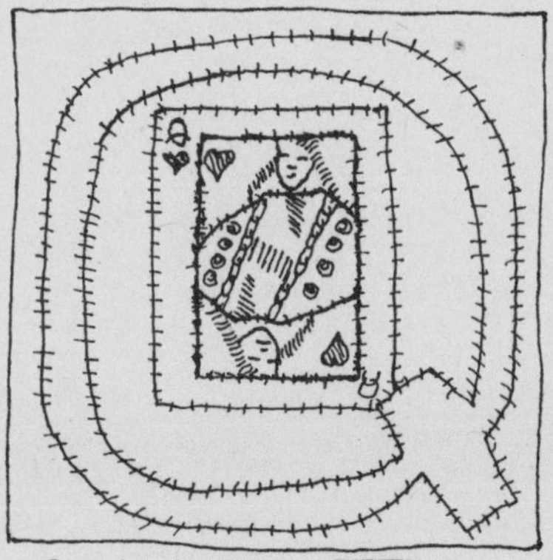

Card appliqué shapes:

Queen's body appliqué shape

Queen's face outline and details: backstitch

Queen's Headdress: satin stitch

Dress details: french knots, chain stitch, satin stitch

Hearts: Satin Stitch "Q": backstitch.

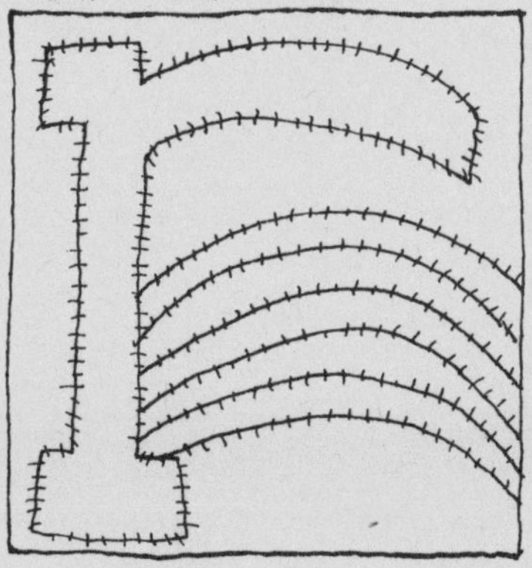

Rainbow appliqué shape:

overlap shapes

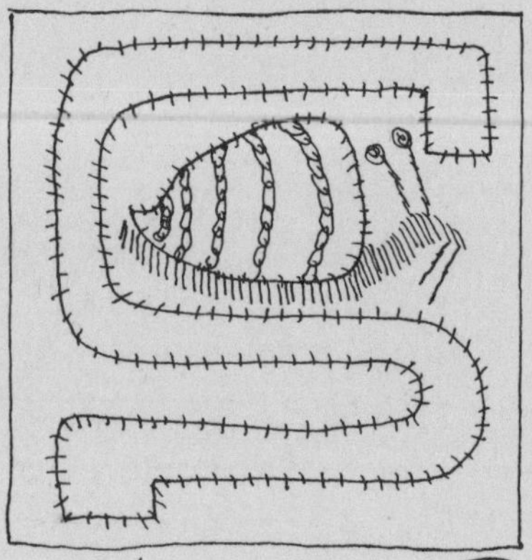

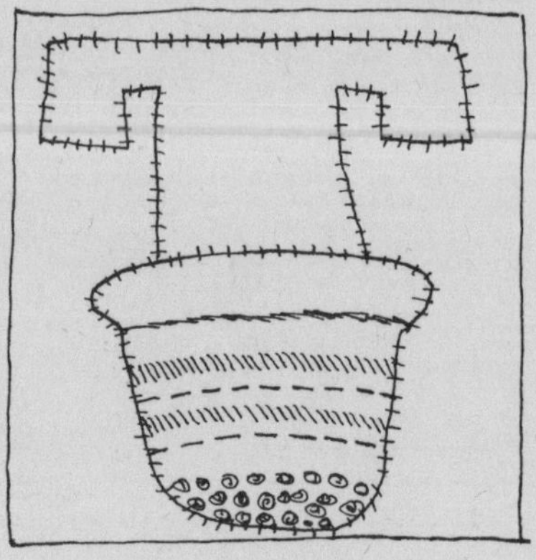

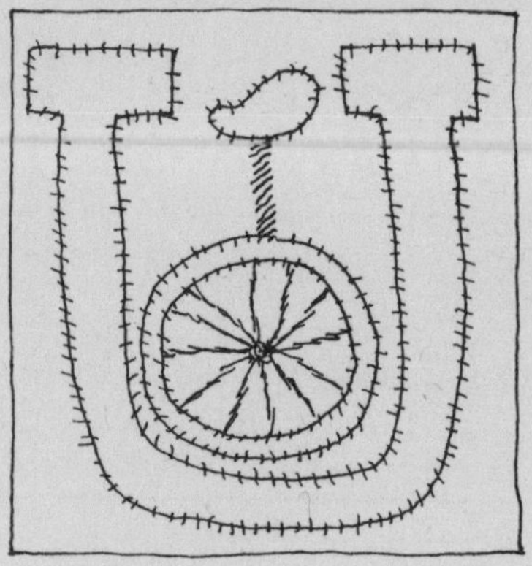

SNail's shell
appliqué shape:

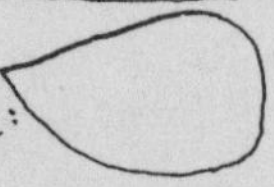

Snail's body: satin stitch
Shell creases: chain stitch
Protrusions: backstitch
and french knots

Thimble appliqué
shape:

Details, in order, top to bottom:
backstitch, satin stitch,
straight stitch, Satin stitch,
straight stitch, French knots

Unicycle seat
appliqué shape

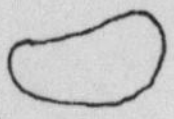

wheel appliqué
shape

Seat bar: Satin stitch
Spokes: backstitch with
french knot at center

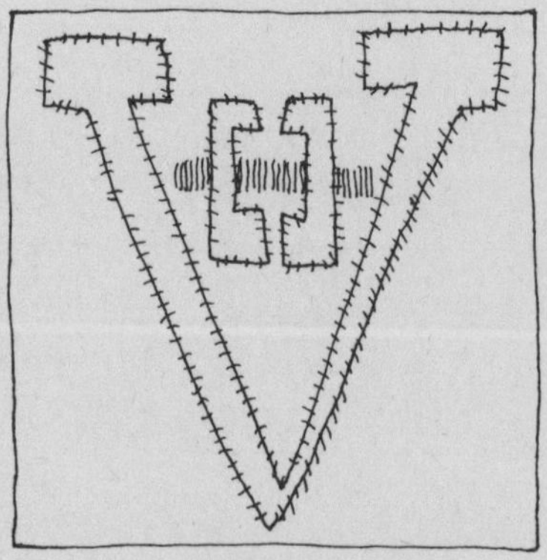

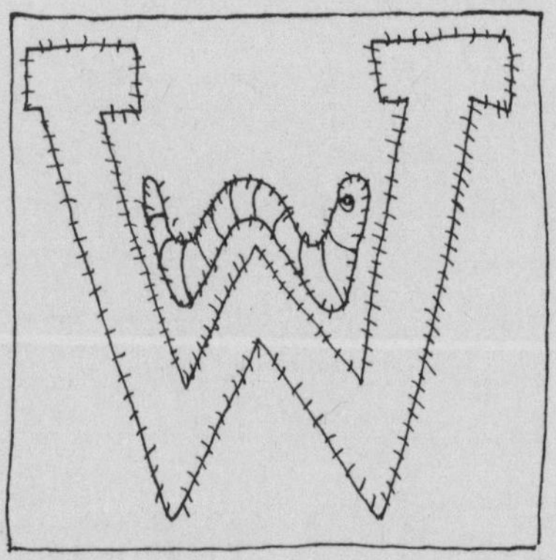

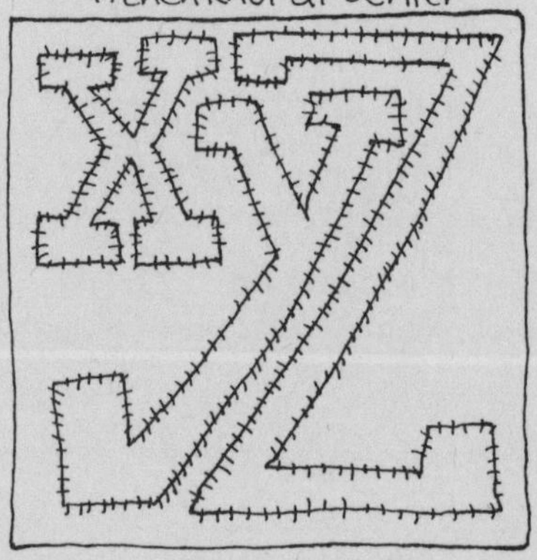

Vise appliqué
shapes:

Screw bar: Satin stitch

Worm appliqué
shape

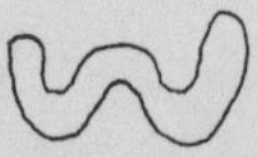

Lines on worm: backstitch
Eye: French Knot

The letters of the ABC quilt are intended to be informal to add to the whimsical and warm quality of the scheme. Also, because color is such a personal matter, particular choices have not been mentioned.

•This quilt also has a large border around the patchwork (originally 12 inches wide; but can be altered). Cut the top and bottom widths equal to the dimension of the patchwork. Sew together with a straight stitch or blind stitch. Cut the side widths of border, the length of the patchwork and first two borders. Sew together.

Patchwork Clothing

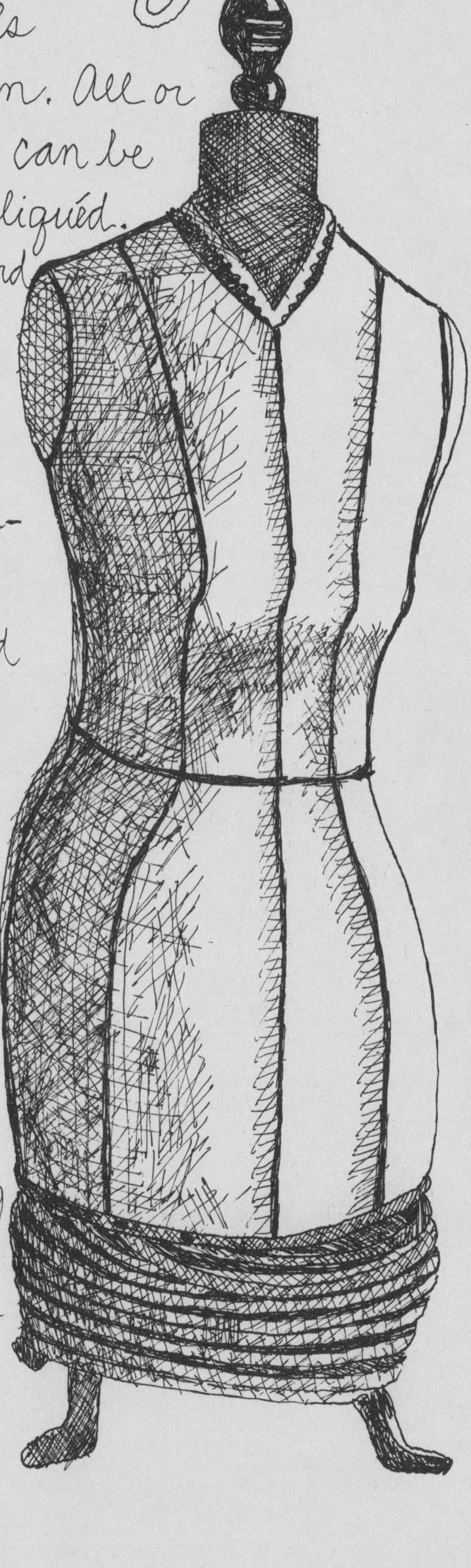

Patchwork clothing reveals itself as an expressive medium. All or merely sections of a garment can be patched, embroidered, or appliquéd. Those interested in recycling and avid disciples of "waste not-want not" delight in its beauty. Garage sales, second-hand clothing stores, and auctions often offer an array of old clothes at extremely mild prices. The clothes can be refurbished to meet your own tastes; or cut up and transformed into an entirely new character.

The following pages include patchwork clothing for all types of weather. It's such a flexible medium for making unique and personal clothes for yourself and others, that you may never return to single fabric clothing.

Lightweight clothing for the warm months

Begin with a pattern that is light and airy; and select one of the following methods of construction:

METHOD 1 Make a patchwork length of material large enough for all the pattern pieces (Use Steps 2, 3, 5, and 6 of Quilt 1; pages 9-10.

- Place and pin pattern pieces on patchwork.
- Cut out pattern and proceed sewing the garment as normal, following pattern instructions.

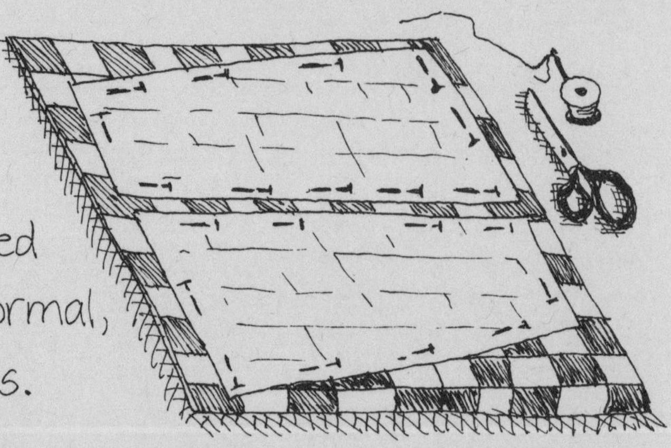

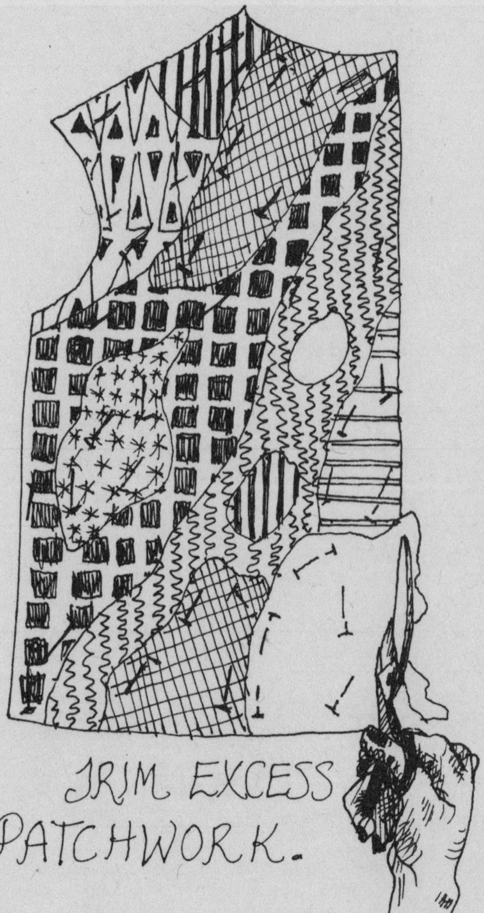

TRIM EXCESS PATCHWORK.

METHOD 2 Place, pin, and cut out pattern pieces on thin muslin or any lightweight fabric, (old-fashioned transparent type curtains are particularly good - although they make nice shirts on their own, too.)

- Unpin pattern and lay out fabric.
- Cut and pin shapes of patchwork (geometric or free form) onto the fabric pattern pieces. A ¼" seam allowance is needed ~ fold under the overlapping pieces.
- Sew patches onto garment pieces using a blind stitch.
- When all patches are sewn; continue constructing the garment following pattern instructions.

METHOD 3 This method is similar to method 2, but the muslin underlining is eliminated. Patches of geometric or free-form shapes are pinned and sewn to each other, with overlapping shapes having the 1/4" seam allowance folded under. Use the pattern pieces as a guide, laying the patches atop.

- Pin the patches together securely; trim excess fabric.
- Sew edges of shapes together with a blind stitch.
- When patchwork pattern pieces are completed, continue constructing garment according to pattern instructions.

Clothes for a cool breeze

In the days when leaves are returning to the trees or the colors of autumn are making their full appearance, lightweight patchwork clothing with an added lining offers the perfect comfort. Use any of the methods for making lightweight clothing and cut out a duplicate of the pattern pieces for the lining. Use muslin, a cotton print, or medium-weight fabric such as Kassha for the lining. For torso garments, slip-stitch the constructed lining at neckline, cuffs, and bottom hem; and sew a few stitches at the armhole. For pants and skirts, slip stitch lining at waist.

Winter Clothing

People who use coal or wood as their resource for heat realize that sometimes warm clothing worn indoors is a part of cold winter nights and sunless days. And of course, dressing warm for the outdoors is important to health and comfort. Patchwork clothing accommodated for winter wear is truly ideal and can be made using the 3 methods of light-weight clothing. The warmth arrives from varied layers of fabric and overlapping patchwork; and use of heavy or warm materials such as: wool, corduroy, flannel, upholstery material, denim, knits, furs + leathers, nylon (for inner linings).

A coat can be made as a patchwork of furs and leathers; which can be surprisingly inexpensive if you look awhile.... leather shops often sell scraps of leather for various prices; old fur coats are seen at garage sales, auctions, and used clothing stores (I got a mink, knee-length coat, in utterly perfect condition recently at an auction for .....$6. That's an incredible deal but it could happen to you!).

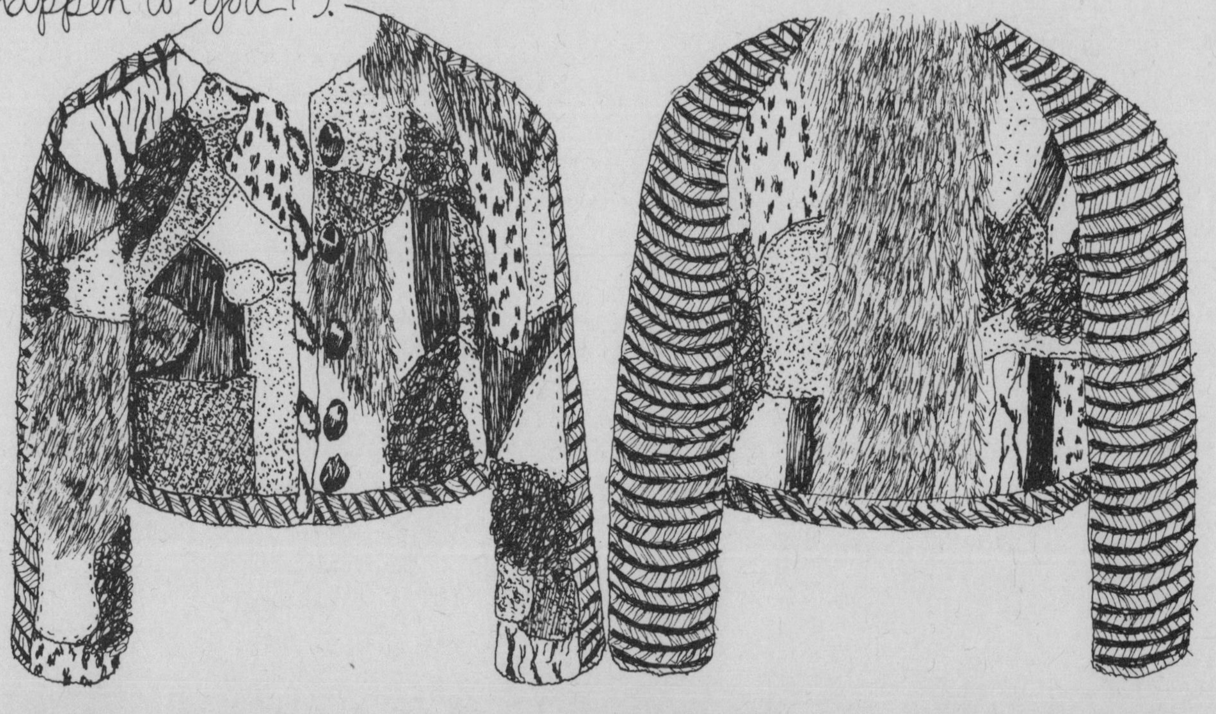

- Cut fur from the back using a razor blade; leather can be cut with scissors ..... to save the upper part of the thumb from becoming 'raw' from cutting heavy fabrics or leather, wear a leather glove with the fingers cut off.
- Hold the patchwork fur and leather together with masking tape— pins are next impossible to insert thru layers and leave holes.
- Use method 2, under lightweight clothing.
- Sew by hand, using carpet thread or heavy-duty polyester thread, and a STURDY Needle with a Straight stitch, slip stitch, or blind stitch.

LEATHER
EDGE

On the sewing machine, use heavy-duty polyester or silk thread with the appropriate needle for the model of sewing machine — (sometimes Size 14, or specified: 'needle for leather.')

- Leather does <u>not</u> require a ¼" seam allowance folded under, so to make the process easier, use leather to overlap fur.

The coat shown on the previous page is made of a variety of fur and leather scraps given by friends and family. The patches are sewn onto bleached muslin, without any lining – the pattern of the stitches on the muslin brings forth its own design quality. Because it is unlined, it is more comfortable in fall but not warm enough when the winter settles. The back sleeves and waist edge are of a tweedy wool, primarily because of a limited amount of fur and leather; but the arm sleeves are nice and flexible because of the fabric. Button loops can be made of fabric, heavy cord, or crochet strands. The buttons are buckeyes which are transformed easily:

Take an ice pick or nail and hammer the point thru the buckeye. It's easiest to work on the ground. Use carpet thread to sew thru hole onto garment.

Clay beads or shaped buttons can be made, too. (See Natural Clay, pages 136-7).

This sheep-skin and natural rawhide coat is SO warm to wear, even on the coldest of cold days. There are 5 layers and because of this, use a pattern a size larger than you wear, or enlarge a coat pattern that you have.... otherwise your circulation will stop particularly in the arms. I found this out the hard way and kept hoping the pressure of the sleeves would adjust my arms to fit the coat or vice-versa. After a few stubborn days of being unable to bend my arms, I reassembled the sleeves minus a couple layers.

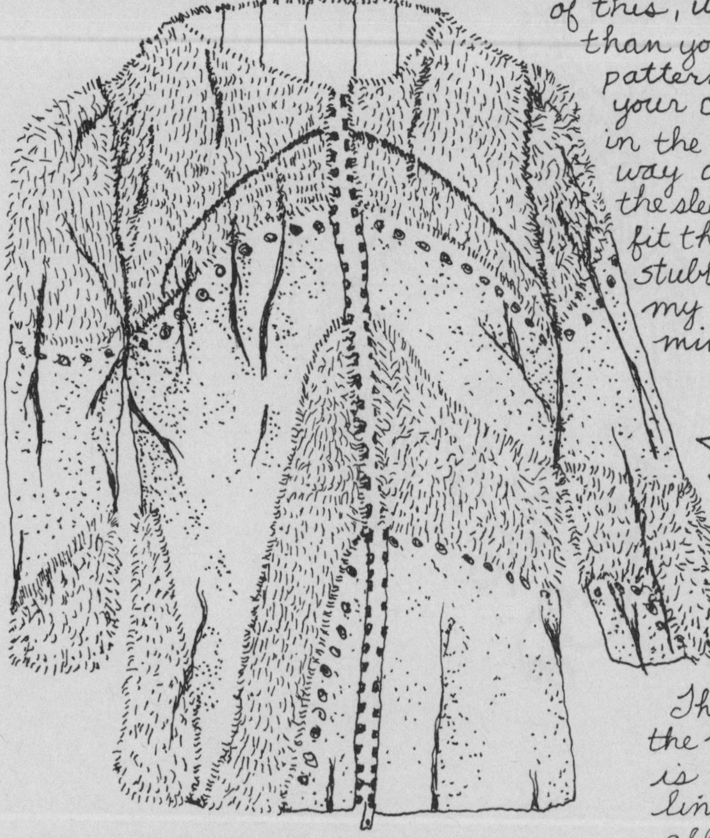

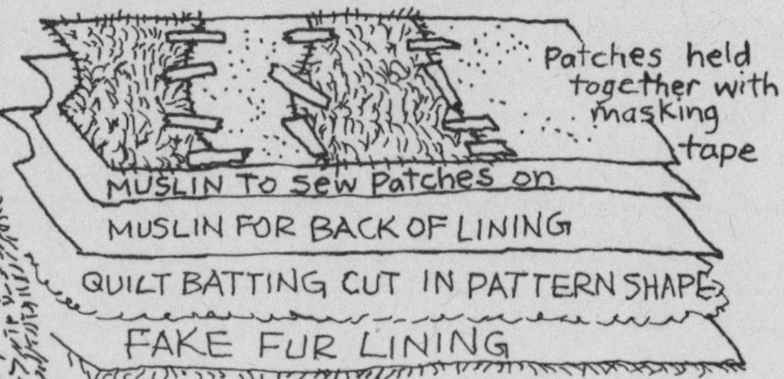
Patches held together with masking tape
MUSLIN TO SEW PATCHES ON
MUSLIN FOR BACK OF LINING
QUILT BATTING CUT IN PATTERN SHAPE
FAKE FUR LINING

The leather and fur are sewn onto the muslin pattern piece which is cut slightly larger than the lining (about 1/4"-1/2" larger along all edges.)

For fur and leather patchwork coats, buy a pattern of a simple style.

The lining is made of fake fur, batting, and muslin — sewn together with rows of straight stitches.

The 3-layered-lining pieces are then constructed according to pattern directions and inserted into the constructed coat. Slip stitch coat to lining at neck, cuffs, and hem.

The design of the coat flows from front to arms to back, with french knots of embroidery thread along some of the rawhide edges.

As shown, a heavy-duty coat zipper is used, which is inserted and sewn between the patchwork and lining layers.

Patchwork Sweater

To make a patchwork sweater, you need at least four old sweaters. Method 2 or 3 under lightweight clothing are used; although a variation of 2 is the easiest: take a sweater of loose-fit and sew the knit patches directly onto this 'lining' sweater. Regardless of method:

1. Patches and lining should be of a sweater-type knit. Try to retain the proper knit direction for patches.
2. Allow for a ½" seam allowance to be folded under. 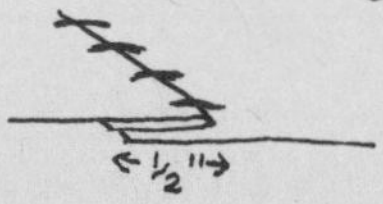
½"
3. Use yarn and a large needle to sew blind stitches.

The patchwork sweater with the lining is very cozy and comfortable on crisp winter days.

Patterns

The following pages include patterns for use with patchwork, (to avoid confusion, illustrations are shown without patchwork). The patterns are uncomplicated and the clothing is designed to use for any size. With accurate measuring, and always keeping in mind seam allowances, you can design and construct more complicated patterns. To avoid frustration, make a paper pattern first and pin the pieces together to assure proper fit. Of course, each season, pattern companies add to their repertoire of designs for the styles of everyone and accessory-type sewing. A few patterns can open doors to variety by adding or subtracting, lengthening or shortening: sleeves, collars, cuffs, buttons, embroidery, appliqué, feathers, beads, and hemlines; OR enlarging areas and then gathering or sewing down pleats. Changing fabrics and patchwork shapes or colors can make the same pattern appear quite unique.

When handsewing, button holes are made using a small piece of fabric, placed with right sides together on the garment. Straight stitch as shown with small stitches. Bring the edges through the hole and slip stitch folded edges to wrong side of garment.

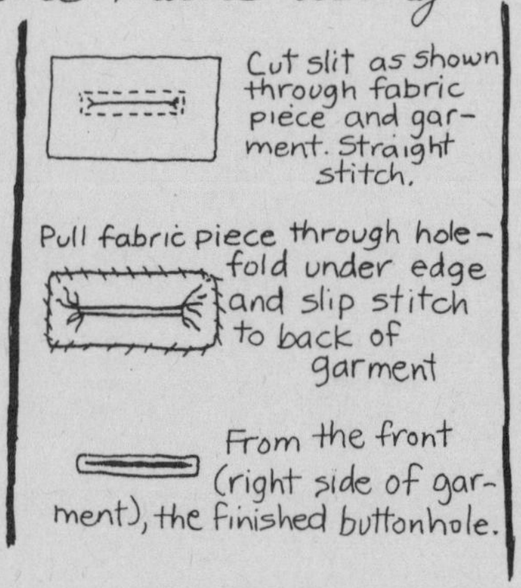
Cut slit as shown through fabric piece and garment. Straight stitch.
Pull fabric piece through hole-fold under edge and slip stitch to back of garment
From the front (right side of garment), the finished buttonhole.

Two more methods of closure are: **1.** use snaps as seen on baby clothes (the gadget for attaching comes with the snaps); **2.** Cut lengths of cord or folded-sewn fabric and sew loops into the seam.

Smocks – for work or play

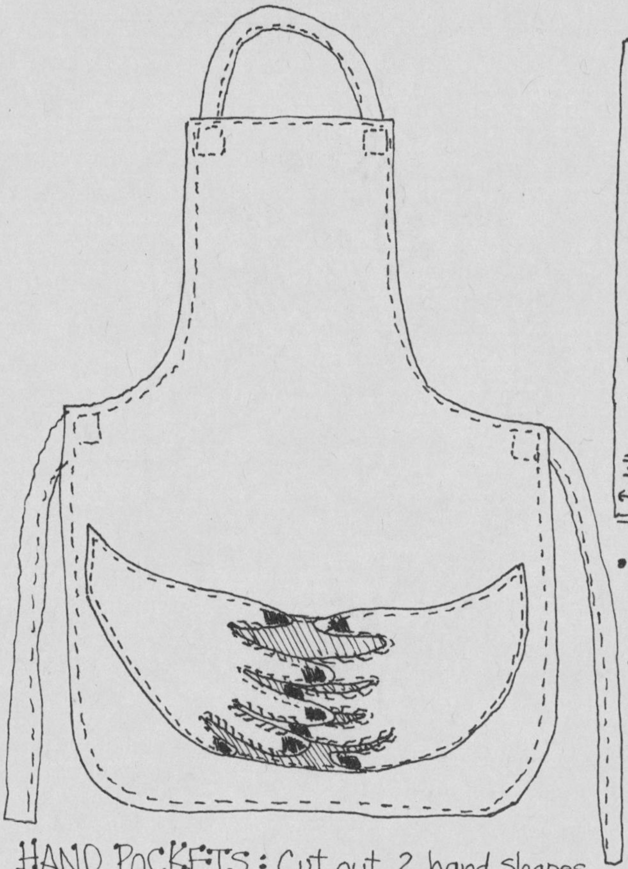

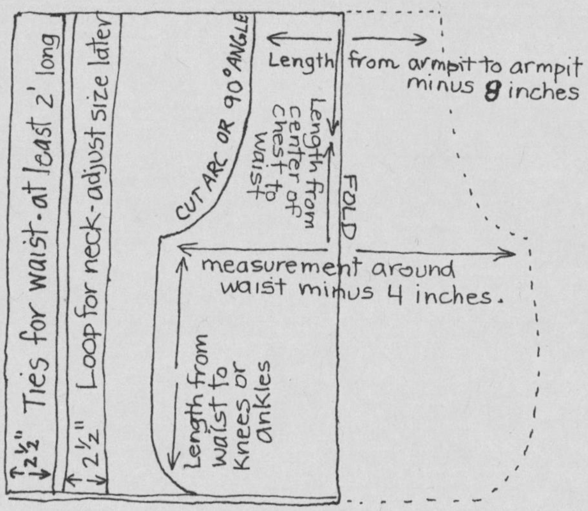
Ties for waist - at least 2' long
$2\frac{1}{2}$"
Loop for neck - adjust size later
$2\frac{1}{2}$"
CUT ARC OR 90° ANGLE
Length from armpit to armpit minus 8 inches
Length from center of chest to waist
FOLD
measurement around waist minus 4 inches.
Length from waist to knees or ankles

- Fold material in ½, and mark with tailor chalk, the measured and arced lines shown. Cut out.
- Fold and press a ½" hem around the smock; fold inside ¼" of the rough edge. Sew down with a straight or slip stitch.
- Fold ties in half lengthwise, and insert rough edges inside fold: Sew together along edge with a straight stitch. Then sew to apron.
- Sew loop as for ties. Sew 1 end to top of smock; adjust to personal size and; cut and sew.

HAND POCKETS: Cut out 2 hand shapes and a center square. Fold under ¼" edge of fingers and sew to the square with a blind stitch. Embroider nails with satin stitch, Fold and press ½" around; straight stitch top edge with ¼" rough edge folded in; sew the rest to smock.

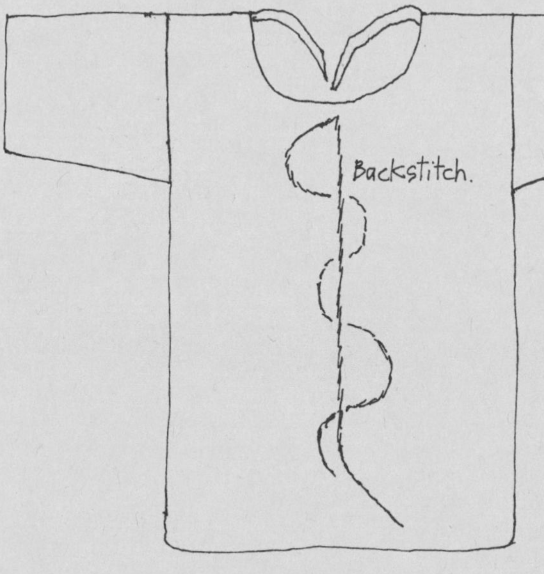
Backstitch.

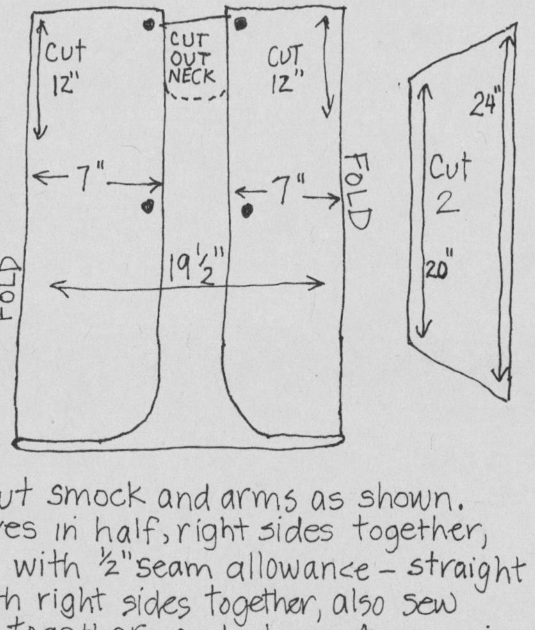
CUT 12"
CUT OUT NECK
CUT 12"
7"
7"
FOLD
$19\frac{1}{2}$"
FOLD
24"
Cut 2
20"

Hem around roughedges as for smock 1. Stitch ribbons of desired length to back at points shown on right (•).

Fold and cut smock and arms as shown. Fold sleeves in half, right sides together, and sew with ½" seam allowance – straight stitch. With right sides together, also sew shoulders together, and sleeve to opening. Hem sleeves using ½" edges folded. (elastic could be inserted.)

Here are two basic Skirt patterns that can produce numerous styles.

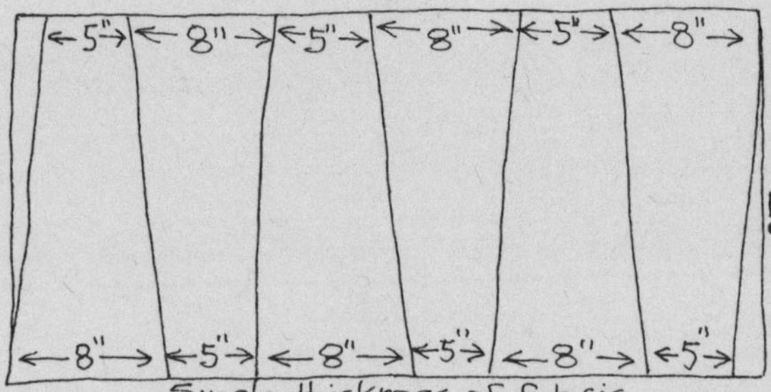
5"
8"
5"
8"
5"
8"
8"
5"
8"
5"
8"
5"
Single thickness of fabric

On a single thickness of fabric, mark the trapezoidal shapes or draw and cut one on paper first, and use as the pattern piece.

1 • For a form-fit A-line skirt with a zipper, cut as many trapezoids as needed, keeping in mind that 1/2" on each side is a seam allowance. Alter trapezoid dimensions or enlarge seam allowance if necessary. Sew the zipper to the first two pieces, as the package describes. With right sides together, sew pieces along seam allowance with a straight stitch. Add bias tape or a fabric strip to the waist, right sides together, straight stitch. Fold strip to inside and slip stitch inside skirt. Hem skirt.

BACK

2 • For a gathered skirt, cut enough trapezoid pieces to allow the waist to slide easily past hips... remember there is a 1/2" seam allowance on each side. With right sides together, sew pieces on seam allowance with a straight stitch. Add a waist band (about 3" wide) to the skirt—right sides together, using a straight stitch. Leave an opening for the elastic, as shown; fold waist band in with a 1/4" or 1/2" folded under and slip stitch to inside. Cut elastic to waist measurement, plus 1". Attach a safety pin to one end of elastic and run through waistband. Sew ends of elastic with 1/2" seam allowance. Hem skirt.

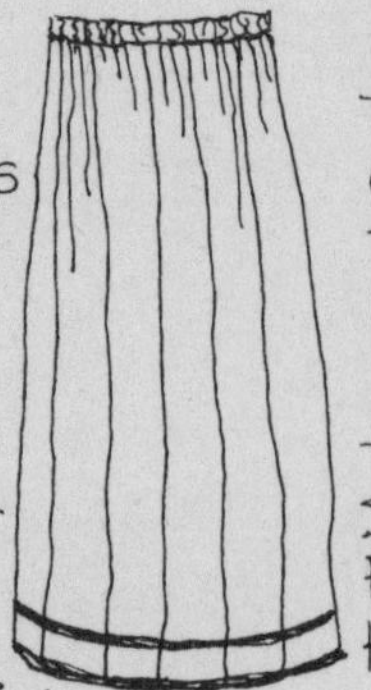

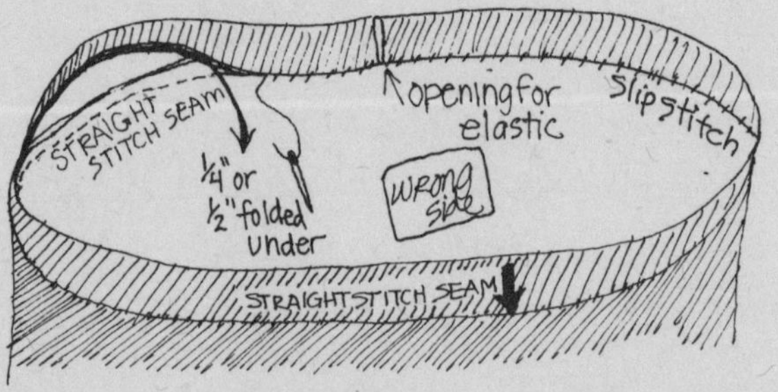
STRAIGHT STITCH SEAM
opening for elastic
slip stitch
1/4" or 1/2" folded under
WRONG side
STRAIGHT STITCH SEAM

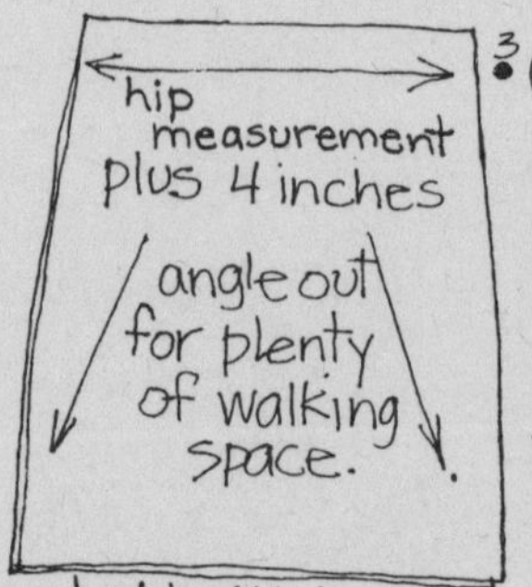
hip measurement plus 4 inches
angle out for plenty of walking space.
double thickness of fabric

3 • Cut out the double thickness of fabric as shown. With right sides together, sew sides with a 1/2" seam allowance using a straight stitch. Attach a waist band (at least 3" wide) to the top, as for 2 •, and insert elastic. A fabric draw string could be used instead of elastic. Hem skirt.

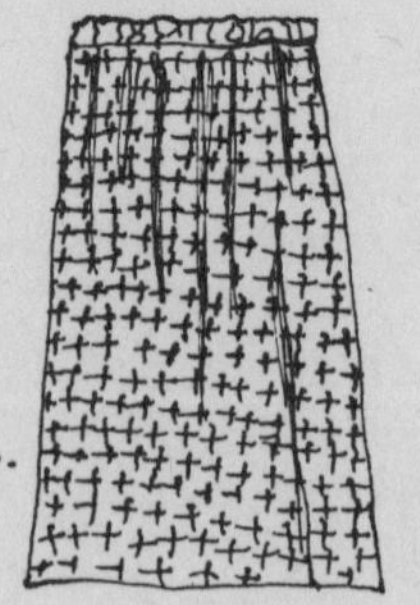

The length of the skirts can vary — or cut the desired length shorter and add a ruffled edge... A ruffle 6-7 inches wide and about 1 foot longer than the bottom hem circumference, lies most naturally.

Knee-length, 1 • with zipper and waistband.

ankle-length, 1 • with zipper and a wide waistband

Calf-length 2 • with ruffle and drawstring

ankle-length 2 • with long ruffle

Knee-length, 3 • with gathered fabric sewn into shaped waistband with zipper.

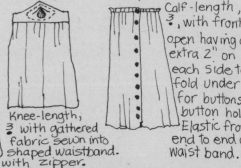

Calf-length, 3 •, with front open having an extra 2" on each side to fold under for buttons + button holes. Elastic from end to end of waist band.

YUKATA

The Japanese **YUKATA** *is a more informal kimono, worn by men, women, and children. The fabric sold in Japan for its making is the appropriate width of the pieces, so there is little cutting. The traditional method of construction requires laborious sewing and a beautiful simplicity of folding. Here is a revised version which retains the basic format of the yukata.*

1. Fold and cut pieces according to dimensions shown.
2. With right sides together, sew the back seam with a straight stitch (½" seam allowance) by joining one side of the 2 lengths to FOLD line. Press open seam.

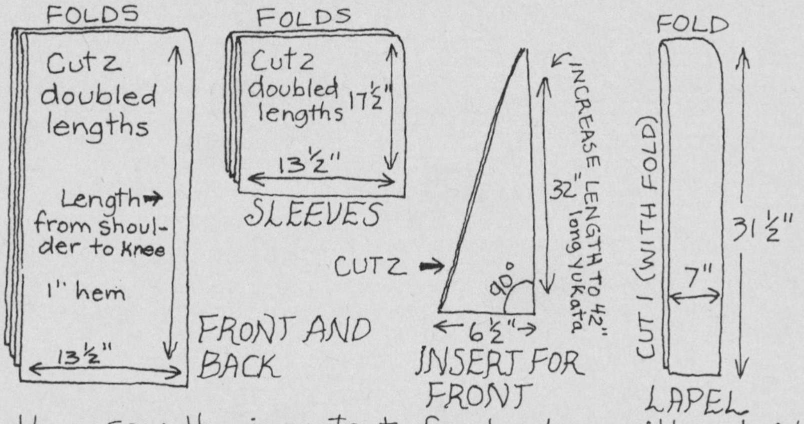
FOLDS
Cut 2 doubled lengths
Length from shoulder to knee
1" hem
13½"
FRONT AND BACK
FOLDS
Cut 2 doubled lengths
17½"
13½"
SLEEVES
INCREASE LENGTH TO 42" long yukata
32"
CUT 2
90°
6½"
INSERT FOR FRONT
FOLD
CUT 1 (WITH FOLD)
31½"
7"
LAPEL

3. With right sides together, sew the inserts to front edges with a straight stitch. Line up base of triangle with lower front edge.

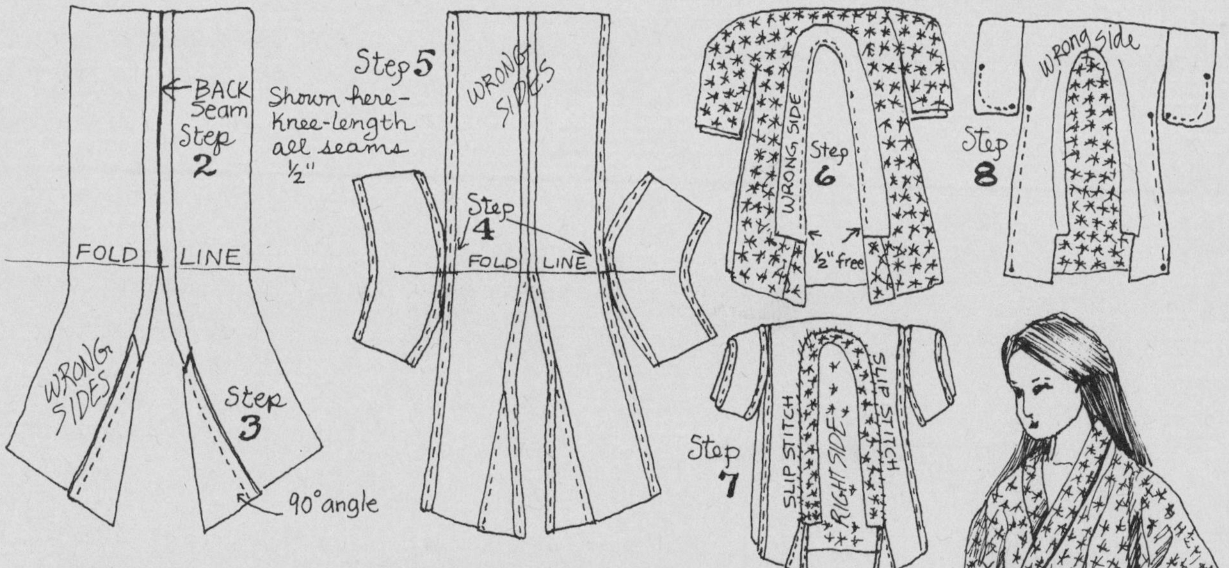
BACK Seam
Step 2
FOLD LINE
WRONG SIDES
Step 3
90° angle
Step 5
Shown here - Knee-length all seams ½"
WRONG SIDES
Step 4
FOLD LINE
WRONG SIDE
Step 6
½" free
wrong side
Step 8
Step 7
SLIP STITCH
RIGHT SIDE
SLIP STITCH

4. With right sides together, join fold lines of front & back to fold lines of sleeves and sew with a straight stitch a length ½ the distance of the sleeve.
5. Fold & press ½" seam allowance under to wrong side of fabric, on the 8 edges shown. (All rough edges can also be folded in ¼": ). Stitch with a straight stitch.
6. With right sides together, pin center fold line of lapel to the top opening point of front. Sew together with a straight stitch — leaving ½" free at ends of lapel.
7. Fold lapel in half and fold ¼" rough edge under. Slip stitch bottom edge closed, and continue sewing lapel edge to the wrong side of the front on the seam line — lapel extends from front.
8. With wrong sides together, straight stitch sides and sleeves to points shown. Trim sleeve curve. Hem ½" at bottom (fold as seen in Step 5.)

Wear as a jacket, shirt, or traditionally with a fabric tie.

Pillows for furniture or pure relaxation are made using any of the methods of quilt 1 or 2, or lightweight clothing. Use polyester filling, shredded or solid foam, or styrofoam pellets depending on the sensation you wish to achieve. The baby bed couch, shown above, uses regular bed-pillows and polyester filling for the bottom cushions, covered with an upholstery plaid and jute webbing for upholstery sewn together. Following, are pattern shapes which are cut, sewn with right sides together using a straight stitch—leaving enough space to turn the fabric inside out and stuff; and finished up with small slip stitches. **OR** fold under 1/4" or 1/2" seam allowance (if using the jute webbing this is unnecessary), place wrong sides together, and slip stitch edges, stuff and continue stitching.

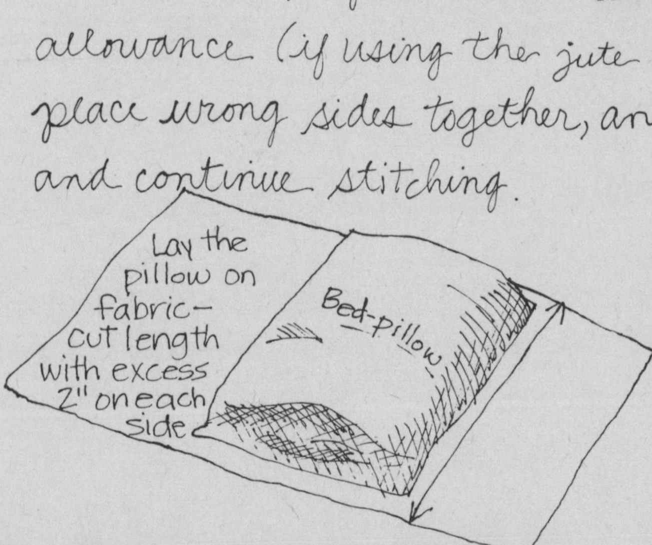
Lay the pillow on fabric—cut length with excess 2" on each side
Bed-pillow

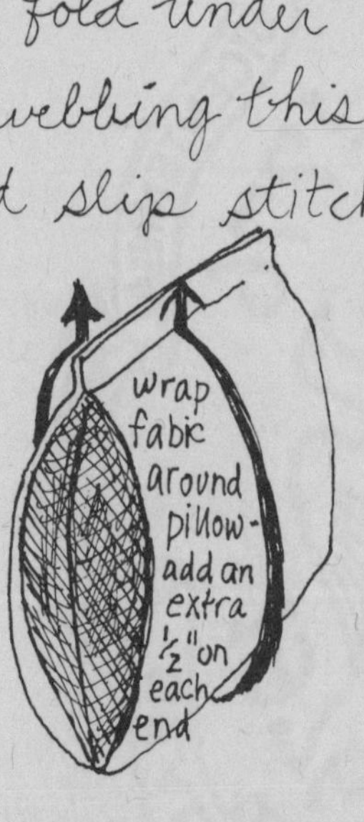
wrap fabric around pillow-add an extra 1/2" on each end

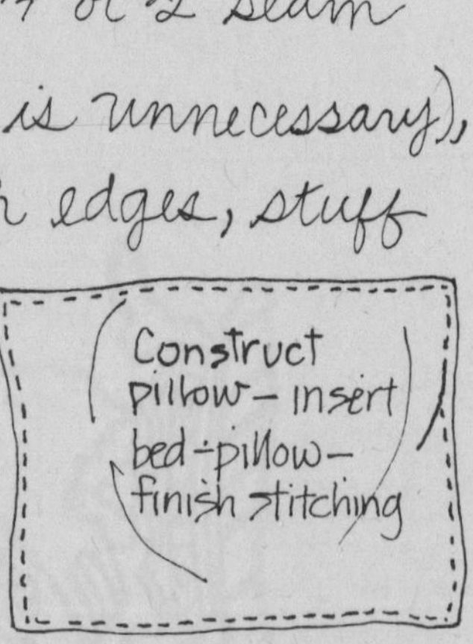
Construct pillow—insert bed-pillow—finish stitching

This one includes straight stitches on the border of the completed pillow.

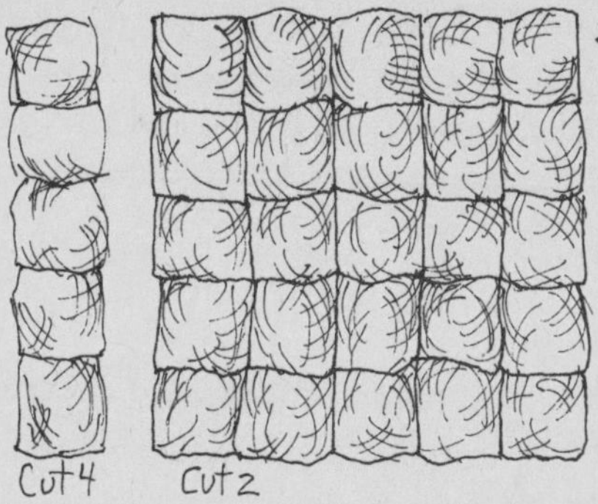
Cut 4
Cut 2

The pillow to the left incorporates construction as for quilt 2, as well as stuffing inside.

Form side lengths equal to dimensions of top and bottom.

Sew all edges with corner points meeting as illustrated. Stuff before finishing last edge.

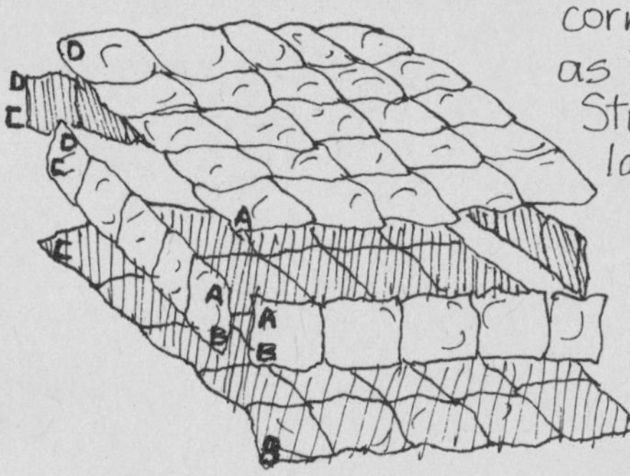
D
D
C
D
C
A
C
A
B
A
B
B

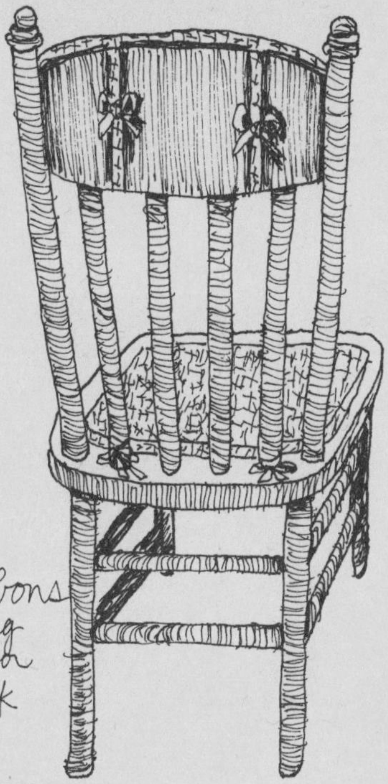

Add fabric ribbons when stitching seam edges for seat and back cushions.

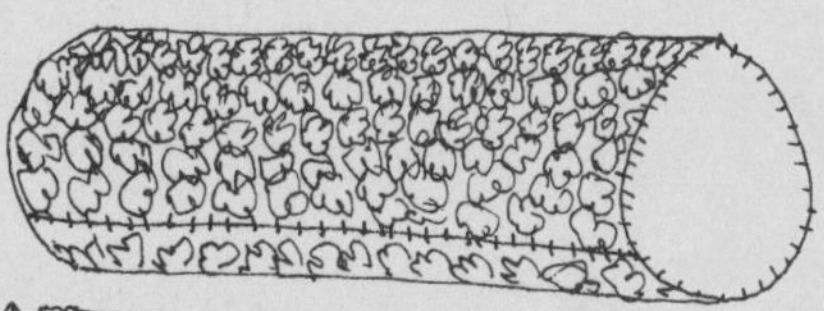

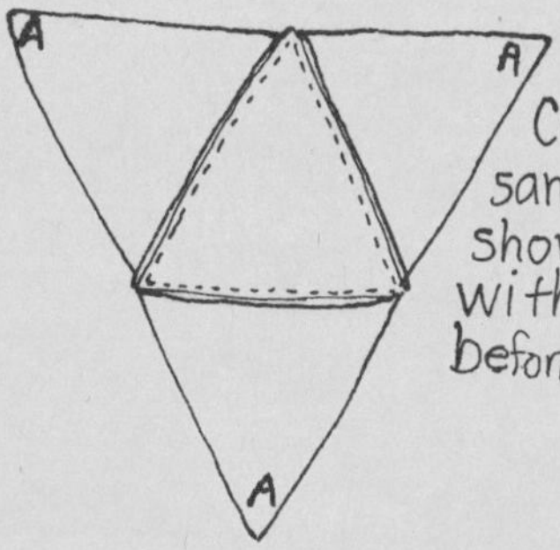
A
A
A

Cut individual triangles of the same size. Sew together as shown, then sew other sides with point A's meeting. Stuff before sewing last side.

Circumference ½" ½"

Foam shapes are sold for use in pillows. Cut 2 circles with an extra ½" seam allowance around, folded under. Cut fabric the length of the pillow and the width of the circle circumference plus ½" at each end.

Circumference plus ½"

Sew the seam of the rectangle first, and then sew the circle ends.

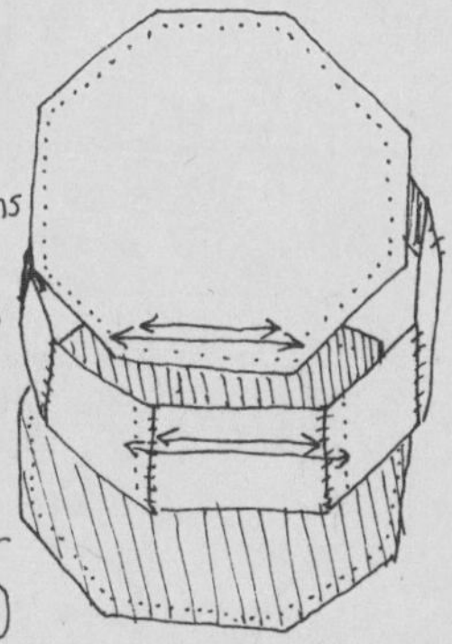

Cut out 2 identical octagons (allowing for a ½" seam allowance.) Cut 8 rectangles having the length of an octagon side (on illustration—smaller arrow shows finished length after sewing + longer shows actual fabric length.) Sewing with ½" seam allowances, join the rectangular sides, and then the sides to the top and bottom. Stuff before final stitches.

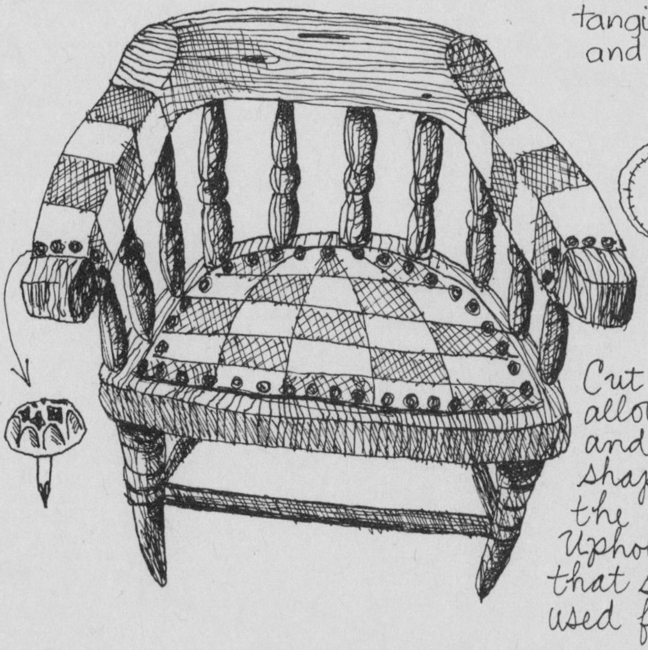

Any shape of pillow can be made by simply cutting two identical shapes and sewing together or adding side panels also, as illustrated above.

Cut out desired shapes with a ½" seam allowance to fold under. Apply batting and muslin backing directly to the shapes (as for quilt 1 or 2) or stuff the cushions as you tack down fabric. Upholstery tacks are used to secure edges that show, while carpet tacks can be used for fastening fabric underneath.

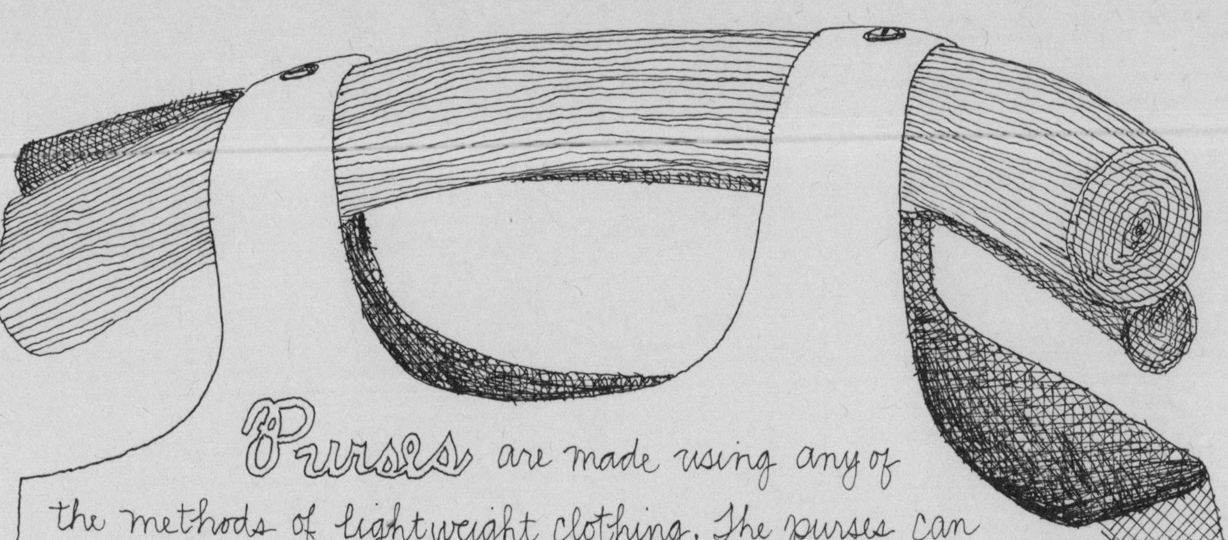

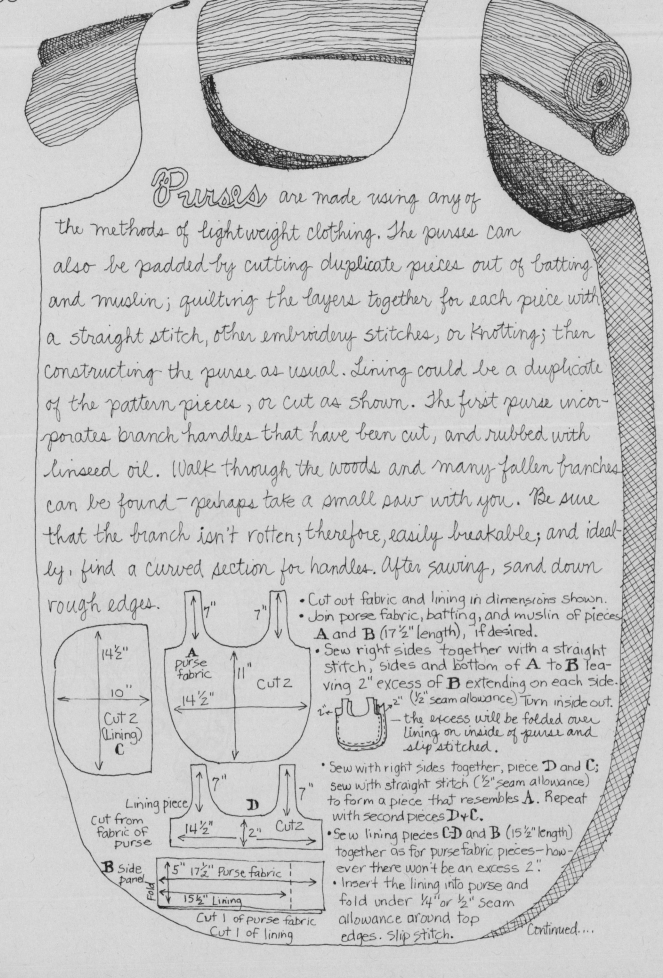

Purses are made using any of the methods of lightweight clothing. The purses can also be padded by cutting duplicate pieces out of batting and muslin; quilting the layers together for each piece with a straight stitch, other embroidery stitches, or knotting; then constructing the purse as usual. Lining could be a duplicate of the pattern pieces, or cut as shown. The first purse incorporates branch handles that have been cut, and rubbed with linseed oil. Walk through the woods and many fallen branches can be found — perhaps take a small saw with you. Be sure that the branch isn't rotten; therefore, easily breakable; and ideally, find a curved section for handles. After sawing, sand down rough edges.

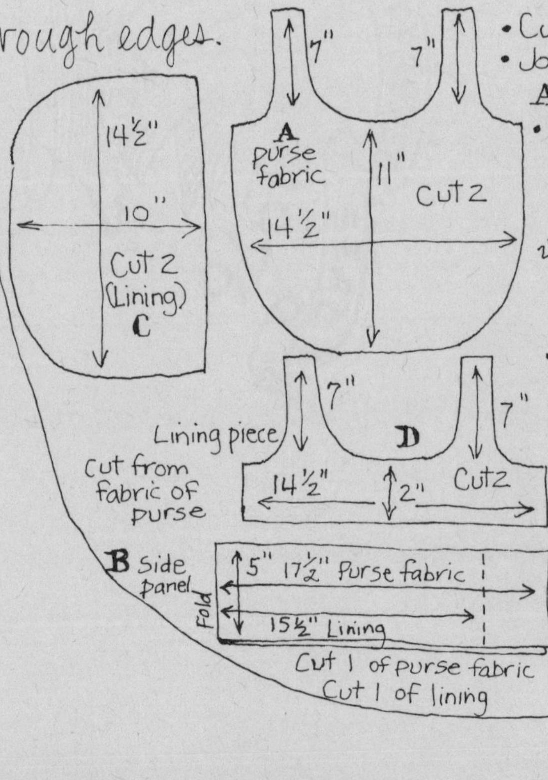

7"
7"
14½"
A
purse
fabric
11"
Cut 2
10"
14½"
Cut 2
(Lining)
C
7"
7"
Lining piece
D
Cut from
fabric of
purse
14½"
2"
Cut 2
B Side
panel
Fold
5" 17½" Purse fabric
15½" Lining
Cut 1 of purse fabric
Cut 1 of lining

- Cut out fabric and lining in dimensions shown.
- Join purse fabric, batting, and muslin of pieces **A** and **B** (17½" length), if desired.
- Sew right sides together with a straight stitch, sides and bottom of **A** to **B** leaving 2" excess of **B** extending on each side. (½" seam allowance) Turn inside out.

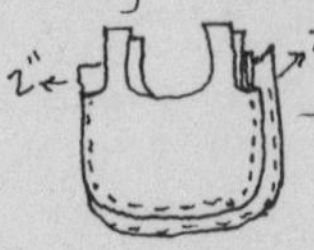

2"
2"

— the excess will be folded over lining on inside of purse and slip stitched.

- Sew with right sides together, piece **D** and **C**; sew with straight stitch (½" seam allowance) to form a piece that resembles **A**. Repeat with second pieces **D** & **C**.
- Sew lining pieces **C-D** and **B** (15½" length) together as for purse fabric pieces — however there won't be an excess 2".
- Insert the lining into purse and fold under ¼" or ½" seam allowance around top edges. Slip stitch.

Continued...

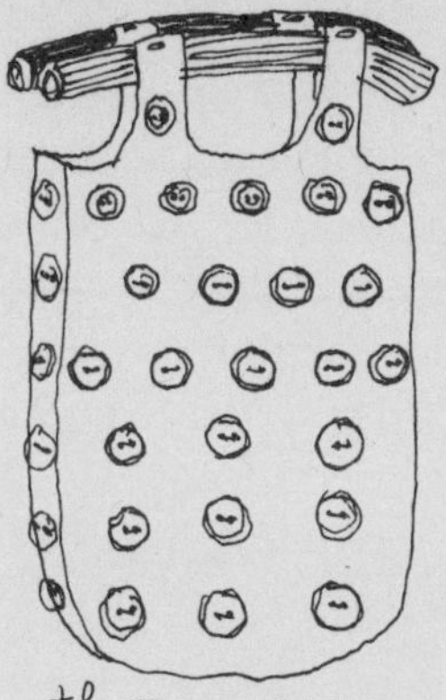

• Add 1 rivet to each handle strap at a point where the strap wrapped around the handle meets the top of the handle as shown:

Strap

(A special tool can be purchased to apply rivets,

Rivet
Rivet tool

when applying the smaller size rivet, the tool cuts a hole in the fabric and covers the rough edge with the metal.

AND/OR use white glue to attach straps to wooden handes. Then, sew the end of the strap to the point where it meets the strap— (the strap area wrapped around the handle should be firmly held), use a slip stitch.

• If using rivets, add 5/8" long, round head screws through each rivet and into wood.

ACTUAL SIZE

the purse can also be cut longer; this one uses buttons to connect, batting & muslin, & purse fabric.

A variation of the branch-handle purse can be made using wooden knitting bag handles — if a relative doesn't have an old bag for acquired handles, they can be purchased in craft or fabric stores. Just shorten the length of the straps on pieces **A** and **D** of the previous pattern to 3" long and cut the straps together as a solid piece of fabric:

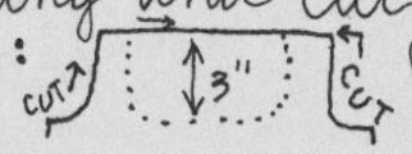
CUT
3"
CUT

(Dotted line shows cut of previous pattern)

Sew pattern pieces and lining as for branch handle purse. Slip strap extension through slits of handle and slip stitch on inside.

this purse hasn't any padding - and embroidered with the satin, & backstitch, & french knots.

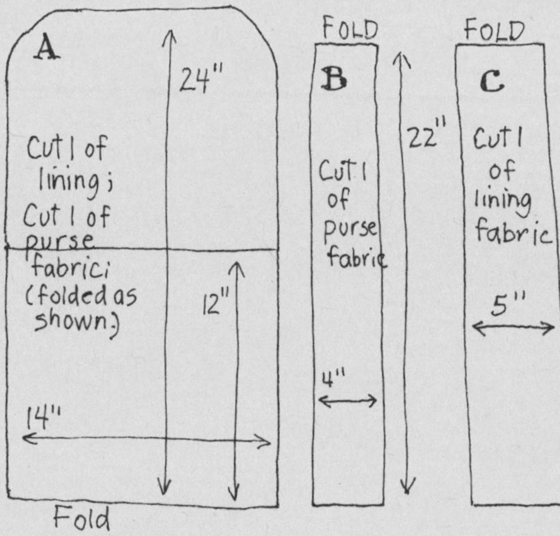
A
24"
Cut 1 of lining; Cut 1 of purse fabric; (folded as shown.)
12"
14"
Fold
FOLD
B
22"
Cut 1 of purse fabric
4"
FOLD
C
Cut 1 of lining fabric
5"

This purse uses a lining that harmonizes well with with the actual purse fabric.

• With wrong sides together, pin **B** in center of **C**. Fold under edges so that the lining shows on the outer edge:
Join with blind stitch.

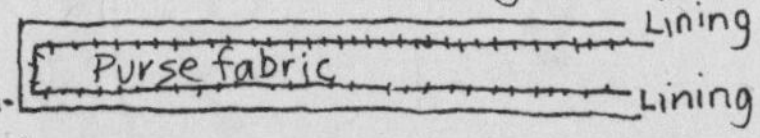
Lining
Purse fabric
Lining

• With wrong sides together, pin lining piece **A** to purse fabric **A**. Fold edges under with an equal 1/4" or 1/2" seam allowance; or fold as for shoulder strap. Sew together with a blind stitch; all around.

• Pin shoulder strap to purse, joining the ends of the strap to the fold line of **A**. Use a blind stitch to join front, bottom, and back of purse to strap.

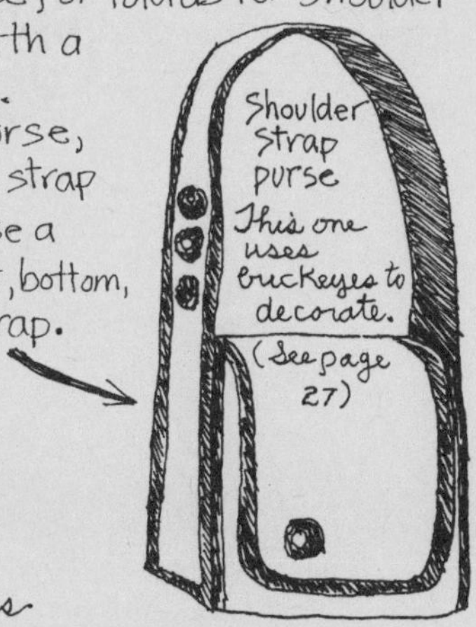
Shoulder Strap purse
This one uses buckeyes to decorate.
(See page 27)

To make a carpet bag you need 1 rectangular length or 2 squares of carpet samples. Occasionally, a garage sale will sell them and often rug & carpet stores sell samples for a dollar or two. If using squares, first slip stitch the purse bottom with right sides together with carpet thread. Fold sides in 3 inches and fold carpet in half. Work inside the purse, slip stitching edges of sides together with carpet thread. One inch from the top, insert a handle strap of fabric or leather and stitch to sides and top edge of purse.

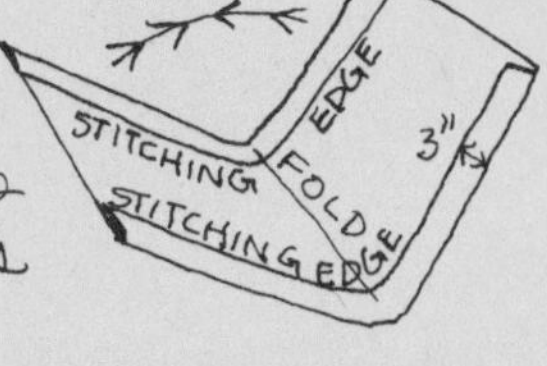
EDGE
3"
STITCHING
FOLD
STITCHING EDGE
EDGE

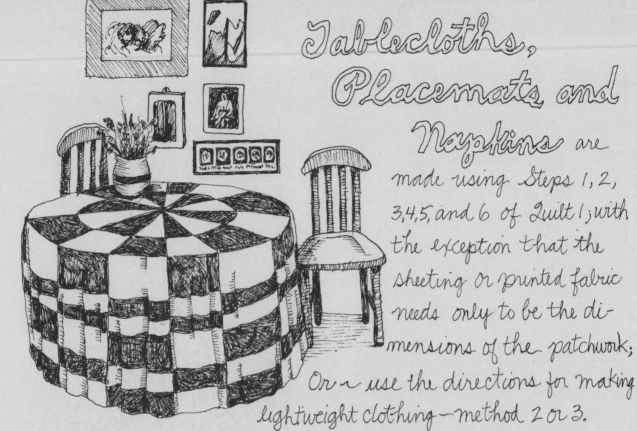

Tablecloths, Placemats and Napkins

are made using Steps 1, 2, 3,4,5, and 6 of Quilt 1; with the exception that the sheeting or printed fabric needs only to be the dimensions of the patchwork; Or ~ use the directions for making lightweight clothing—method 2 or 3.

Adjust size of squares or free form shapes relative to the size of the item. When working with circles, measure the diameter of the circle needed and circumference.

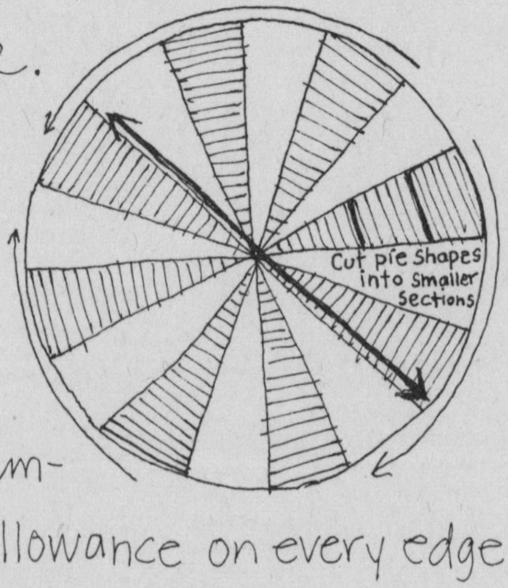
Cut pie shapes into smaller sections

Divide as desired and cut a paper pattern of 1 of the pie shapes with proper dimensions. Cut the shape into varied or uniform sections. Use each section for cutting out the appropriate number of fabric pieces, ADDING ½" seam allowance on every edge. With <u>right</u> sides together, sew with a straight stitch 1. first, sections; 2. then, ½ the pie shapes; 3. then, other half; 4. finally sew 2 halves together.

Regardless of the shape, use a straight stitch to sew ½" seam allowance of patchwork to lining—right sides together—leaving enough length free for turning patchwork inside out. Then, use a slip stitch to close the open length.

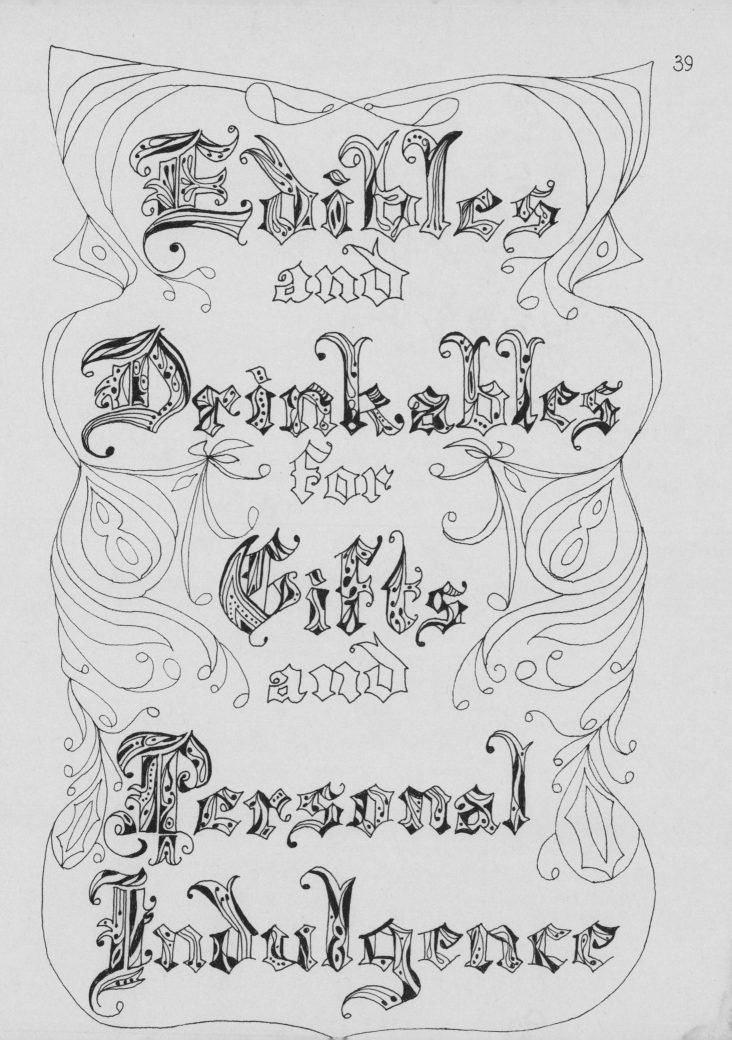

Edibles and Drinkables for Gifts and Personal Indulgence

Edibles and Drinkables for Gifts and Personal Indulgence

Food and drink always make for fine times; and gifts from the kitchen retain the warmth of thought that go into their creation. All of the following recipes are appropriate as gifts and many also mail well (if so noted on the recipe.) To insure proper **mailing**, pack the wrapped item snugly with small wads of newspaper in the smallest box possible.

All recipes include label designs which can be traced or used as a spark for new ideas. **Labels** added to the containers of food you've made or gathered makes them all the more special on the kitchen shelf or when presented as a gift. Draw and cut out labels on light-or-medium weight paper (typing paper is good). Use white glue to attach labels to fabric bags or other porous containers ~ White glue will also make a temporary bond on glass; after a few months moisture in the air loosens the label. For glass and plastic containers, there are glues on the market which adhere to porous & non-porous materials. Dimestores also carry various sizes of blank labels on gummed paper. And, many bookstores sell a <u>wide</u> variety of gorgeous bookplate designs which allow a space for writing and are on gummed paper. If you have your own design in mind, a small block print is a solution ~ remember to carve all lettering backwards on the block (pages 120-3).

Last Christmas—Chanukah, my husband and I made up what became known in our minds as **Nature Packs.** Each gift package contained an ample quantity of delux Granola; a sampling of teas which we picked, dried, and packaged in cloth bags; jams; wine (if the package was not mailed); and a hand-dipped candle. [The candles are made by tying strands of string or wick on a stick, about 6-10 inches apart. One at a time, dip each string into a pot of melted wax (a coffee can works fine.) Continue to dip each candle string, consecutively, until the desired thickness has been reached. To make long candles, allow the string to slither around the bottom of the pot each time it is dipped.] The Nature Pack is then contained in muslin bags (tied with a ribbon), with the name of the friend written with a wide marker (see page 51, for further ideas for the bag). Of course, any combination of the following recipes, or your own favorites can make a nature pack: Jam & a nut butter; Zucchini Bread and teas; Aunt Odell's Applesauce Nut Bread and a hand-made potholder (Make the potholder as for 1 square of a quilt, adding appliqué or embroidery. Sew together, front, batting (or other stuffing), and printed or muslin back, using a slip stitch. Quilt stitch, if desired.)

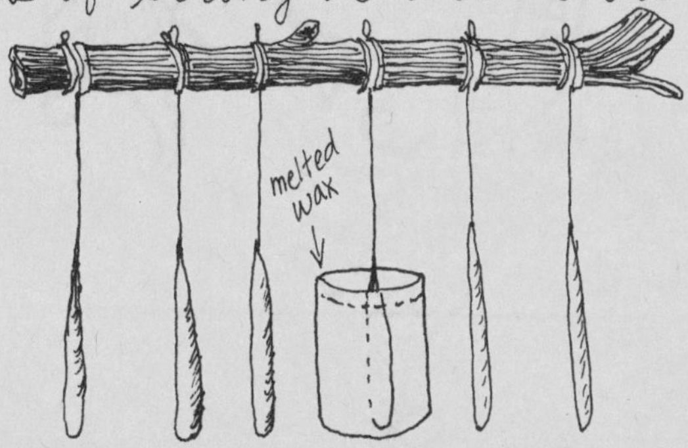
melted
wax

All this talk of Nature Packs is not meant to take any charm away from a single food or drink offering. Individually, any of the items will delight the receiver.

Some of the recipes call for canning jars & lids and **water-bath**. With such a sharp increase in canning in the last few years, there are many sources for obtaining information concerning standard canning procedures:

- Any all-purpose cookbook includes a chapter or two on canning and other methods of preserving food.
- Pamplets on canning are included when purchasing a box of jars and lids, which will also specify the manufacturer's instructions for use of the particular lid.
- New water-bath canners come with information about water-bath.
- The U.S. Department of Agriculture in many areas across the country has a cooperative Extension Service which handles any questions you may have. They also offer many informative pamphlets on many preserving and cooking topics.
- There are many books which can be used as your daily guide during the canning and freezing season.
- As for jams, all boxes of pectin contain a pamplet of instructions for making any type of jam or jelly.

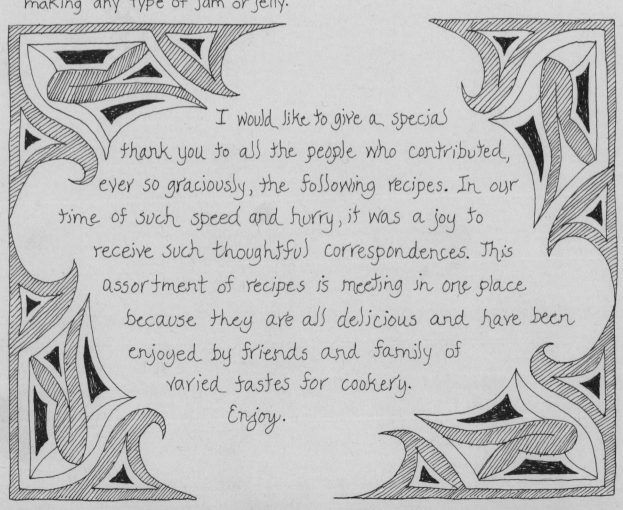

I would like to give a special thank you to all the people who contributed, ever so graciously, the following recipes. In our time of such speed and hurry, it was a joy to receive such thoughtful correspondences. This assortment of recipes is meeting in one place because they are all delicious and have been enjoyed by friends and family of varied tastes for cookery.

Enjoy.

Aunt Odell's APPLESAUCE NUT BREAD

MAILS WELL

~ good with cream cheese or butter on top.

2 cups flour
3/4 cup sugar
2 tsp. baking powder
1 tsp. salt
1/2 tsp. baking soda
1 cup nuts
1 egg
1 cup applesauce
2 tsp. melted shortening
1/2 tsp. cinnamon

COMBINE ALL THE INGREDIENTS IN A BOWL AND STIR TIL BLENDED. POUR INTO GREASED LOAF PAN.... (9" x 5" x 3"). BAKE AT 350° IN OVEN FOR 45-50 MINUTES.

APPLE
SAUCE
NUT
BREAD

When the bread is completely cooled, package in clear plastic wrap or bag.

Try substituting the 1 cup of applesauce with a cup of mashed paw-paws (see page 131).

JAM

Mail jam jars with the rings and pack well.

A piece of toasted bread with sweet butter and homemade jam is an experience to be revisited. Wild blackberries, black raspberries, elderberries, and wild apples are the free-for-the picking ingredients that can be used in these recipes.

Jam requires the least complicated of canning procedures: Use ½-pint or pint canning jars with no cracks or chips.

Clean jars in soapy water—rinse well.

Fill jars with boiling water while making the jam.

Prepare lids according to the manufacturer's directions—usually, metal lids with sealing compound are put into boiling water.

Make jam and fill jars to within ⅛-inch of top.

Wipe rim with a clean, damp cloth; place metal lid on jar and screw on ring-tight. Allow jam to cool upright.

WILD APPLE

APPLE RELISH ✻

4 ½ cups finely chopped red apples (takes about 3 lbs.)
½ cup water
¼ cup lemon juice
½ cup raisins
1 package powdered pectin
5½ cups sugar
½ cup chopped nuts

Select tart apples. Sort and wash apples. Remove stem and blossom ends and core; do not pare. Chop apples fine. Combine the apples, water, lemon juice, and raisins in a kettle. Add the pectin and stir well. Place on high heat and, stirring constantly, bring quickly to a full boil with bubbles over the entire surface. Add the sugar, continue stirring, and heat again to a full bubbling boil.

CONTINUED

APPLE RELISH CONTINUED...

Boil hard for 1 minute, stirring constantly. Add the nuts. Remove from heat. If desired, add 3 or 4 drops of red food coloring. Skim. Fill and seal containers. Makes about 7 half-pint jars.

BLACKBERRY JAM*

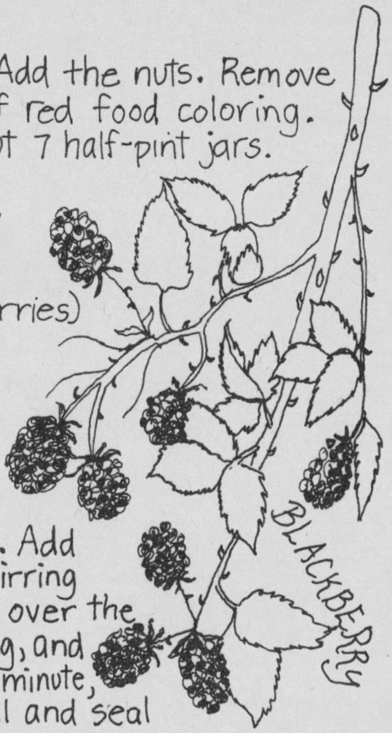
BLACKBERRY

6 cups crushed blackberries (about 3 qt. boxes of berries)

1 package powdered pectin
8½ cups sugar

Sort and wash fully ripe berries; remove any stems or caps. Crush the berries. If they are very seedy, put part or all of them through a sieve or food mill. Measure crushed berries into a kettle. Add the pectin and stir well. Place on high heat and, stirring constantly, bring quickly to a full boil with bubbles over the entire surface. Add the sugar, continue stirring, and heat again to a full bubbling boil. Boil hard for 1 minute, stirring constantly. Remove from heat; skim. Fill and seal containers. Makes about 10 half-pint jars.

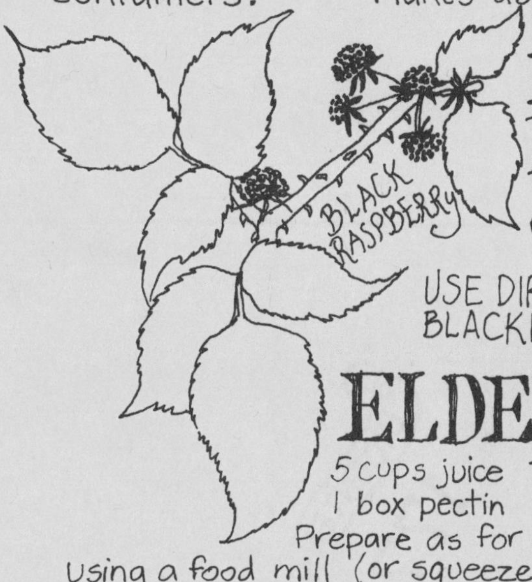
BLACK RASPBERRY

BLACK RASPBERRY JAM

USE DIRECTIONS FOR BLACKBERRY JAM.

ELDERBERRY

ELDERBERRY JAM

5 cups juice
7 cup sugar
1 box pectin

Prepare as for blackberry jam — definitely using a food mill (or squeeze out juice using a muslin bag after simmering crushed berries for 15 minutes.)

APPLE RELISH

BLACKBERRY
JAM

BLACK
RASPBERRY
JAM

Elderberry
Jam

* Courtesy *Complete Guide to Home Canning, Preserving and Freezing*: U.S. Dept. of Agriculture; Dover Publications Inc.

NUTS AND THEIR BUTTERS

MAILS WELL

The traditional nut butter: **PEANUT BUTTER**, is easily made in an electric blender or a mortar & pestle. Use salted or unsalted nuts (if using unsalted peanuts, add salt to taste, after the butter is made). **OR**, plant your own peanuts: plant Virginia peanuts in the spring, 2" in sandy soil, 18" apart — takes 120 days. Grind peanuts until the butter forms. I don't add peanut oil, but some recipes do; if using oil, add a little at a time until the desired creaminess is reached. Store peanut butter in CLEAN jars with lids tightly closed — after a few months oil will rise to the top, but the peanut butter will remain edible. Other nuts need added oil (and salt to taste, unless previously salted). Grind nuts in a blender or a mortar & pestle as for peanut butter. When the nuts are ground enough that they make an attempt to become a butter, add olive or peanut oil a little bit at a time to create the desired creaminess. Make a small sample of the nut butter first, as taste buds differ: I found **WALNUT BUTTER** to be rather unappealing although others have found it luscious. On the other hand, **CASHEW BUTTER** is an indubitably fine butter, very rich and palatable. Experiment with **WILD NUTS**: walnut, hickory, and hazelnuts. The nuts are gathered in the fall and for storage of the nuts, it is best to hull them first (to avoid worms). Be sure the nuts are ripe: the ripened nuts fall to the

ground. Here are some pointers about **gathering and preparing nuts:**

1. Gather nuts that have fallen to the ground — this is not only the best but the easiest method.
2. After removing the hulls, drop the unshelled nuts into a bucket of water — nuts that are rotten will immediately float to the top. Wash the nuts, changing the water every so often.
3. Dry the nuts with a coarse towel and place them in single layers on cheesecloth hung canopy-style or on a dehydrator (See page 57) in an airy room. In 3-4 weeks, taste a few nuts, checking for crispness.
4. Store nuts in muslin or burlap sacks hanging in a cool place — shell small quantities of about one quart as needed. Hickory and hazelnuts open easily with a nut cracker; walnuts take a good tap with a hammer.

NOTE: THE HULLS OF NUTS ARE USED IN NATURAL DYEING (See pg. 110-1).

Black Walnuts

★ Be SURE to hull walnuts SOON after gathering, to keep the incredible staining powers of the hulls from seeping into the nut. ★

Wear rubber gloves when hulling walnuts — otherwise, hands & finger nails will be stained for a week or more. Cut the hulls in half with a knife and twist the halves off the shell. If the hulls are too hard to twist off, then hit with a hammer, and peel off. Remove as much hull-pulp as possible and place the unshelled nuts in the sun for 1 day or in a WARM oven for ½ hour, to dry up the stain. Dry and store as described above. Black walnuts are particularly fine for baking.

Black Walnut Stain

THE HULLS OF THE BLACK WALNUT MAKE A BEAUTIFUL STAIN FOR WOOD WHICH WILL VARY IN COLOR DEPENDING ON THE METHOD OF APPLICATION. AFTER HULLING THE NUTS, PLACE THE HULLS IN

A LARGE ENAMEL KETTLE. ADD ENOUGH WATER TO AVOID BURNING — ABOUT 2 INCHES OF WATER. COOK THE HULLS OUTSIDE OR IN A WELL-VENTILATED ROOM. PLACE THE KETTLE OVER MEDIUM HEAT AND SIMMER FOR 30-45 MINUTES, STIRRING AND SMASHING HULLS OFTEN WITH A WOODEN SPOON. WHEN HULLS ARE SOFT, REMOVE FROM HEAT AND LET COOL. WEARING RUBBER GLOVES, TAKE HANDFULS OF HULLS AND SQUEEZE OUT ALL THE JUICE. REMOVE ALL THE HULLS AND SIMMER THE JUICE OVER MEDIUM HEAT, STIRRING OCCASIONALLY, UNTIL THICK (APPROXIMATELY 2 HOURS; REDUCED TO ABOUT ½ THE ORIGINAL VOLUME). WHEN COOL, FILL TO 2" OF TOP IN SEALED JARS. USE CLOTH TO APPLY STAIN. FOR A **DARK STAIN**, APPLY STAIN WHILE WARM, **OR** APPLY AS MANY COATS OF STAIN AS DESIRED TO ACHIEVE DARKER AND DARKER TONES, ALLOWING ONE MINUTE BETWEEN EACH APPLICATION. THEN WIPE WITH A CLEAN CLOTH, OR DIP THE CLOTH IN LINSEED OIL AND RUB. A **LIGHT STAIN** IS MADE BY EITHER A SINGLE COAT OF WALNUT STAIN OR BY MIXING 4 PARTS STAIN TO 1 PART LINSEED OIL AND APPLYING THE MIXTURE WITH A CLOTH. **NOTE:** This stain is neither an edible nor a drinkable.

Hazelnuts

The husk of the hazelnut during summer is green and camouflages itself amid the leaves of this small tree. During the fall, the husk turns brown and the nuts are easily husked. It's not only a favorite of people, but also of squirrels who have an uncanny knack for knowing the first days that the nuts have fallen to the ground. I have a friend who picks the brown-husk nuts from the tree instead of competing with the squirrels for the fallen hazelnuts. This seems to be the best method of gathering. Wash, dry, and store the nuts as described in general notes about nuts on the previous page.

Hickory Nuts

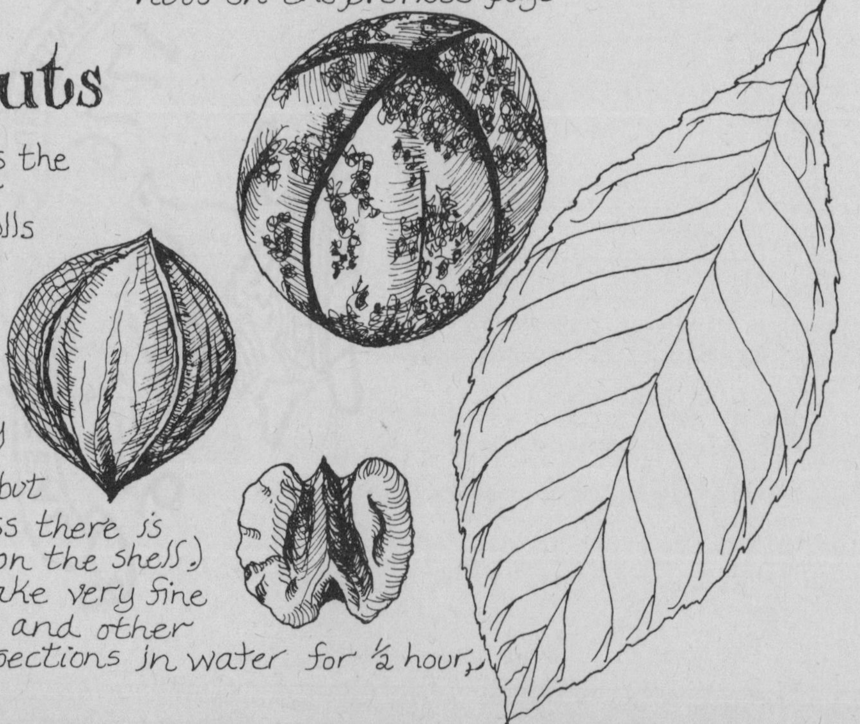

Hickory trees (such as the Shagbark Hickory) bear delicious nuts — the hulls of the ripe nut begin to separate. Pushing away colorful leaves to uncover hickory nuts is a WONDERFUL way to know and enjoy autumn. Gather nuts with the hulls still on, but also nuts alone (unless there is obviously a wormhole on the shell.) The hull sections make very fine objects for macramé and other crafts: Boil the hull sections in water for ½ hour, rub with linseed oil, or leave them as they are. Dry the hulls in the sun, or in a light room. Then drill a hole. Wash, dry, and store hickory nuts as directed on page 47.

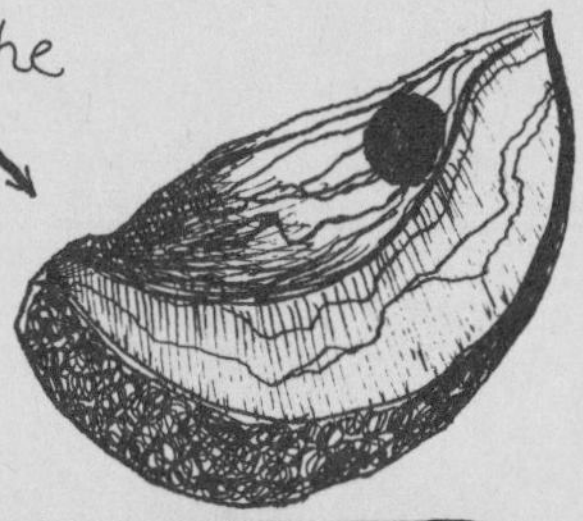

An invaluable book full of knowledge about preparing and storing food from the garden and outdoors is:

STOCKING UP-HOW TO PRESERVE THE FOODS YOU GROW, NATURALLY, by the Editors of Organic Gardening and Farming; Edited by Carol Stoner. Emmaus, Penna.: Rodale Press, Inc., Book Division, 1975.

Black Walnut Stain
FOR USE ON WOOD ONLY

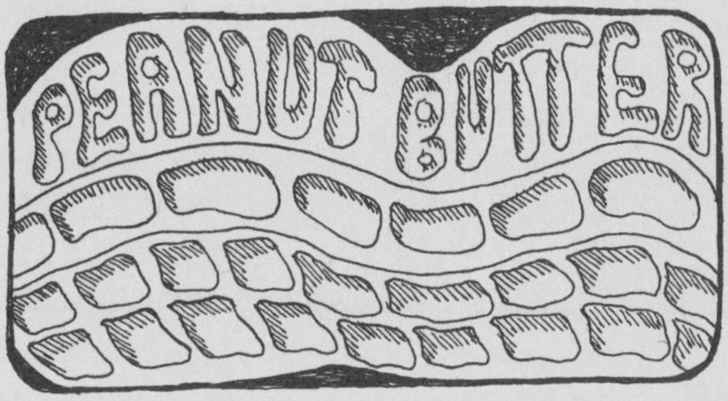
PEANUT BUTTER

Walnut Butter

HAZELNUTS

CASHEW BUTTER

BLACK WALNUTS

hickory Nuts

PECAN BUTTER

Sunflower Seeds

DATES
SUNFLOWER SEEDS
ROLLED OATS
ALMONDS
BUCKWHEAT

Homemade Granola*

Mails well

4 cups rolled oats
1/2 cup sesame seeds
1/2 cup sunflower seeds
1/2 tsp sea salt
1/4 cup honey or maple syrup
1/4 cup safflower or corn oil
1 tsp vanilla
1/2 cup raisins

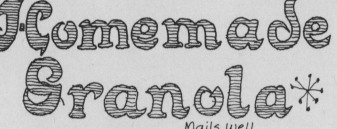

In a large mixing bowl combine oats, sesame and sunflower seeds and salt, mixing well. In another bowl mix together sweetener, oil, and vanilla, then add to dry ingredients. Mix thoroughly to an even consistency and spread out in a shallow baking pan. Set in a 325° oven to bake for about 40 minutes or until fairly dry and golden brown. Be sure to stir regularly, at least every 10 minutes, to prevent burning on top and sides. When baking is complete, remove from oven and add raisins. Granola will become crispier and crunchier as it cools; after cooling it is ready to eat as is or with hot or cold milk or other beverage.

Makes 5-6 cups

SOY GRITS
FILBERTS
CURRANTS
MIXED DRYED FRUIT
PUMPKIN SEEDS

RAISINS
CASHEWS
SESAME SEEDS
WHEAT GERM
COCOANUT

Granolas Galore*

The basic ingredients for granola are cereal, oil, sweetener, and "extras". Using the same basic proportions as given in this recipe, you can vary one or more of these

CONTINUED....

* Courtesy © 1973 natural recipes
94 Bourne Street, Jamaica Plain, MA. 02130

ingredients to create many different granolas. Here are some of the possibilities for "extras."

Sunflower Seeds · Sesame Seeds · Almonds · Buckwheat · Dates · Wheat Germ · Filberts · Cocoanut · Soy Grits · Cashews · Raisins · Pumpkin Seeds · Dried Fruits · Currants

Granola is a healthful delight and can also be used with favorite recipes. For instance, substitute granola for plain oats in your oatmeal cookie recipe. To store on the pantry shelf or to package for a friend.... cover an oats box OR place a plastic bag within a fabric bag and tie with cord. For a special Granola Bag: A) PRINT YOUR OWN FABRIC (See pages 120-3); B) EMBROIDER THE LABEL WITH THE SATIN STITCH & THE BACKSTITCH (See pgs. 4-5); OR C) BATIK THE FABRIC (See pgs. 100-3).

GranoLa
GranoLa

GranoLa
Ingredients ~ from list and lettering above

SUNFLOWER SEEDS

Mails well

Sunflowers are an outstanding addition to any garden or yard. Plant seeds in early spring, ½" deep. Sunflowers grow easily with little weeding ... birds may drop seeds while feeding and unexpected flowers appear. Pick out the seeds when the central area of the flower contains seeds with the black and white pattern. Dry seeds on a dehydrator rack (see page 57) or stretched out cheesecloth, until the shells are hard to the touch. Store seeds in jars, for eating & beauty. (Don't forget the birds in the winter!)

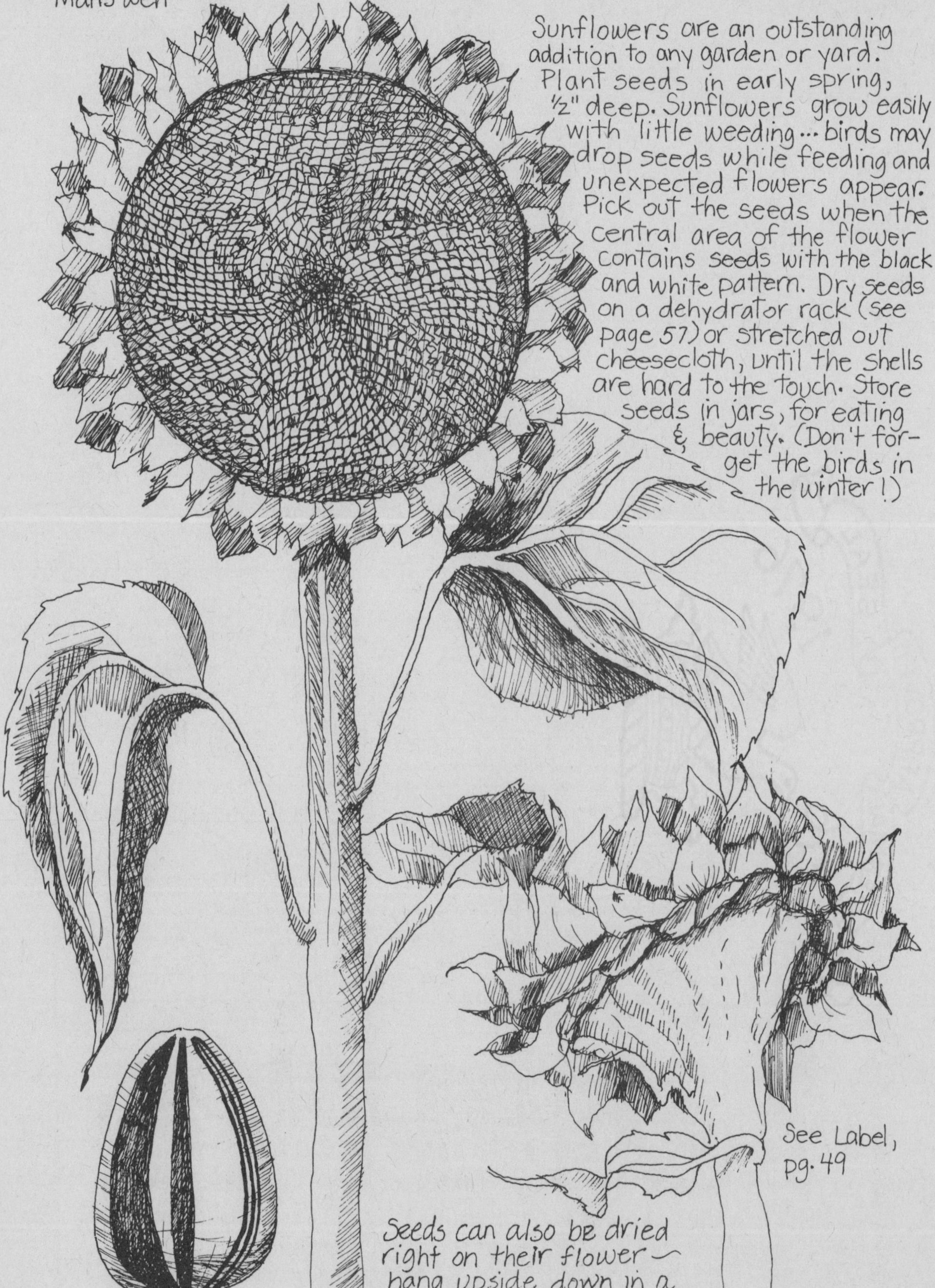

See Label, pg. 49

Seeds can also be dried right on their flower — hang upside down in a light, airy room.

MAILS WELL

DRYING TEAS

YELLOW CLOVER
WHITE CLOVER

During the summer, particularly early summer before many of the flowers have dried from the heat, observe and read of wild flowers and plants that can be dried as teas. Some specimens are native to the land and the book, **A Field Guide to Wildflowers** by Roger Tory Peterson and Margaret McKenny (Houghton Mifflin Company), identifies rapidly by an arrangement of color, form, and detail. Common to most regions are: chamomile, red clover, mint, and white & yellow clover.

Mint has tiny white flowers on top
MINT

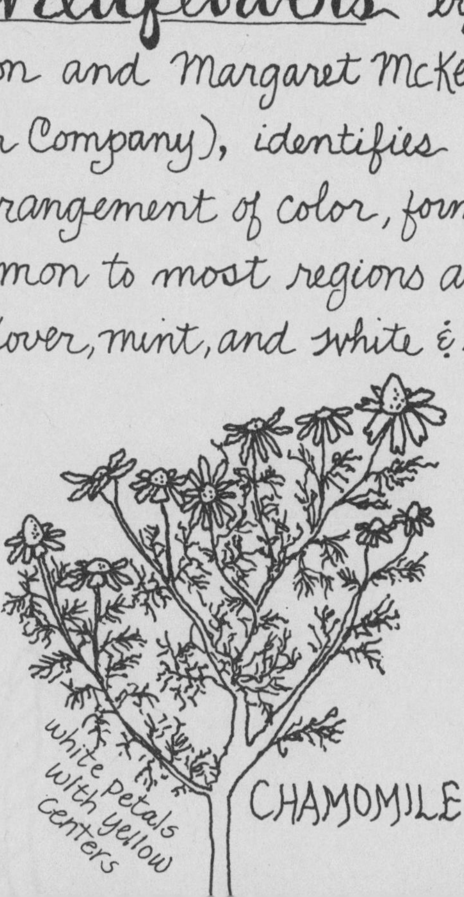
white petals with yellow centers
CHAMOMILE

red-purple flowers
RED CLOVER

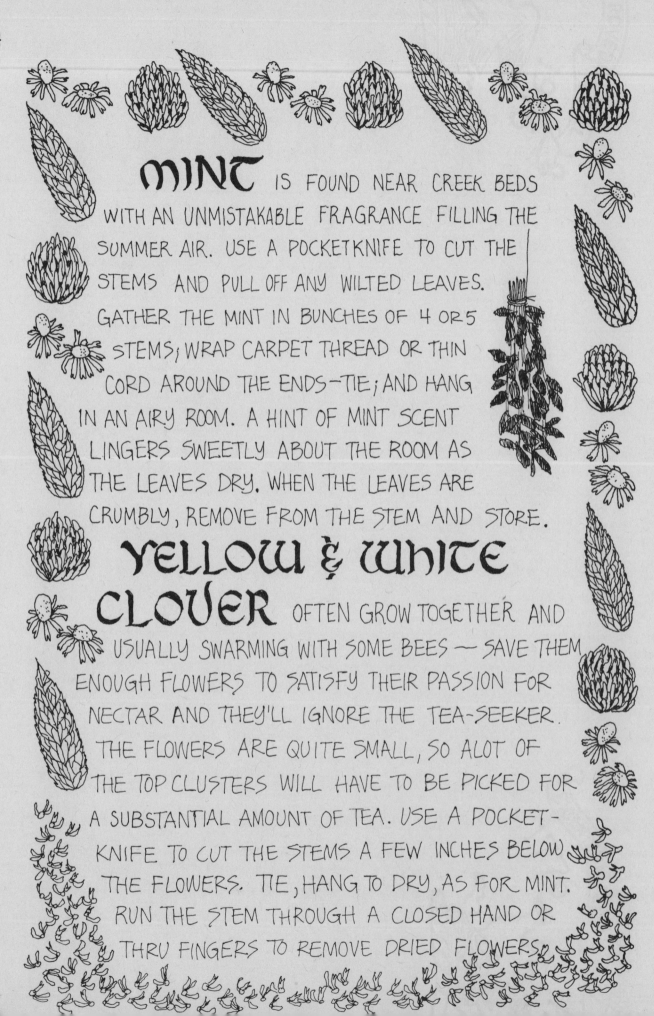

MINT IS FOUND NEAR CREEK BEDS WITH AN UNMISTAKABLE FRAGRANCE FILLING THE SUMMER AIR. USE A POCKETKNIFE TO CUT THE STEMS AND PULL OFF ANY WILTED LEAVES. GATHER THE MINT IN BUNCHES OF 4 OR 5 STEMS; WRAP CARPET THREAD OR THIN CORD AROUND THE ENDS—TIE; AND HANG IN AN AIRY ROOM. A HINT OF MINT SCENT LINGERS SWEETLY ABOUT THE ROOM AS THE LEAVES DRY. WHEN THE LEAVES ARE CRUMBLY, REMOVE FROM THE STEM AND STORE.

YELLOW & WHITE CLOVER OFTEN GROW TOGETHER AND USUALLY SWARMING WITH SOME BEES — SAVE THEM ENOUGH FLOWERS TO SATISFY THEIR PASSION FOR NECTAR AND THEY'LL IGNORE THE TEA-SEEKER. THE FLOWERS ARE QUITE SMALL, SO ALOT OF THE TOP CLUSTERS WILL HAVE TO BE PICKED FOR A SUBSTANTIAL AMOUNT OF TEA. USE A POCKET-KNIFE TO CUT THE STEMS A FEW INCHES BELOW THE FLOWERS. TIE, HANG TO DRY, AS FOR MINT. RUN THE STEM THROUGH A CLOSED HAND OR THRU FINGERS TO REMOVE DRIED FLOWERS.

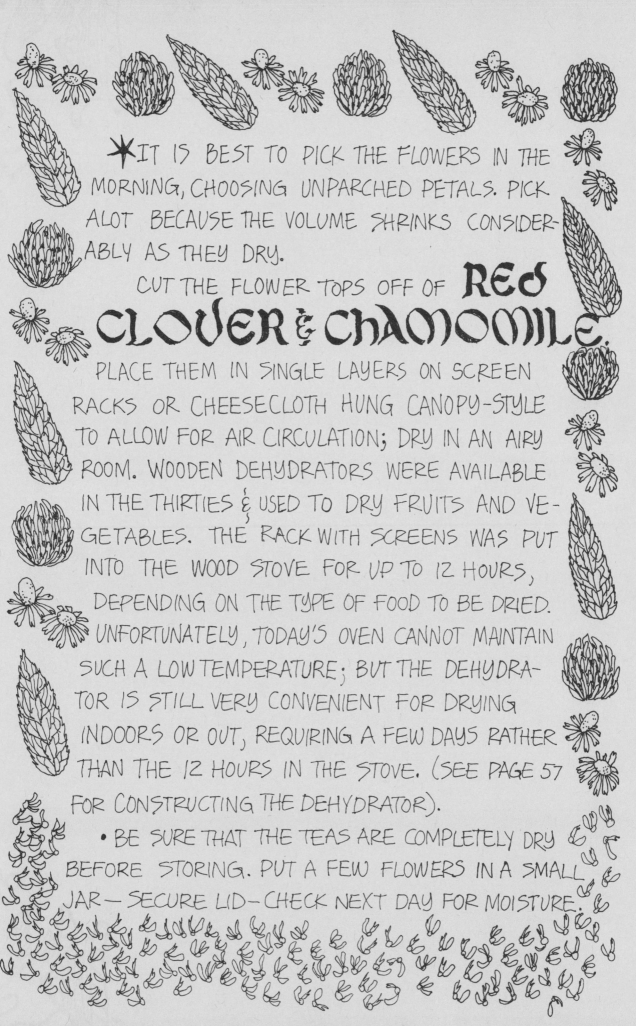

✶IT IS BEST TO PICK THE FLOWERS IN THE MORNING, CHOOSING UNPARCHED PETALS. PICK ALOT BECAUSE THE VOLUME SHRINKS CONSIDERABLY AS THEY DRY.

CUT THE FLOWER TOPS OFF OF **RED CLOVER & CHAMOMILE.**

PLACE THEM IN SINGLE LAYERS ON SCREEN RACKS OR CHEESECLOTH HUNG CANOPY-STYLE TO ALLOW FOR AIR CIRCULATION; DRY IN AN AIRY ROOM. WOODEN DEHYDRATORS WERE AVAILABLE IN THE THIRTIES & USED TO DRY FRUITS AND VEGETABLES. THE RACK WITH SCREENS WAS PUT INTO THE WOOD STOVE FOR UP TO 12 HOURS, DEPENDING ON THE TYPE OF FOOD TO BE DRIED. UNFORTUNATELY, TODAY'S OVEN CANNOT MAINTAIN SUCH A LOW TEMPERATURE; BUT THE DEHYDRATOR IS STILL VERY CONVENIENT FOR DRYING INDOORS OR OUT, REQUIRING A FEW DAYS RATHER THAN THE 12 HOURS IN THE STOVE. (SEE PAGE 57 FOR CONSTRUCTING THE DEHYDRATOR).

• BE SURE THAT THE TEAS ARE COMPLETELY DRY BEFORE STORING. PUT A FEW FLOWERS IN A SMALL JAR — SECURE LID — CHECK NEXT DAY FOR MOISTURE.

Serve the **TEAS** separately, mixed, hot or cold, with lemon, honey, cream, sugar, or a sprig of fresh mint in the summer.

— SEE INDEX FOR MORE TEAS —

Store tea in tins or package smaller "samplers" for gifts.... For each sampler bag, cut 2 pieces of fabric 3 inches by 7 inches and 2 pieces of polyethylene plastic (such as a plastic bag) of the same dimensions. Place right sides of fabric together, with the plastic lined up on the outside. Sew the 4 thicknesses together with a straight stitch on 3 sides, as shown. Turn bag inside out. Fill with tea and close with cord or wire. Use labels, if desired; attach with white glue.

PLASTIC

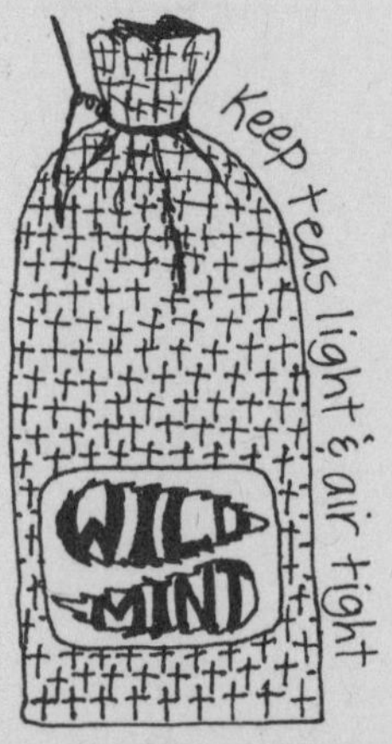
Keep teas light & air tight
WILD MINT

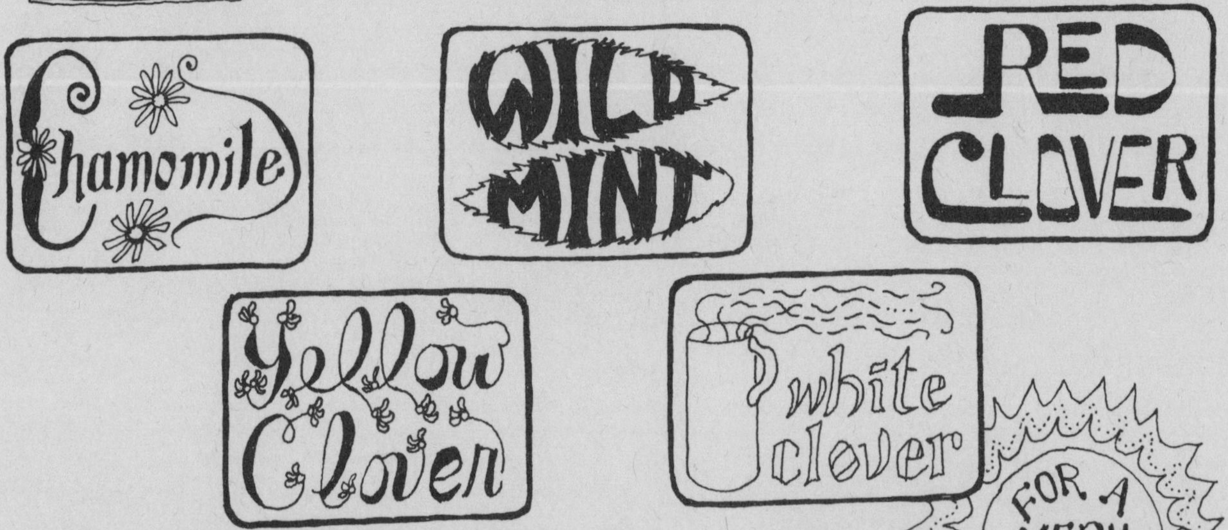
Chamomile
WILD MINT
RED CLOVER
Yellow Clover
white clover

FOR A VERY CLEAR TEA

For Hot Tea
Use a tea strainer or tea ball — Fill with tea and pour boiling water over both.

Use about 3 TBsp. tea per ½ gallon of water; put tea in a coffee filter or thin muslin and tie with cord. Put teabag & water in glass jar with lid just set on top. Rest jar in sun all day!

FOR ICED TEA....

SUN TEA

a very good book on the many uses of plants:

THE HERBALIST by Joseph E. Meyer; publication of the Indiana Botanic Garden, Hammond, Indiana 46325; 1972 (9th printing)

The Dehydrator

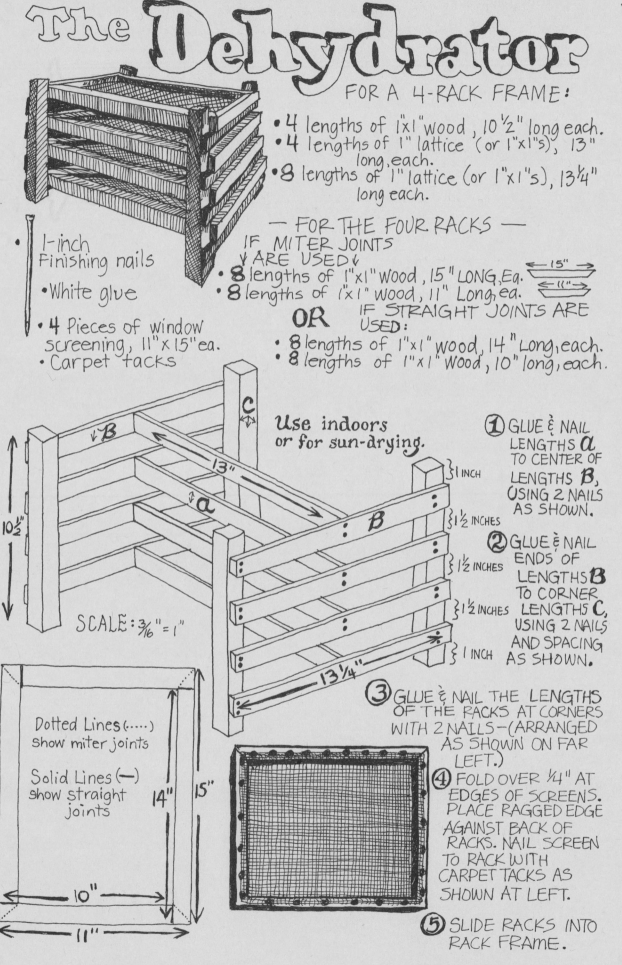

FOR A 4-RACK FRAME:

- 4 lengths of 1"x1" wood, 10½" long each.
- 4 lengths of 1" lattice (or 1"x1"s), 13" long, each.
- 8 lengths of 1" lattice (or 1"x1"s), 13¼" long each.

- 1-inch Finishing nails
- White glue
- 4 Pieces of window screening, 11" x 15" ea.
- Carpet tacks

— FOR THE FOUR RACKS —

IF MITER JOINTS ARE USED:

- 8 lengths of 1"x1" wood, 15" LONG, Ea.
- 8 lengths of 1"x1" wood, 11" Long, ea.

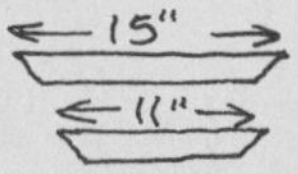
15"
11"

OR IF STRAIGHT JOINTS ARE USED:

- 8 lengths of 1"x1" wood, 14" Long, each.
- 8 lengths of 1"x1" Wood, 10" long, each.

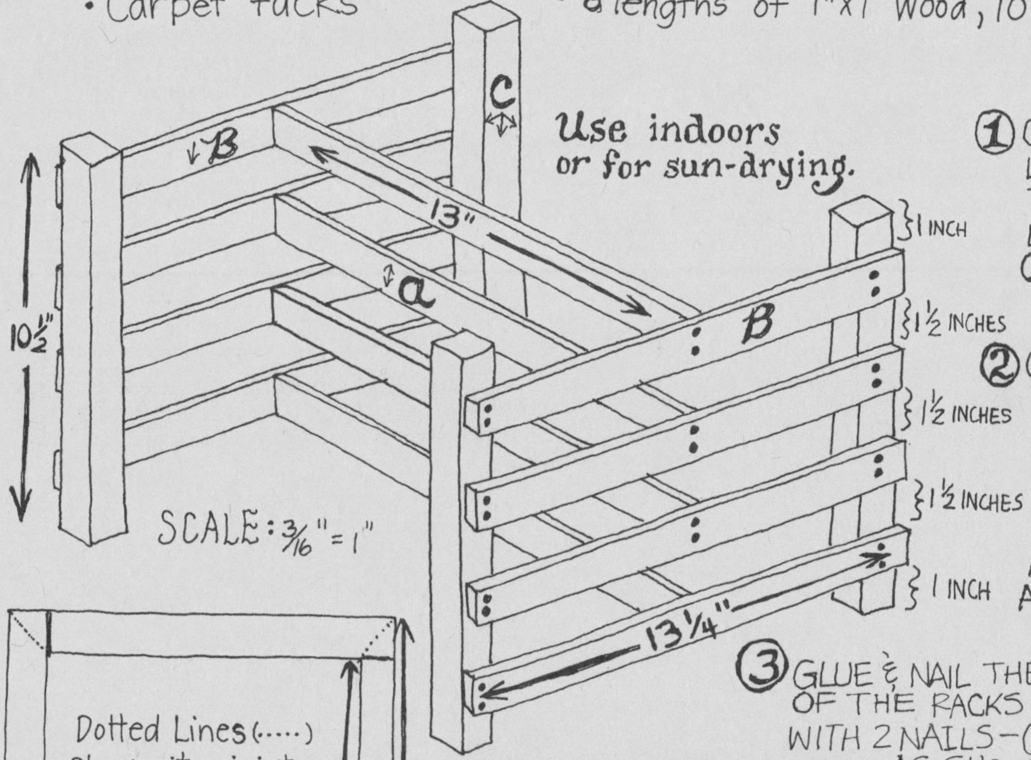
C
B
13"
a
B
10½"
1 INCH
1½ INCHES
1½ INCHES
1½ INCHES
1 INCH
13¼"
SCALE: 3/16" = 1"

Use indoors or for sun-drying.

1. GLUE & NAIL LENGTHS *a* TO CENTER OF LENGTHS *B*, USING 2 NAILS AS SHOWN.
2. GLUE & NAIL ENDS OF LENGTHS *B* TO CORNER LENGTHS *C*, USING 2 NAILS AND SPACING AS SHOWN.
3. GLUE & NAIL THE LENGTHS OF THE RACKS AT CORNERS WITH 2 NAILS—(ARRANGED AS SHOWN ON FAR LEFT.)
4. FOLD OVER ¼" AT EDGES OF SCREENS. PLACE RAGGED EDGE AGAINST BACK OF RACKS. NAIL SCREEN TO RACK WITH CARPET TACKS AS SHOWN AT LEFT.
5. SLIDE RACKS INTO RACK FRAME.

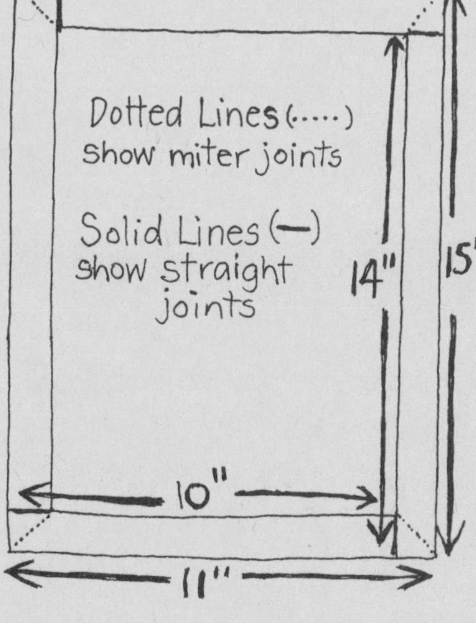
Dotted Lines (.....) show miter joints
Solid Lines (—) show straight joints
14"
15"
10"
11"

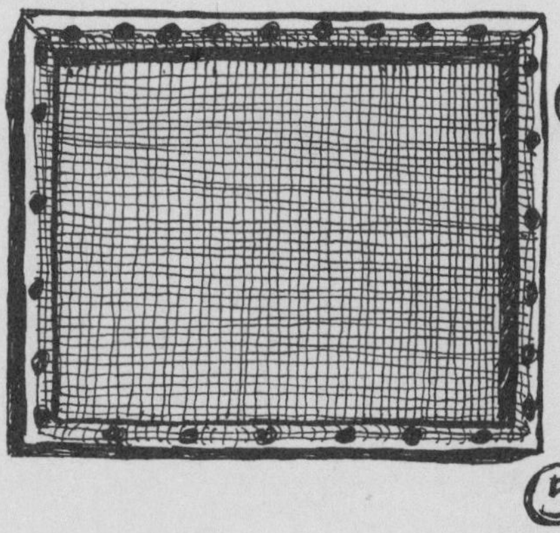

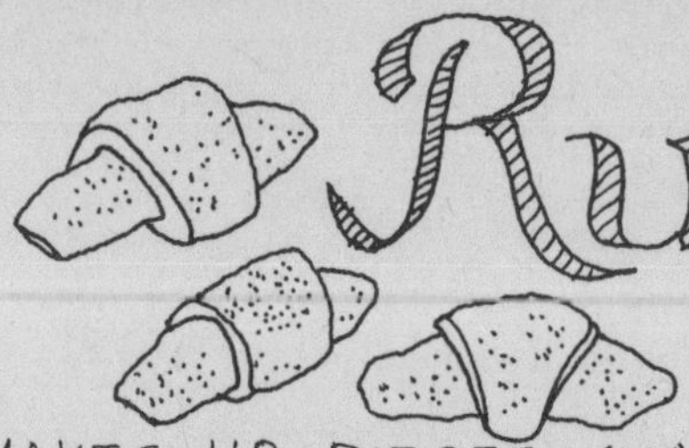

Ruggles*

(pronounced: **RUG**-lahs)

MAKES 48 PIECES (MAILS WELL)

1½ tsp. powdered yeast
1 tsp. granulated sugar
½ pound butter or margarine
¼ cup lukewarm water
2 Tbsp. granulated sugar
2 eggs-thoroughly beaten
3 cups flour

YEAST
FLOU
SUGAR

Melt ½ lb. butter and let cool; set aside.

Dissolve 1½ tsp. yeast in ¼ cup lukewarm water in bowl.

Add 1 tsp. sugar and mix.

Add melted butter to yeast mixture.

Add 2 Tbsp. sugar and mix.

Add 2 thoroughly beaten eggs.

Add 3 cups flour and mix thoroughly.

Place dough in shallow bowl, cover and chill in refrigerator overnight.

Cut dough into six parts. Form each section into a ball, and roll out into a circle on mixture of cinnamon and sugar. Cover each circle with a mixture of sugar, cinnamon, ground nuts, and raisins or any desired filling... (try sesame seeds, jam, a section of a chocolate bar for each crescent, cocoanut...). Cut circles of dough into 8ths (⊛), and roll from outside to point. (Keep rest of dough in refrigerator while baking.) Bake in 350° oven for 25 min., on cookie sheet, spaced 1-in apart.

RUGGLES

Package in plastic-lined fabric bag.
See page 51

*Courtesy Mrs. Selma Abeles

OLD·FASHIONED * HARD CANDY

MAILS WELL

2 CUPS SUGAR
1 CUP WATER
3/4 CUP LIGHT CORN SYRUP
FOOD COLORING
FLAVORING TO TASTE (found at drug stores)
Suggested flavorings:
Oil of peppermint, cinnamon, anise, Clove, wintergreen
CONFECTIONERS' SUGAR

Mix sugar, water, and corn syrup together; cook to 300° on a candy thermometer. Remove from heat; add coloring and about 1/8 tsp. of flavoring. Mix well. Pour into well-greased plate or pan. When cool enough to handle, cut into 1/2" strips, then cut strips into chunks. Drop candy in a greased cookie sheet. When cold and brittle, sprinkle lightly with confectioners' sugar.

Store in jars, or plastic bags.

old fashioned
Hard Candy

*Courtesy
Isabelle Martin & Chagrin Falls United Methodist Youth Fellowship

Kosher Dills*

Here is a quick and easy kosher dill pickle recipe, that transforms cucumbers into crispy, garlic pickles — right in the jar.

4 pounds 4-inch pickling cucumbers
14 cloves garlic, peeled, split
1/4 cup salt .... USE PURE GRANULATED SALT
2-3/4 cups Heinz Distilled White Vinegar
3 cups water
12-14 sprigs fresh dill weed
28 peppercorns

WASH CUCUMBERS; CUT IN HALF LENGTHWISE. COMBINE GARLIC AND NEXT 3 INGREDIENTS; HEAT TO BOILING. REMOVE GARLIC AND PLACE 4 HALVES INTO EACH CLEAN JAR, THEN PACK CUCUMBERS, ADDING 2 SPRIGS DILL WEED AND 4 PEPPERCORNS. POUR HOT VINEGAR SOLUTION OVER CUCUMBERS TO WITHIN 1/2 INCH OF TOP.
ADJUST COVERS.
MAKES 6-7 PINTS.
PROCESS IN BOILING WATER BATH FOR 10 MINUTES.

Kosher
Dills

*Courtesy H.J. Heinz Company

PUMPKIN RELISH *

2 QUARTS SHREDDED PUMPKIN
2 CUPS SWEET GREEN PEPPERS
3 CUPS CABBAGE
2 CUPS ONION
2 CUPS CELERY — CHOPPED-NOT TOO FINE
5 CUPS WHITE (4%) VINEGAR
1 CUP WATER
2½ CUPS GRANULATED SUGAR
4 teaspoons SALT
2 TABLESPOONS DRY MUSTARD
1 TABLESPOON TUMERIC
1 SMALL HOT PEPPER

Mix all ingredients in a stainless steel pan (6 qt. or larger). Bring to simmer and cook 20 minutes. Pack hot into clean jars leaving ⅛ inch head space; adjust caps. Process 15 minutes in water bath after water is boiling. Makes 8 pints.

Pumpkin
Relish

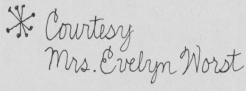

* Courtesy
Mrs. Evelyn Worst

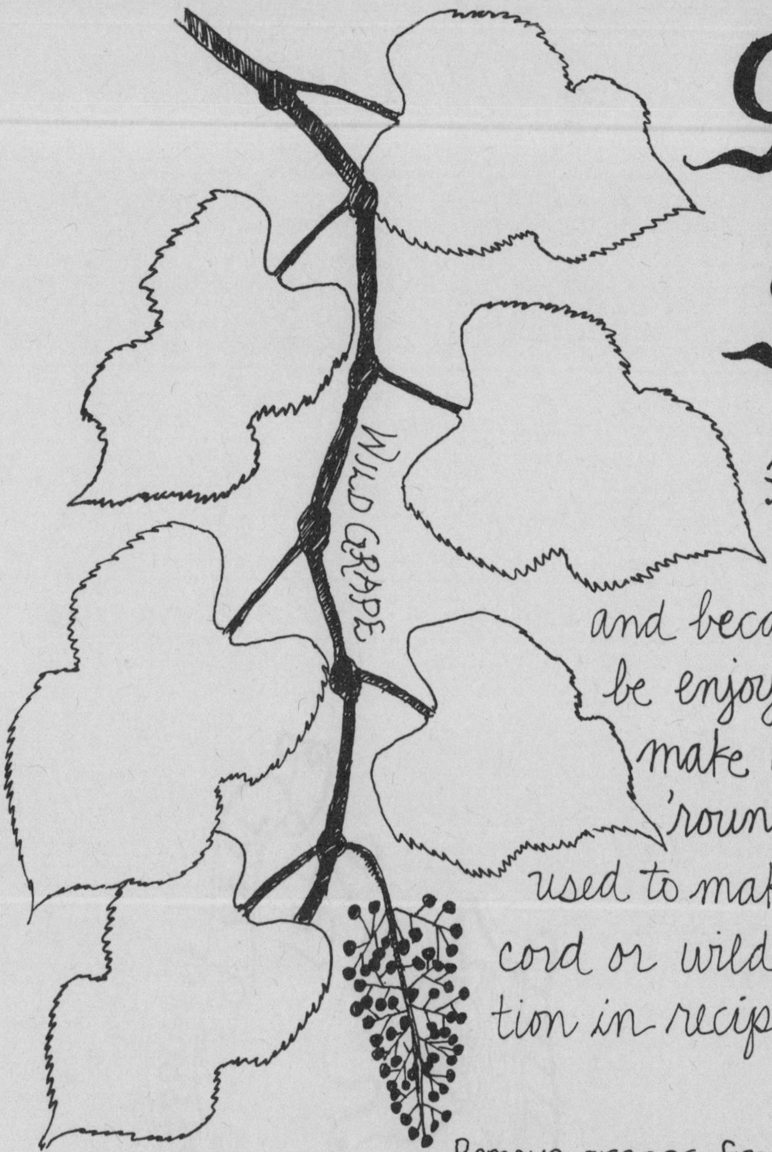
WILD GRAPE

Grape Juice*

Homemade grape juice is incredibly tasty; and because it's canned, may be enjoyed as a drink or to make grape jelly all year 'round. Firm grapes are used to make juice, such as Concord or wild grapes..... See alteration in recipe for wild grapes.

Remove grapes from stems after washing. Put grapes in a kettle and cover with water. Heat slowly to simmering.

DO NOT BOIL

Cook slowly until fruit is very soft. Strain through cloth (such as a large square of cotton flannel or an old cotton sheet). Twist and squeeze as much juice as you can...Don't try to squeeze too large a quantity of grapes at one time as it is hard to get all the juice out. Let the juice stand over night in refrigerator and strain again; or skip this step and just add 1/2 cup sugar to one quart of juice. Bring to boil, stirring to dissolve sugar. Pour into clean jars; seal and process in water bath for **20** minutes after water is boiling. Allow jars to cool, upright.

NOTE: Grape juice can be made without sugar, but the flavor is not as good; even when the sugar is added when you use it.

CONTINUED...

*Courtesy Mrs. Evelyn Worst

Wild Grapes make wonderful juice or jelly, but are stronger, so more water should be added. After covering a large kettle (6 to 8 quart) of washed grapes, add 1½ quarts more of water. Continue with directions of grape juice recipe on preceding page.

Use lemon juice to remove grape stains on hands.

HOME MADE GRAPE JUICE

Below is a grape jelly recipe which can be altered a bit in order to use the canned grape juice. If the grape juice was made omitting the overnight refrigeration step, restrain the juice for making a clear jelly. (The jelly will also taste good without straining, though.) Begin with directions for jelly, marked with •.

Because the grape juice has sugar already added, use only 6 ½ cups minus 2 Tablespoons of sugar in the jelly recipe.

GRAPE JELLY*

MAIL WITH RING ON LID

5 CUPS GRAPEJUICE (TAKES ABOUT 3½ POUNDS CONCORD GRAPES AND 1 CUP WATER)
1 PACKAGE POWDERED PECTIN
7 CUPS SUGAR

Sort, wash, and remove stems from fully ripe grapes. Crush grapes, add water, cover, and bring to boil on high heat. Reduce heat and simmer for 10 minutes. Extract juice. To prevent formation of tartrate crystals in the jelly, let juice stand in a cool place overnight, then strain through two thicknesses of damp cheesecloth to remove crystals that have formed.

• Measure juice into a kettle. Add the pectin and stir well. Place on high heat and, stirring constantly, bring quickly to a full rolling boil that cannot be stirred down. Add the sugar, continue stirring, and bring again to a full rolling boil. Boil hard for 1 minute. Remove from heat; skim off foam quickly. Pour jelly immediately into hot containers and seal (See page 44 for instructions pertaining to jars). Makes 11 or 12 six-ounce glasses.

Grape Jelly

* Courtesy *Complete Guide to Home Canning, Preserving and Freezing*; U.S. Dept. of Agriculture; Dover Publications, Inc.

Date & Nut Bread*

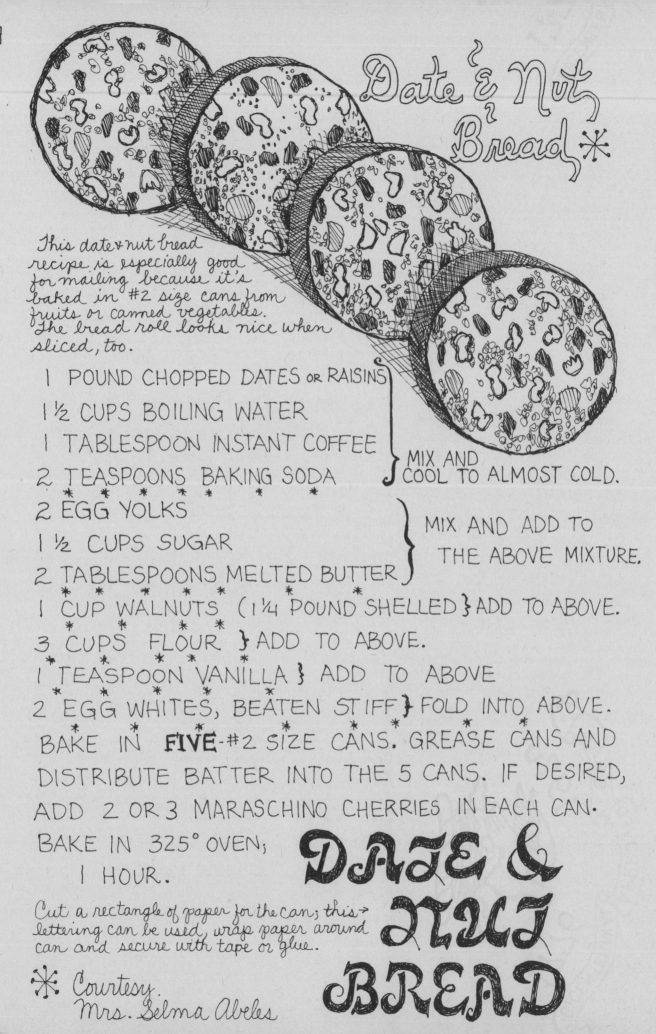

This date & nut bread recipe is especially good for mailing because it's baked in #2 size cans from fruits or canned vegetables. The bread roll looks nice when sliced, too.

1 POUND CHOPPED DATES OR RAISINS
1½ CUPS BOILING WATER
1 TABLESPOON INSTANT COFFEE
2 TEASPOONS BAKING SODA
} MIX AND COOL TO ALMOST COLD.

* * * * * * *

2 EGG YOLKS
1½ CUPS SUGAR
2 TABLESPOONS MELTED BUTTER
} MIX AND ADD TO THE ABOVE MIXTURE.

* * * * * * *

1 CUP WALNUTS (1¼ POUND SHELLED } ADD TO ABOVE.

* * * *

3 CUPS FLOUR } ADD TO ABOVE.

* * * * *

1 TEASPOON VANILLA } ADD TO ABOVE

* * * * *

2 EGG WHITES, BEATEN STIFF } FOLD INTO ABOVE.

* * * * * * * *

BAKE IN **FIVE**-#2 SIZE CANS. GREASE CANS AND DISTRIBUTE BATTER INTO THE 5 CANS. IF DESIRED, ADD 2 OR 3 MARASCHINO CHERRIES IN EACH CAN. BAKE IN 325° OVEN; 1 HOUR.

DATE & NUT BREAD

Cut a rectangle of paper for the can; this→ lettering can be used, wrap paper around can and secure with tape or glue.

* Courtesy
Mrs. Selma Abeles

ROOT BEER*

This rootbeer is easy to make using Hires Rootbeer Extract. It's refreshing, really foams up, and costs much less to make than store-bought rootbeer. The complete recipe comes inside the box along with instructions for use with making popcicles, ice cream, milk shakes, instant ade, candy kisses, and low-calorie rootbeer.

A bottle capper and caps can be purchased for sealing the rootbeer in clean soda or beer bottles. The capper is a nice gadget to have in the kitchen for recipes that require bottling. Caps are sold very inexpensively by the gross.

The bottle capper, caps, and Hires Rootbeer Extract can be ordered from:

CAP
BOTTLE CAPPER

Mother's General Store
Box 506
Flat Rock
North Carolina
28731

Mother's General Store handles many items and old-time tools, large and small, & of such variety that their catalogue is a joy to review.

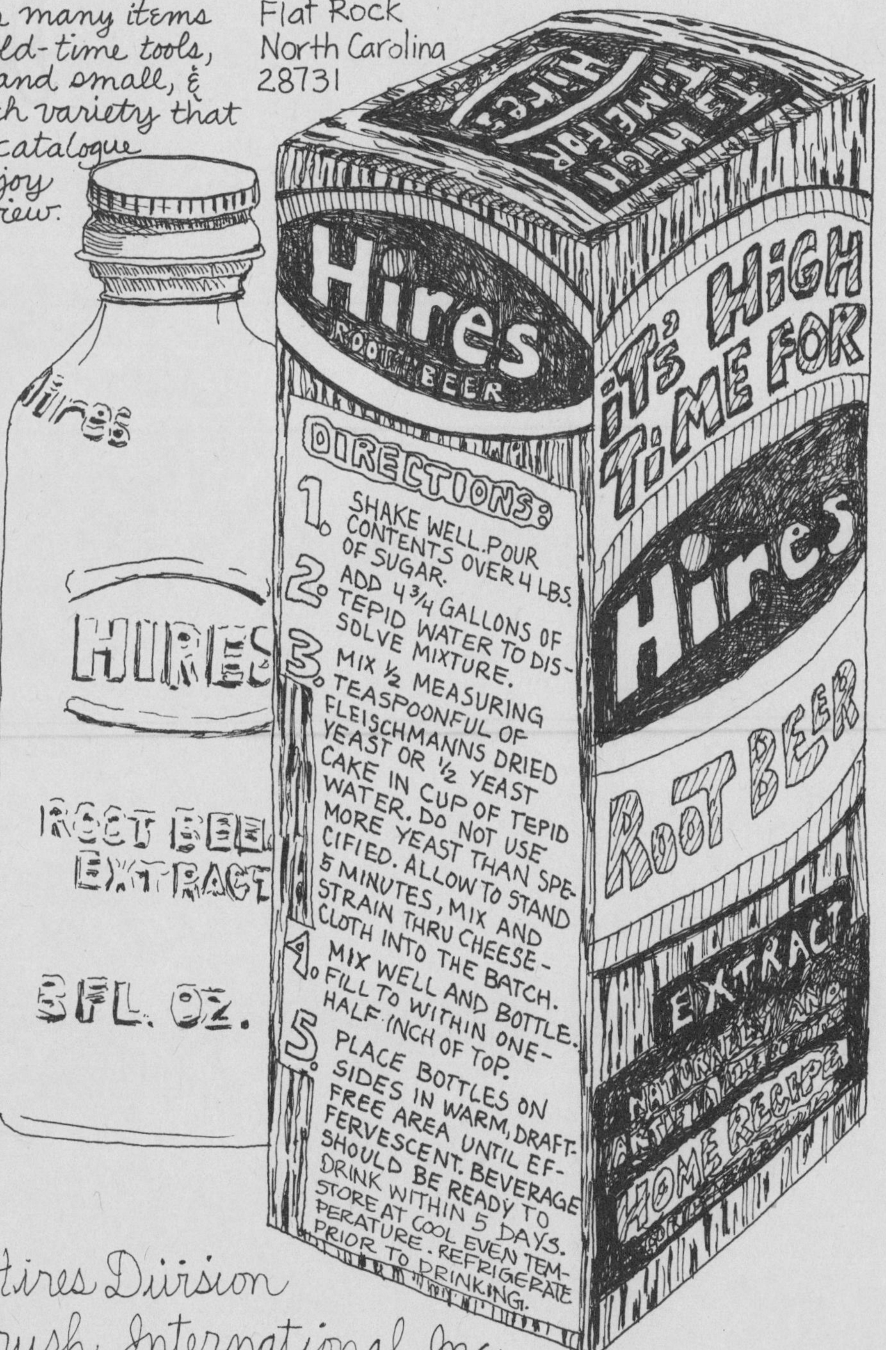
Hires
HIRES
ROOT BEER EXTRACT
3 FL. OZ.
Hires
ROOT BEER
IT'S HIGH TIME FOR
Hires
ROOT BEER
DIRECTIONS:
1. SHAKE WELL. POUR CONTENTS OVER 4 LBS. OF SUGAR.
2. ADD 4 3/4 GALLONS OF TEPID WATER TO DISSOLVE MIXTURE.
3. MIX 1/2 MEASURING TEASPOONFUL OF FLEISCHMANNS DRIED YEAST OR 1/2 YEAST CAKE IN CUP OF TEPID WATER. DO NOT USE MORE YEAST THAN SPECIFIED. ALLOW TO STAND 5 MINUTES, MIX AND STRAIN THRU CHEESE-CLOTH INTO THE BATCH.
4. MIX WELL AND BOTTLE. FILL TO WITHIN ONE-HALF INCH OF TOP.
5. PLACE BOTTLES ON SIDES IN WARM, DRAFT-FREE AREA UNTIL EFFERVESCENT. BEVERAGE SHOULD BE READY TO DRINK WITHIN 5 DAYS. STORE AT COOL EVEN TEMPERATURE. REFRIGERATE PRIOR TO DRINKING.
EXTRACT
HOME RECIPE

Bottles of root beer are sure to be consumed by family and friends before labels can be applied. But, the case containing the rootbeer could be decorated with paint, crayons, or paper as a permanent holder for the bottles.

ROOT
BEER

* Courtesy Hires Division
Crush International, Inc.

Zucchini Bread*

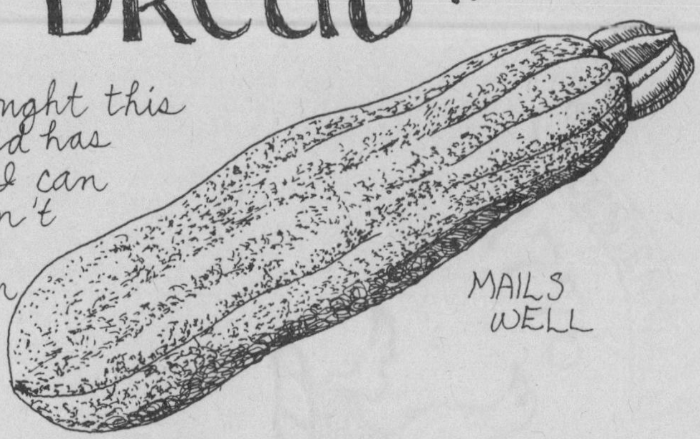

Ever since my friend, Debbie, brought this recipe to our area, zucchini bread has been baked in more ovens than I can count. Even those people who don't like anything about zucchini as a vegetable have made loaf after loaf, even freezing some for winter enjoyment.

MAILS WELL

- 3 eggs
- 2 cups sugar
- 1 cup oil
- 1/4 teas. baking powder
- 2 teas. baking soda
- 1 teas. salt
- 3 teas. cinnamon
- 3 teas. vanilla
- 2 cups, raw, unpeeled, shredded, & packed zucchini
- 3 cups flour
- 1 cup chopped nuts (optional but delicious)

ZUCCHINI BREAD

Beat eggs till light and fluffy. Add sugar, oil, & vanilla; Blend well. Stir in zucchini. Add dry ingredients to creamed mixture. Fold in nuts. Pour into 2, 9"x5", well-greased loaf pans and bake at 350° for 1 hour.

Applesauce**

Grandma Flossie's Applesauce has to be THE BEST tasting and most unique recipe that I have ever come across. A small amount of butter and vanilla transforms plain applesauce into a luscious delight.

Peel, core, and slice apples into chunks. Put into a kettle and add enough water to keep it from burning. Let simmer until apples become a sauce— stir occasionally. Add sugar or honey to taste. For a 4-qt. batch, add 1 Tablespoon vanilla and 1 Tablespoon butter (The butter makes it smooth).

For canning applesauce, fill clean, hot jars to 1/4 inch of top and process in boiling water-bath for 10 min. (for qts. & pts.)

APPLE
SAUCE

* Courtesy Deborah Valentour

** Courtesy Cindy Thorpe

Hungarian Coffee Cake*

MAILS WELL

(ARANY HALUSKA)

1 CUP SOUR CREAM OR CANNED MILK (the sour cream is particularly good)

1/2 CUP SUGAR

1 tsp. SALT

2 CAKES YEAST (small ones, 1" sq.)

3 EGGS

1/2 CUP BUTTER

1 tsp. VANILLA

4 1/2 CUPS FLOUR

1/2 CUP MELTED BUTTER

1 CUP FINELY GROUND WALNUTS

1/2 tsp. CINNAMON

1 CUP SUGAR (for walnut mixture)

MELT BUTTER; ADD SOUR CREAM. WHEN COOL, ADD EGGS, VANILLA, AND CRUMBLED YEAST; BEAT WITH EGG BEATER. ADD THIS MIXTURE TO DRY INGREDIENTS. WORK DOUGH UNTIL SMOOTH. PLACE IN GREASED BOWL AND LET RISE UNTIL DOUBLE IN BULK (ABOUT 1 1/2 HOURS). PUNCH DOWN AND LET RISE AGAIN FOR 30-45 MINUTES. WHILE DOUGH IS RISING FOR SECOND TIME, COMBINE WALNUTS, SUGAR AND CINNAMON; SET ASIDE. ALSO MELT 1/2 CUP BUTTER. AFTER SECOND RISING, DIP TEASPOON INTO MELTED BUTTER AND FORM DOUGH INTO WALNUT SIZE BALLS (NOT TOO LARGE). DIP EACH INTO MELTED BUTTER; ROLL INTO SUGAR-WALNUT-CINNAMON MIXTURE. PLACE IN LAYERS IN A 10" TUBE PAN (NO NEED TO GREASE PAN.) LET RISE AGAIN ABOUT 45 MINUTES. BAKE IN 375° OVEN FOR 40-50 MINUTES.

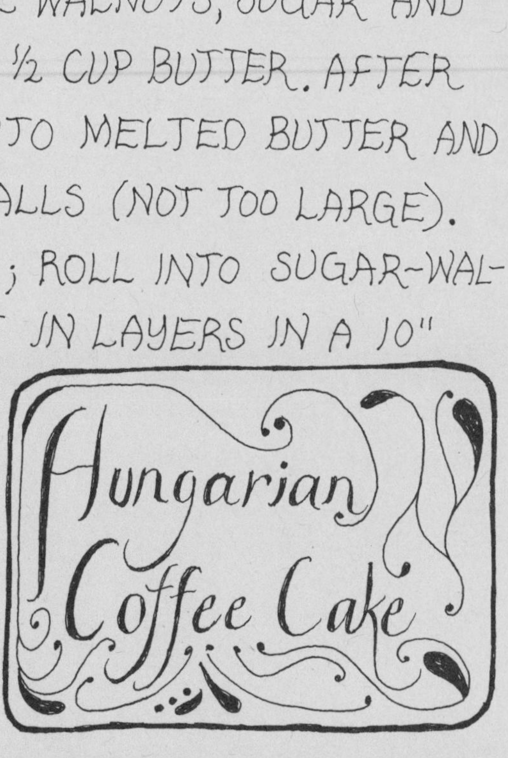
Hungarian
Coffee Cake

*Courtesy Margaret Loprire

WINE

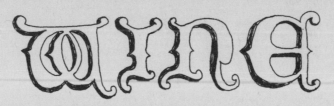

Folk wines or country wines are made from an extensive variety of fruits, grains, and flowers. Winemaking is an enjoyable and soothing hobby which does not necessarily require any expensive utensils.

There are quite a few books on the market which are filled with enough recipes to utilize any season's bounties. Two books which I have found useful are:

FOLK WINES, CORDIALS, & BRANDIES by M.A. Jagendorf; New York: Vanguard Press, Inc., 1963.

WINEMAKING AT HOME by Homer Hardwick; (paperback edition) New York: Cornerstone Library, 1972.

Some books include much of the nomenclature of the experienced and traditional winemaker. Following are some pointers to enable you to use any wine recipe with a minimum of supplies.

1. All **utensils** when working with wine should be of plastic, glass, wood, enamel or stainless steel. Keep everything **clean** that comes in contact with the wine. Sulphite crystals (dissolved in water) can be used over and over for cleaning utensils; however 'sterilizing' all tools and containers with boiling water is adequate.
2. The main ingredients of the wine are put into a **fermenting vat**, first; usually from a few days to a few weeks. A ceramic crock makes a marvelous vat. Crocks are expensive new, but second-hand crocks at farm auctions sell for a reasonable price. Plastic waste baskets and garbage cans (plastic!) are fine for a vat. 5-8 gallon volumes will serve most recipes.
3. When ever **mashing of fruit** is called for, use a stainless steel potato masher, a wooden kitchen utensil such as a large spoon, or make a mashing tool: drill a hole through a piece of wood for insertion of a 3/4" dowel; use white glue if necessary.

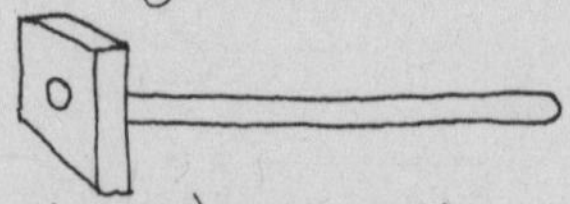

4. Place a few layers of cheesecloth (found at fabric stores) or cotton muslin on the crock **to prevent dirt and bugs** (particularly fruit flies invade) from getting into the must. The **must** is the juice before it has become wine.
5. Sodium Meta Bisulphide, often found as **Campden Pills**, are used to sterilize the must (1 Campden Pill per gallon). I have made wine successfully without them—however the pills are very inexpensive and avoid unnecessary failures in winemaking that are due to bacteria. Dissolve the pills in warm water before adding to the must.
6. **Enzyme Pills** keep the wines of any small stone fruit (plums, cherries, peaches, and so on) from becoming cloudy. Add to must when the Campden Pills are added. As with Campden Pills, the Enzyme Pills are inexpensive, and although my friend makes her wonderful PLUM WINE without them, you may decide to buy them.

7. Special wine **yeasts** are available but regular baking yeast works fine and is very inexpensive — in general, use 1 pkg. per 1-5 gallons (the recipe will usually specify). Dissolve yeast in warm water.
8. To remove juice and to **strain** out flowers, fruits, and grains, use a muslin bag, squeezing out the juice; OR use a plastic strainer if you have one.
9. The **first fermentation** takes place in the crock or plastic can. The **second fermentation** occurs in a **cask** (barrel — usually of wood) or a **carboy** (large glass bottle). Traditional casks and carboys are expensive. Instead the 5-gallon water bottles from distilled water bottling companies can be used (ask for "strays".) Also, most easily attainable are ½ gallon or gallon wine bottles which friends will most likely be glad to give you. Any glass juice bottles (½-1 gallon size) will also do. Avoid use of plastic bottles, as the wine will be in the cask at least a month or two, the taste of plastic may get into the wine.
10. **Water-seals** are used on the glass bottles to let the carbonic gas of the fermentation to escape while eliminating air from entering the bottle. If you plan to buy one, get a plastic water-seal; the glass type breaks too easily. Some recipes do not mention the use of a water-seal, however a home-made version costs only pennies and moments to make and is worthwhile for preventing the wine from turning into vinegar. Shown at the right is a water-seal using a cork. Be sure to brush melted wax over the cork so it is air-tight. Drilled rubber stoppers are available from wine-making suppliers.

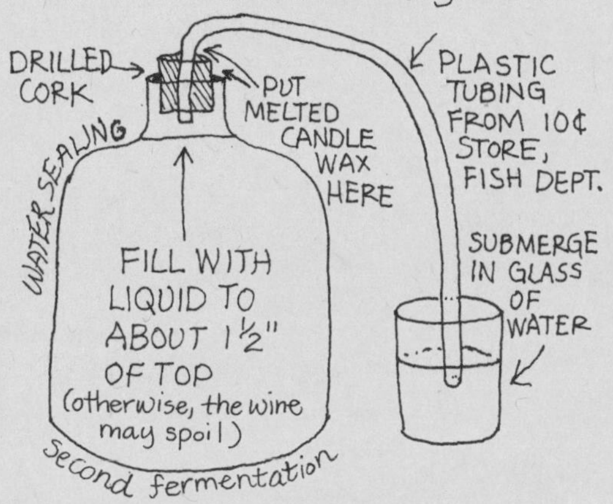
DRILLED CORK
PUT MELTED CANDLE WAX HERE
PLASTIC TUBING FROM 10¢ STORE, FISH DEPT.
WATER SEALING
FILL WITH LIQUID TO ABOUT 1½" OF TOP (otherwise, the wine may spoil)
SUBMERGE IN GLASS OF WATER
Second fermentation

11. During the second fermentation, bubbles will continue to rise to the top. When the bubbling has stopped, remove the watersea), and cap the bottle, giving the wine time to **fine** or become clear. This step varies with each recipe. Leave the wine in a closed container, undisturbed, to enable the yeast sediment to drift to the bottom. Egg shells with the moist egg white residue can be added - remove the shells when they are coated with the sediment (usually a few days to to a week). Wine will usually fine itself naturally, it just takes time (I'm speaking in terms of months).
12. When the wine is clear, **siphon** it into clean **bottles** (See #1.). Clean wine bottles, beer or soda bottles are easily saved. I prefer clear glass, in order to be able to see what's going on with the wine. To siphon wine into bottles, use plastic tubing, sucking on one end to start the flow of the wine through the tube. Prevent the sediment of the wine from entering the **tube** by keeping the tube end away from the bottom. Further fining of the wine will often occur after bottling, so it is best to put a temporary seal on them. The **bottle capper** (see page 65) is ideal and convenient. **Corkers** and corks can also be used for bottling (fill bottle to within 1" of cork bottom). Store wine bottles on their side, and resyphon if sediment appears.

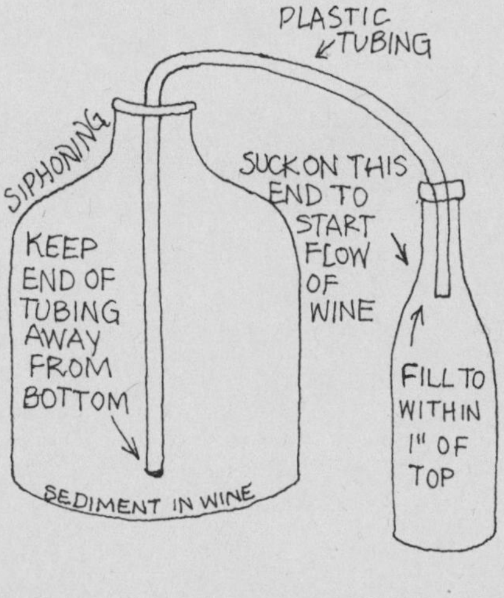
PLASTIC TUBING
SIPHONING
SUCK ON THIS END TO START FLOW OF WINE
KEEP END OF TUBING AWAY FROM BOTTOM
FILL TO WITHIN 1" OF TOP
SEDIMENT IN WINE

13. **Label** all bottles with the name of the wine and the date. (See page 40 about types of labels).

The previous pages speak of the basics of wine-making tools and procedures. There are many more gadgets, supplies, and chemicals available to the winemaker.

All winemaking supplies can be ordered from:

E.S. KRAUS
BOX 451
NEVADA, MISSOURI 64772

(E.S. Kraus has reasonable prices and very fast service.)

Plum Wine*

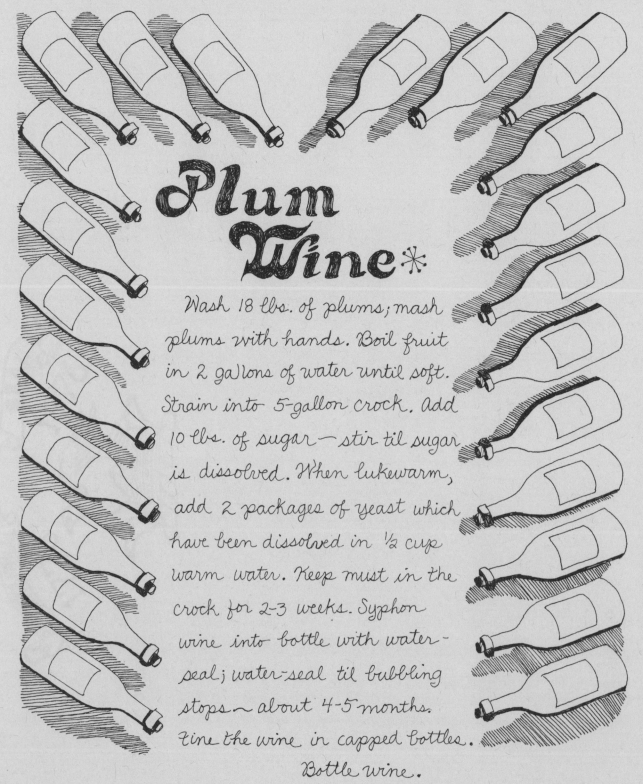

Wash 18 lbs. of plums; mash plums with hands. Boil fruit in 2 gallons of water until soft. Strain into 5-gallon crock. Add 10 lbs. of sugar—stir til sugar is dissolved. When lukewarm, add 2 packages of yeast which have been dissolved in 1/2 cup warm water. Keep must in the crock for 2-3 weeks. Syphon wine into bottle with water-seal; water-seal til bubbling stops—about 4-5 months. Fine the wine in capped bottles.

Bottle wine.

* Courtesy Deborah Valentour

DRY CHERRY TABLE WINE*

4 lbs. Cherries per gallon
2 lbs. Sugar per gallon
1 Enzyme Pill per gallon
Yeast (if using wine yeast, use according to package directions)

Put cherries in a large plastic waste basket with ABOUT a quart of water and 50 mls. 10% sulphide solution made by melting 1/4 lb. Sodium Meta Bisulphide in 1 quart warm water (or 1 Campden Pill). Let stand overnight — this will kill all the natural yeast and other bad bacteria. You don't have to mash the cherries or pit them. Put in the Enzyme Pill when the sulphide goes in. Boil 1 quart of water and dissolve 2 lbs. of sugar in it to make a syrup. After the sulphide has worked for 24 hours, add the yeast, the room temperature sugar syrup; and tie plastic cover tightly over the top of the pail. Let ferment for a good 3 days. By this time, the cherries will be bleached and leathery. Squeeze the pulp out and put the wine into a gallon jug with a waterseal. Let the wine ferment out — it may take a couple of months (you can also keep it in the water-seal for 1 year.) If the jug is not full after you have squeezed out the pulp, you can add enough plain water to bring the wine up to about 1 1/2 inches of the top. Fine the wine after second fermentation has stopped; then bottle.

* Courtesy
Al Jenkins

Plum
Wine
date

Dry
Cherry
Table
Wine
date

On the Wall....

On the Floor

RUGS

Following, are four methods of making rugs that do not require expensive equipment. The amount of money spent on supplies varies with the type of rug and the size. Room size rugs are costly and/or time consuming, so it is best to begin with throw rugs which are an attractive addition to a room and can be cleaned easily. A handmade rug makes a fine house-warming gift. Or, use it as a wall-hanging. In the winter, tacking a rug you have made over a door or using one as a roll up & tie window "shade" protects a home from unnecessary chills when the temperature drops.

Arts & crafts stores carry many rug-making supplies. TRIARCO ARTS & CRAFTS, INC. sells rug backing compound as well as a numerous line of arts & crafts supplies. Below is a list of TRIARCO service locations and addresses:

Creative Hands Division
4146 Library Road
Pittsburgh, Pennsylvania
15234

Delco Craft Division
1000 Troy Court
Troy, Michigan 48084
(Detroit area)

Gager's Handicraft Division
3516 Beltline Boulevard
St. Louis Park, Minnesota 5516
(Minneapolis area)

J.C. Larson Division
110 West Carpenter Avenue
Wheeling, Illinois 60090
(Chicago area)

Cavalier Handicrafts Division
Richmond Leather Division
1839 West Broad Street
Richmond, Virginia 23220

220 Carillon Tower East
13601 Preston Road
Dallas, Texas 75240

5737 38TH Avenue North
St. Petersburg, Florida 33710

Write to the nearest Triarco address.

Braided Rug

A nice way to use up remnants of fabric is to make a braided rug of any size. The rug should be of any type heavy-weight fabric, although I made a braided throw rug of medium-weight cotton that is colorful and easily washed. However, the heavier fabrics make a more durable rug, particularly for a room size rug.

The braided rug uses strips of fabric <u>about</u> 2 inches wide which are sewn together on the bias to avoid excessive lumping:

BIAS

There are three methods for folding the strips:

1. Rug braiders for cotton and wool fold the strips as you braid. The strips are inserted through the slits, curve with the metal, and the raw edges are thus folded in.

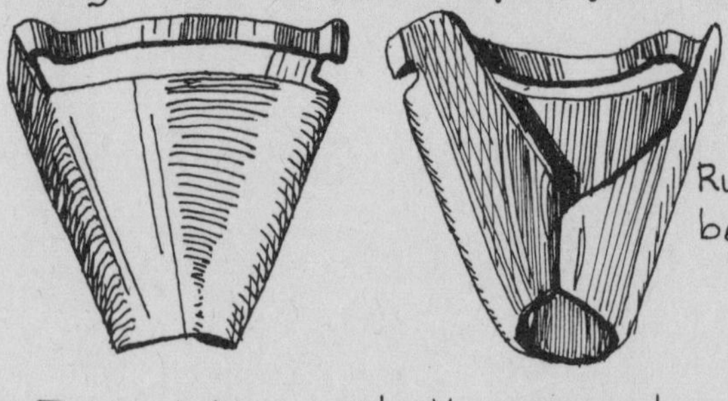

Rug Braiders and other braiding supplies can be ordered from:

NU-FLEX COMPANY
246 First Avenue South
St. Petersburg, Florida 33701

2. Fold strips with the raw edge in, and press lightly with an iron.

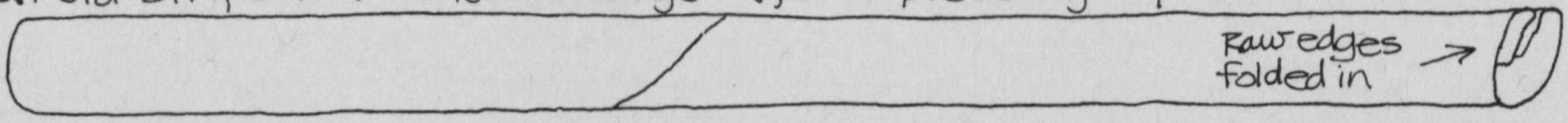
Raw edges
folded in

3. Particularly with thicker fabrics, it may be well to slip stitch the folded edge with regular sewing thread.

The strips of fabric are rolled into balls—small balls are easier to handle. Slip stitch the ends of 3 balls of strips and use a safety pin to attach the ends to a fabric surface. The strips can be braided as one braids hair, or 'encouraged' to fold in a flat rather than twisted manner. **Note:** If using the rug braiders, they are positioned for folding as shown in the next illustration.

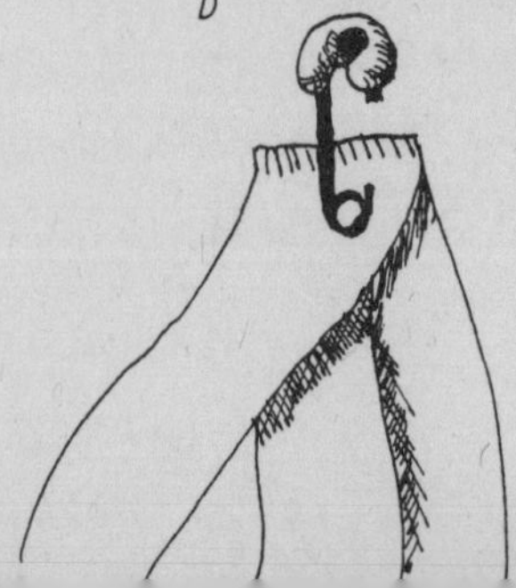

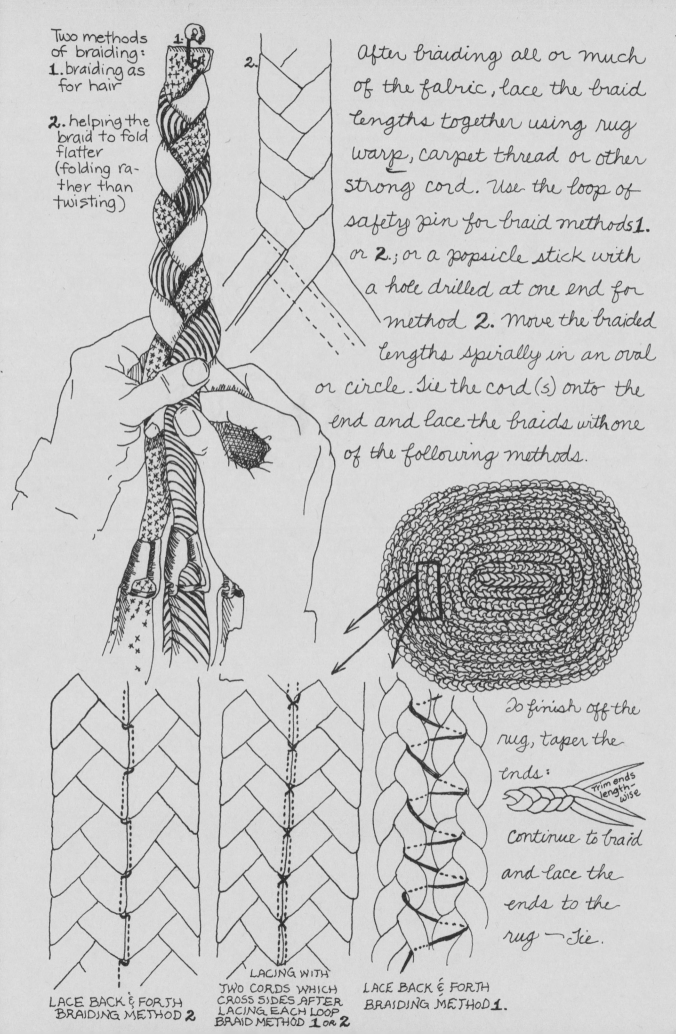

Two methods of braiding:
1. braiding as for hair

2. helping the braid to fold flatter (folding rather than twisting)

1.
2.

After braiding all or much of the fabric, lace the braid lengths together using rug warp, carpet thread or other strong cord. Use the loop of safety pin for braid methods 1. or 2.; or a popsicle stick with a hole drilled at one end for method 2. Move the braided lengths spirally in an oval or circle. Tie the cord(s) onto the end and lace the braids with one of the following methods.

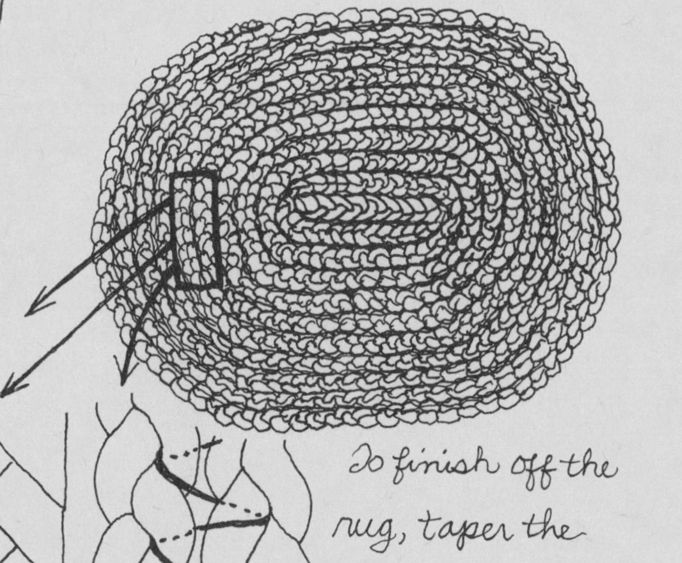

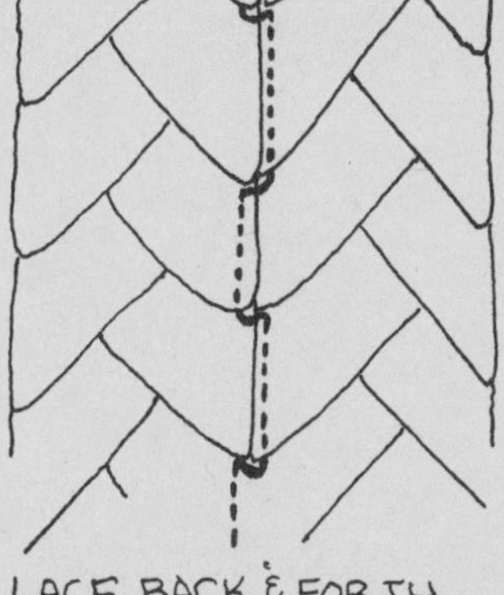

LACE BACK & FORTH BRAIDING METHOD 2

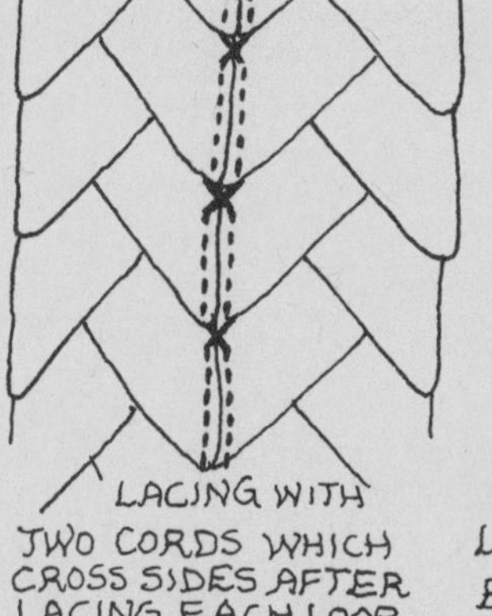

LACING WITH TWO CORDS WHICH CROSS SIDES AFTER LACING EACH LOOP BRAID METHOD 1 OR 2

LACE BACK & FORTH BRAIDING METHOD 1.

To finish off the rug, taper the ends:

Trim ends lengthwise

Continue to braid and lace the ends to the rug — Tie.

Macramé Mat

The macramé mat or throw rug is made using the wrapping technique (pages 89-93) with rope of any thickness used as the guide cord. Any type of cord can be used for the wrapping cords as long as it is durable. The basic scheme is to leave an excess 6 inches at the end of the rope, and begin attaching cords with the lark's head to the desired length of the rug. Because adding on to the wrapping is easy and efficient, the length of the cords is optional (4 ft. for each strand extending from the lark's head is a good length). Turn the excess 6" of rope towards the cord and clove hitch. Now, begin turning the rope back and forth, wrapping the cords around the rope with the clove hitch. The flexibility of the cord and rope enables the curve caused by the excess 6" of rope to straighten out after a few rows of wrapping. Finish off the last row by subtracting cords into the wrap (See page 93) Variations of the rectangular rug are made by changing the route of the rope and inserting other macramé knots between the flow.

LARK'S HEADS
EXCESS 6" OF ROPE SHOW AS DARKENED AREA. TURN IT BACK INTO THE RUG AND CLOVE HITCH.
Secured behind

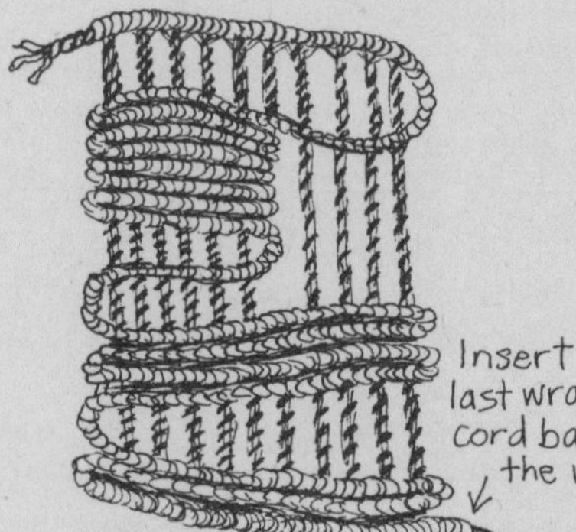
Insert the last wrapping cord back into the wrap

This mat uses twirl lengths of half knots between the flow of rope. The curving edges of rope are wrapped with the half-hitch. The rope ends are left free.

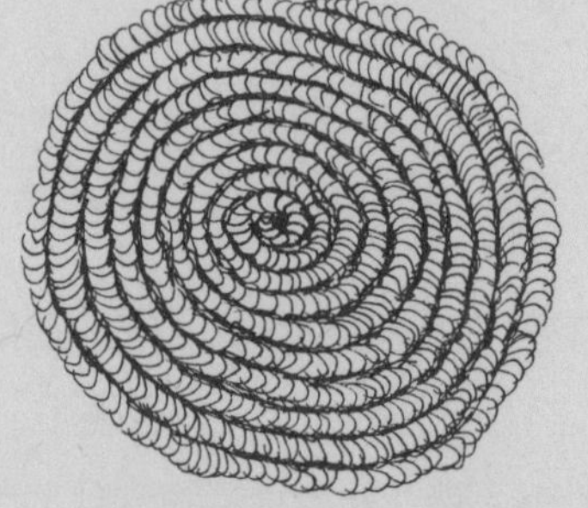
Insert behind

The circular mat is made by attaching and adding cords with lark's heads, starting at the center as for the base of macramé baskets (See pg. 119). Cords are wrapped into the last row.

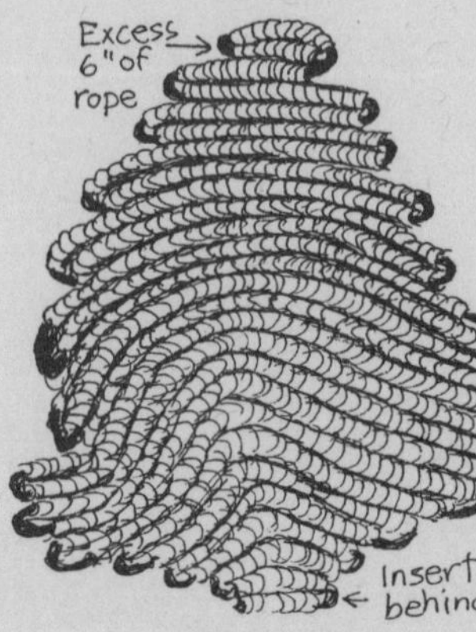
Excess 6" of rope
Insert behind

This mat enlarges from the top by adding on new strands with the lark's head at the sides; and subtracting strands at the sides to shorten the bottom.

PUNCH RUGS

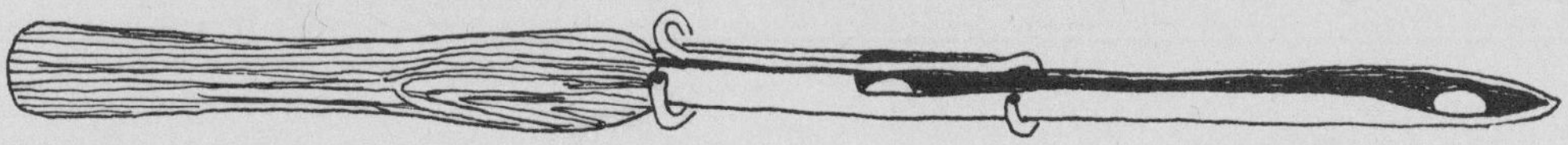

SUPPLIES: Rug punch • Burlap (color of the main yarn color, if any) • Rug yarn • Scissors • wooden frame (see page 107) • carpet tacks & hammer or staple gun • screwdriver • tailor chalk or other marker • carpet thread • rug backing compound

INSTRUCTIONS:

1. Design the rug on paper and decide on the size. Cut the burlap to the size PLUS 3 inches around.
2. With a marker, draw the design on the burlap, leaving the 3" space untouched. The side with the drawing will be punched, with the rug appearing on the other.... Keep in mind any lettering will be reversed.

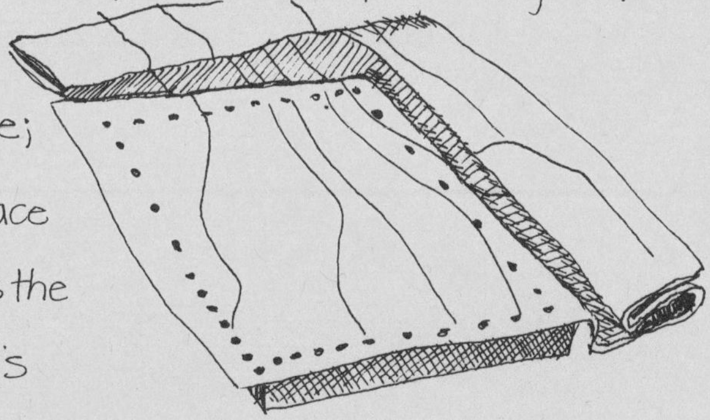

3. Tack the burlap to a wooden frame; the burlap must be held firmly in place without sagging. Ideally, the frame is the size of the rug; but a smaller frame is portable and used by shifting and tacking the burlap as each section is completed. Use the screwdriver for carefully removing tacks or staples.
4. Thread the punch with the desired color, rug yarn leaving about 2"-3" of excess to start. Punch between the weave of the burlap — each punch produces a loop on the front. As you work, check the front for correct spacing of loops (generally every 3RD to 5TH weave opening is punched) A longer loop can be made by removing the wire catch on the punch.

2"-3"
MOVE FORWARD

5. To finish off an area of color, pull extra yarn from the tip of the

punch, as shown with 2 inches excess. Rethread punch and continue.

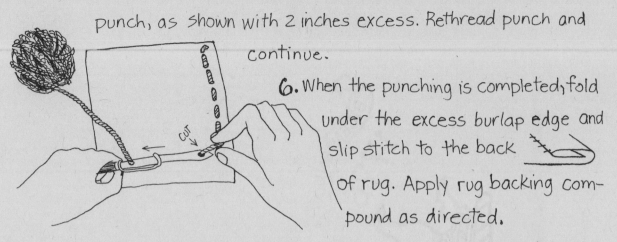

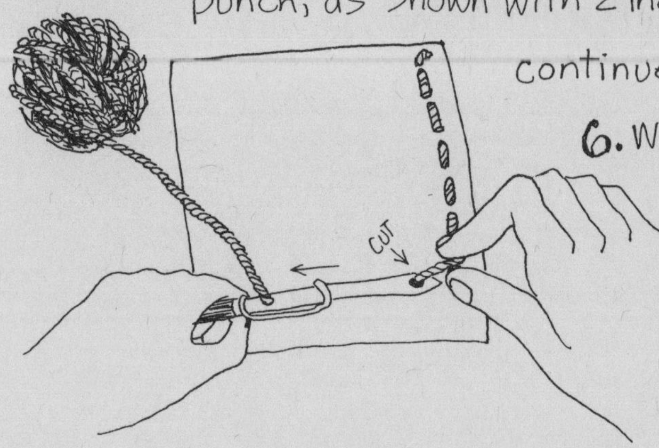
CUT

6. When the punching is completed, fold under the excess burlap edge and slip stitch to the back 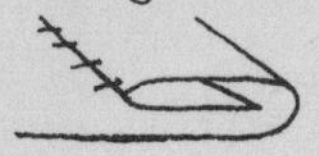 of rug. Apply rug backing compound as directed.

7. After the rug backing compound has been applied, loops may be cut to create a shag.

During the 40's a rug looking similar to the shag-type, punch rug was made using cording, such as string, and canvas. When my mother was in the opera, she and her friends used to sit making the rugs while waiting for their cues. The resulting rugs are handsome, off-white shags; and very washable. Today, many colors of cording are available for multi-color designs.

1. Cut canvas to the desired size plus 2 inches extra around.
2. Use a curved needle to sew a single thickness of cording thru the canvas. Cut even lengths of cording— 6-10 strands, <u>about</u> 2 inches long.

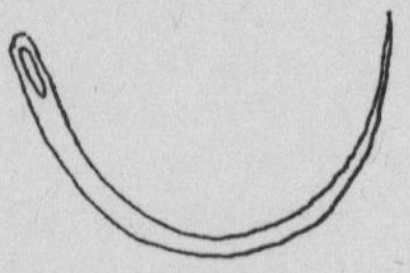

3. Tie the stitched cord (from 2) around the loose strands. Trim.

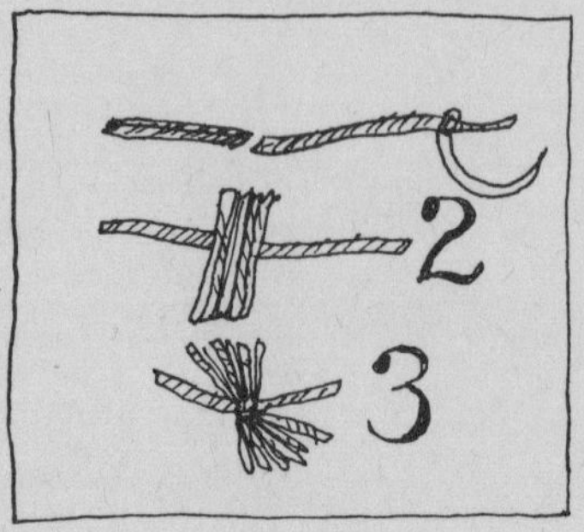
2
3

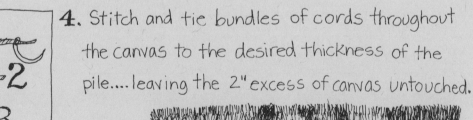

4. Stitch and tie bundles of cords throughout the canvas to the desired thickness of the pile.... leaving the 2" excess of canvas untouched.

5. When the shag is completed, fold under the 2" excess of canvas and slip stitch to back of rug. ()

1.

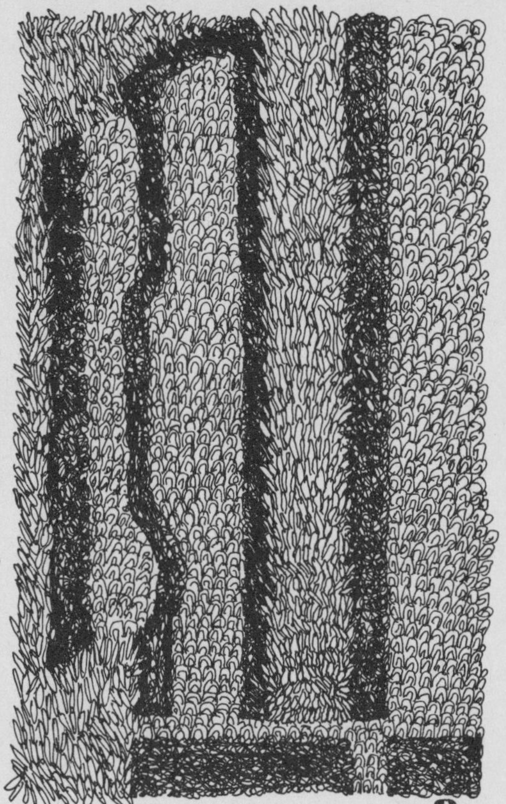

2.

PUNCH RUG DESIGNS

1. PARTICULARLY WHEN MAKING A RUG WITH LARGE COLOR AREAS, BUY A QUANTITY OF YARNS AT ONE TIME, AS DYE LOTS MAY DIFFER SLIGHTLY.
2. CUTTING LOOPS TO FORM SHAGS IN SOME AREAS CREATES TACTILE VARIETY.
3. RUGS MAY BE OF ANY SHAPE—JUST BE SURE THERE ARE NOT TOO MANY IRREGULARITIES SO THAT HEMMING IS IMPOSSIBLE.
4. MAKE THIN LINES WIDE ENOUGH SO THEY ARE NOT 'LOST' IN THE DESIGN.

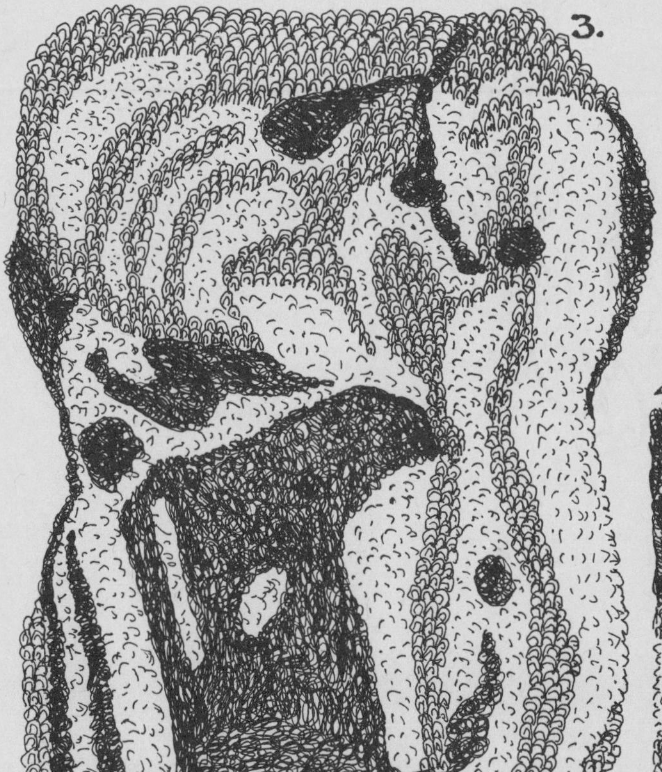

3.

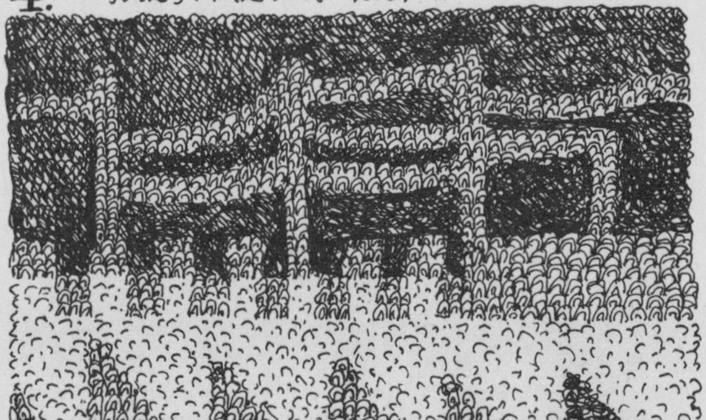

4.

WOVEN RUGS

SUPPLIES: wooden frame of desired size (see page 107)—to make a large rug, weave throw rug-size sections sewn together with carpet thread....

Hammer and small nails (
about 1 inch) .... Cotton carpet warp or other cotton cord...

actual size

tapestry needle...thread•yarn or other cord... wide-toothed comb

Instructions:

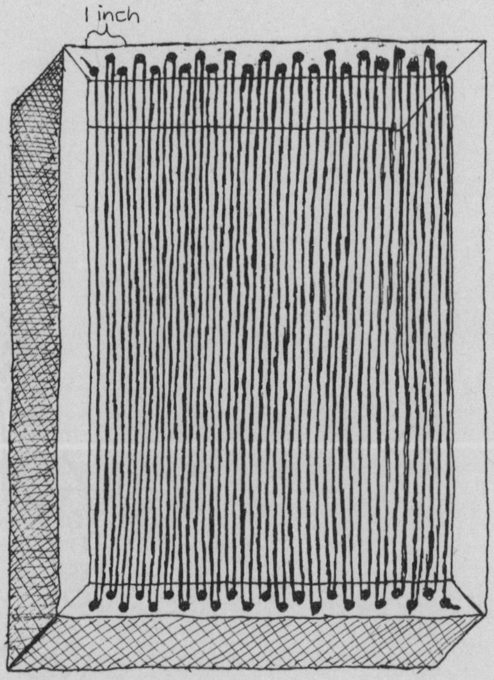
1 inch

1. Hammer nails to the top and bottom lengths of the frame, as shown, with 3 nails per inch, and nails extending 1/4"–1/2" from wood. 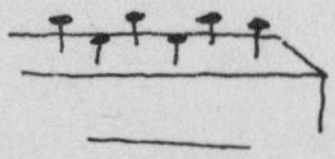

2. Tie the end of the cotton cord to the upper left nail. Bring the cord down to the lower left nail, looping the cord once around the nail (
CORD). Then, take the cord back up to the second nail, looping the cord once... continue moving the cord up and down to form the **warp** along the frame. The warp should be taut—springing back when an open hand is press against the cords. Tie the cord to the last nail.

3. To begin weaving the **weft**, horizontally through the warp; thread the tapestry needle with any color of yarn or cord. Use as much cord as you can handle (about 6–8 ft.). Single weave for 8 rows, moving the needle over and under the warp. On the first row, pull the cord leaving a 6 inch excess extending from the warp. Use the wide-toothed comb to push the weft up. **BE CAREFUL NOT TO PULL THE WEFT TOO TIGHT OR THE WEAVING WILL EXCESSIVELY BOW.**

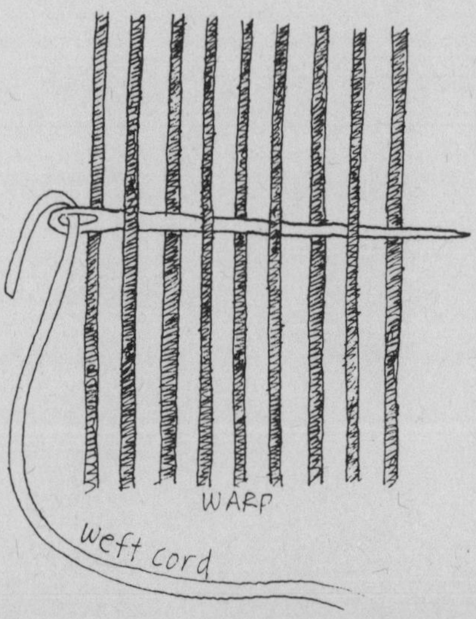
WARP
weft cord

3. CONTINUED Leave an excess 6 inches of the weft cord extending from the 8th row of weaving. The 8 rows of single weaving at the top, as well as 8 similar rows to be woven at the bottom, are folded under as hems when the weaving is completed.

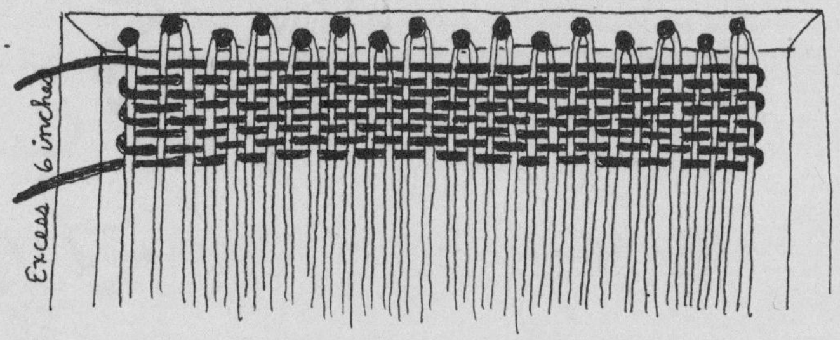
Excess 6 inches

4. Start the weaving design; as for the hem, leave an excess of 6 inches of cord at the ends, extending from the weaving. Use a wide-toothed comb to push up the weft and DO NOT PULL THE WEFT CORDS TOO TIGHT. Use the illustration and explanation on the next two pages to form combinations in the weaving.

5. Add 8 rows of straight weaving (as in Step **3**) below the weaving design. Take the weaving off of the frame. Fold under the 2 woven hems and stitch the loops to the back of the weaving with regular sewing thread: If the weaving is for a **WALL-HANGING**, use dowels through the 2 hems. Also, a wallhanging does not have to be as durable as a rug, so any type of cord or yarn can be used for the warp and weft.

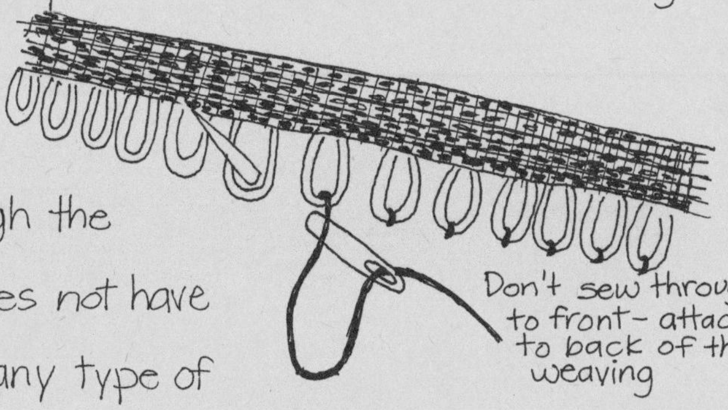
Don't sew through to front - attach to back of the weaving

6. Finish the weaving by inserting all 6" excess cords through the weave in the Back. Use the tapestry needle, or better - a smaller needle with a large eye. Since the excess length is short, push the needle through the Back weave and then thread the eye with cord.

BACK
Insert needle across back, or down

A wide variety of yarns — wools, rayons, handspun yarns, novelty synthetics, cottons, linens, jute, and more — as well as looms, can be purchased from:

WEAVING and WHAT-NOT
5702 Royalton Road
North Royalton, Ohio 44133

Send a stamped, self-addressed envelope for samples of current stock.

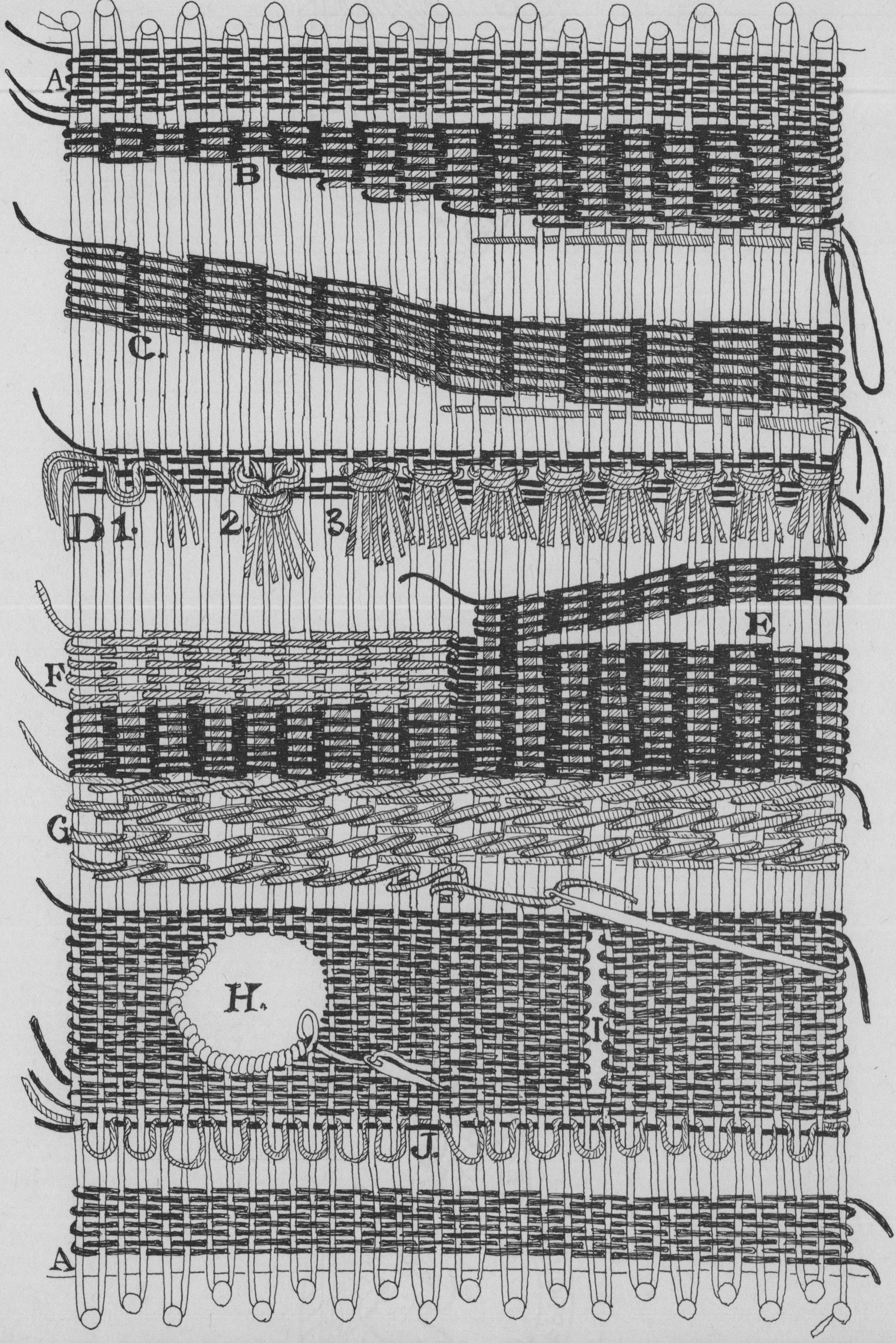
A
B
C.
D 1.
2.
3.
E
F
G
H.
I
J.
A

The opposite page illustrates some methods of weaving on a frame; for the sake of clarification, warp and weft cords are shown more spaciously than an actual weaving. The book, WEAVING - A CREATIVE APPROACH FOR BEGINNERS, by Clara Creager; Garden City, New York: Doubleday & Co., Inc., 1974, contains further ideas about weaving.

NOTES ABOUT WEAVING ILLUSTRATION

A.
- 8 rows of single weaving for hem
- single weaving allows the warp cords to show, forming a checkerboard pattern with the weft

B.
- double weaving under and over 2 strands of warp — in actual weaving, the warp does not show
- form a slanted area by eliminating consecutive warp strands from the weave, row by row.

C.
- triple weaving under and over 3 warp strands — in actual weaving, the warp does not show
- weaving the weft cord at a slant or curve

D.
- forming shag with 3 warp cords (or more)
  1. cut desired lengths of cord — insert around warp cords, as shown
  2. insert the shag ends through the frontal loop
  3. tighten shag, trim, continue to form next shag.
- secure shag in place with 2 rows of straight weaving above and 2 rows below — the straight weave does not show in actual weaving.

E.
- leaving the warp open as part of a design

F.
- changing color or texture of cord — VERTICALLY, by looping the weft of 1 color (or both) around the last warp cord of the other — HORIZONTALLY, rethread the needle with the new color and begin next row.

G.
- forming a slant pattern of the weft with 4 warp strands (or more, or less)
- Bring the weft cord back and under the previous warp strands, as shown
- Secure slant pattern into place with 1 row of straight weaving above and 1 row below — the straight weave does not show in actual weaving

H.
- Cutting shapes from the weaving, when the weaving is completed
- Fold under raw edges, and use yarn or cord in a close slip-stitch

I.
- weaving a slit between warp cords
- Straight weave 2 rows above and 2 below slit — weave warp cords to left of slit separately from warp cords to the right.

J.
- Looping by straight weaving and pulling out excess weft
- Secure above and below with 1 row of straight weaving — the straight weave does not show in actual weaving.

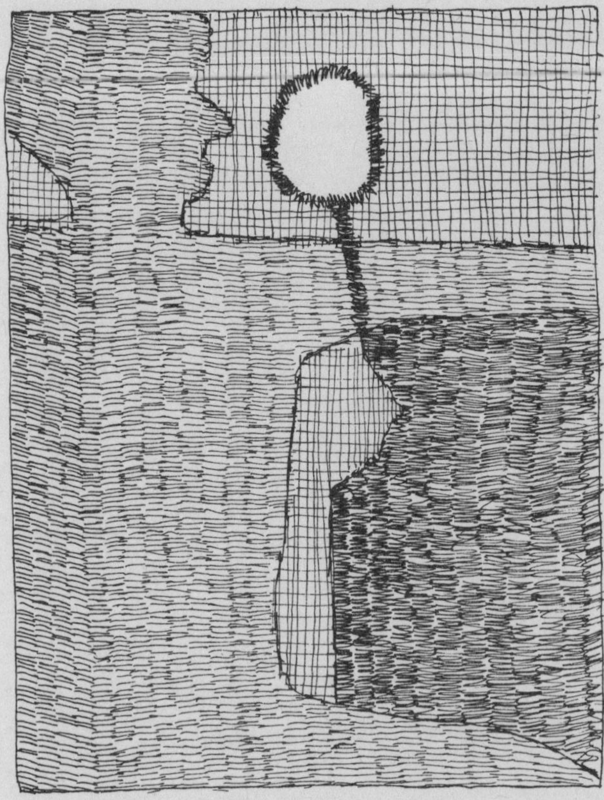

Incorporating a single and double weave. A hole was cut after completion of weaving, with a satin stitch of yarn extending as the hole was stitched.

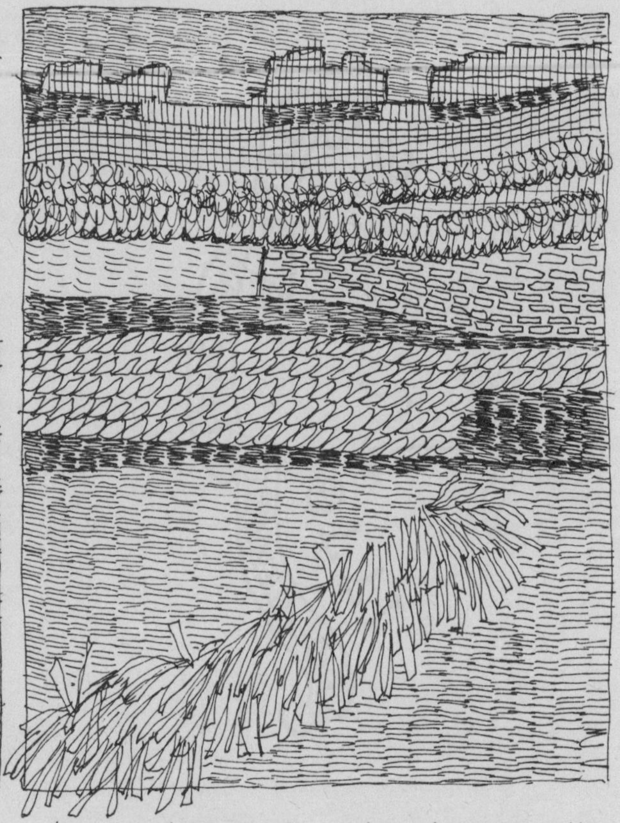

Various types of cord and yarn with many weaving techniques stimulate tactile as well as visual sensations.

Weaving Designs

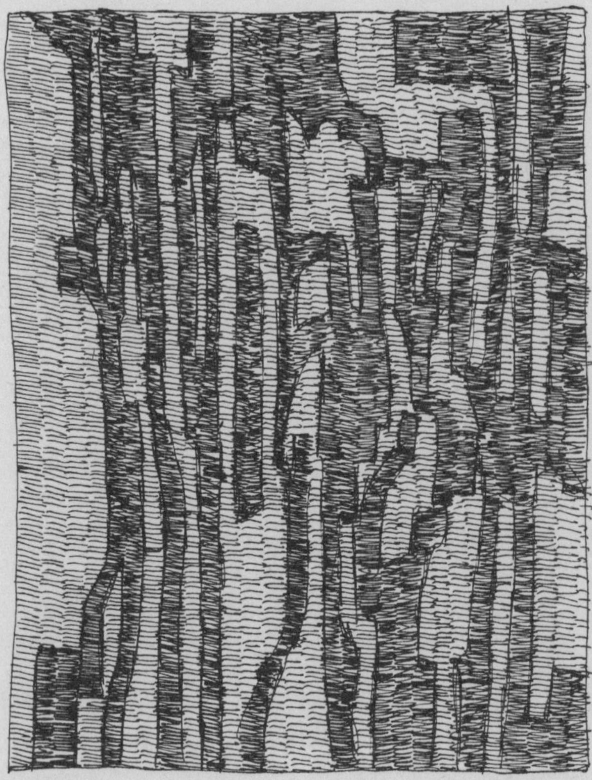

Double weaving with 2 colors as described in F. of the weaving instructions.

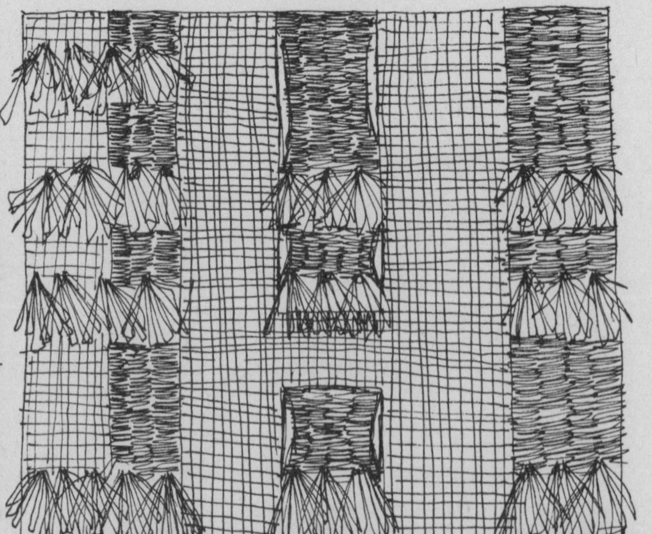

Use of slits, single & double weaving, and shag—A totally shagged rug using weaving is also a possibility.

MACRAMÉ

Macramé utilizes a few basic knots and the flexibility of cord for an endless number of design possibilities. There are many types, thicknesses, and colors of cord to use:

JUTE · SISAL · COTTON · POLYOLEFIN · YARN · NYLON · MACRAMÉ SUEDE · RAFFIA · ROPE

Some types can be purchased in stores, including hardware stores. Most macramé supplies can be ordered from arts and crafts suppliers (See page 73) or from a company specializing in this sort of product such as: Central Ohio Bag & Burlap Co., Inc.
1010 E. Starr Avenue
Columbus, Ohio 43203

More unconventional materials for macramé could also be used, such as strips of fabric (as on page 74); fishing line; thin, flexible wire; crochet cording; cattail leaves or vines—soaked 'til pliable; and, if you possess great deliberation and patience— strips of rice paper glued together to an adequate length.

Besides cord, the only necessary tool is a pair of scissors or a pocketknife. Some people also prefer to work on a styrofoam, fiberboard, or celotex board, pinning down the macramé as it progresses, (T-shape pins are easiest to handle.) However, the following page includes two other alternatives that are cost-free.

The best way to become familiar with macramé is to make a sampler with a few rows of each knot and its variations. As mentioned, special boards can be purchased to pin the macramé while working. • Instead, a scrap of plywood or any wood of at least 1'x1' with nails hammered to the upper left and right hand corners can be used. Some wood will take pins or push-pins. OR • wrap a piece of the cord around a pillow, or a chair back if you prefer to work upright.

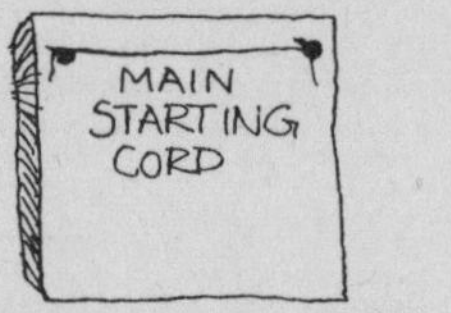
MAIN
STARTING
CORD

MAIN STARTING CORD
TIED IN BACK

MAIN STARTING CORD

- Attach cords that are folded in half with a **LARK'S HEAD**.

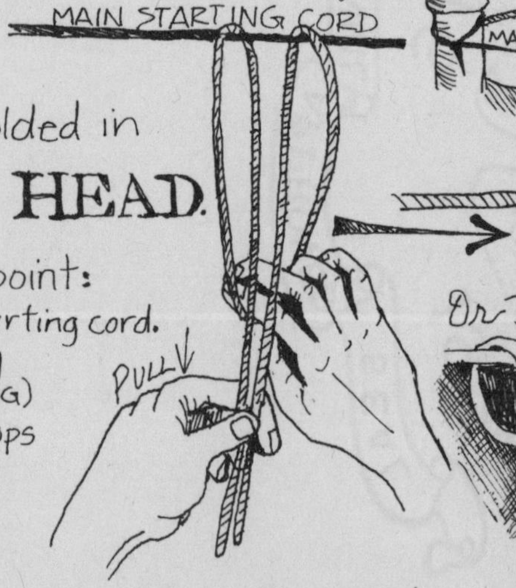
MAIN STARTING CORD
PULL

Or

The lark's head is a starting point:
1. to attach cords to the main starting cord.
2. to add on cords while wrapping with clove hitches (See: WRAPPING)
3. to start the wrapping of groups of cords

- **The number of single strands extending from the lark's heads should be a multiple of 4** (an exception to this is a macramé that uses the wrapping technique ONLY.)

- If cords longer than are manageable are used, fold strands (single or in pairs), as shown. Secure bundles with rubber bands or tie with cord.

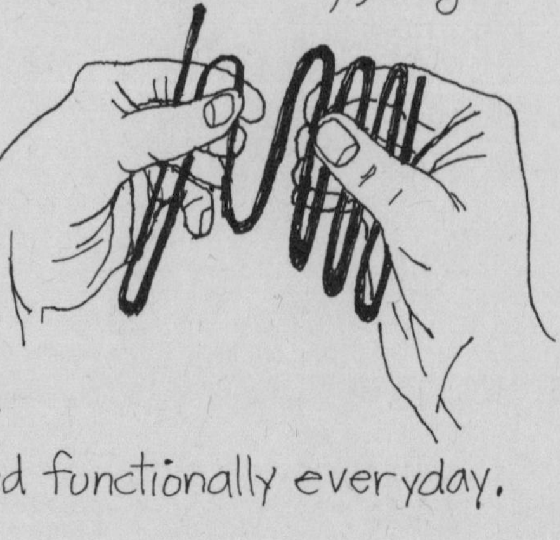

- The **OVERHAND KNOT** is used functionally everyday.

Used in macramé, the overhand knot serves several purposes: 1. to tie a bundle of cords together with one knot—for functional purposes such as putting aside a group of cords while concentrating on another section; for

decorative purposes with the macramé — tie knot and pull each strand individually to tighten.

2. to tie 1 cord around a number of strands

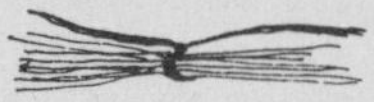

3. to secure beads or objects at top and bottom

4. to create a decorative spacing of cords:

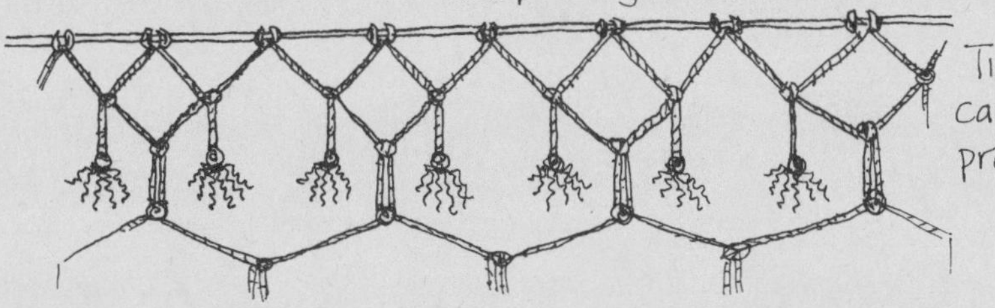

Tie overhand knots carefully to assure proper placement.

- As seen above, a method of finishing of ends of most types of cord is to unravel trimmed ends by twisting plies free.

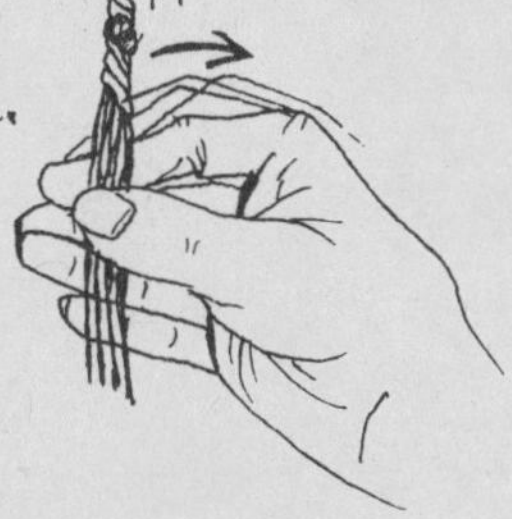

- **To add on** to an overhand knot, insert the new cord as shown and tighten knot. Any number of strands can be added to a single overhand knot.

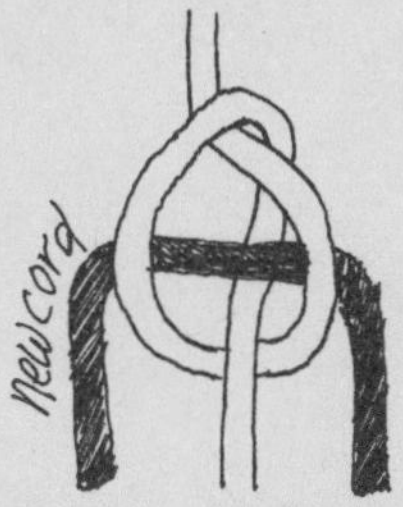
new cord

- The **SQUARE KNOT** is a very versatile macramé knot made up of 2 **half-knots**. *Different books and people explain renditions of which half-knot is made first. The difference is very slight, as shown:*

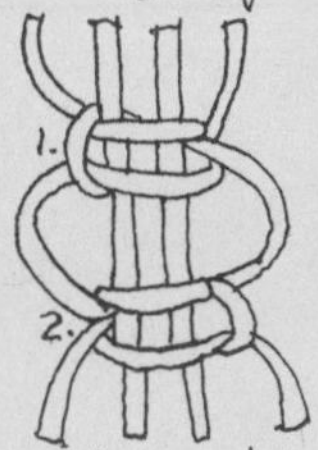
1.
2.

Regardless of which half-knot you wish to make first, the easiest way to learn the square knot is to say the steps aloud as they are made. After a while, the very movements of the hands and fingers become unconscious and natural.

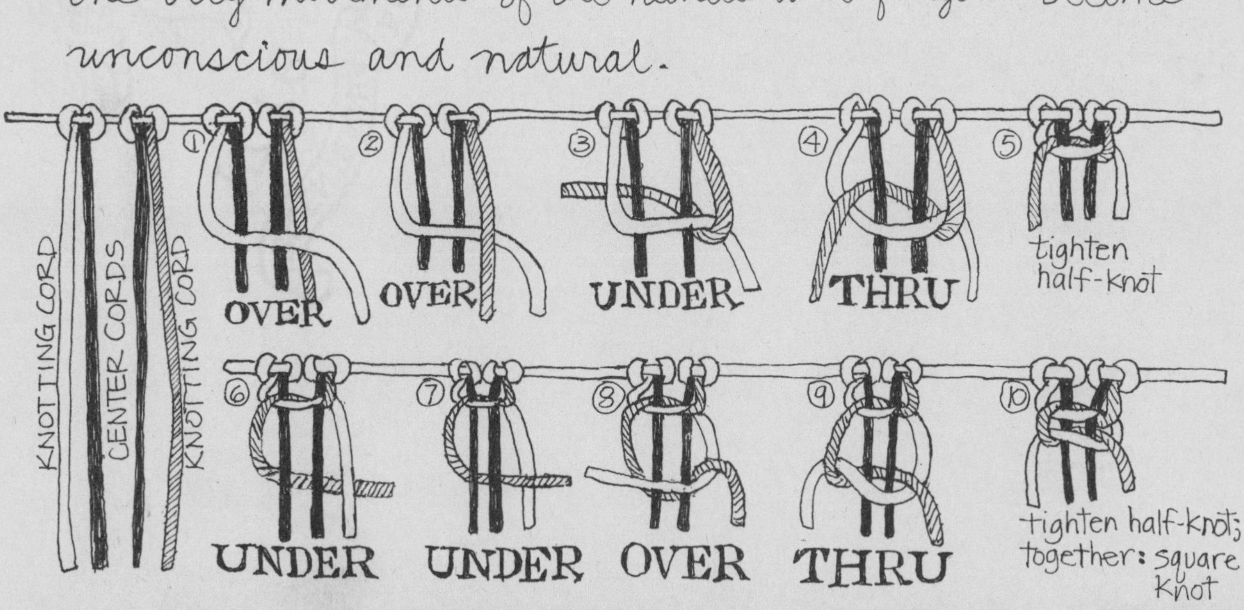
KNOTTING CORD
CENTER CORDS
KNOTTING CORD
① OVER
② OVER
③ UNDER
④ THRU
⑤ tighten half-knot
⑥ UNDER
⑦ UNDER
⑧ OVER
⑨ THRU
⑩ tighten half-knot; together: square knot

The square knot can be used several ways:

1. to make a length of square knots using groups of strands

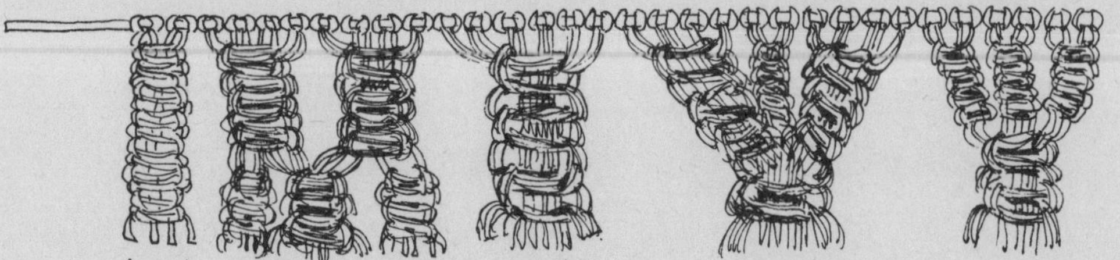

2. to decoratively space cords

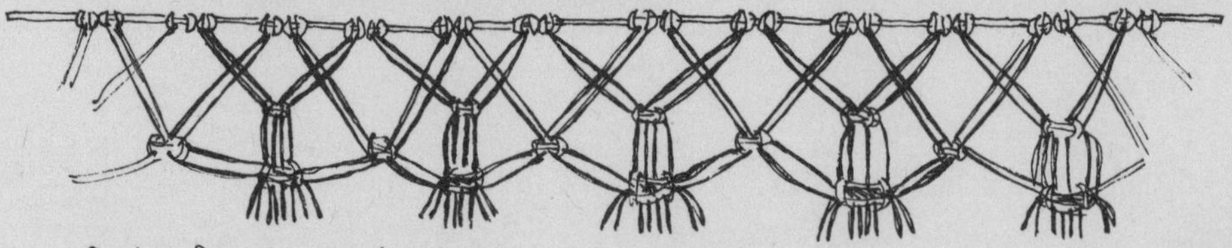

3. to form solid areas of square knots

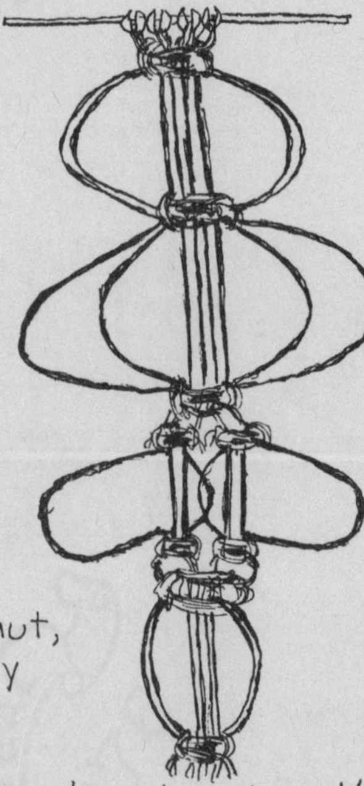

the standard format for solid areas is to **a)** knot the first row **b)** on the next row skip the knotting cord(s) and the center cord(s) on the left and knot the remaining strands **c)** on the third row, knot all strands, and so on:

square knot
row a)
row b)
row c)

4. To curve strands by keeping the center cords taut, as the knotting strands are curved, and carefully square knotted

5. To secure beads or other objects through the center strands and/or knotting strands, using the square knot on the bottom and top.

- The **SQUARE KNOT BUTTON** is a very attractive addition for detail of design. Making the square knot button requires at least 4 pairs of strands, knotted to form a solid area as shown on far left. The space (★) made as the result of square knotting secures the square knot length as it is pulled through. The number of knots for the length depends on the thickness of the cord (4-ply twine requires 4 square knots, for example.) When the button has been formed, square knot at least 1 row, as seen.

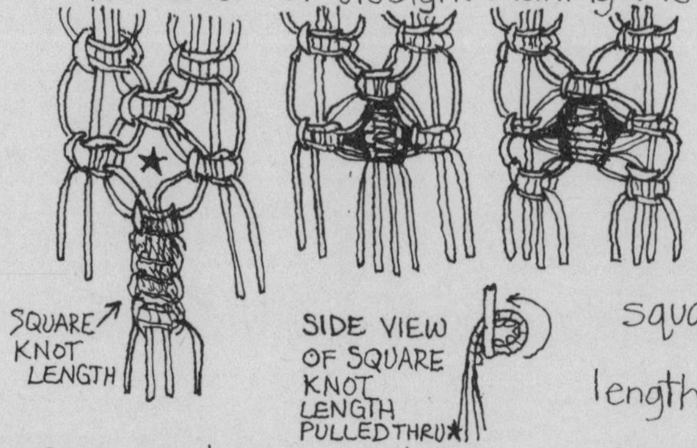
SQUARE KNOT LENGTH
SIDE VIEW OF SQUARE KNOT LENGTH PULLED THRU★

A more loopy variation of the square knot button is described on page 153.

● **To add on** to a square knot, insert the new strands to their midpoint as shown; then tighten the knot. *(Add 4 strands when replacing short, original knot cords—square knot with new strands, including all short ones with the new center cords.)*

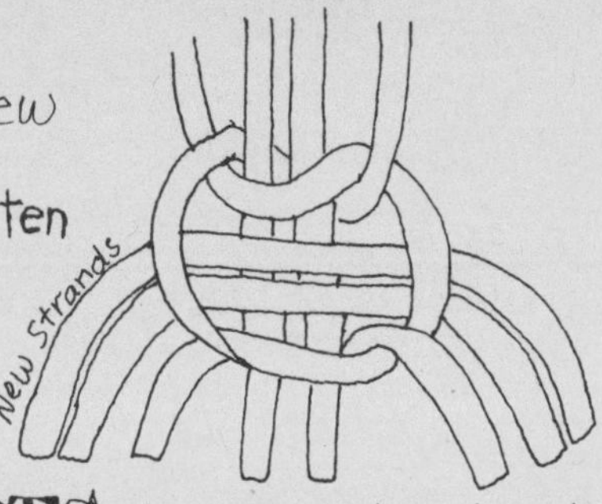
New strands

● **TWIRLING** with **HALF-KNOTS** is a most enjoyable method of macramé, as the length of knots actually twirls itself. Either half of the square knot can be used; the only difference appears as the direction of the twirl:  — twirls to the right  — twirls to the left

At least 4 strands are needed to twirl half-knots; more strands or thicker cord will twirl slower with longer, resulting curves. Retaining

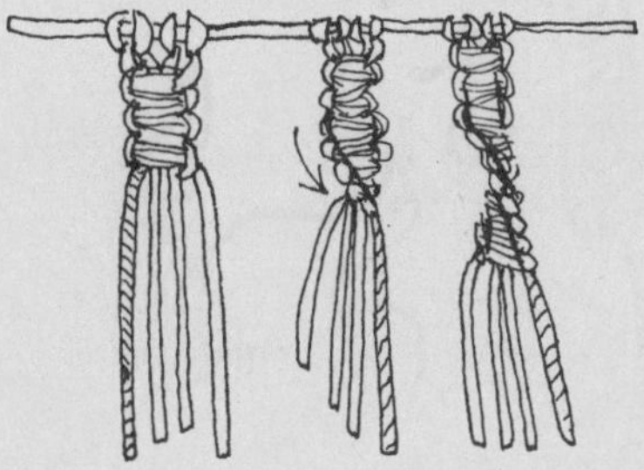

the same center cords, half-knot with the knotting strands. The length will naturally turn, altering the positions of the knotting strands. When the strands have completely changed places, continue with half-knots, until more twirling and change of places occur.

● **To add on** to a half-knot, insert the new strand(s) as shown, between two, like halfknots - tighten knots.

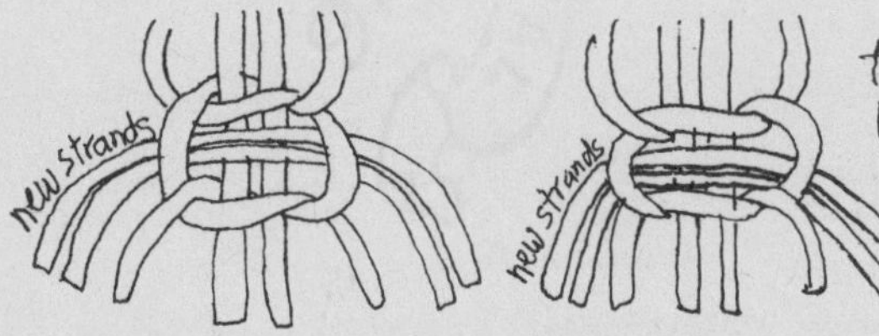
new strands
new strands

Add on strands to form intermediate twirl lengths.

When cutting strands to be used for twirling, keep in mind that the center cords remain straight, while the knotting cords are used up in forming the half-knots. When possible, arrange the strand lengths accordingly. If the knotting strands, only, become too short, add new knotting cords as shown and include all short ends in with the center cords while half-knotting.

● **WRAPPING** with the **CLOVE HITCH** is undoubtedly my favorite method of macramé because of its strength of design. Strands are wrapped around any thickness of cord or rope to create a wide variety of lines and forms.

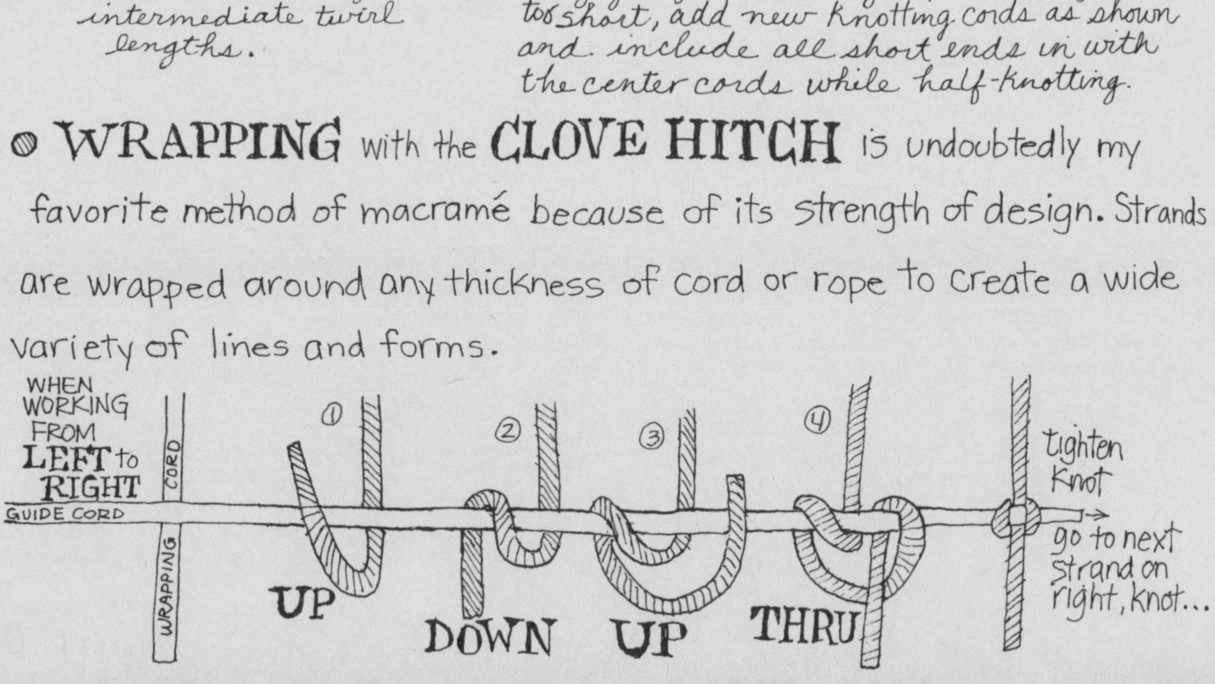
WHEN WORKING FROM LEFT to RIGHT
CORD
GUIDE CORD
WRAPPING
①
②
③
④
UP
DOWN
UP
THRU
tighten Knot
go to next strand on right, knot...

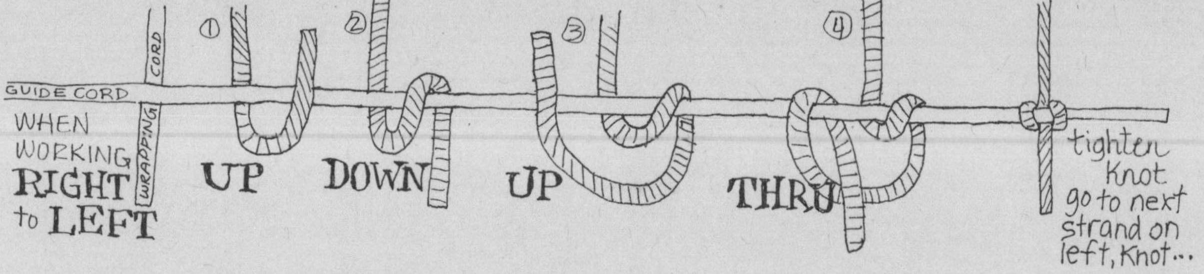
GUIDE CORD
CORD
WRAPPING
WHEN WORKING RIGHT to LEFT
① UP
② DOWN
③ UP
④ THRU
tighten Knot go to next strand on left, Knot...

As you can see, the clove hitch for moving left to right or right to left along the guide cord within a macramé is the same knot with only the direction of the looping altered. The same holds true for the many other paths that the wrapping involves:

1. Horizontal paths are made using a guidecord of any thickness, that has been added to the macramé with a lark's head (See 'adding on...') or that is already a strand of the macramé.

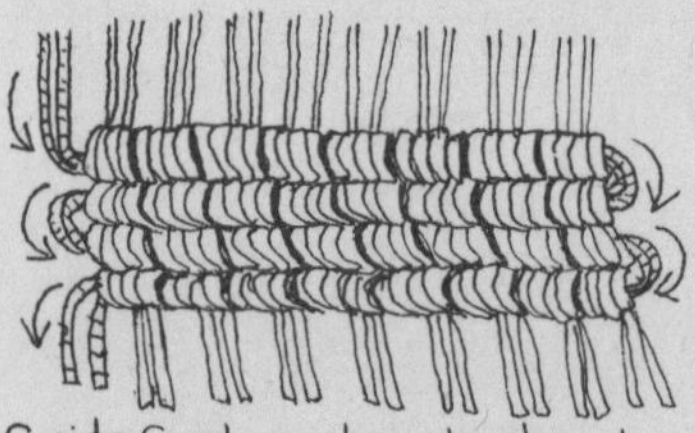

Guide Cord as strands already in macramé (2 strands)

After turning back guide cord to other direction, clove hitch end strands again to make rows even.

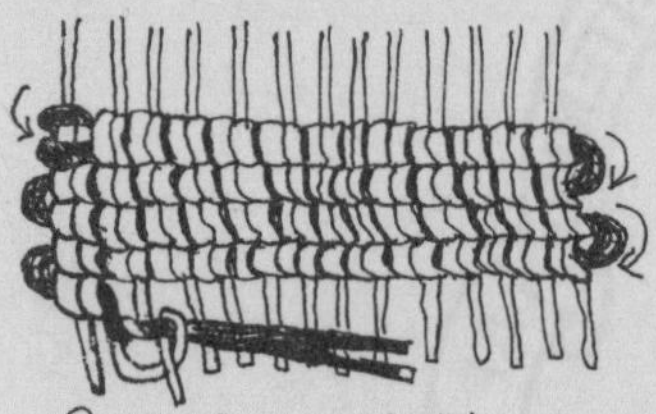

Guide Cord added to macramé with a lark's head

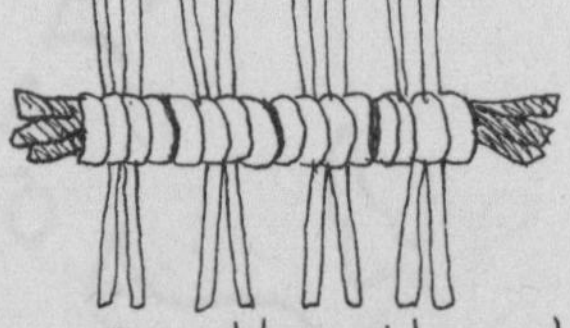

Or, add a guide cord with ends free.

2. Diagonal Paths and numerous free form directions follow the same instructions for horizontal paths; the only change being the route of the guide cord. When used in conjunction with vertical paths, the design possibilities are limit-less.

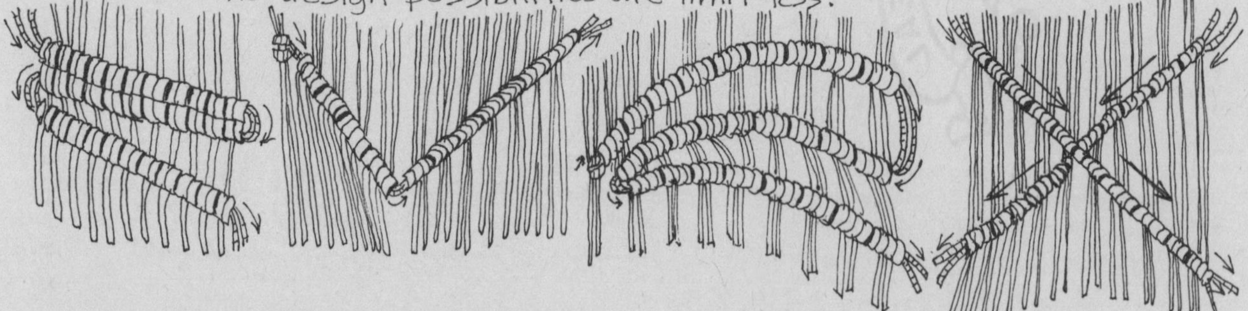

3. Consecutive Clove Hitching is made using each strand (s) consecutively as a guide cord.

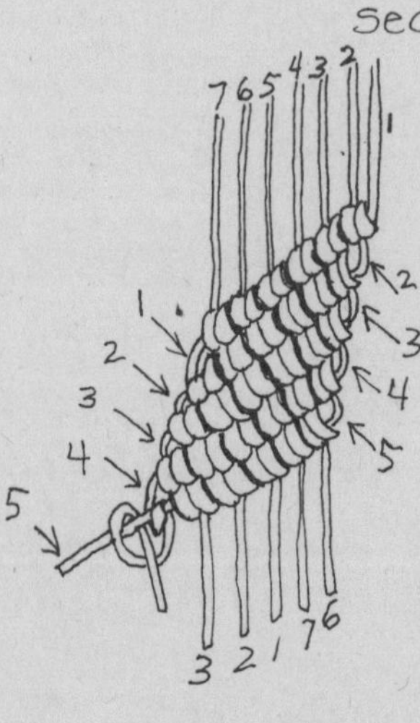
7 6 5 4 3 2
1
1.
2
3
4
5
2
3
4
5
3 2 1 7 6

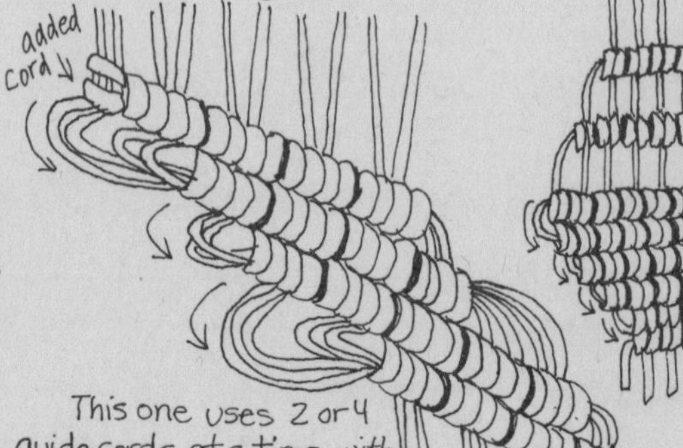
added cord

This one uses 2 or 4 guide cords at a time, with 2 strands in each wrap. Strands are wrapped and then the guide cords are pulled and shaped into loops.

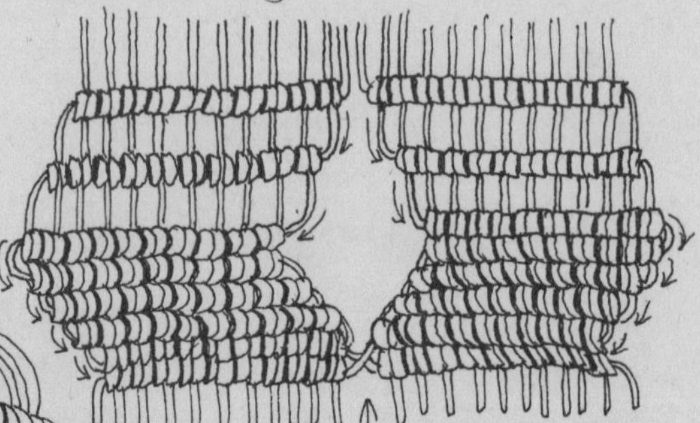

GUIDE Cords crossed over and switched to other side

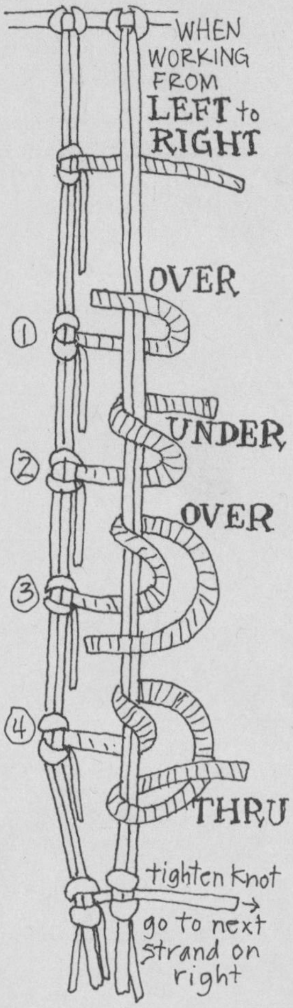
WHEN WORKING FROM LEFT to RIGHT
OVER
UNDER
OVER
THRU
tighten knot
go to next strand on right

4. Vertical paths use the strands of the macramé as guide cords, with the wrapping cord added on to the first strand with a lark's head (see below, 'adding on....') or using the first strand as the wrapping cord. The formation of the clove hitch is the same as shown for horizontal paths — only the angle for working has changed.

When the last strand (s) has been wrapped, turn the wrapping cord under and to the other direction; begin the next row by again wrapping the last strand(s) and then continuing in the new direction:

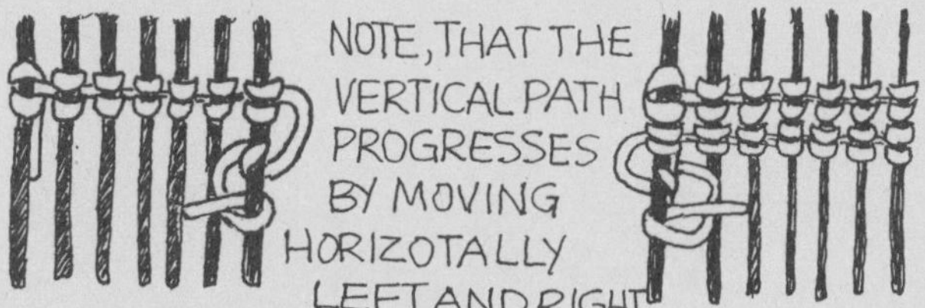
NOTE, THAT THE VERTICAL PATH PROGRESSES BY MOVING HORIZOTALLY LEFT AND RIGHT

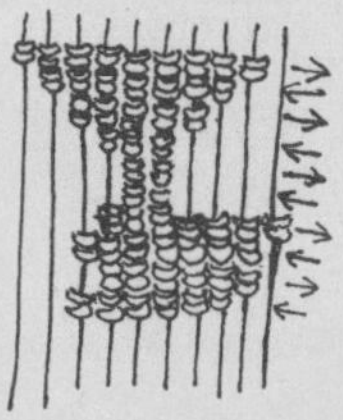

To form curves, do not rewrap the last strand(s), instead turn the wrapping cord under and to the other direction, wrapping the next guidecord.

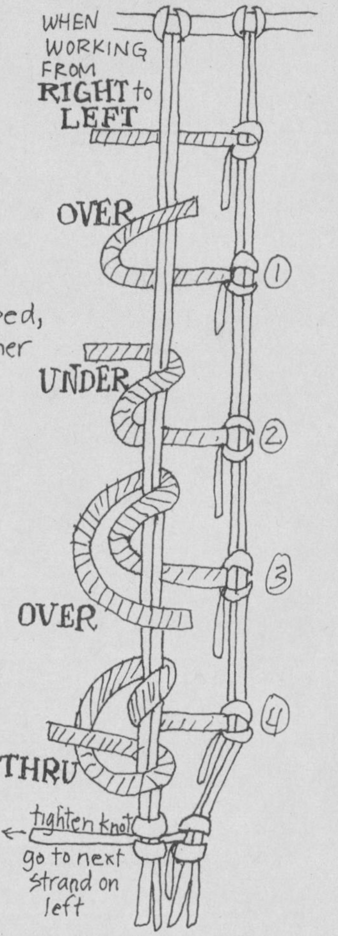
WHEN WORKING FROM RIGHT to LEFT
OVER
UNDER
OVER
THRU
tighten knot
go to next strand on left

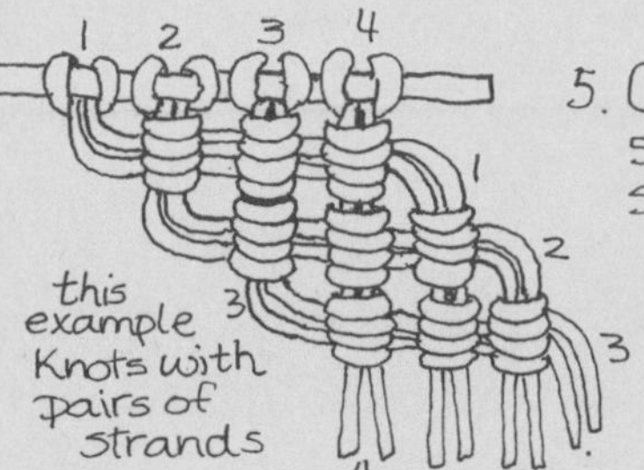
this example knots with pairs of strands

5. Consecutive Clove Hitching for verticals, uses each consecutive macramé strand(s) as a wrapping cord, as shown at left.

6. Incorporating the various directions of clove hitch wrapping enables limitless combinations. Basically, anything can be created as long as there is a guide cord and a wrapping cord; and the cords may interchangeably wrap or be wrapped. Square knots, half knot twirl lengths, or overhand knots can also be added between wrapped areas.

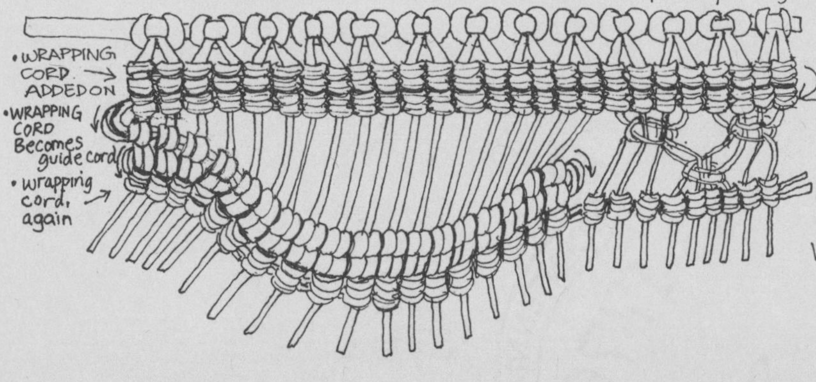
• WRAPPING CORD ADDED ON
• WRAPPING CORD Becomes guide cord
• wrapping cord, again

To add on when wrapping, attach strands with a lark's head, to the guide cord. Strands are added on when wrapping for various reasons:

1. to add a wrapping cord for Vertical paths, as seen at top of this page. In this example the added cord pairs are split; one of the strands is used to wrap while the other strand will be wrapped in with the guide cord as the macramé progresses. To save cord, fold the added cord with the stationary strand shorter:

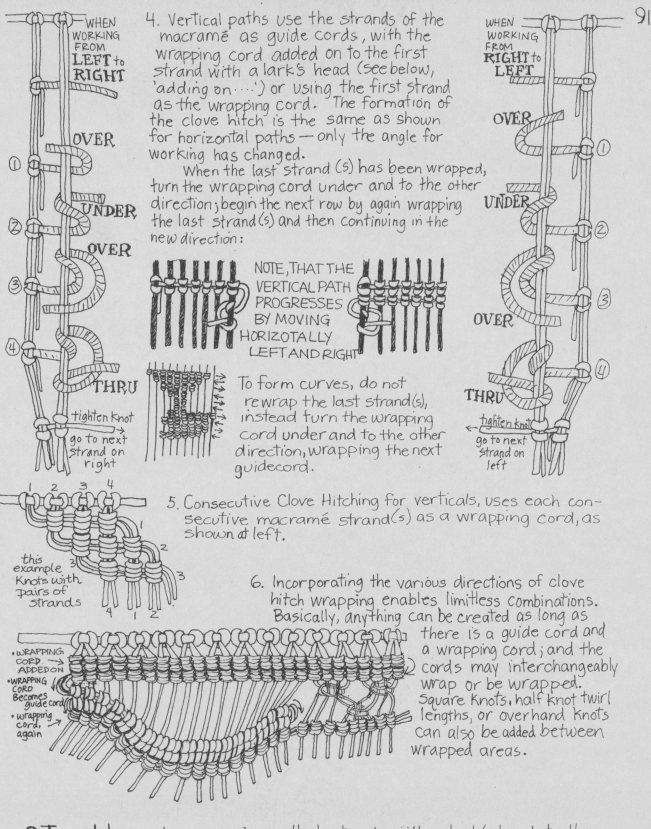

WRAPPING STRAND

2. to add a guide cord for horizontal paths

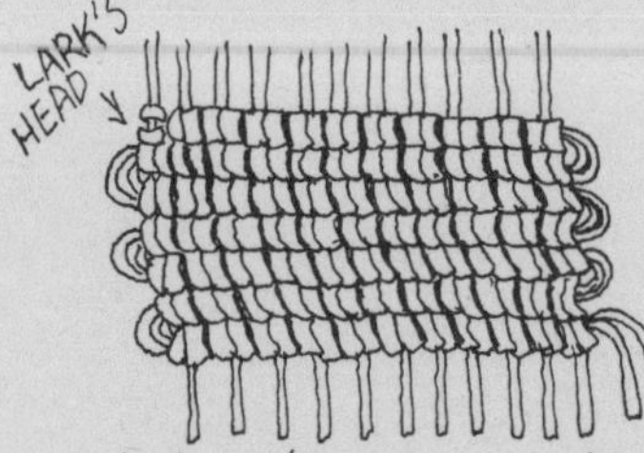
LARK'S HEAD

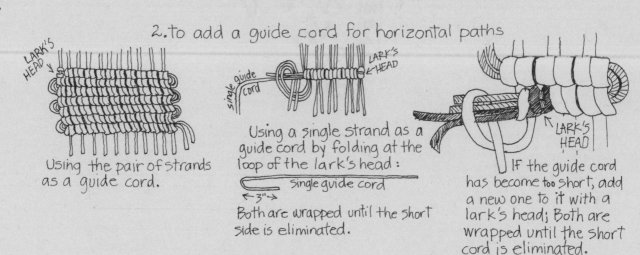

Using the pair of strands as a guide cord.

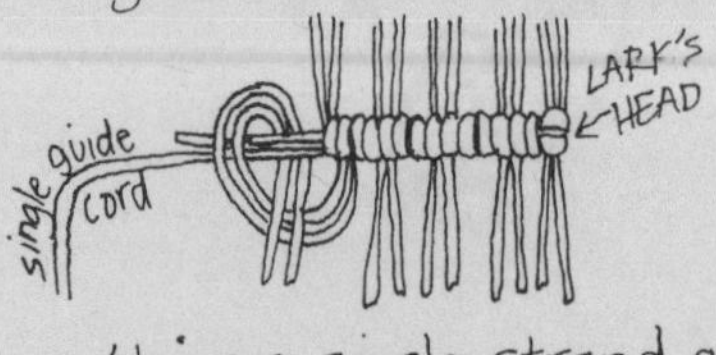
single guide cord
LARK'S HEAD

Using a single strand as a guide cord by folding at the loop of the lark's head:

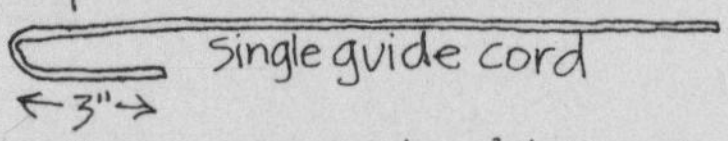
single guide cord
3"

Both are wrapped until the short side is eliminated.

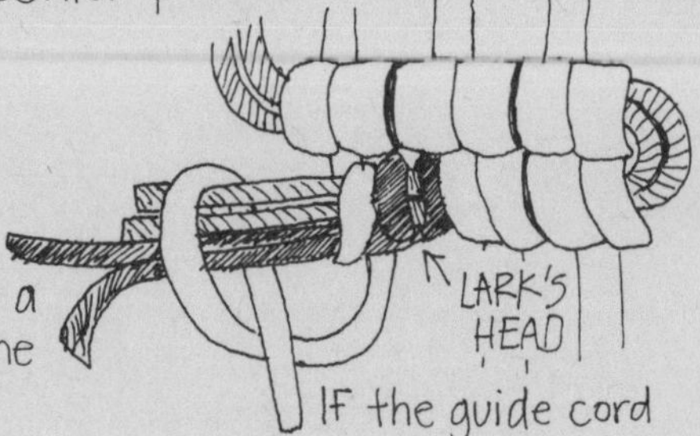
LARK'S HEAD

If the guide cord has become too short, add a new one to it with a lark's head; Both are wrapped until the short cord is eliminated.

3. to replace a wrapping cord that has become too short

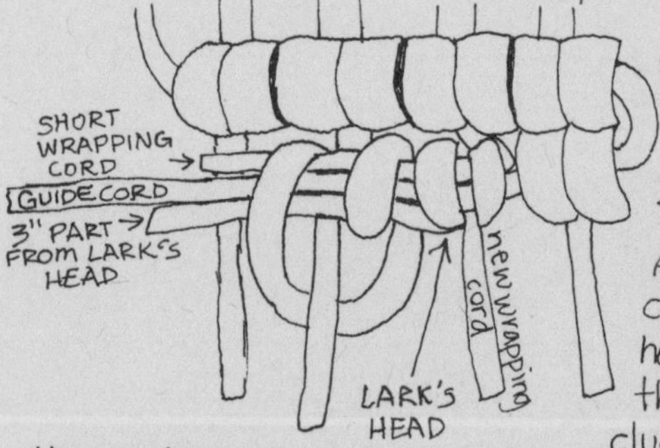
SHORT WRAPPING CORD
GUIDE CORD
3" PART FROM LARK'S HEAD
new wrapping cord
LARK'S HEAD

Using single wrapping cords (See also, page 95)

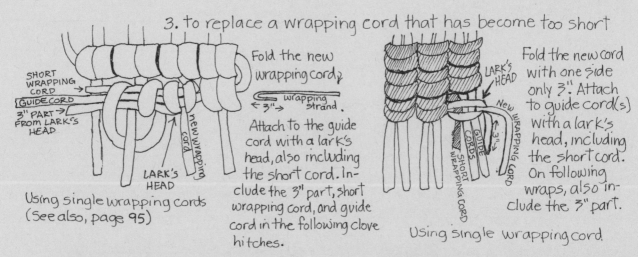

Fold the new wrapping cord.

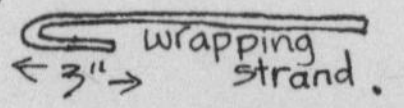
wrapping strand
3"

Attach to the guide cord with a lark's head, also including the short cord. Include the 3" part, short wrapping cord, and guide cord in the following clove hitches.

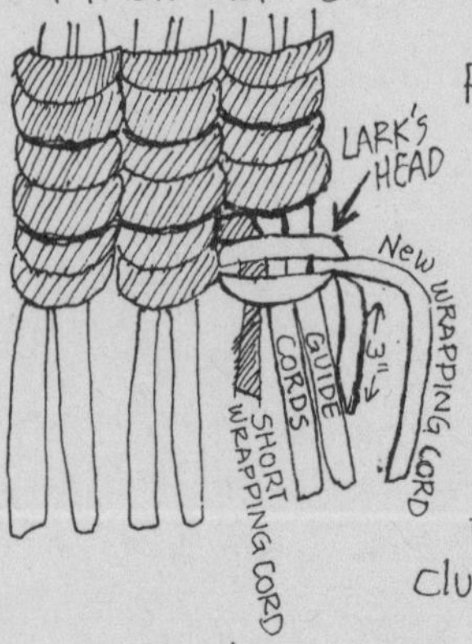
LARK'S HEAD
New WRAPPING CORD
GUIDE CORDS
SHORT WRAPPING CORD
3"

Fold the new cord with one side only 3". Attach to guide cord(s) with a lark's head, including the short cord. On following wraps, also include the 3" part.

Using single wrapping cord

When pairs of strands are used for wrapping, add a half-hitch next to the added lark's head, so it is even with the rest of the wrapping.

WHEN WORKING FROM LEFT to RIGHT
WHEN WORKING FROM RIGHT to LEFT
WHEN WORKING FROM LEFT to RIGHT
WHEN WORKING FROM RIGHT to LEFT.

The lark's head with the half-hitch equals the double-strand clove-hitch.

4. to increase the wrapping row, by attaching new strands to the guide cord with a lark's head.

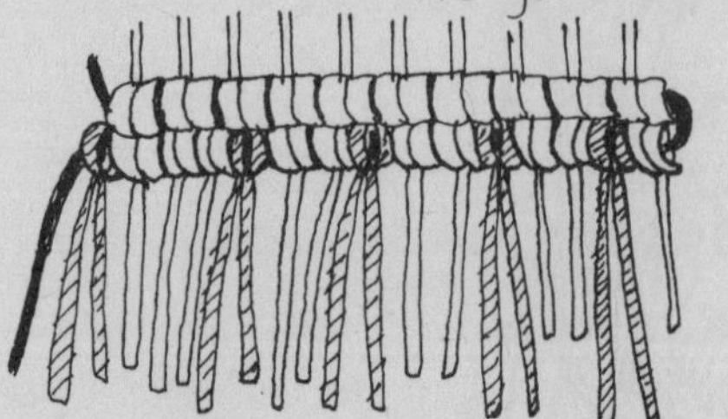

as the new strands wrap the next row, the wrapping row will increase further.

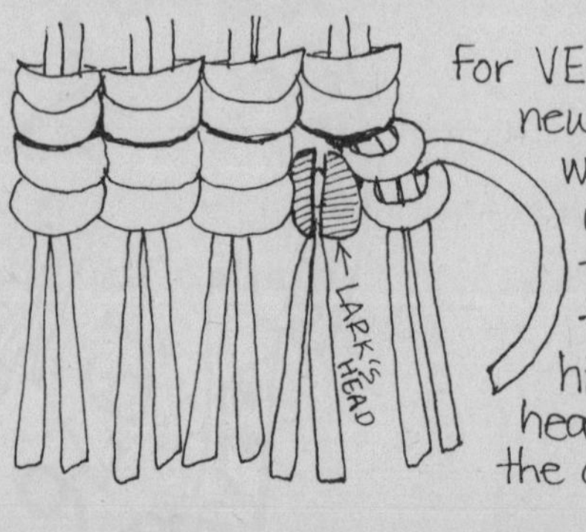
LARK'S HEAD

For VERTICAL PATHS, add new strands to the wrapping cord(s) with a lark's head. On the following wrap, tighten the clove hitch so that lark's head is <u>hidden</u> behind the adjacent hitches.

5. to wrap a group or bundle of strands together, using any four of the **half-hitches** seen on the previous page. Use a crochet hook or unfold and form a small hook on a paper clip to pull the wrapping cord back into the wrap.

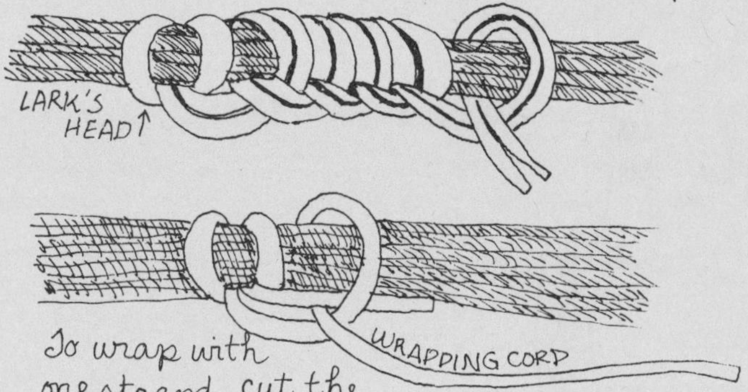
LARK'S HEAD
WRAPPING CORD

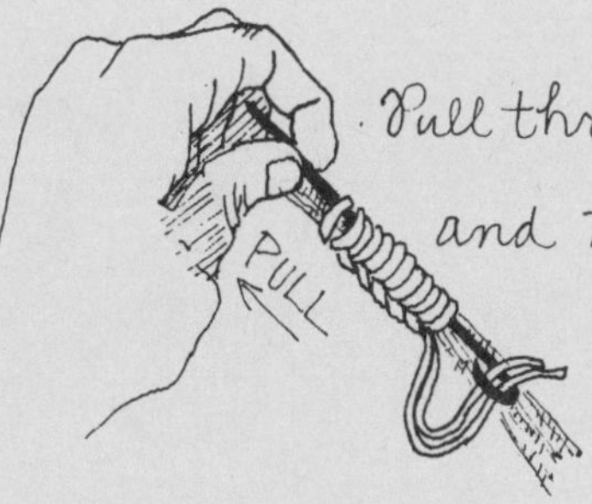
PULL

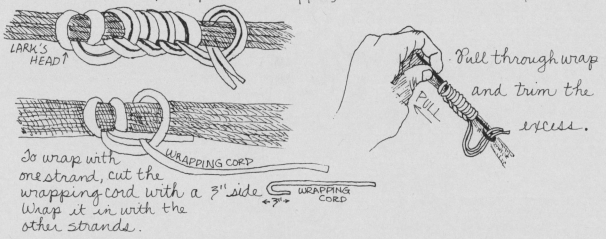

Pull through wrap and trim the excess.

To wrap with one strand, cut the wrapping cord with a 3" side. Wrap it in with the other strands.

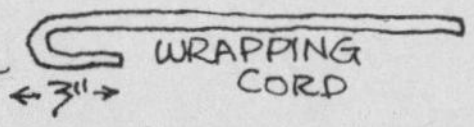
WRAPPING CORD
3"

To subtract cords or to finish off the last horizontal row without any loose strands, insert cords into the wrap after clove hitching. Trim the inserted cords to about 3 inches.

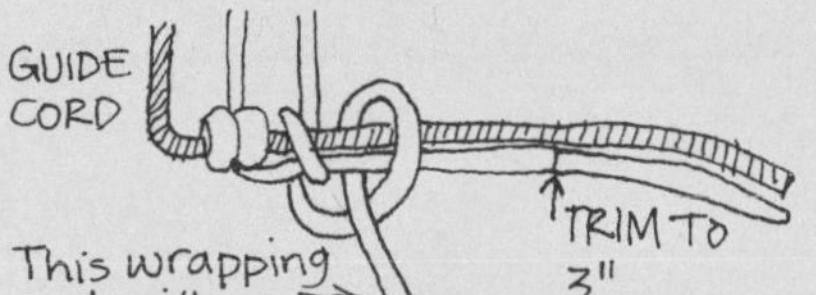
GUIDE CORD
TRIM TO 3"

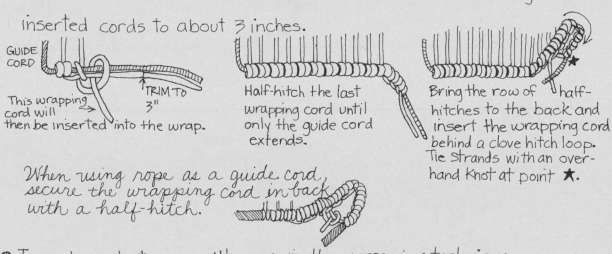

This wrapping cord will then be inserted into the wrap.

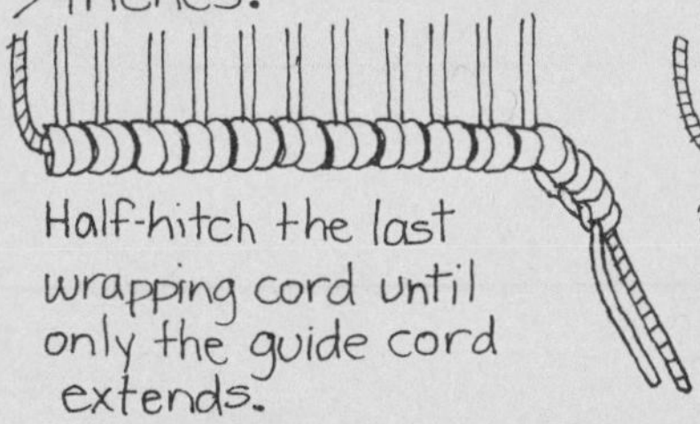

Half-hitch the last wrapping cord until only the guide cord extends.

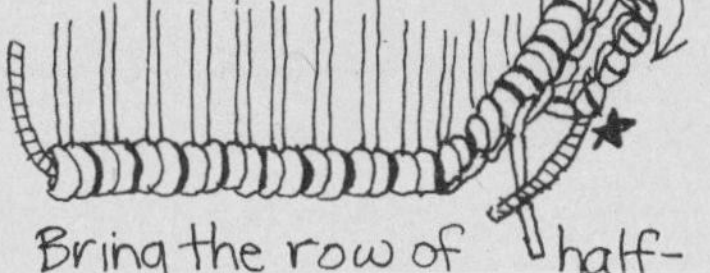

Bring the row of half-hitches to the back and insert the wrapping cord behind a clove hitch loop. Tie strands with an overhand knot at point ★.

When using rope as a guide cord, secure the wrapping cord in back with a half-hitch.

To replace short rope with new, in the wrapping technique

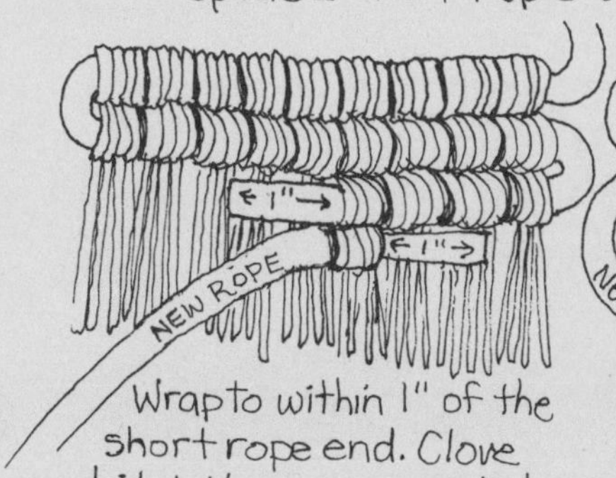
1"
1"
NEW ROPE

Wrap to within 1" of the short rope end. Clove hitch the new rope below to within 1" of end.

New Rope

Place the 1" rope ends behind macramé strands. Wrap the new rope snugly, hiding the 1st 1" end.

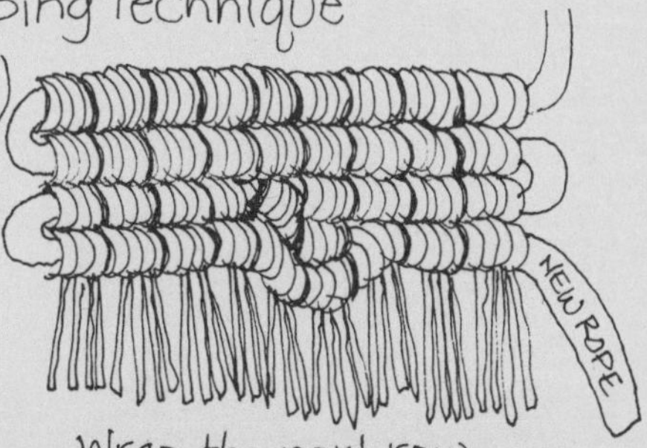
NEW ROPE

Wrap the next row snugly, hiding the 2nd 1" end.

For more information and ideas about macramé:

MACRAMÉ–CREATIVE DESIGN IN KNOTTING by Dona Z. Meilach; New York: Crown Publishers, Inc., 1972.

MACRAMÉ–ADVANCED TECHNIQUE AND DESIGN by Norman and Lilian Rack; Garden City, New York: Doubleday & Co., Inc., 1972.

MACRAMÉ WALL HANGINGS

Macramé wallhangings offer more freedom than any other macramé project — all it really has to 'do' is hang and not necessarily against a wall. The first attempt may not correspond to the glorious vision of how the macramé would look on completion. Cord and rope project their own characteristics and life that the craftsperson may not have planned on — such is part of the neverending fascination for materials. As with all media, the more experimental the process, the more delightful the surprises are; and by all means, remember that failure is a big part of learning.

Use any of the types of cord mentioned on page 85, separately or in combination. Keep an eye open for other materials that could be incorporated. Because new cords can be added on to all the knots, the length of the first strands is optional. I prefer to work with lengths about 3-5 feet (distance from fold to end ↕∩), adding on new strands as needed. Although some people cut long lengths to accommodate the size of the wallhanging, securing the cord in bundles (see page 86)...Because of changing knots and design, only a rough estimate is possible for how long strands should be ~ on an average, the cord length should be 5-6 times longer than the desired wallhanging dimension.

Generally, a wall hanging uses a dowel, tree branch, metal length, or ANY object which meets two criteria: 1. macramé cords can be attached; 2. the object can hang from wall or ceiling, alone or by use of an attached hanging cord or wire. Within the macramé, other objects can be incorporated such as: **buttons**, **buckeyes** (page 27), **clay beads** (pages 132-3, 136-7), **plastic tile** (shriveled and curled on tin foil in a low oven), **gourds** (plant the seeds in the spring and watch the vines travel <u>so</u> far; harvest and wash the gourds gently; let them dry in a well-lit room), **dried lemons** and **small oranges** (while drying, turn frequently to avoid rotting), **hickory nut hulls** (page 49), **horseshoe crab tails** (page 131), various lengths of **copper tubing**, and found objects of humans and nature.

To change color or type of cord, insert the new cord as explained in the sections: **to add on** for the various knots. An alternative method when wrapping with pairs of strands is to include the first cord into the wrap; under the absent space add the new strand with a lark's head on the following row:

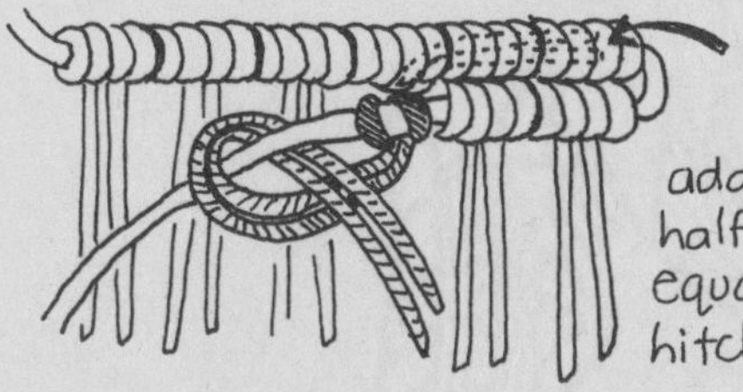

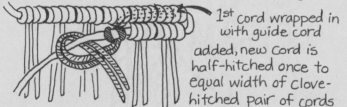

1st cord wrapped in with guide cord added, new cord is half-hitched once to equal width of clove-hitched pair of cords

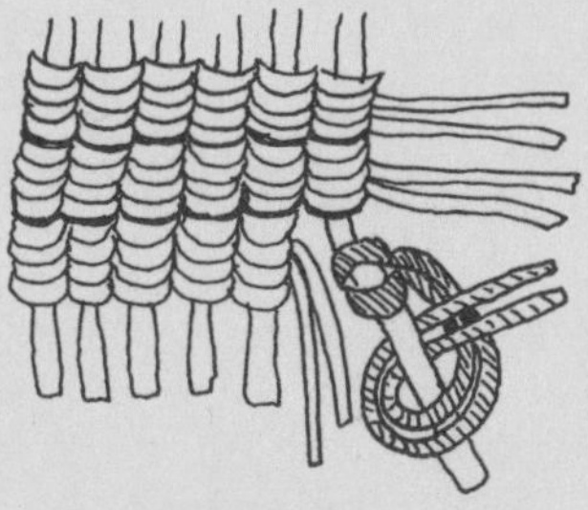

wrap the subtracted cords into the following rows of clove-hitches.

Because of the aspects of flexibility, I have not included knot by knot instructions of macramé wall-hangings. The following pages show a few possible schemes with written descriptions of knots and techniques. I have chosen examples which illustrate the nature of rope, and cord; and utilize a variety of objects as starting lines for macramé.

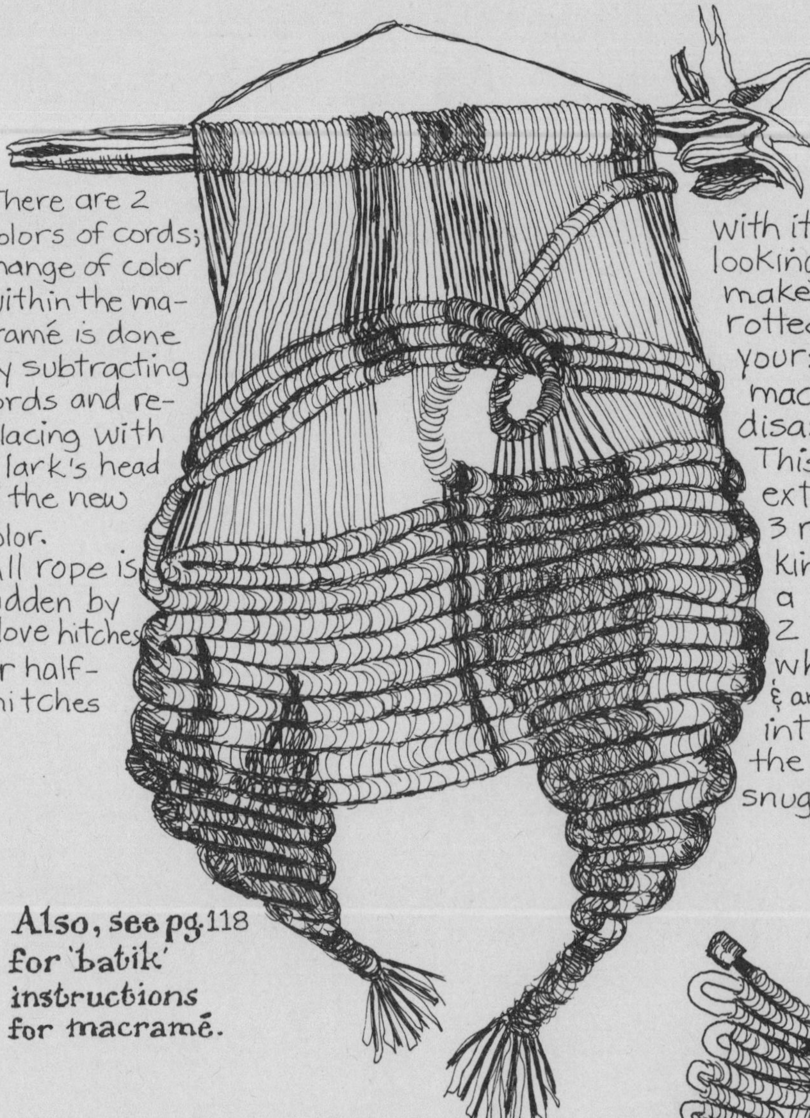

Unique branches make a fine main starting line. A friend gave me this weathered branch with its 'goat's head' end. When looking for branches, just make sure they are not rotted out or you may find yourself in the middle of a macramé when the branch disastrously breaks.

SIDE VIEW

This hanging actually extends out; there are 3 reasons why: **1.** working upright rather than on a flat surface, **2.** there are 2 separate pieces of rope which interchange rows & are drawn tightly back into the macramé, and **3.** the wrapping cords are snugly clove-hitched.

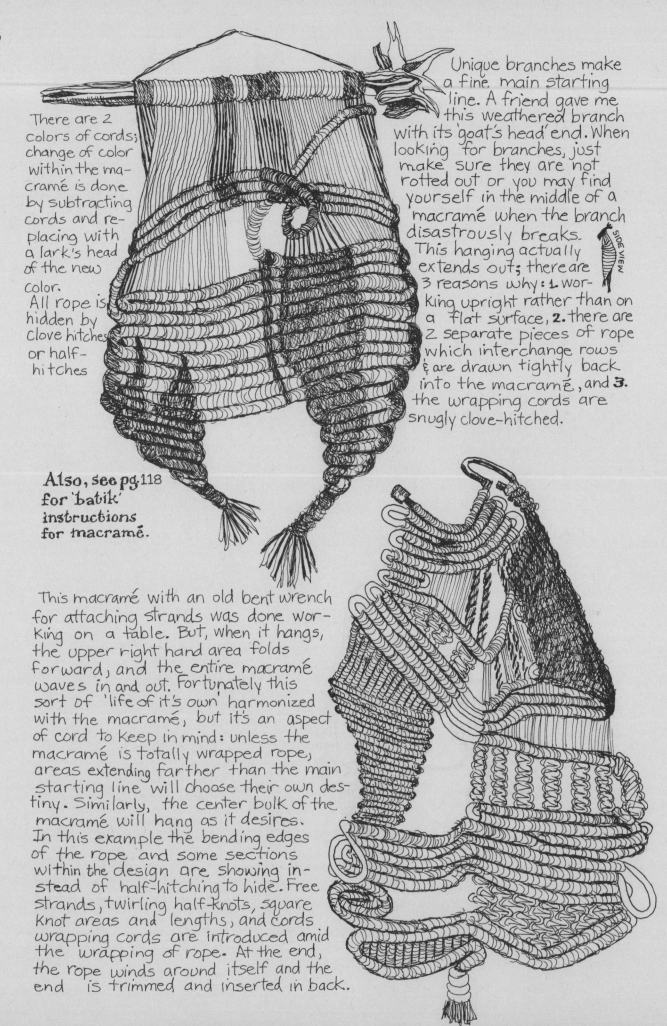

There are 2 colors of cords; change of color within the macramé is done by subtracting cords and replacing with a lark's head of the new color.

All rope is hidden by clove hitches or half-hitches

Also, see pg. 118 for 'batik' instructions for macramé.

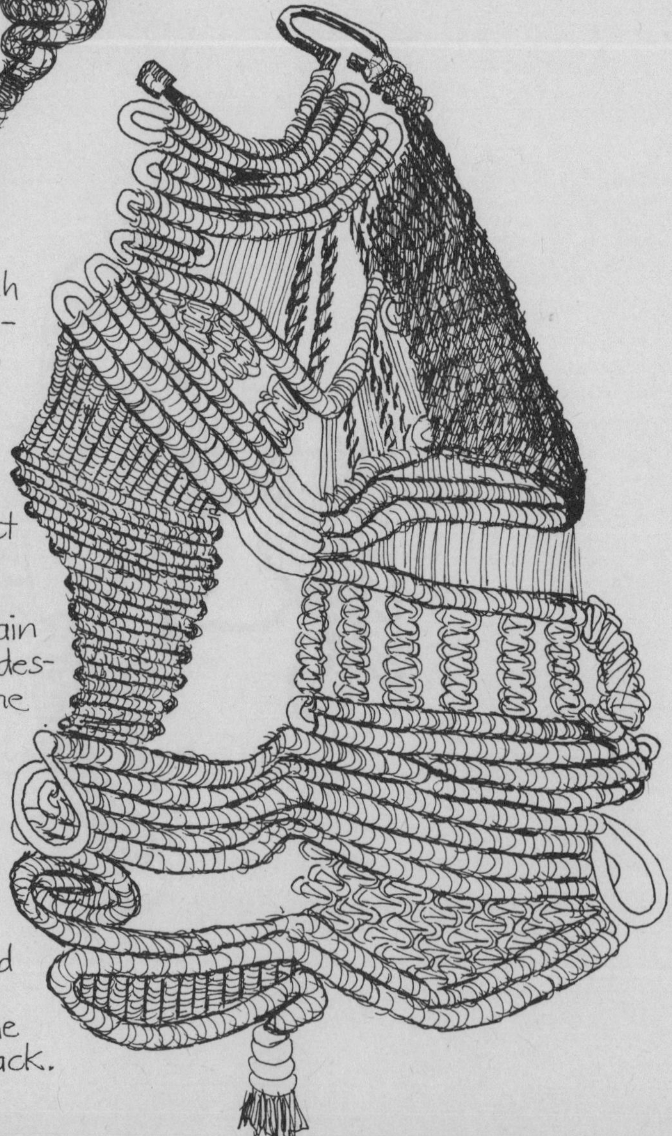

This macramé with an old bent wrench for attaching strands was done working on a table. But, when it hangs, the upper right hand area folds forward, and the entire macramé waves in and out. Fortunately this sort of 'life of it's own' harmonized with the macramé, but it's an aspect of cord to keep in mind: unless the macramé is totally wrapped rope, areas extending farther than the main starting line will choose their own destiny. Similarly, the center bulk of the macramé will hang as it desires. In this example the bending edges of the rope and some sections within the design are showing instead of half-hitching to hide. Free strands, twirling half-knots, square knot areas and lengths, and cords wrapping cords are introduced amid the wrapping of rope. At the end, the rope winds around itself and the end is trimmed and inserted in back.

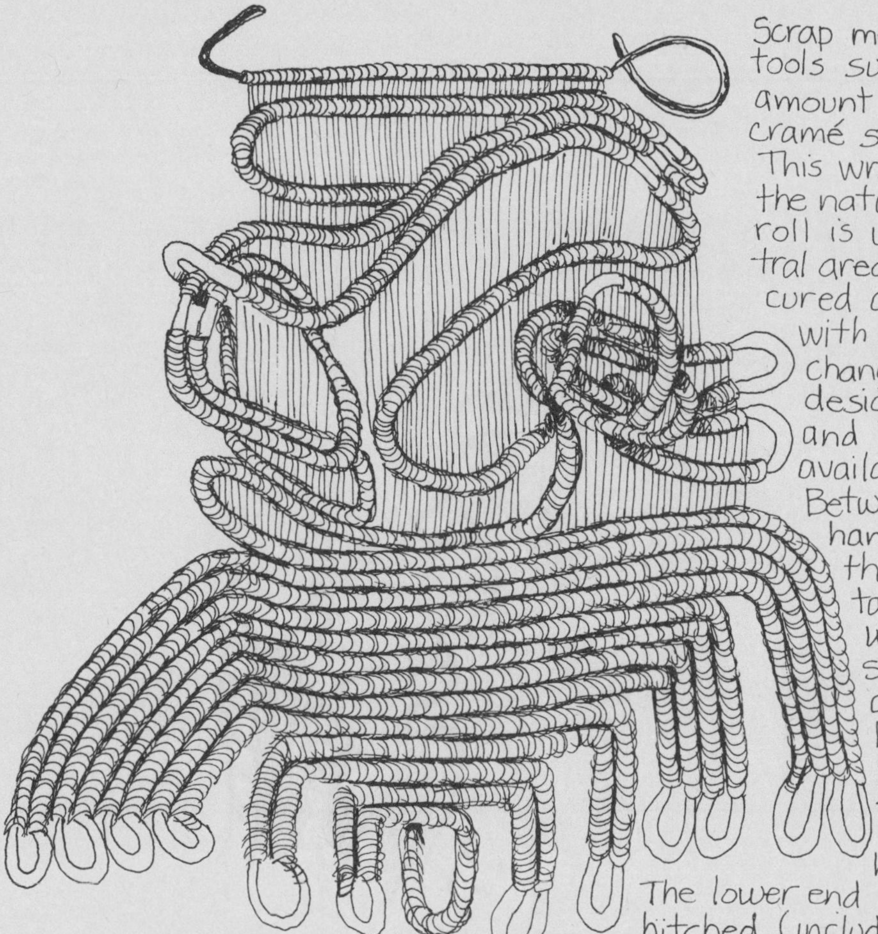

Scrap metal and old farm tools supply an endless amount and types of macramé starting lines. This wrapping incorporates the nature of rope as the roll is unwound. In the central area, the rope is secured as it naturally fell with only a few minor changes for the sake of design. The rope is clove- and half-hitched with available and added cords. Between the rope, strands hang free as part of the design—hanging taut because of the weight of the lower section. The lower area is a continuous length of rope moving back and forth; secured and hidden by clove-+ half hitches. The lower end of the rope is half-hitched (including last strands into the wrap) and secured in back.

This wallhanging uses 2 branches, weathered and varnished, as main starting lines. Square knots, clove hitches and free strands are used with oven-baked linoleum looped with twine and tied in back. At the bottom of the smaller section, new cords are added to square knots and the old cords are tied 2 together with an overhand knot, trimmed, and unraveled. All clove-hitches use one of the macramé strands as a guide cord; the lower left section is a consecutive vertical clove-hitching. The large area of square knotting deletes the 2 right strands on each row. This macramé can be hung from the ceiling—the back of any macramé has its own personality—less dramatic than the front, but presentable.

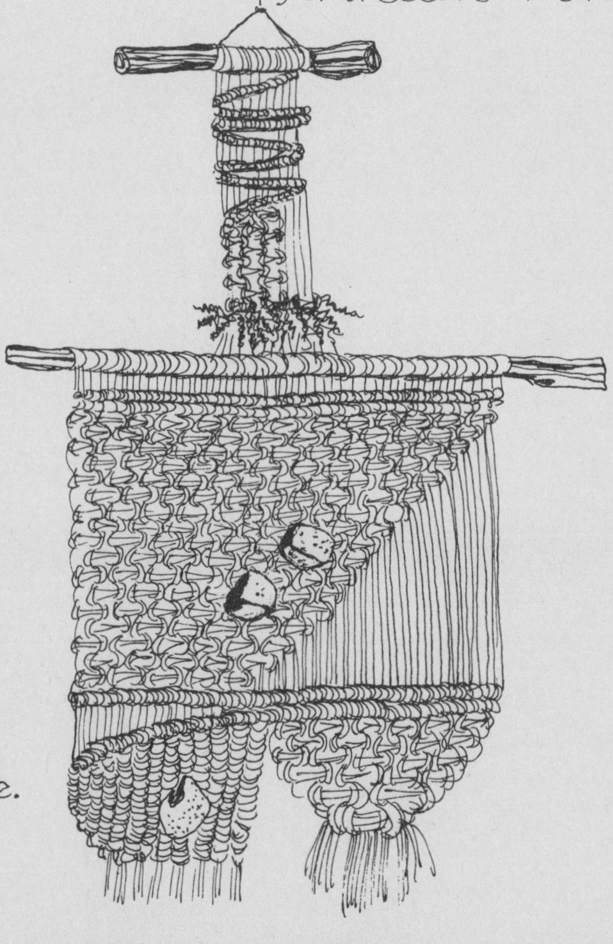

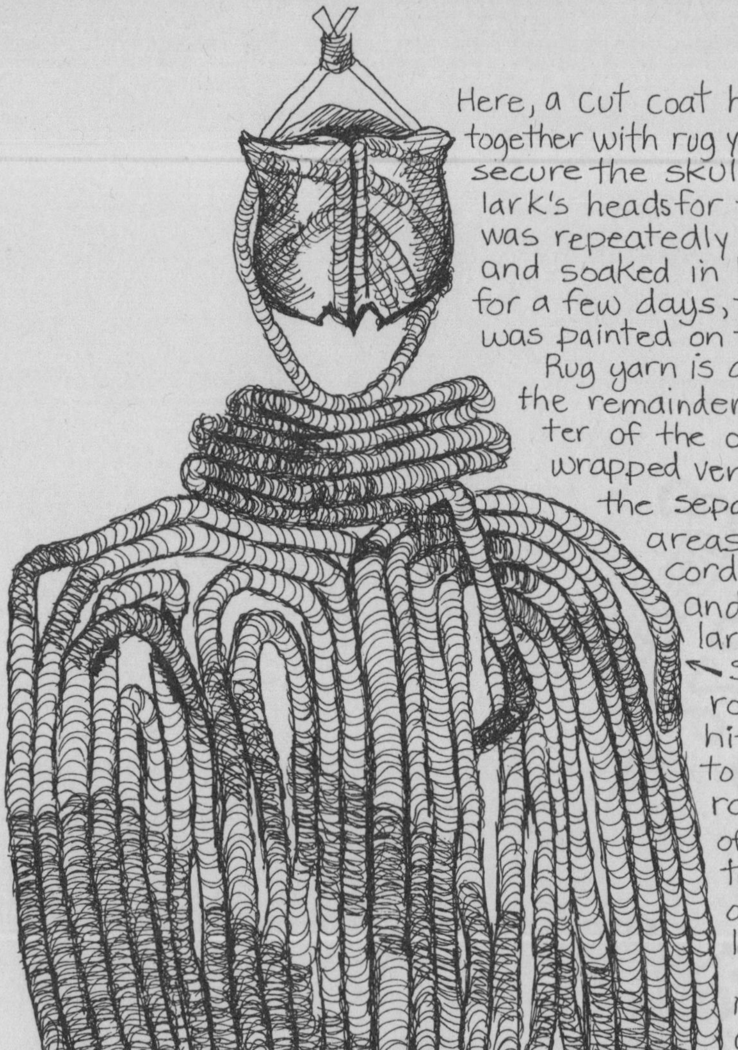

Here, a cut coat hanger and rope are half-hitched together with rug yarn, as a hanging device, to secure the skull into place, and for attaching lark's heads for the macramé. The cow's skull was repeatedly strubbed with a stiff brush and soaked in bleach; after drying in the sun for a few days, the visage of wrapped rope was painted on the surface with acrylic paint.

Rug yarn is attached with lark's heads, to the remainder of the top, and sides to center of the outer ∩∩-shapes. Cords are wrapped vertically and horizontally onto the separate rope ∩-shapes. Void areas are formed by subtracting cords from one length of rope—and attaching new cords with lark's heads to the adjacent rope. ←Separate lengths of wrapped rope are formed by half—hitching the cord. (Note the length to the upper left, where the rope overlaps another.) Change of yarn color is made by subtracting the yarn and on the next row, adding the new color with a lark's head.

All cord ends are subtracted into the wrap—the last cords are pulled back into the wrap with a crochet hook.

This ceiling hanging uses a recycled lamp shade frame—so it could be functional as well. A smaller version of working in the round uses embroidery hoops or shaped coathangers (hook ends and secure with thin wire.) And, although I've never done it, using a hoola hoop would make a magnificent hanging. Cords are attached to the first circle of wire with lark's heads—if using a lamp frame rather than 2 separate rings, the connecting wires should be hidden into or behind the macramé. In this one, the connecting wires (there are usually 3-5 of them) are included in with the center cords of the twirling half-knots—the strands will need just a bit of encouragement to twirl. The following square knots with square knot buttons, and then the larger square knots, hide the remaining wire. Below the last ring, large twirling half-knots become divided into thinner ones with beads pulling the strands somewhat taut.

NATURAL WOOD CLOCK*

THE NATURAL WOOD CLOCK IN OUR HOME HAS RECEIVED COMPLIMENTS FROM NEARLY EVERY VISITOR. IT'S EASY TO MAKE, USING THE TIME MECHANISM TAKEN OUT OF AN OLD OR CHEAP WALL CLOCK. ASK FRIENDS OR PERHAPS A NICE LUMBER MILL EMPLOYEE FOR A SCRAP OF WOOD.... ROUGH-CUT WOOD IS BEAUTIFUL BUT COULD ALSO BE PLANED DOWN AND SANDED. SAW THE WOOD TO THE CORRECT SIZE OR SHAPE DESIRED. USING AN ELECTRIC OR HAND DRILL, MAKE A HOLE IN THE CENTER, LARGE ENOUGH FOR THE SHAFT THAT CONNECTS TO THE HANDS OF THE CLOCK. ON THE BACK OF THE CLOCK, USE A DRILL AND A CHISEL TO CARVE OUT THE AREA AROUND THE HOLE, LARGE ENOUGH TO INSERT THE MECHANISM.

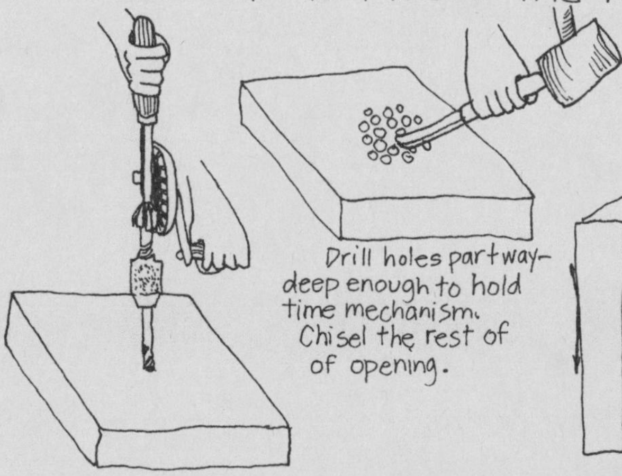
Drill holes partway-deep enough to hold time mechanism. Chisel the rest of of opening.

REMOVE THE HANDS FROM THE SHAFT AND SLIDE IT THROUGH THE HOLE IN THE WOOD. GLUE THE TIME MECHANISM TO THE WOOD WITH EPOXY AND SCREW, IF POSSIBLE. REPLACE THE HANDS, LINING UP TO SIX O'CLOCK TO ASSURE THE HOURS WILL LIE CORRECTLY.

* *Courtesy Kenneth Abeles*

BATIK

Batik is a method of 'painting', utilizing the resistance property of wax incorporated with the dyeing of cloth. Using a brush or a tjanting (See page 106), melted wax is applied to natural fabric, which is then dyed & dried; the process is then repeated; and finally the wax is removed. Although any style of art is possible with batik, it is best to begin with free-form, abstract experimentation. Because 1) the design is established with the wax, 2) the color blooms afterwards, & 3) further dyeing interacts to form new colors; surprise is inevitably an exciting element of batik. In general (and this is by no means a rule), add each wax application in thin lines and small areas, so that there will be enough space allowed for further waxing and dye colors. If a particular scheme is desired, sketch lightly on the fabric with pencil; planning which areas and lines will be waxed and dyed first, second, or more. I must admit that although I have made many such sketches on cloth, when it came time to wax, I usually preferred to apply the wax rhythmically as my mood dictated; then, moving anxiously to the dye bath to see the metamorphosis of the fabric. A batik is rarely awful, particularly from the eyes of the creator, because the process is so lovely and intriguing. However, an excellent batik (from a more critical standpoint of design, color, craftsmanship, and so on) takes practice, trial & error experimentation, and time — I make this statement in homage to the artists of batik who delve into it with great earnest and patience.

In relation to dye baths, begin with lighter colors, working toward the darker hues with each consecutive dye application. You may wish to dye the fabric before the first waxing. The colors resulting from the combinations of dyed fabric will vary somewhat depending on the shades of color and brand ~ keep a notebook of fabric samples and note the brand and names of colors used. The dyed fabric placed in another dye bath will generally create colors in correlation with a basic color chart: for example: red + yellow = orange; blue + yellow = green; blue + red = purple. Color combinations for the specific brand and their dyes are often available with the product.

SUPPLIES:
- Natural fiber fabric such as cotton or silk (NO synthetics or permanent press).
- Beeswax and paraffin — usually used in combinations of varying proportions, but paraffin (which is cheaper) can be used alone (see Step 3)
- Cold water dyes such as DYLON COLD DYES, which can be purchased at crafts stores or arts & crafts suppliers **OR** All-purpose dyes such as RIT HOUSEHOLD DYES, which are found at grocery, drug stores, and others.
- Coffee can to melt wax — some people also prefer to use an old pan with the can as a double boiler — this is much safer (NOTE: the pan will end up waxy inside)
- Stove burner, or a hot plate is ideal
- Stiff, bristle brush (some books also recommend soft brushes but I've never had any luck with them)
- Frame and push-pins or thumbtacks (See page 107); an old picture frame could also be used
- Plenty of newspaper
- Tjanting (optional, but a nice tool to use); these can be purchased at some art & crafts stores and definitely thru suppliers such as TRIARCO (see page 73); or make one (see page 106)
- Iron and ironing board (the removal of wax will not hurt the iron — in fact, the wax will keep the iron smooth.)
- Large pot or container for dye bath (see also STEP 6 if using Household Dyes)

INSTRUCTIONS:

1. Cut fabric to desired size of design plus 2-3 inches around. Wash fabric to remove sizing — dry. Sketch design onto the fabric with pencil if desired. At any rate, have a scheme in mind.

2. Tack the fabric to the frame with push pins or thumbtacks, so that it is fairly taut and not sagging. **NOTE:** Do not batik without a frame—if the cloth is laying against any surface, the wax is pulled off the fabric and the dye will bleed through somewhat, destroying the richness of the colors.

3. Melt the wax in a can which is then placed in a pan of water. The mixture of beeswax and paraffin is variable (beeswax is about 4 x the price of paraffin). I use a mixture of one cake of beeswax to 2 cakes of paraffin. However, remember that paraffin alone can be used—paraffin causes more cracking of wax on fabric, which dyes beautifully. The wax is hot enough when it is brushed on, penetrating the fabric, and appears clear. Keep the wax hot while using.

BEESWAX
3oz.
PARAFFIN 4oz.
4oz.

4. While the wax is heating, lay out newspaper on the work area, for catching dripping wax. If using a tjanting, it may be necessary to keep the tjanting hot by a candle flame, to allow a free flow of hot wax. The metal frame of a fondue pot with a piece of wire attached across the top works well. Or make a cylinder of screening, tack or staple it to a piece of wood, and attach a wire across the top.

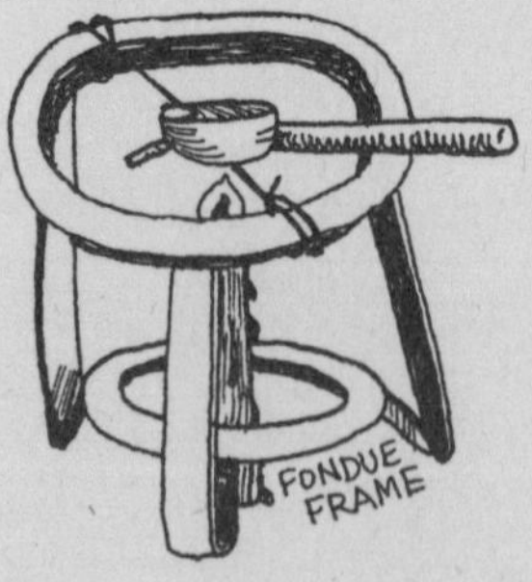
FONDUE FRAME

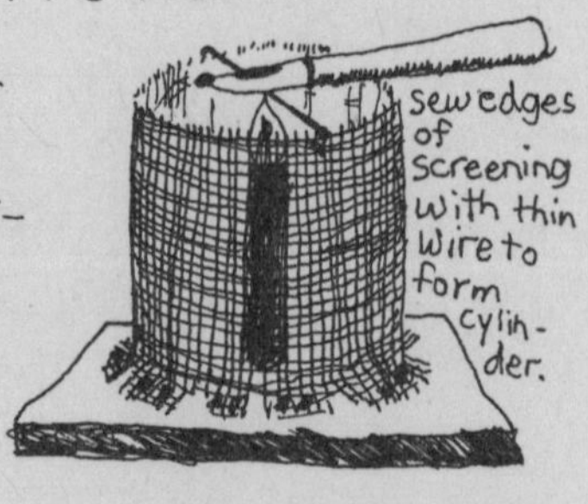
Sew edges of screening with thin wire to form cylinder.

5. Brush on the wax and/or fill the tjanting with wax to form lines, dashes, or dots on the fabric. Wax in all areas that are to retain the color of the fabric. Check the back to be sure the wax has completely penetrated the fabric—if there are any segments that haven't penetrated, wax on the back.

6. Prepare the first (light color) dye bath. Cold water dyes, such as DYLON COLD DYES, supply their own instructions when pur-

chasing the container of dye. All-purpose dye, such as RIT HOUSEHOLD DYES, requires an alteration of the enclosed instructions, because the hot water melts the wax, thus eliminating any resist design. Therefore, in a pint jar combine the packet of dye with hot water; allow the dye to dissolve, stirring a few times. Strain this solution thru a nylon stocking or a few layers of cheesecloth; otherwise, the remaining granules would spot the fabric. Add 2-3 gallons of cool to lukewarm water (lukewarm water is about room temperature) and stir together. **NOTE:** Liquid dye mixes readily with water, without straining.

7. Place wet fabric in the dye bath (encourage cracking of waxed areas, if desired.) Keep the fabric immersed for 1 hour, or longer. Rinse in cold water until the water runs clear. Lay the fabric flat (on an old towel, is ideal) to dry—hanging to dry MAY cause the dye to run, although many people do hang the fabric.
8. When the material is dry, repeat steps **2~7**, waxing new lines and areas; and dyeing with a new color. Repeat again (and again...), if desired.
9. To remove the wax, place the dry fabric between sheets of newspaper and iron. Replace with new paper, as needed, until wax does not melt onto the paper. (This paper makes great fire starters~roll up tightly the waxed, newspaper and tie with string. Wetting the paper before rolling will also make it more of a 'log'.)

FABRIC

10. You may or may not wish to remove the remaining stiffness of the fabric; the cheapest way (if you have quite a few batiks) is to dry clean in the coin-operated machines.

Books for more ideas about batik:

DESIGNING IN BATIK AND TIE DYE by Nancy Belfer; Worcester, Mass.: Davis Publications, Inc., 1972.

CONTEMPORARY BATIK AND TIE DYE by Dona Z. Meilach; New York: Crown Publishers, Inc., 1973.

USE OF COLOR PENCILS OR CRAYONS FOR A SKETCH OF DESIGN WILL ENABLE A CLEARER REFLECTION OF THE FINAL BATIK.

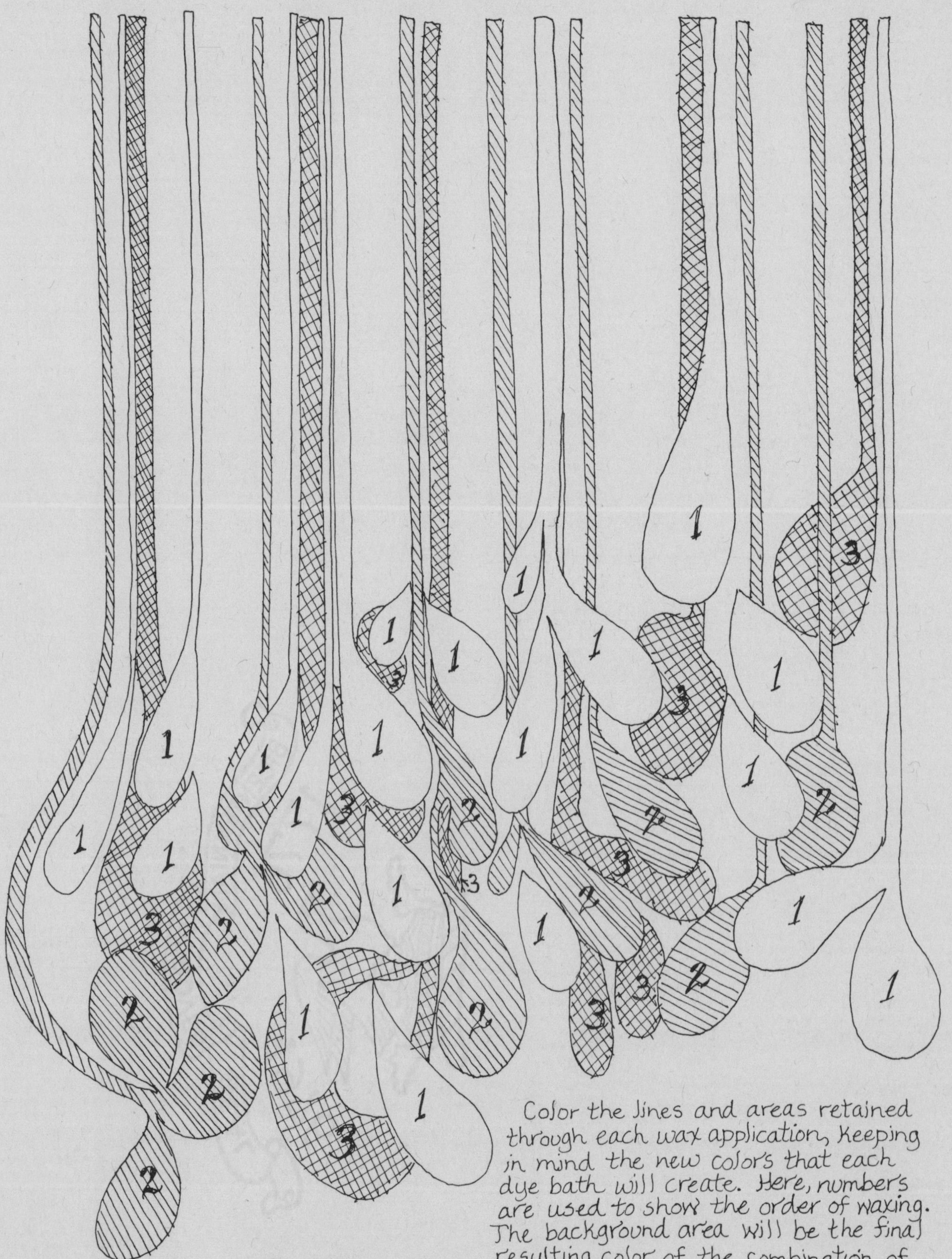
1
3
1
1
1
1
1
1
1
1
1
1
2
1
3
1
1
3
2
1
1
2
3
1
2
1
3
2
1
2
3
3
2
2
1
1
2
2
3
1
2

Color the lines and areas retained through each wax application, keeping in mind the new colors that each dye bath will create. Here, numbers are used to show the order of waxing. The background area will be the final resulting color of the combination of all dye baths.

Abstraction and evaluation of objects around us have been used for centuries in art. Depicting structures, large or small, gives the artist an endless repertoire of designs.

To the right is a sketch of the starting framework for our neighbor's studio and below is the resulting design for a batik. Because of the unique quality of individual interpretation and perception, abstraction is an infinite display of tangible and imaginary objects.

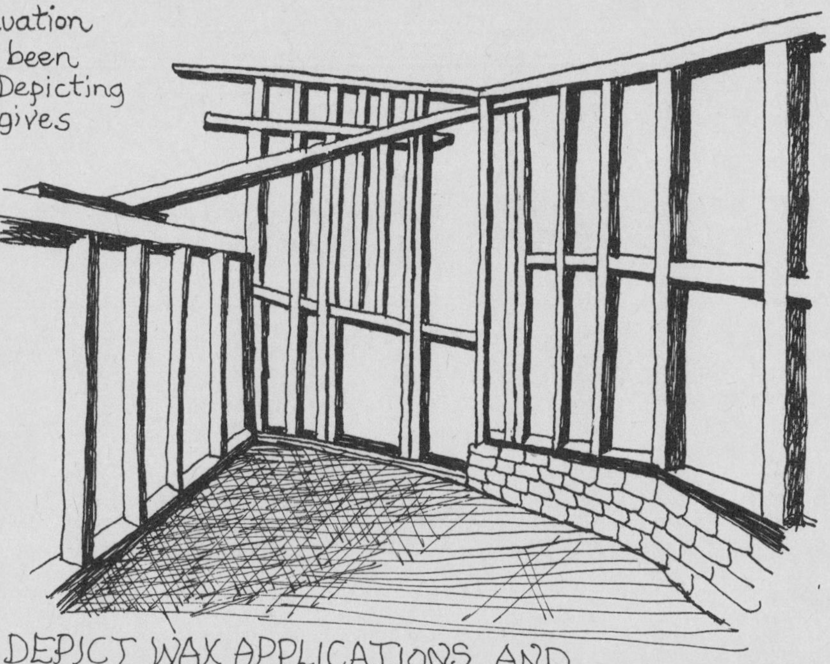

NUMBERS USED TO DEPICT WAX APPLICATIONS AND SUBSEQUENT COLORS.

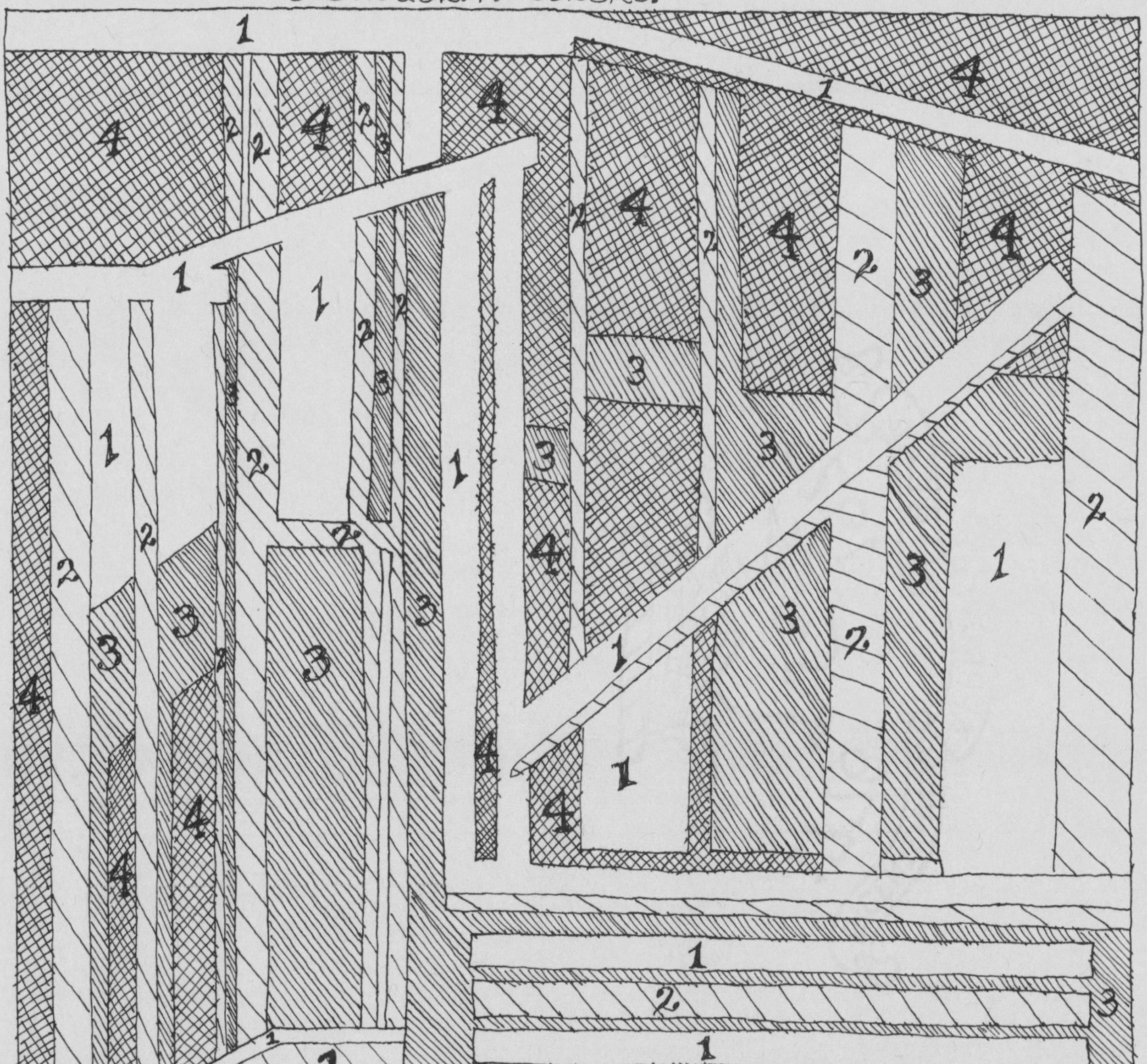
1
4
2
4
2
3
1
4
2
4
2
4
2
3
4
1
1
2
2
3
3
3
2
3
1
1
2
2
2
3
3
4
3
2
3
3
4
1
3
1
2
4
4
4
4
1
1
2
3
1

Tjanting*

The tjanting is a tool of batik used for applying various thicknesses of lines or dots. The following styles are used by heating the tjanting over a candle (see pg 102), filling with hot wax & tilting foward to enable the flow of wax. **NOTE:** Designs with tubing, use <u>flexible</u> copper tubing; ½ inch (outside diameter) tubing is an appropriate size.

1.

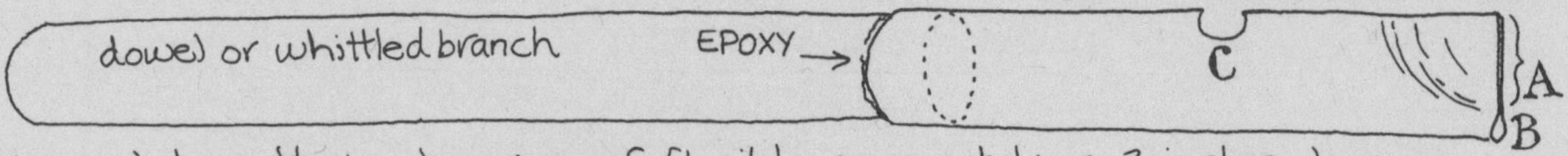

dowel or whittled branch
EPOXY
C
A
B

Using a tube cutter, cut a piece of flexible copper tubing 3 inches long. Hammer one end, with a finishing nail of desired size inserted in tubing to form opening **B** — hammer length **A** tightly together. For a smaller opening **B**, remove nail and carefully hammer further. Fuse **A** together by filing. Drill a hole **C**, at least ¼" in diameter; if using a hand drill, hold the drill at an angle to enable it to bite into the metal. Cut a dowel 5-6 inches long and insert into the tubing, secure with epoxy glue. When using the tjanting keep the epoxy from direct flame.

2.

insert end
insert leather end
C
A
B

Cut a 9-inch length of copper tubing. Hammer and drill as for design **1.** To form the handle, hammer closed 6 inches of tubing. Tightly wrap a leather strand that has been soaked in hot water for ½ hour around the hammered handle.

3.

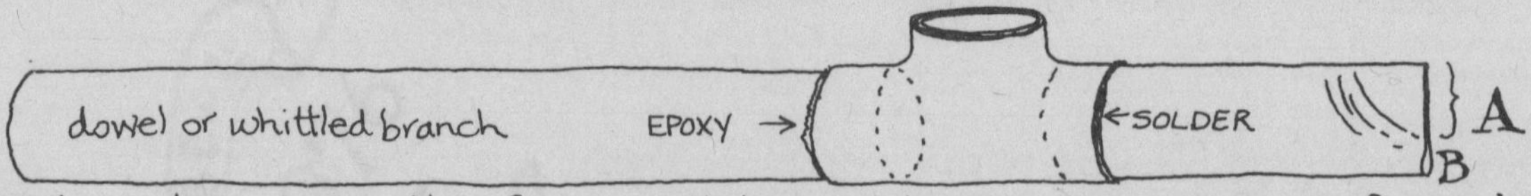

dowel or whittled branch
EPOXY
SOLDER
A
B

Cut a 2½ inch length of copper tubing and prepare end **A**, **B** as for design **1.** Solder a copper T-joint (½ inch, inside diameter) to the flexible tubing: apply flux to the joint; heat the metal with a propane torch; move solder along the hot joint to seal. Cut a dowel 5-6 inches long, and epoxy to T-joint.

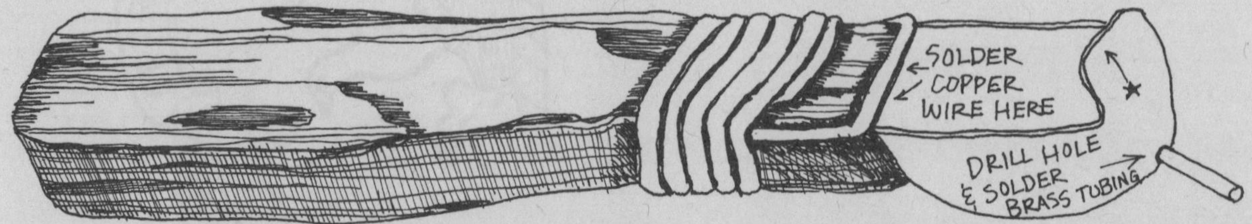

SOLDER COPPER WIRE HERE
DRILL HOLE & SOLDER BRASS TUBING

Using a jeweler's saw, cut a brass circle 2 inches in diameter. Hammer the circle into a hemisphere with a dapping block. Then hammer the front lip forward as shown (★). Drill a hole through the lower front for desired size of brass tubing. Cut the tubing to ¾". Solder the end of the tube to the edge of the hole as described in design **3.** Cut a length of copper wire 3½"; solder to the opposite side of the hemisphere — the extending wire is used to secure a dowel or branch handle. Use epoxy to fasten wire to the handle & wrap with leather as for design **3.**

* a special thanks to Bobbi Renz for her help with ideas.

WOODEN FRAMES

Various crafts require use of a wooden frame with push pins, or tacks securing the project on top. Here are two ways to make frames, both requiring a minimum of tools ~ hammer, saw, and a miter box (optional). The first is a permanent-size frame and the second is adjustable to meet the needs of any project.

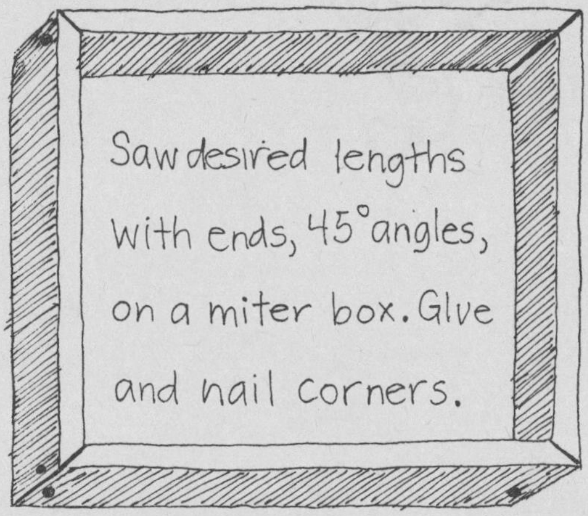
Saw desired lengths
with ends, 45° angles,
on a miter box. Glue
and nail corners.

Use 1"x2"s or 2"x2"s

Use white glue.

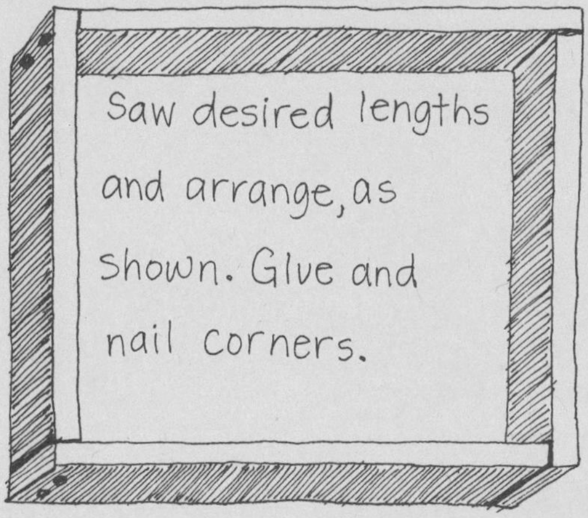
Saw desired lengths
and arrange, as
shown. Glue and
nail corners.

THE ADJUSTABLE FRAME

Saw 1"x2"s in 8 equal lengths (at least 16" long). Miter one end of each length, if desired. Join 2 lengths together with white glue and nails, to form 4 L-shapes. Allow the glue to dry thoroughly. Mark a pencil line along the center of each length. Measure along the line, 4 inches from the corner, and then mark every 2 inches. Drill holes at the points marked, using an electric or hand drill.

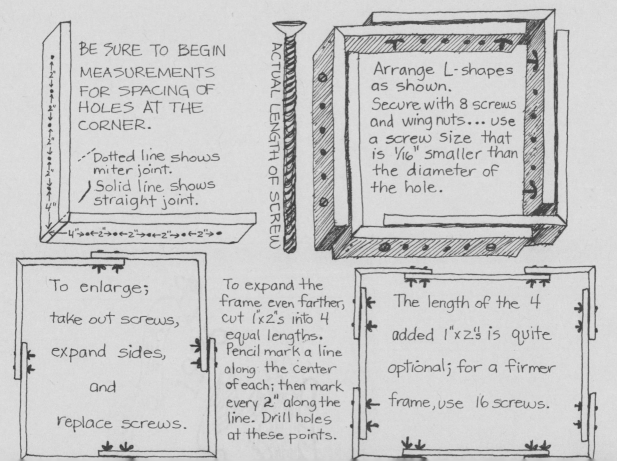

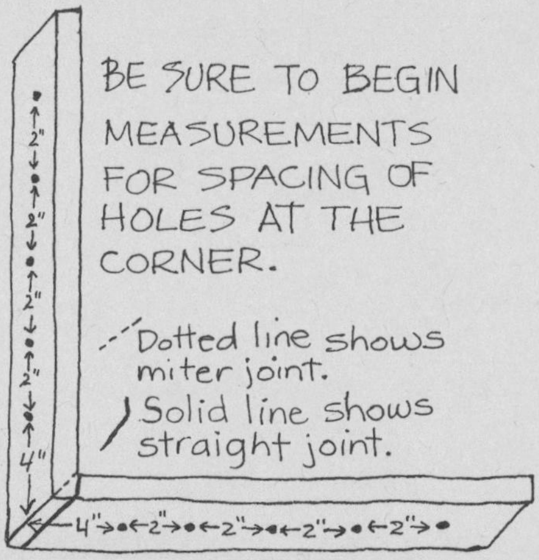
BE SURE TO BEGIN MEASUREMENTS FOR SPACING OF HOLES AT THE CORNER.
Dotted line shows miter joint.
Solid line shows straight joint.
2"
2"
2"
2"
4"
4"
2"
2"
2"
2"

ACTUAL LENGTH OF SCREW

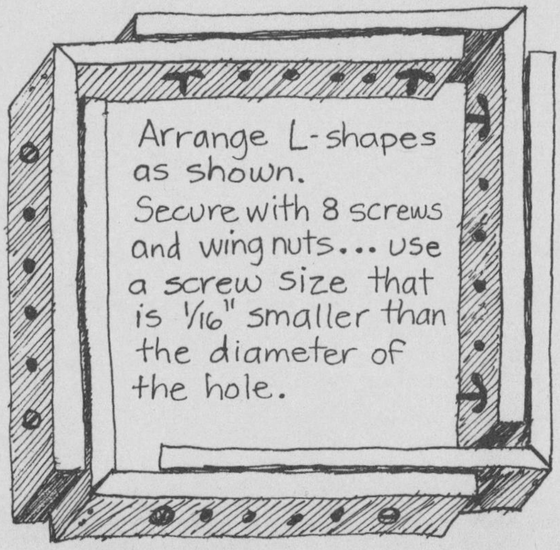
Arrange L-shapes as shown.
Secure with 8 screws and wing nuts... use a screw size that is 1/16" smaller than the diameter of the hole.

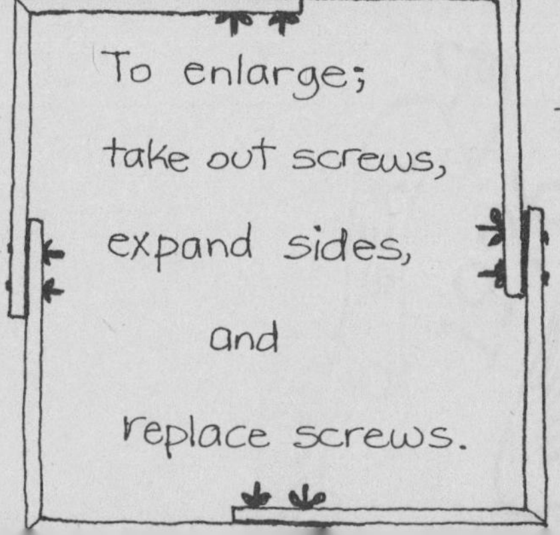
To enlarge;
take out screws,
expand sides,
and
replace screws.

To expand the frame even farther, cut 1"x2"s into 4 equal lengths. Pencil mark a line along the center of each; then mark every **2"** along the line. Drill holes at these points.

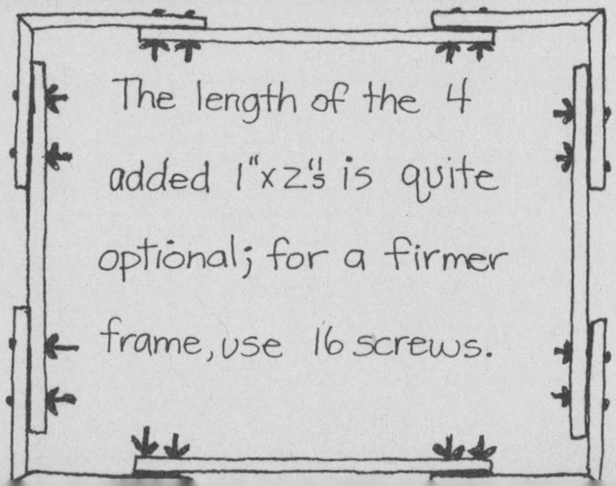
The length of the 4
added 1"x2"s is quite
optional; for a firmer
frame, use 16 screws.

NATURAL DYEING

Natural dyeing makes use of plants and their beautiful coloring powers. The growing seasons bring forth an extensive array of plants, flowers, trees, and berries. I have listed some, although as you walk thru field and forest other plants will undoubtedly fancy your curiosity and end up in a dye bath. As with any endeavor utilizing natural materials, "don't put off 'til tomorrow...", for tomorrow may bring the next plants in the season's flow.

Most natural dyeing must be accompanied by **mordanting** which allows the fabric to take and keep the dye color. Many dye books stress the use of chemicals for mordanting, such as aluminum potassium sulfate, potassium dichromate, and copper sulfate. However, I prefer to use natural mordants found outdoors for these plant materials are gifts of nature which we should enjoy and use. A few of the mordants are items found in the kitchen.

The following information was collected through experimentation on muslin and are applicable for other **vegetable fibers**. You may wish to try wool, however, I can only speculate that the same results will be produced. As with commercial dyes, **washing** will have a tendency to fade or change the colors of the dye after a while. It is best to wash the dyed fabric using a mild soap and sal soda (found at grocery stores.) You might also consider using natural dyed fabrics for items which are not washed often: pillows & upholstery cushions, lined curtains, purses, quilts, and so on. But clothing of the mellow or rich colors should not be bypassed.

General Points:

1. All **utensils** and **containers** should be of wood, enamel, plastic, or glass. Large enamel pots used for canning are good for the cooking steps. Other than that, all you really need is a wooden spoon for stirring, a glass measuring cup for a few of the mordants, a plastic container for soaking plants & for rinsing fabric, and a place to cook. Cheesecloth is also useful.

2. **Wash fabric** before using for dyeing to remove sizing or grime. Use a mild soap and sal soda. Rinse thoroughly.

3. **Rain water** is ideal for natural dyeing — make due with what you have for collecting the water; my neighbor's have a small plastic swimming pool for their children which made a perfect rain water collector (unless our dogs jumped in). If using hard, tap water, add a **water softener** for all soaking, cooking, and rinsing.

4. To enjoy the process of natural dyeing, work in a **well-ventilated room** or, if possible **outdoors.** Although some of the smells from cooking the mordants and dyes are sweet and lovely, others are displeasing odors.

A gas burner with a propane tank is a convenient set-up for out-doors. It's also useful for canning, making black walnut stain, and other cooking activities which are more enjoyable in the open air. Bought new, the gas set-up costs about $50; consider a second-hand tank that you may see at an auction. Two nice friends gave us our gas burner which I've appreciated and enjoyed for all sorts of boiling — the tank is filled for about $2.60 and last 3 months with <u>CONSTANT</u> use.

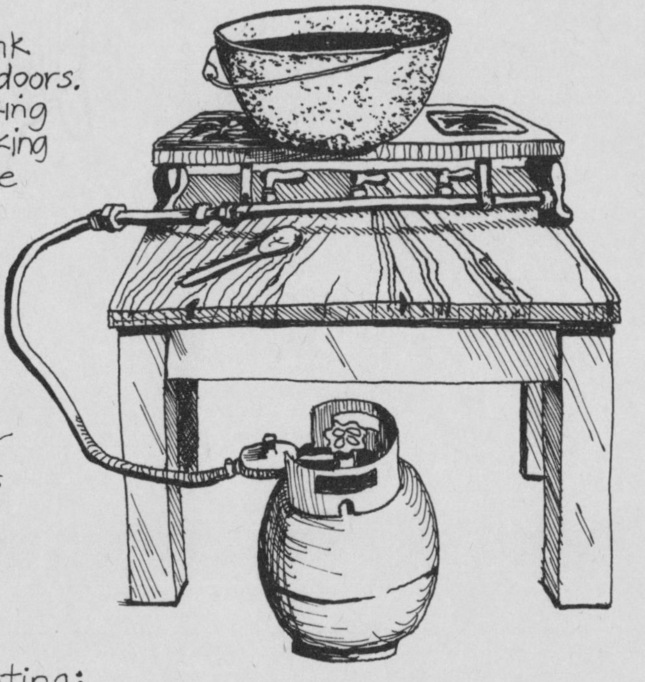

MORDANTS

The general scheme for mordanting:

1. Prepare the mordant bath according to specific instructions. For those using plant materials, be sure to use only enough water to cover. All simmering/boiling times are 45 to 60 minutes. After the mordant bath has been prepared, clean & dampened fabric is immersed — use <u>**about**</u> 1 gallon of bath per 1 yard of muslin; just be sure the fabric

is not packed and can move freely in the water. If necessary, add more water while simmering.

2. With the fabric in the mordant bath, light the fire and begin timing AFTER the water has begun to simmer. Stir frequently for even mordanting. When simmering is completed, keep the fabric in the bath as it cools or overnight.

3. Remove fabric from bath and soak up excess water by rolling it up in a towel — do not wring. Place damp fabric in a paper bag until ready to use for dyeing.

Preparing the mordant baths: (remember to use soft water)

Rust mordanting produces an off-white shade on the muslin, so the basic color of the plant dye will appear. Scrape rust off of metal objects or fill the enamel pot with rusty nails and just cover with water. (If using rust scrapings, add about 1½ cups of rust per 3 gallons of water.) Start fire and begin timing 45-60 min. when the water begins to boil (place a lid on the pot til boiling starts, if desired). Stir now and then. Let cool or sit overnight, then remove nails and strain through cheesecloth.

Oak Bark is a very good mordant which is off-white on fabric and as with rust, brings forth the basic color of the plant dye. I'm not well-versed about trees and there are so many types of oak trees; I let the acorns guide me in the right direction. Collect oak bark and break it into small pieces (the smaller, the better.) Put them in the enamel pot or a plastic container. Just cover with water, and soak the bark for 2 days (weigh down bark with a plate if necessary.) Then boil, stir, cool, & strain as for rust.

Walnut Hulls: (this is BLACK WALNUT—see page 47)
Black walnut hulls not only make an interesting mordant, but they also act as a rich, brown dye on fabric with no previous mordanting. The brown fabric added to plant dye baths transforms into new colors of grays and browns. As examples; the walnut mordanted fabric when added to a goldenrod dye bath becomes more of a yellow-brown
to a rose-hip dye bath becomes a rose-gray
to a pokeweed dye bath becomes a blue-gray. All of the resulting colors are rich and wash well. After hulling the black walnuts, soak the hulls for 2 days in an enamel pot or plastic container — just cover with water. Then boil, stir, and cool as for rust. When straining through the cheesecloth, squeeze out all liquid. **NOTE:** When working with black walnuts, wear rubber gloves to avoid staining hands.

Sumach Leaves: (see page 112). Sumach leaves create a dark, earth-tone of beige on fabric with no previous mordanting necessary. Used as a mordant, the beige color alters when immersed in dye baths. For example, when added to a sassafras dye bath beige moves toward a rose color; added to a wild grape dye bath the sumach-mordanted-fabric becomes a beautiful blue-gray. Gather sumach leaves and cut them into small pieces; just cover with water and soak them in the container for 1 day (weigh down with a plate if necessary). Boil, stir, cool, and strain as for rust.

Hazelnut Husks: (See page 48) Hazelnut husks as a dye make a fine beige on fabric with no previous mordanting. Used as a mordant, the results are beiges with a tint of the dye bath color. For example, the hazelnut-husk-mordanted fabric with an onion skin dye bath becomes an orange-tinted beige; with goldenrod, the fabric becomes a more yellowish beige. Cover husks with water & soak for 2 days. Boil, stir, cool, and strain as for rust.

Hickory Nut Hulls (see page 48) Hickory nut hulls used as a mordant or as a dye on fabric with no previous mordanting are similar to that with hazelnuts. Only a side by side comparison reveals the hazelnut results as a more yellowish beige. Prepare hickory nut hull mordant as for hazelnuts.

Urine (my step-dad calls this T-Pee Dye): I'm still not quite certain how to encourage someone to use urine as a mordant. I will admit that it took me 6 months and a great deal of encouragement from friends before I tried this one. Urine is a very good mordant which will retain the basic color of the dye bath. It was used in the past and is often briefly mentioned in natural dyeing books, but I'd like to get you to use it, not just hear about it. Urine is not only cost-free but makes use of a natural by-product of ourselves which is as constant as the sun. The abhorrence to using urine as a mordant is only a STATE OF MIND and if it is any consolation, you won't even have to touch it. Keep a plastic bucket with a lid or even a portable-type toilet in the barn, garage, or outdoors. After one day, I'll guarantee that saving urine won't make you grimace. As with all mordant solutions have about 1 gallon per 1 yard of muslin. Let it sit for 1-2 weeks then pour the mordant into an enamel pot and immerse clean, dampened fabric. Boil for 45-60 minutes. This mordant will definitely be more pleasant with an outdoor cooking set-up; and on a breezy day, the odor is really not too noticeable.

Tea is a fairly good mordant which acts as a beige dye on fabric with no previous mordanting. As a mordant, it produces tints of beige, as for hazelnut husks. Use 5 tea bags per gallon of water or 1 cup of unpackaged tea such as Japanese green tea per gallon. Boil for 45 minutes, stir, cool, and strain as for rust.

Salt & Baking Soda make a fairly good mordant. Stir to dissolve one cup each of regular table salt and baking soda per 3 gallons of water. Place over heat and enter dampened fabric. Begin timing 45-60 min. when water begins to boil. This mordant will enable the basic dye bath color.

DYE BATHS

Use the general steps in correlation with specific instructions of the plant.

1. Prepare the dye bath according to instructions. Remember to use soft water. If the mordanted material has dried, dampen. As with mordants, use about 1 gallon of water per 1 yard of muslin—add more water while simmering if necessary. Begin timing when the water has begun to simmer — 45-60 minutes. Stir frequently.

2. Place the dampened fabric in the dye bath, start fire, simmer, and then let the material cool with the bath or overnight. Rinse fabric in cool water and soak up excess water in a towel—do not wring. Hang the fabric to dry, out of the sunshine.

Goldenrod basically creates a yellow dye, sometimes toward green, depending on the mordant. Use the unopened flowers, which are a greenish-yellow in comparison with the opened flowers, and the adjacent stems. Cut into small pieces and place in an enamel pot. Just cover with water. Start fire and begin timing 45-60 minutes when the water has begun to boil. Stir frequently. Remove from heat and cool or let sit overnight. Strain through cheesecloth, squeezing out all liquid.

SUMACH BERRIES give tan shades to mordanted fabric. Gather the bunches of berries and break apart into an enamel pot. Just cover with water and soak for 2 days. Place on fire and begin timing 60 minutes when the water boils. Stir frequently. Remove from heat and let cool or sit overnight. Strain through cheesecloth, squeezing out all liquid.

Elderberries: (see page 45) Elderberries have a reddish-purple color when rinsed but when washed, the dye becomes beige. Prepare dye bath as for Sumach berries.

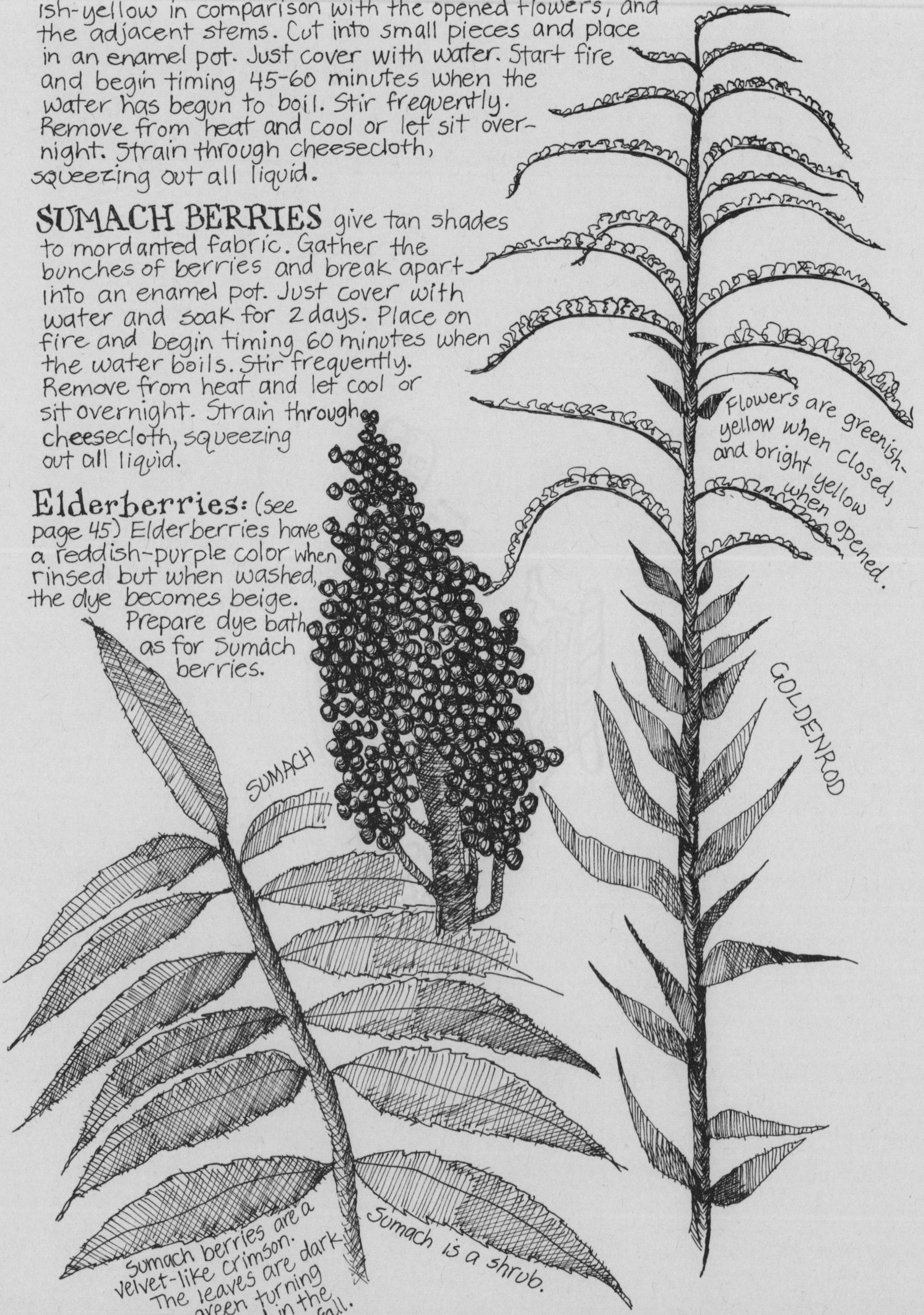
Flowers are greenish-yellow when closed, and bright yellow when opened.
GOLDENROD
SUMACH
Sumach berries are a velvet-like crimson. The leaves are dark green turning red in the fall.
Sumach is a shrub.

Chicory gives various shades of a rich yellow-beige depending on the mordant used. Use a pocketknife to gather the stem, leaves, and flowers. Chop into small pieces, put in an enamel pot and cover with water; soak for 1 day. Place on heat and begin timing 45-60 minutes when the water begins to boil. Remove from heat, let cool or sit overnight; then strain through cheesecloth squeezing out all liquid. Chicory also makes a fine hot drink: pull up roots of the young chicory. The roots are usually slender; but if not, cut lengthwise. Dry in an airy room by stringing together or on a dehydrator rack. (See 'Teas'). The dried roots make a mellow tea OR when baked on a cookie sheet for 1 hr. at 375° (check for brownness) the chicory is a hearty addition to coffee.

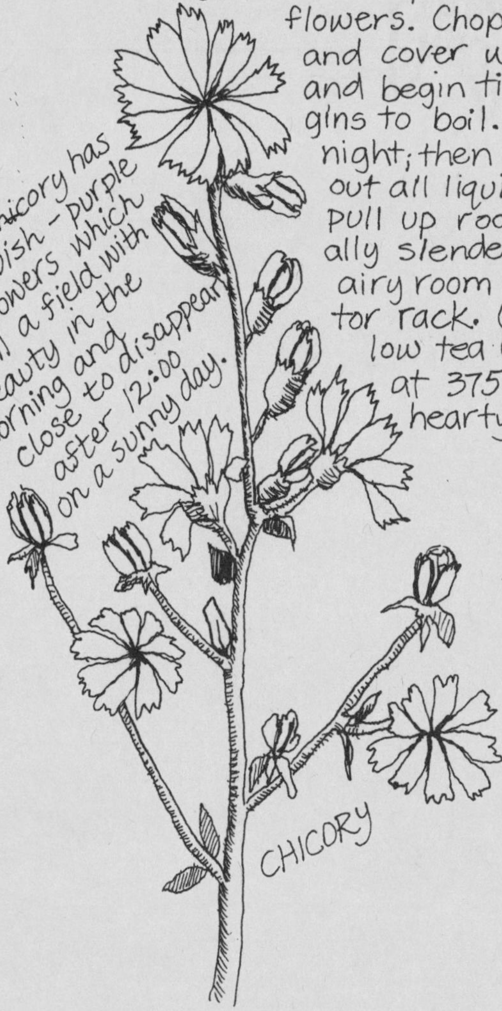
Chicory has bluish-purple flowers which fill a field with beauty in the morning and close to disappear after 12:00 on a sunny day.
CHICORY

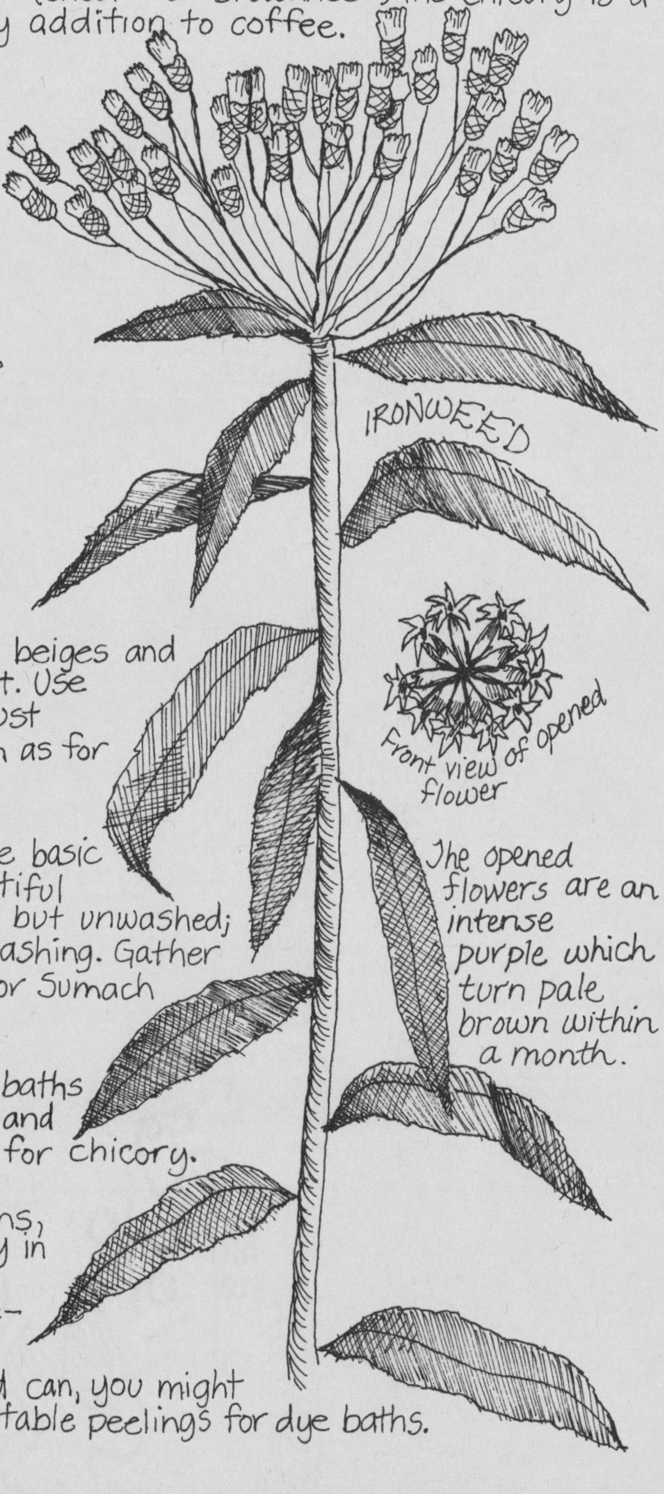
IRONWEED
Front view of opened flower
The opened flowers are an intense purple which turn pale brown within a month.

IRONWEED produces reddish beiges and browns depending on the mordant. Use the top clusters of unopened or just opening flowers. Prepare dye bath as for goldenrod.

Wild Grapes: (see page 62) The basic dye color of wild grapes is a beautiful purple when the fabric is rinsed but unwashed; and becomes a blue-gray after washing. Gather grapes and prepare dye bath as for Sumach berries.

MINT: (see page 53) Mint dye baths are a khaki color. Gather leaves and stems and prepare dye bath as for chicory.

Onion skins: Save onion skins, allowing any fresh cuttings to dry in the open air for a few days. The basic resulting dye is an orange-beige. Prepare the dye bath as for goldenrod. If you garden and can, you might consider experimenting with vegetable peelings for dye baths.

Wild Carrot, also called Queen Anne's Lace, produces a golden yellow dye on fabric. Gather the flowers, leaves, and stems. Prepare the dye bath as for chicory.

SMARTWEED gives a dye bath for fabric resulting in tones of yellow and yellow-beige depending on the mordant used. Gather stems, flowers, and leaves. Prepare dye bath as for chicory.

Sassafras leaves and bark make a reddish or orange tint of tan. (As with most natural dyeing the exact resulting dye color cont. below

WILD CARROT
Wild Carrot has small white flowers with one deep purple flower at the center of the bunch. The root has an obviously carrot smell and can be cooked as for garden carrots.

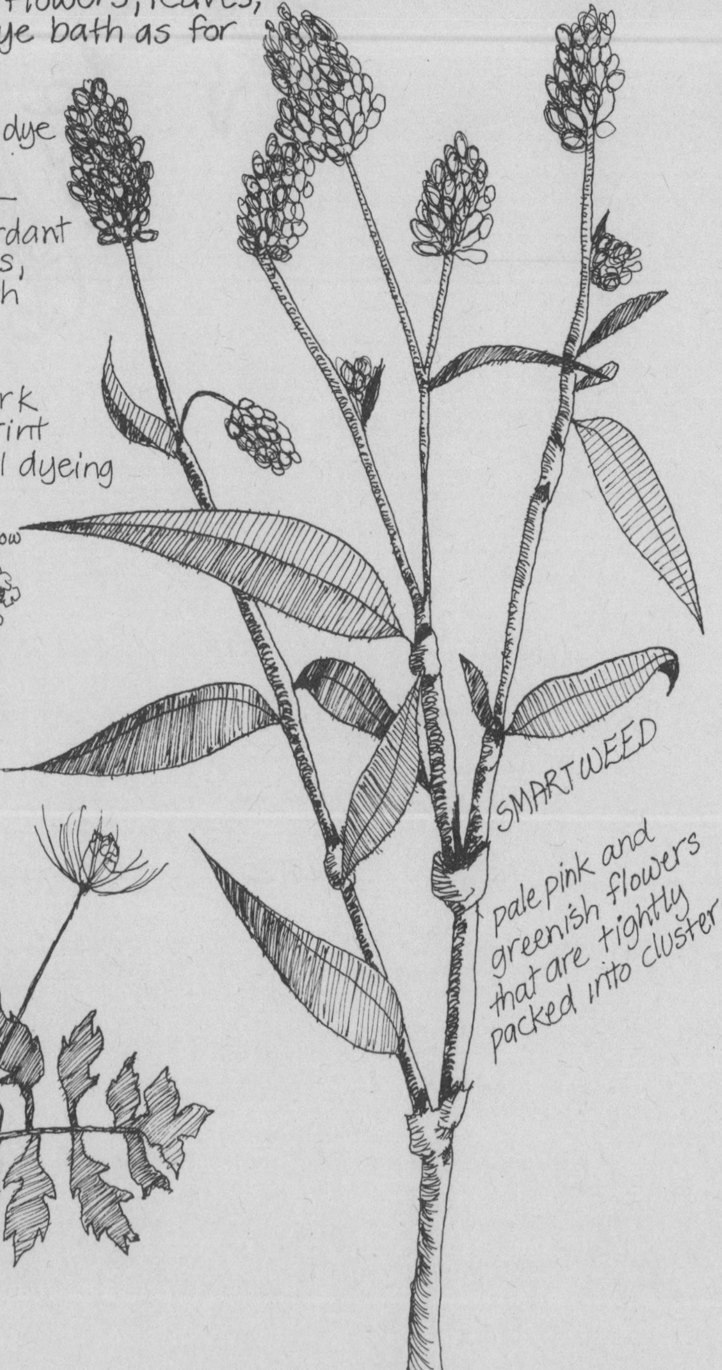
SMARTWEED
pale pink and greenish flowers that are tightly packed into clusters.

depends on the plants gathered & the general weather conditions of the season.) Chop leaves and break the bark into small pieces. Prepare dye bath as for Sumach berries. Sassafras bark or roots are dried for tea. I've been told that sassafras trees grow quickly, so digging up the roots of a small one seems alright. Dry as mentioned under chicory. Use a knife to shave the orange <u>inner</u> bark for tea. Dry the bark on cheesecloth or a dehydrator rack in the sun.

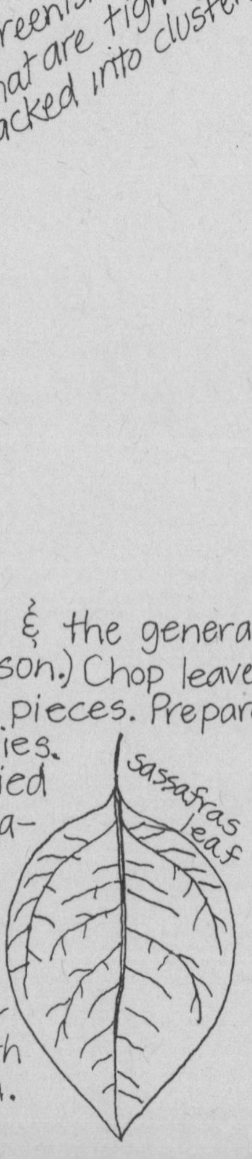
sassafras leaf

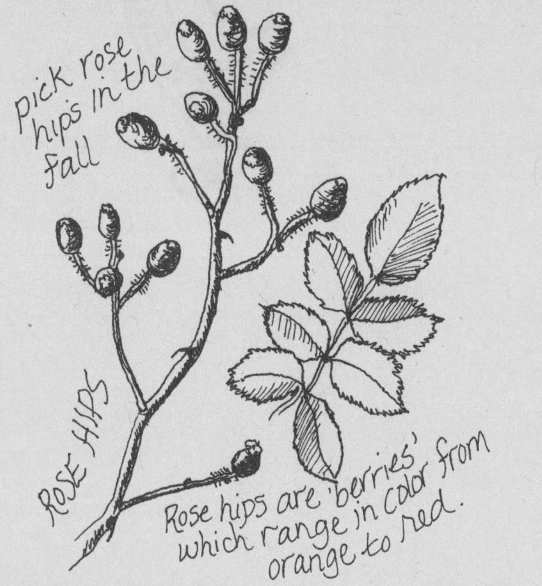
pick rose hips in the fall
ROSE HIPS
Rose hips are 'berries' which range in color from orange to red.

Rose hips and the surrounding stems produce various tones of rose-beige. Prepare as for sumach berries; crush the hips as they soften in the water. Rose hip tea is full of Vitamin C and a good drink for colds. Remove the stems and dry the hips on cheesecloth or dehydrator racks (see pg. 57) in the sun or over a wood stove. When the hips begin to dry break them open (in a mortar & pestle is convenient); continue drying.

Pokeweed gives a red cast to the various mordanted fabrics. Prepare a dye bath of the ripe berries and surrounding stem as for sumach berries.

Using the instructions under MORDANTS, prepare dye baths and dye the fabric (with no previous mordanting necessary) with:

Sumach leaves • Tea • Walnut Hulls • Hazelnut Hulls • Hickory Nut Hulls

Dyeing **plants** can be **dried** and stored (no more than 1 year), however the brilliance of the dye color may fade a bit. In general, dry plants by tying up small bunches & hang to dry; place leaves, berries, and flowers on cheesecloth or dehydrator racks — dry all in a light, airy room. Store in air & light-tight container. The deeper dyes can be prepared and stored in light & air tight jars for use within one month.

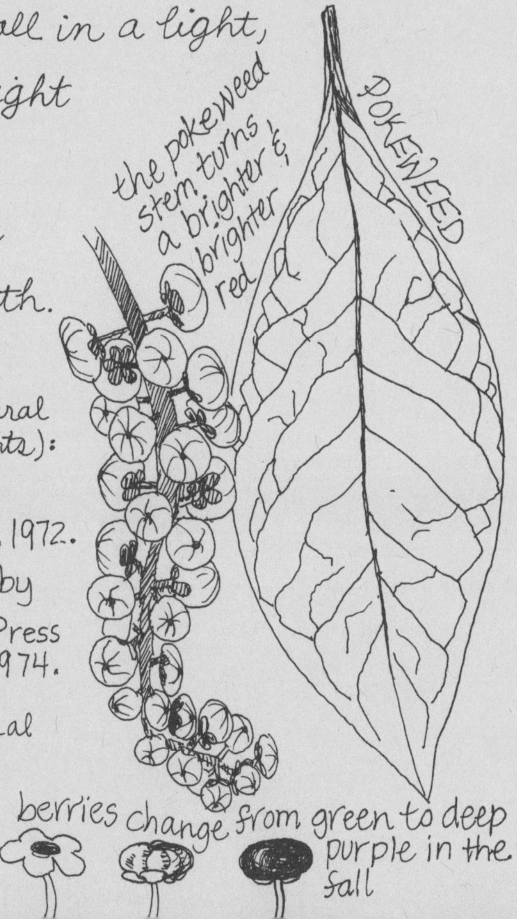
POKEWEED
the pokeweed stem turns a brighter & brighter red
berries change from green to deep purple in the fall

Two books with information concerning natural dyeing with wool (using chemical mordants):

NATURAL DYES, PLANTS, & PROCESSES by Jack Kramer; New York: Charles Scribner's Sons, 1972.

STEP BY STEP SPINNING AND DYEING by Eunice Svinicki; Racine, Wisconsin: Golden Press a division of Western Publishing Company, Inc., 1974.

A good book with many old mordant and natural dyeing recipes:

NATURAL DYES AND HOME DYEING by Rita J. Adrosko; New York: Dover Publications, Inc., 1971.

Miscellany

The Cat Pouch

Using the instructions for Quilt 1 or 2, (PAGES 9-12), create a cat pouch ~ so that the cat can be as warm as you in the wintertime. Sew 2 mini-quilts* together on 3 sides with a blanket stitch or a straight stitch. The size of the pouch depends on the cat ~ just be sure it is roomy.

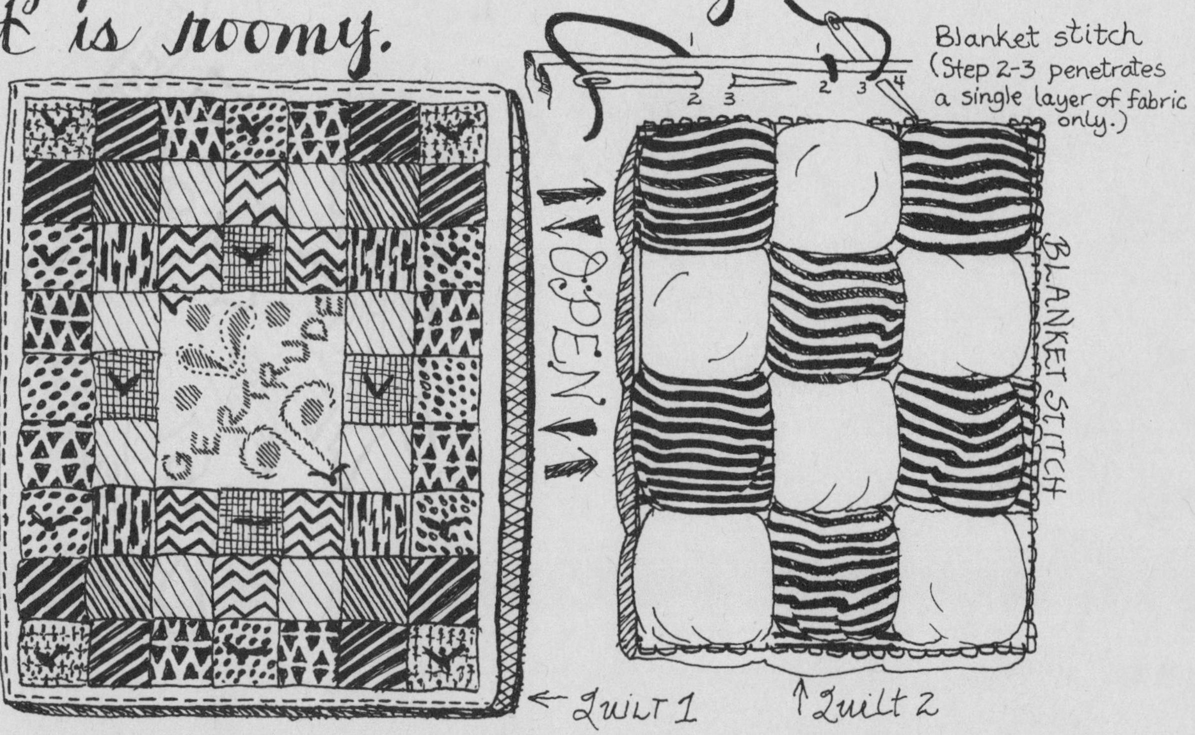
Blanket stitch
(Step 2-3 penetrates a single layer of fabric only.)
1 2 3
1 2 3 4
STRAIGHT STITCH
OPEN
BLANKET STITCH
← Quilt 1
↑ Quilt 2

* The bottom of the pouch could also be a solid piece of fabric instead of patchwork ~ line with batting & sheeting also.

Macramé Baskets

This method of making baskets uses the wrapping technique of macramé (See pages 89-90) with any thickness of rope and cord listed on page 85. White cord or jute can be dyed with cold or hot water dyes before or after completion of the basket. Or brush melted paraffin (or any mixture of paraffin and beeswax) on the completed basket, in a design as for batik, and place the basket in a dye bath — the waxed areas resist the dye and need not be removed.*

Light areas—waxed; dark areas—dyed
*Excess wax is removed after dyeing by drying the basket by a heat source.

Hundreds of shapes, sizes, and color variations are possible using the basic instructions. The amount of cord needed depends on the type used & size of rope and basket; but short cords are easily replaced by subtracting short ends into the wrap and adding on new cords with a lark's head as on page 95 ... (new colors are added on in the same way). In general, begin with cords that are 5 times longer (5x 5x) than the height of the desired basket. **NOTE:** At most, add and subtract only on 2 or 3 adjacent wrapping cords; unless slits are desired — however, too many long slits weaken the structure of the basket.

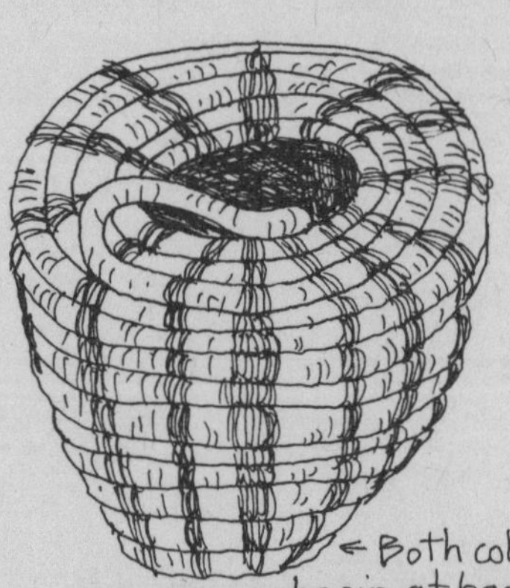
← Both colors begin at base of basket.

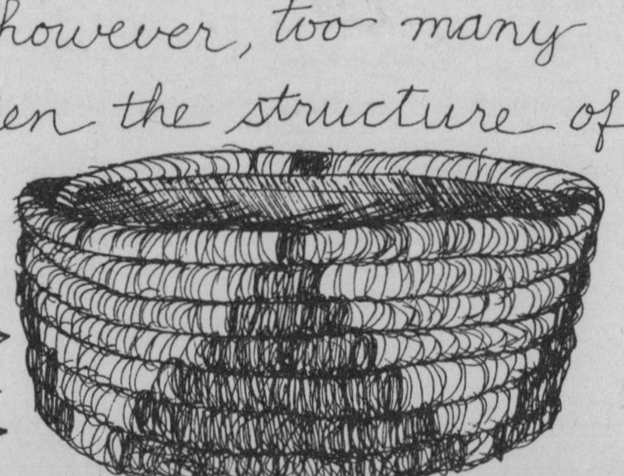
Dark color subtracted and new color cord → added on consecutive rows →

1. 1 inch from the end of the rope, attach 6-10 pairs of cords with lark's heads.... the number of pairs depends on the thickness and type of cord used.

1"
5 X
height
of
basket

2. Begin the base of the basket by securing the 1" end with the rope ★, with a lark's head of a new pair of cords. Make the hole formed, as small as possible.

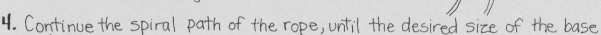

3. Move the rope spirally, wrapping it securely with snug clove hitches. (Note: wrap with single cords or pairs.) Add new strands with lark's heads as needed; on the first few spirals, generally, a new pair of cords is added between original cords.

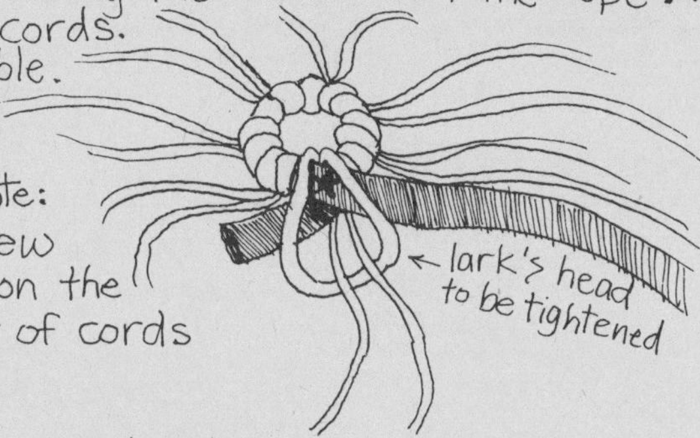

lark's head
to be tightened

4. Continue the spiral path of the rope, until the desired size of the base has been formed.

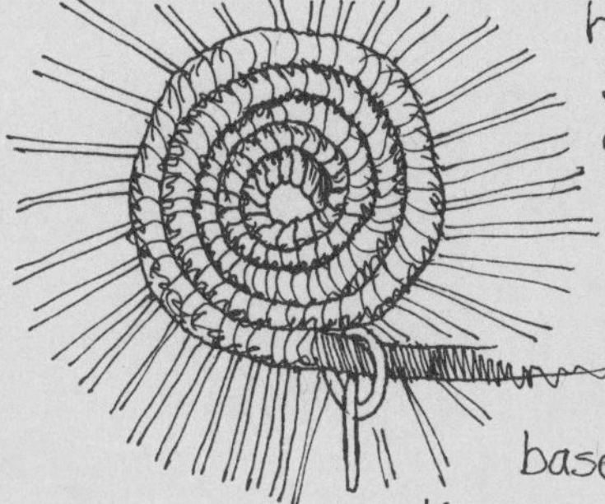

Starting the sides of the basket is a matter of the position while working. The easiest method is to hold the base between bended knees, with the wrapping cords hanging down. Clove hitch the rope snugly in place with a spiral path forming the sides of the basket. Check, now and then, the even movement of the sides, if symmetry is desired: since the cord and rope are somewhat flexible, sides can be pushed and pulled more evenly if necessary.

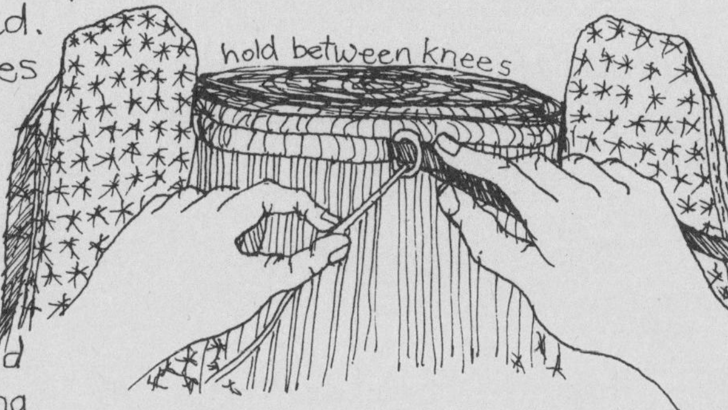

hold between knees

TO INCREASE the sides: add new cords with lark's heads at even intervals around the basket. Add a few or many on one or each consecutive row depending on how abrupt you want the side to move out.

TO DECREASE the sides: Subtract cords at even intervals around the sides by including the clove-hitched strand into the wrap.— On the following row, pull the rope and clove hitch snugly with the strand adjacent to the now subtracted space so that the side moves in.

TO ADD ON NEW ROPE, SEE PAGE 93 .

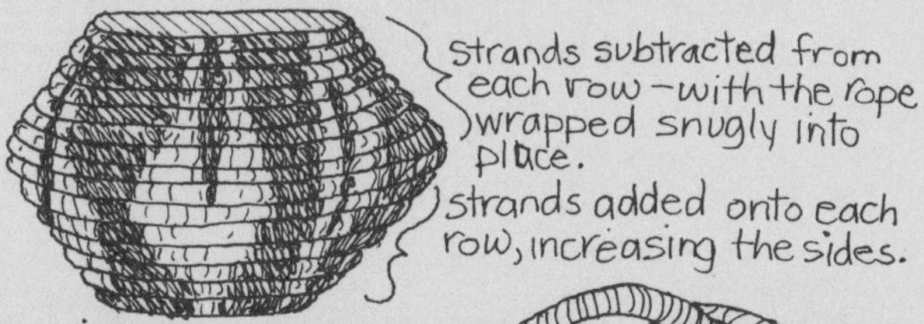

strands subtracted from each row – with the rope wrapped snugly into place.
strands added onto each row, increasing the sides.

5.a Finish off the top edge of the basket as illustrated on page 93, by including each strand into the wrap after it has been clove hitched (trimming the ends to 2-3 inches after inclusion.) The remaining few strand ends are half-hitched into the wrap with the last cord. Trim the rope and secure into the basket side by pulling the last cord through a loop of the back of the macramé with a crochet hook – tie into place.

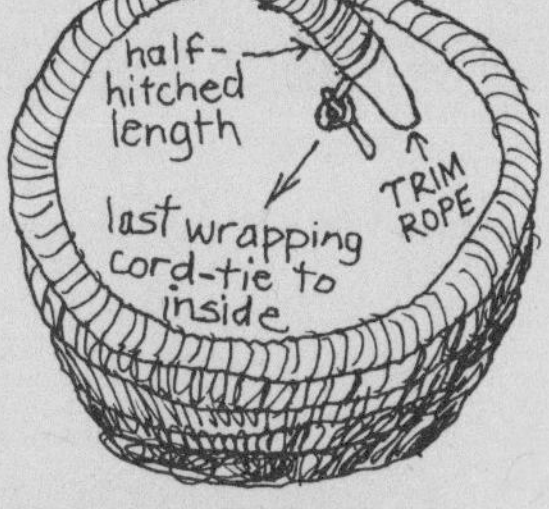

half-
hitched
length
TRIM
ROPE
last wrapping
cord-tie to
inside

5.b OR – let the strands hang down, securing into place with overhand knots and trimming.

The macramé basket lends itself to vertical color patterns. To make horizontal or free-form designs, apply the wax-resist-dye method as previously mentioned.

white
areas
waxed

WOOD CUT AND LINOLEUM PRINTS

The major differences between wood cut and linoleum prints are the materials and tools used. The HUNT MANUFACTURING CO. produces fine Speedball printing supplies, including linoleum blocks and cutters; and hand wrought steel woodcutting tools and wood blocks. The prices are quite reasonable ~ with proper care, woodcutting tools will last forever and the lino cutters have wooden handles with interchangeable and replaceable blades. All Hunt products (also, brayers, teflon-coated baren, inks, and many more) are found in art stores or mail order houses, such as:

DICK BLICK CO.
PO BOX 1267,
GALESBURG, IL.

SAX ARTS & CRAFTS
PO BOX 2002
MILWAUKEE, WI.

NASCO
FORT ATKINSON,
WI.

I've made many linoleum prints in the past and it does have a positive quality of being easy to cut, but to my nature, woodcut holds more charm and beauty of process and product. I learned the art of wood cutting years ago in Japan, from a most noble and wise man named Kōsai Kobari. To this day, he sends me one of his beautiful wood cut prints with each letter; Kosai's prints reflect the tranquility that the act of wood cutting creates. The wood is cut with shallow strokes to the desired depth ~ NEVER hack away with deep cuts, for the beauty of the block itself is as important as the final print. The wood used in Japan is called a magnolia hypoleuca plate. It is marvelous to work with, cutting smoothly in any direction. I've never come across it in the states, but if you do — enjoy! Here, hard woods will cut adequately in both directions because of the close grain. Some hard woods to look for are CHERRY, APPLE, PEAR, PEACH, WALNUT, MAPLE, OAK. There are more — I tend to use whatever scraps we have or that friends donate. Soft woods, particularly the various types of PINE, will cut more easily than the hard wood, however they will only cut smoothly in the direction of the grain. Therefore, outlines of areas traveling against the grain are first cut with a straight skew chisel and then the area is carved away in the direction of the grain.

SOFT WOOD

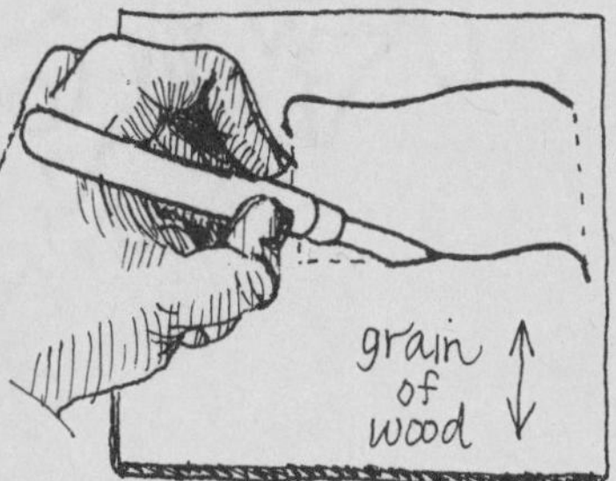
grain of wood

First, cut outlines that go against the grain.
Then carve away the area with the grain — the incised outline will stop the cut.
Cut with shallow strokes

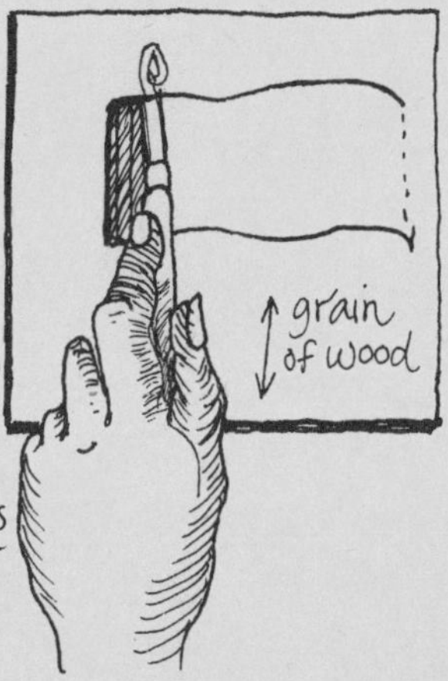
grain of wood

In some ways, this method adds to the feeling for wood. To make **lines** against the grain, cut the outlines of the lines (as for areas) and use the straight skew or straight chisel to remove the small space between.

My view on whether to use water or oil-base printing ink corresponds with my attitude on wood versus linoleum. Water-base ink is easier to clean up with soap and water, and oil-base requires turpentine or a similar solvent; but the quality of the final print is far superior when using oil-base ink. Oil-base can also be used for fabric printing, whereas water-base washes out. And from a personal standpoint, I like the rich aroma of the oils and experience the history of its work. Acrylic and oil paint can also be used if you happen to have some or come across a sale. Otherwise, use the paint for canvas. (Other information about tools and process is found on the following pages.)

SUPPLIES: (Read the preceding pages about wood, cutting, and inks)

WOOD:

Wood, cut to the desired size
Woodcutting tools (as mentioned; or a small set for about $1.50 is sold in most arts & crafts stores.)

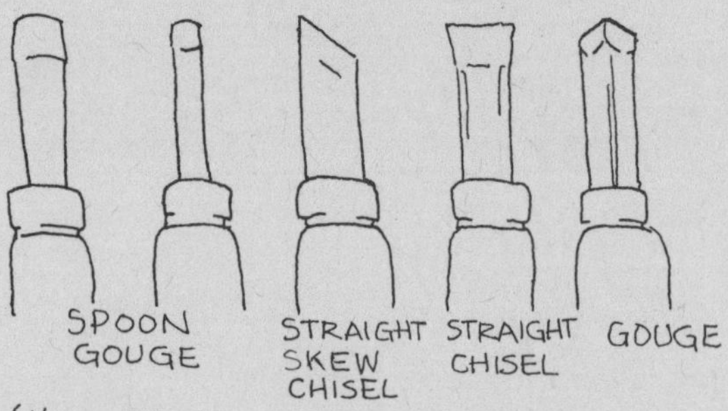

SPOON GOUGE
STRAIGHT SKEW CHISEL
STRAIGHT CHISEL
GOUGE

(Keep blades sharp with a sharpening stone)

LINOLEUM:

linoleum blocks, or a sheet of linoleum cut to the desired size
linoleum cutters: handle with various blades.

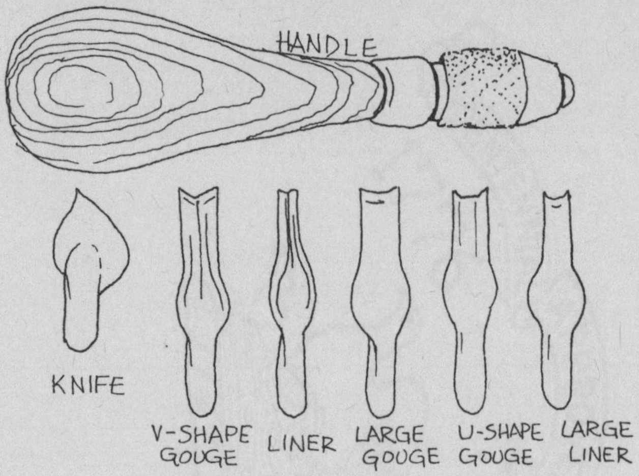

HANDLE
KNIFE
V-SHAPE GOUGE
LINER
LARGE GOUGE
U-SHAPE GOUGE
LARGE LINER

SUPPLIES FOR WOOD & LINOLEUM:

newspaper (for catching chips and when printing) • ink or paint, as previously mentioned • brayer to roll up ink (an inexpensive model costs $1.50) • a piece of plexiglass or other non-porous surface to roll up ink • a baren to rub the back of the paper while printing ~ in Japan, the baren is heavy cardboard covered with bamboo sheath; Teflon-coated barens can be purchased at art stores; or cut a circle out of heavy cardboard, like illustration board • paper for printing - rice paper or the various types of printing paper are best.

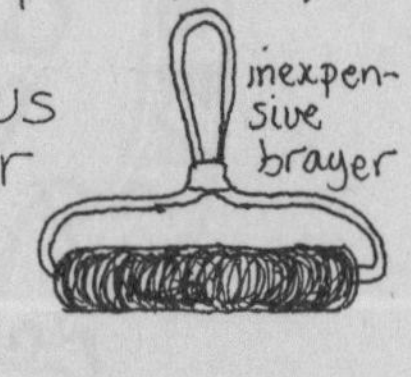

inexpensive brayer

instructions:

1. Draw or trace the design onto wood or linoleum. Keep in mind that the print will be reversed. Decide which areas and lines should take ink and which should retain the color of the paper.

2. Lay out newspaper on table to catch scraps and begin cutting. ALWAYS CUT **AWAY** from you with the free hand **BEHIND** the carving hand. Regardless of whether you want carving lines to show or to be totally absent on the print, cut with shallow strokes, slowly working deeper. Experience and logic are the best teachers as to which blade to use for what job.

3. When the carving is completed, it's time to print. Lay out newspaper on a table. Gather the ink, brayer, baren, wood or linoleum cut, and the non-porous surface (wax paper taped down to a piece of wood works fairly well). Cut paper to the desired size.

4. Squirt about 4 inches of ink at the top of the non-porous surface. Roll the ink down with the brayer — roll brayer back and forth in the ink; allowing the roller to spin in the air every so often for the brayer to be evenly coated. The ink is ready to apply to the block when it begins to make a crackling noise.

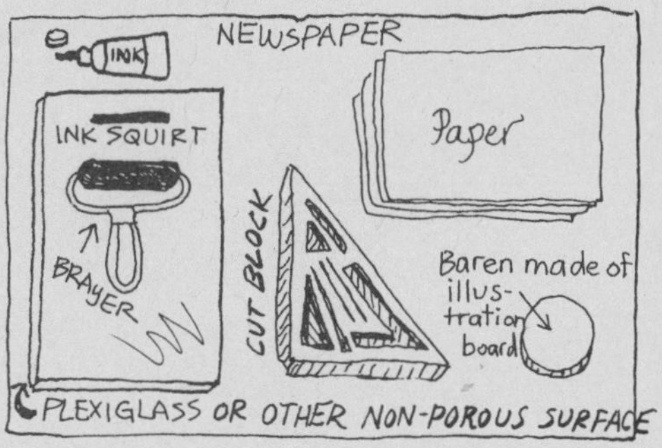
INK
NEWSPAPER
INK SQUIRT
Paper
BRAYER
CUT BLOCK
Baren made of illus-tration board
PLEXIGLASS OR OTHER NON-POROUS SURFACE

5. Roll ink onto the block. Roll up brayer again in the ink — reapply onto the block. Repeat again, if the block has not been evenly coated with ink.

6. Carefully place paper on top of inked block so as not to smear. Rub the back of the paper with the baren until the ink vaguely shows through (If using thick paper, carefully lift up a corner to check the printing).

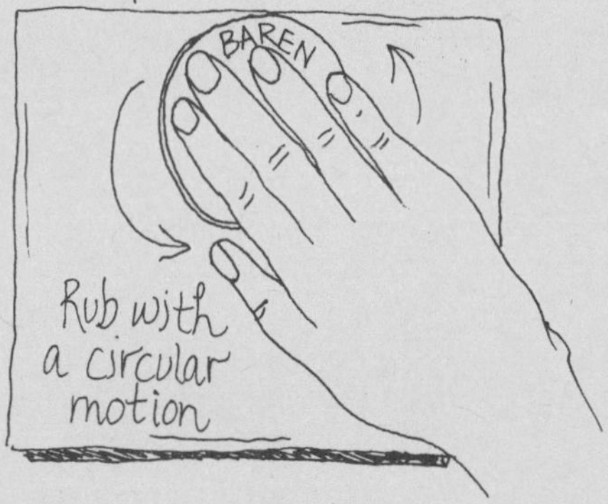
BAREN
Rub with a circular motion

7. Pull off paper. Often, the first print will be rather light. Check the print to see if there is any deeper cutting you wish to do. If so, clean the block with soap and water (for waterbase) and turpentine or similar product (for oil base). Lay or hang wet prints to dry — either ink will take a day or two to dry.

ideas for any of the ink printing methods:

- Print cards, or stationery, or wrapping paper, or fabric (oil-base ink) Repeat prints side by side to form a pattern. Print the first area, then line up one edge with the newly, inked block edge — carefully fold the rest of the paper or fabric onto the block. Repeat.
- If you want the block to be perfectly centered on the paper; before inking up the block, lay the block on the paper and mark the corners lightly with pencil. When printing, lay the inked block on the paper (lining up with corner marks), and carefully turn both upside down and rub the back of the paper with the baren, as usual.
- To print with 2 or 3 colors of ink, squirt the colors side by side on the plexiglass (about 1-2 inches long, each) and roll side by side with brayer.
- A cheap and easy way to hang prints for drying is to string cord from wall to wall and use paper clips to hold paper and attach to cord.

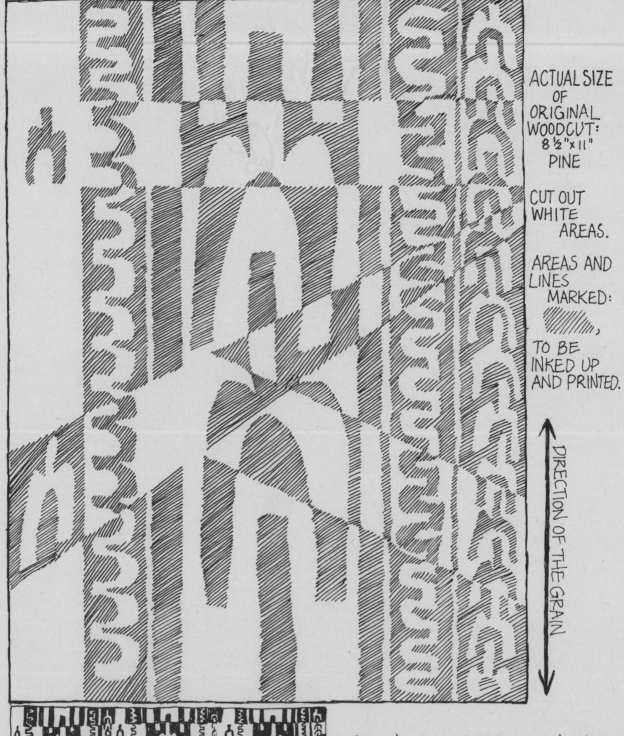

ACTUAL SIZE OF ORIGINAL WOODCUT: 8 ½" x 11" PINE

CUT OUT WHITE AREAS.

AREAS AND LINES MARKED: [hatched area], TO BE INKED UP AND PRINTED.

DIRECTION OF THE GRAIN

The design of this woodcut lends itself well for multiple printing; thus, suitable for a fabric print or wrapping paper.

A uniform pattern of the print is shown here, although other directional or random sequences are possible.

ACTUAL SIZE OF LINOLEUM BLOCK SHOWN.

ACTUAL SIZE OF LINOLEUM BLOCK SHOWN.

CUT OUT WHITE AREAS.

AREAS AND LINES MARKED

TO BE INKED UP AND PRINTED.

ACTUAL SIZE OF LINOLEUM BLOCK 10"x 3½".

ACTUAL SIZE OF LINOLEUM BLOCK 6" x 5".

STRING & CARDBOARD PRINTS

SUPPLIES: STRING (ANY OR VARIOUS THICKNESSES) • SCISSORS • ILLUSTRATION BOARD OR OTHER THICK CARDBOARD • UTILITY KNIFE • WHITE GLUE • SPRAY PAINT OR VARNISH (See below) • WATER- OR OIL-BASE PRINTING INK OR ACRYLIC- OR OIL PAINT • BRAYER AND/OR PAINT BRUSH • PAPER FOR PRINTING NON-POROUS SURFACE FOR ROLLING UP INK

instructions: *This method works well with rather simple line drawings — any areas to be printed should be divided into cardboard shapes no larger than 8" x 8" (larger shapes make it difficult to produce a good solid print).*

1. With a pencil, draw on any size of illustration board.
2. Lay string on line segments of the drawing and cut to the appropriate size. For thicker lines use 2 or more lengths of string side by side or thicker cord. Run the string thru a dish of white glue and attach to board.

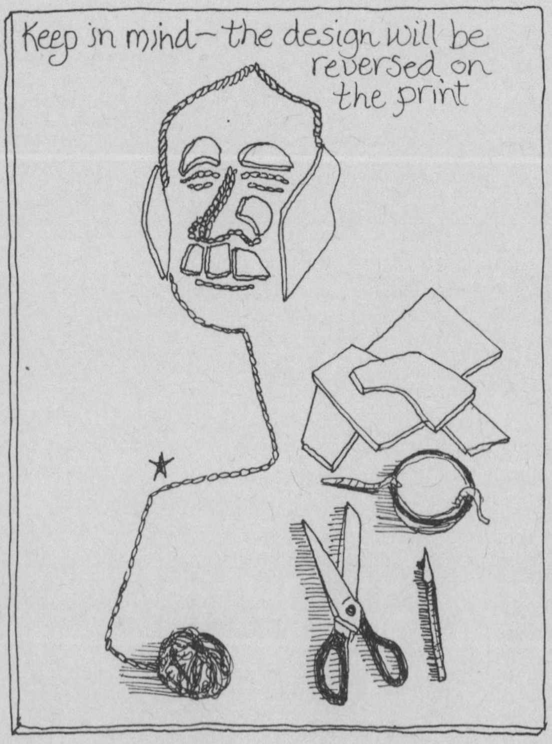
Keep in mind – the design will be reversed on the print

3. Cut shapes from scraps of illustration board using a utility knife. To cut the precise shapes you had drawn, trace the shape onto paper – lay the paper on the scrap of cardboard – and cut through both. Glue shapes to board.
4. Some people eliminate this step, but I've always found it to result in a better print: Apply 2 coats of spray paint or varnish over the entire surface. Let dry.
5. Roll up ink with a brayer as for Steps 3&4 of woodcut prints. Roll the inked brayer across the string and cardboard – BRUSH on to lines such as ★ above, that find themselves alienated. Lay paper atop and rub.

SMALL CIRCLES FOR PRINTING ARE MADE WITH A PAPER PUNCH AND THIN CARDBOARD (SHIRT CARDBOARD FROM THE CLEANERS IS PERFECT) — PASTE LAYERS OF THIN CARDBOARD.

When cutting areas, be sure each is not excessively large. Below, the hair section has been segmented to add rhythm, but also to assure a cleaner print. Use of two (or more) thicknesses of string adds to variety in design.

To the left is an abstraction of a corner section of a woven chair seat.

FOUND OBJECT

PRINT PRINT PRINT PRINT PRINT PRINT PRINT

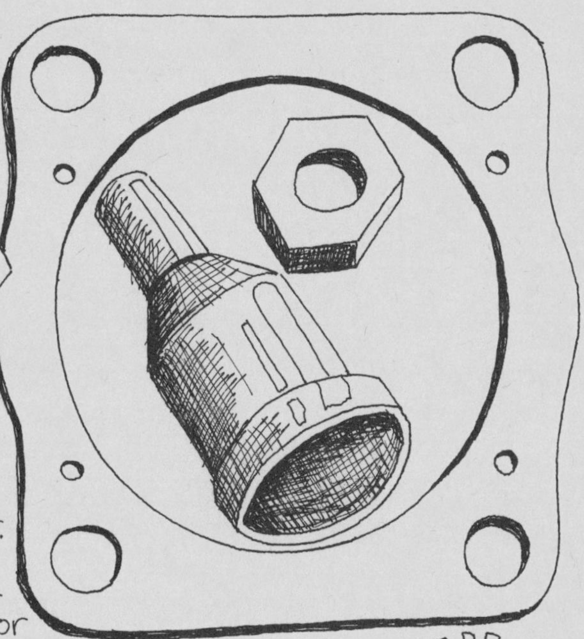

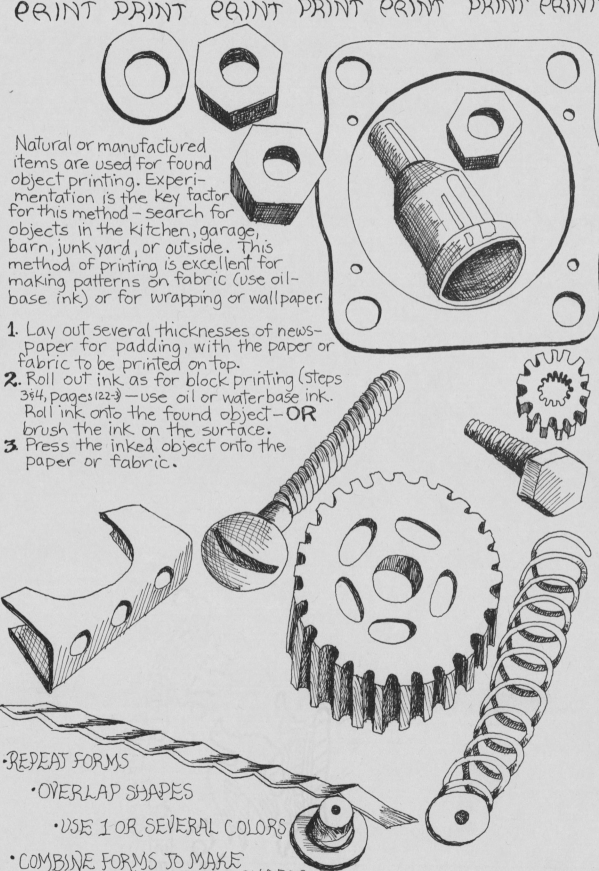

Natural or manufactured items are used for found object printing. Experimentation is the key factor for this method – search for objects in the kitchen, garage, barn, junk yard, or outside. This method of printing is excellent for making patterns on fabric (use oil-base ink) or for wrapping or wallpaper.

1. Lay out several thicknesses of newspaper for padding, with the paper or fabric to be printed on top.
2. Roll out ink as for block printing (steps 3&4, pages 122-3) — use oil or waterbase ink. Roll ink onto the found object – **OR** brush the ink on the surface.
3. Press the inked object onto the paper or fabric.

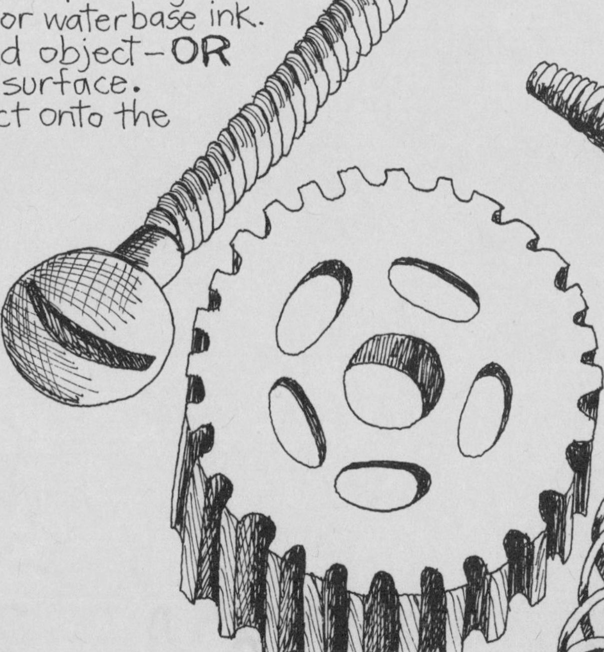

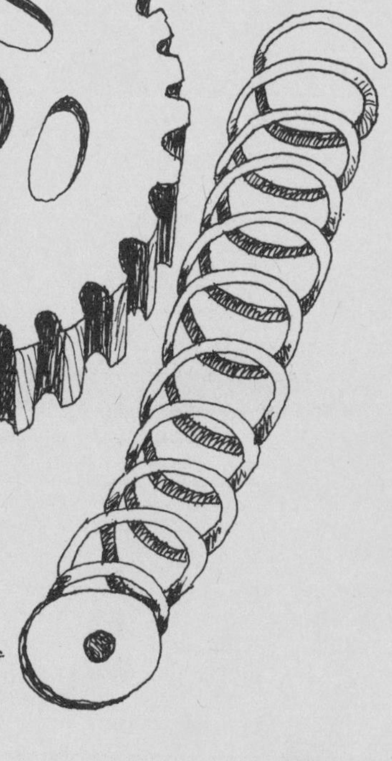

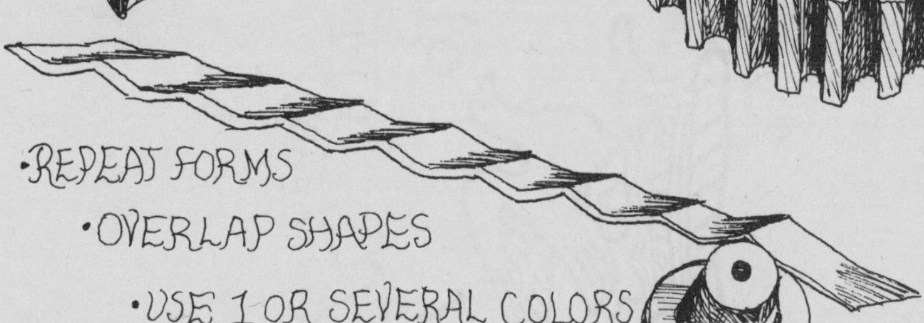

- REPEAT FORMS
- OVERLAP SHAPES
- USE 1 OR SEVERAL COLORS
- COMBINE FORMS TO MAKE LARGER SHAPES

Wild Plants

Pack a small shovel, a few plastic bags, and a lunch if you want to make a day of it; and walk through the woods. Looking down at the ground, you will see beautiful plants and ground cover growing in the cool shade of the forest.

Dig up the plant, carefully as not to injure roots. Usually dead leaves and such surround the soil; dig up enough of this rich soil for potting the plant. Place all in the bags for the journey home. Always give the plant plenty of water to assimilate the wooded environment— they usually don't need much light. Experiment with plants in your area of the country— some won't survive the change of scenery and others will flourish. Below, are three types that thrive well indoors.

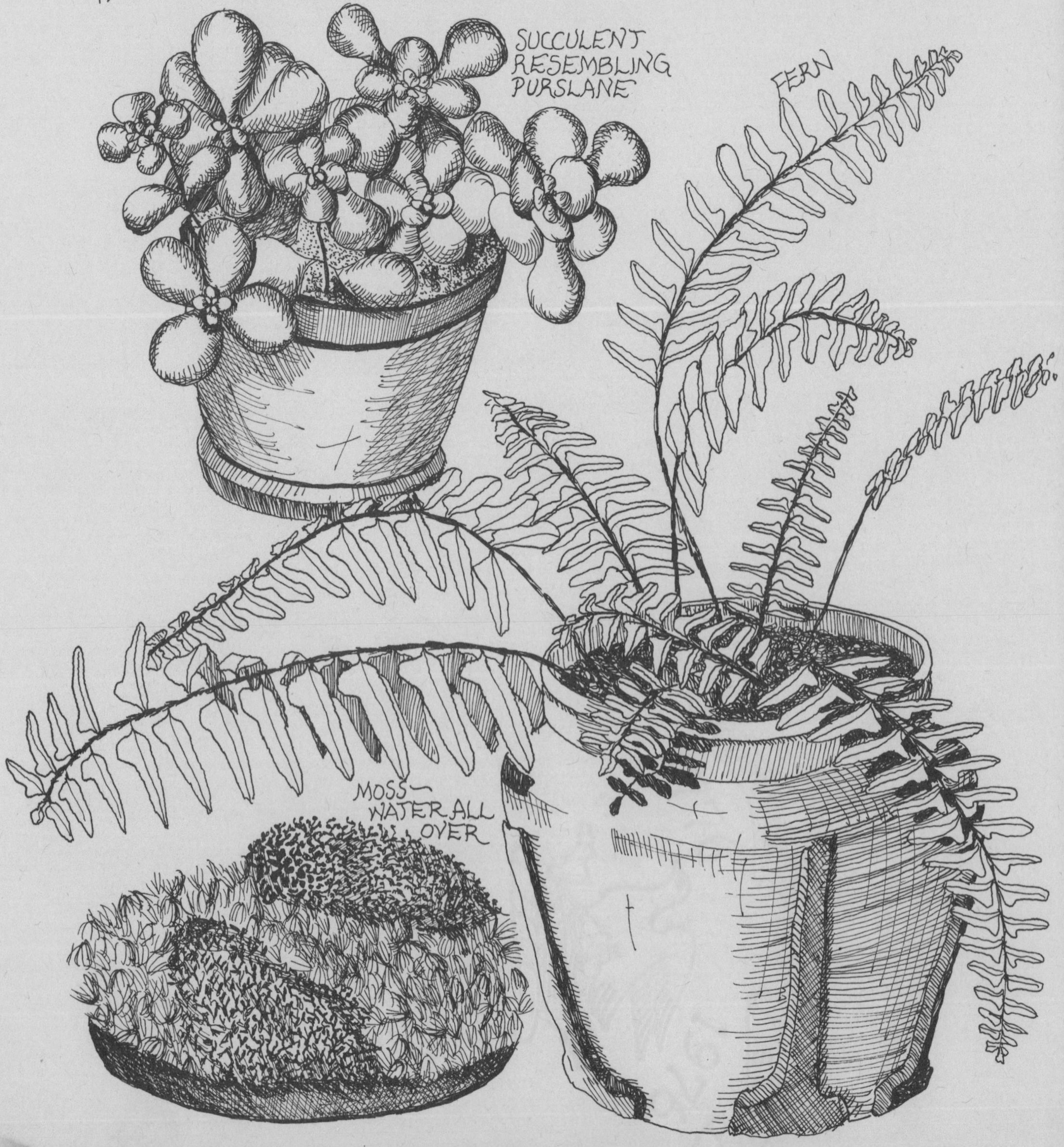
SUCCULENT RESEMBLING PURSLANE
FERN
MOSS— WATER ALL OVER

Macramé Jewelry

A COMPLETELY MACRAMÉD NECKLACE OR JEWELRY & BELTS INCORPORATING MACRAMÉ WITH OTHER MATERIALS ARE MADE USING CROCHET CORD OR OTHER THIN CORDING. AS WITH WALLHANGINGS, FREEDOM OF DESIGN USING ANY OF THE KNOTS AND THEIR COMBINATIONS IS LIMITLESS ~ SO LONG AS THE PIECE CAN BE WORN. (SEE MACRAMÉ SECTION)

The tails of the horseshoe crab are earth-tones of browns & green and make sturdy beads.

Bend sturdy wire or thin metal tubing with a simple loop and hook for closure.

The fruit of the paw-paw tree is a delicious combination of the taste of banana-strawberry-& apple ~, depending on whose eating it.

LEAF & FRUIT
Paw-Paw tree

ACTUAL SIZE OF SEEDS SHOWN

Use a jewelers' saw or other small saw to cut many lengths of beads.

Wash the tails in soapy water and dry in the sun for a few days. Smooth out the small spikes on the back of the tail with sandpaper, or a metal file for larger tails. Beads can also be shellacked. Drill holes if desired in full-length tails; or as shown in the necklace above, pull cord through, forming a loop at the sawed tip.

The seeds of the paw-paw are reddish brown and make lovely beads. Make a hole with a sewing needle—then ream out with a larger one.

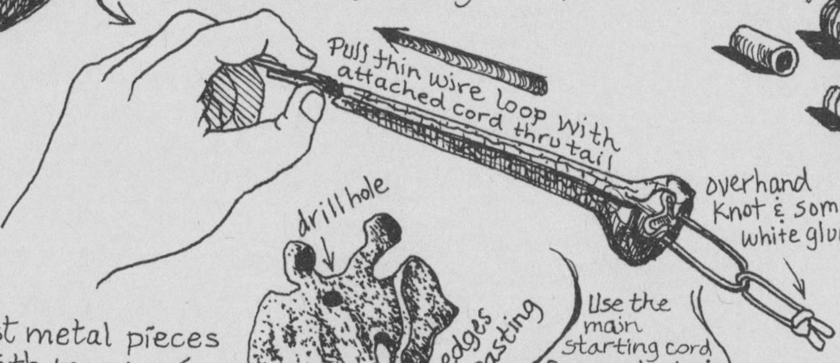
Pull thin wire loop with attached cord thru tail
overhand knot & some white glue

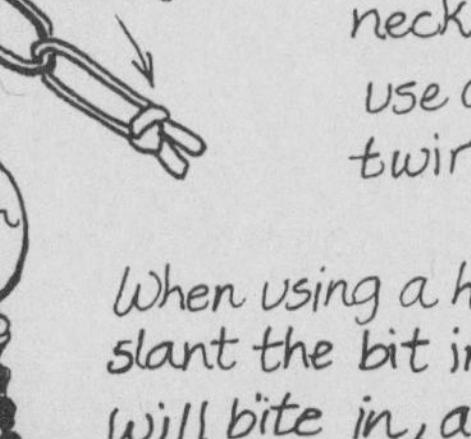

Use a tube cutter to cut and mark decorative lines on copper or brass tubing.

To make an attractive neck chain for objects, use crochet cord and twirl with half-knots.

drill hole
File edges after casting

Use the main starting cord for neck chain

Sand cast metal pieces for use with macramé jewelry. Wet sand (beach sand is best) and make impressions using any available objects. Pewter melts so easily that small pieces can be placed directly on the impression and melted with a propane torch. For silver, brass, or copper, melt the metal in a cast iron container first and pour the hot metal into the sand.

When using a hand drill on metal, slant the bit into the metal so it will bite in, and drill steadily.

Holes are easily drilled through seashells. Varnish or shellac to strengthen.

Books for many more jewelry techniques and ideas:

JEWELRY YOU CAN MAKE, a Sunset Book, Menlo Park, Calif.: Lane Publishing Co., 1975

STEP BY STEP JEWELRY by Thomas Gentille; Rascine, Wisconsin: Golden Press a Division of Western Publishing Company, Inc., 1968

CLAY

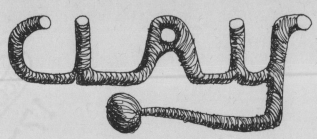

Here are two clay recipes using items found in the kitchen pantry. Food coloring can be added to the water of either recipe **OR** the clays can be painted when dry, using tempura, acrylic, or watercolor paint — a thick but brushable consistency is best **OR** felt tip pens. Then, brush on varnish, shellac, or clear nail polish — **NOTE:** when using felt tip pens to color, a spray varnish or shellac is best, to prevent bleeding of colors.

This KITCHEN CLAY

has been used for years by families across the country.

4 cups flour
1 cup salt
1½ cups water (food coloring optional)

Combine flour, salt, and water in a large bowl; mix thoroughly. Form clay into desired shapes, or roll out clay and cut shapes. Bake on a cookie sheet in a 350° oven for 40 minutes. Cool; color; and varnish. (See above)

PLAY CLAY*

2 cups Arm & Hammer baking soda
1 cup cornstarch
1¼ cups cold water

Mix 2 cups baking soda with 1 cup cornstarch. Blend. Then add 1¼ cups of cold water and mix until smooth. Boil one minute to consistency of moist mashed potatoes. Stir constantly. Spoon out on plate. Cover with damp cloth and cool. Knead lightly and roll out on waxed paper. Cut out designs with cookie cutter, bottle caps, or shape by hand. Etch in pattern. Let dry until hard (24 – 48 hours). Paint with tempura or watercolors. Dry. Coat with clear shellac or clear nail polish. Mount pins or clips with white glue.

Either clay can be used to make the objects illustrated here and the next page. Store left-over clays in a closed plastic bag in the refrigerator for later use.

BEADS (ACTUAL SIZE OF BEADS SHOWN)

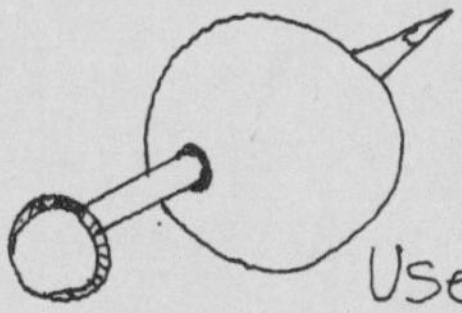

Use a nail to make holes.

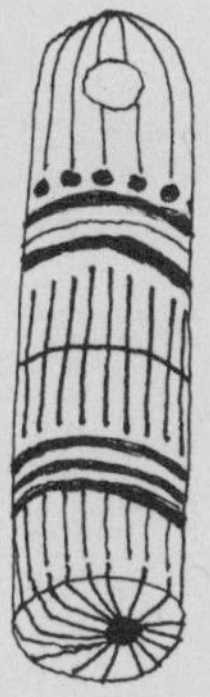
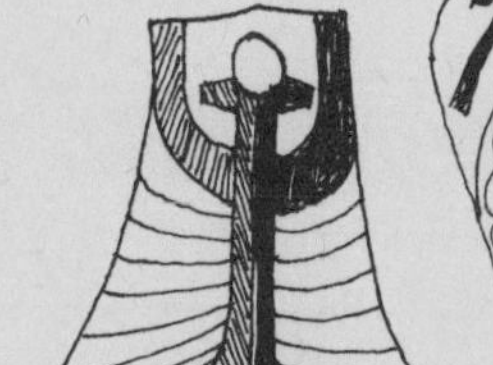

IF using **PLAY CLAY**, dried clay can be shaved with a knife for a smoother finish.
For jewelry, string beads using plain or color cord or elastic cording.

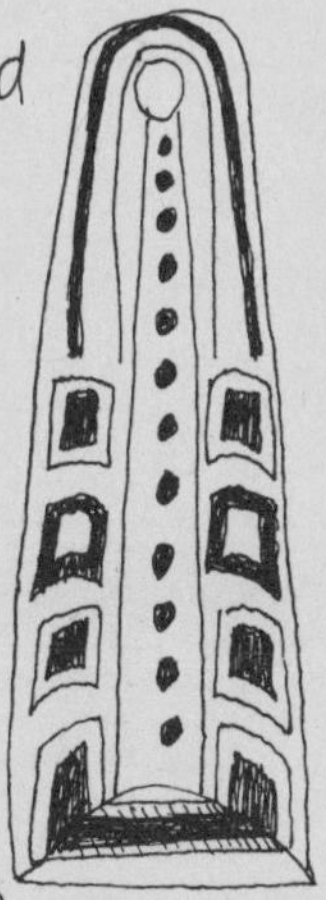

* *Courtesy Church & Dwight Co., Inc.*

window and tree decorations

SHOWN 1/2-SIZE

Insert curved, stiff wire while forming the clay,

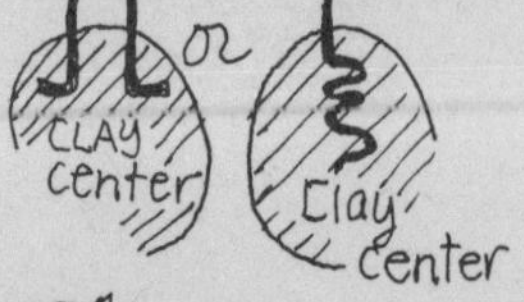
or
CLAY center
Clay center

for hanging cord.

Etch in circles with knife. Details painted on.

Hanging hook and curled wire "wind" inserted while forming clay. Details painted.

Insert wire in to fish and sea while forming clay. Tie hanging cord to center fish. Details painted.

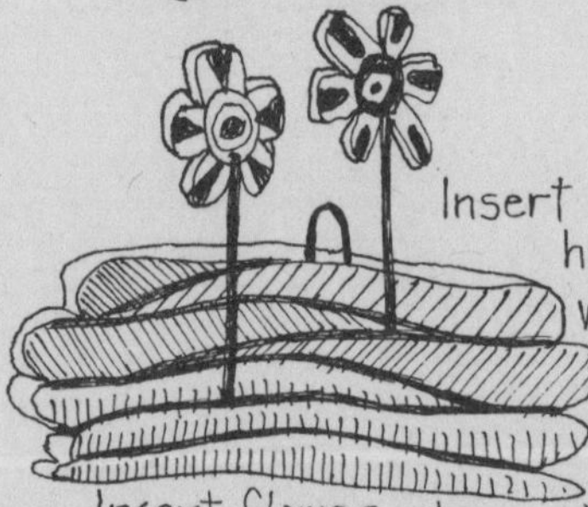

Insert hanging hook while forming clay.

Insert flower stem wires into flowers and earth when forming clay. Etch earth layers with knife. Details painted.

Form man with fingers or cut with gingerbread man cookie cutter. Insert hook while forming. Details painted.

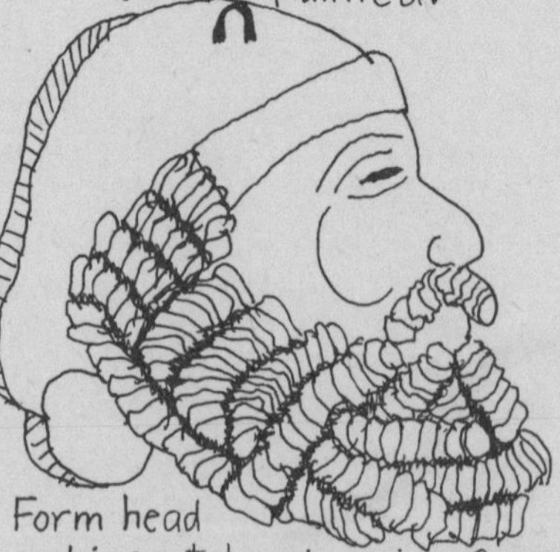

Form head and insert hanging wire. Squeeze moistened clay thru large holes of garlic press – place on beard area. Paint details.

DO A CARICATURE OF A FRIEND.

Insert hanging hook while forming clay. Paint details

Insert hanging hook while forming clay – this example also shows wire whiskers. Etch ear and jaw with knife. Details painted.

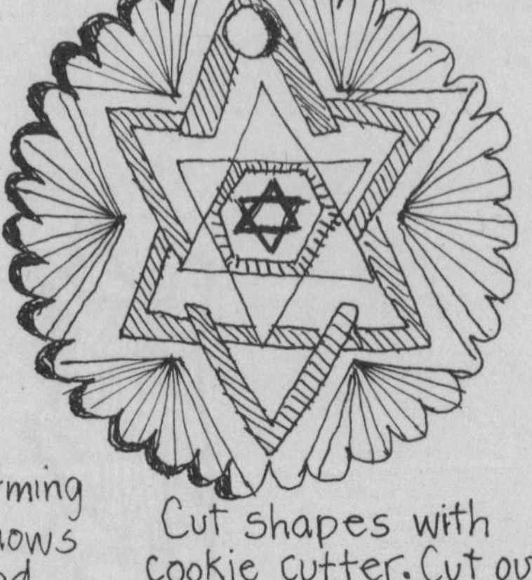

Cut shapes with cookie cutter. Cut out hole with funnel end. Paint details.

Paint details.

Form dancer and insert hanging wire. Squeeze moistened clay thru small holes of garlic press & place on head.

Mobile

The movement of the **Mobile** shows the gestures of a breeze flowing indoors and out. A variety of materials can be used for the balancing rods, such as: cut coat hangers, dowels, thin brass tubing, or twigs. The example below uses clay for the dangling objects, but there are many items and materials to be incorporated, such as: tin cans and/or lids - cut and painted, found objects of the city or country, cardboard 2-Dimensional or 3-Dimensional shapes, test tubes tied around the upper lip, and many more.

Tie fishing line or string to a main rod, and then add on more rods, cords, and objects (the mobile below is just an example). The lengths of the cords are ambiguous - just be sure all parts of the mobile have free movement. The placement of the strand knots along the rods is important for balance. Placement follows the principle of the fulcrum and lever:

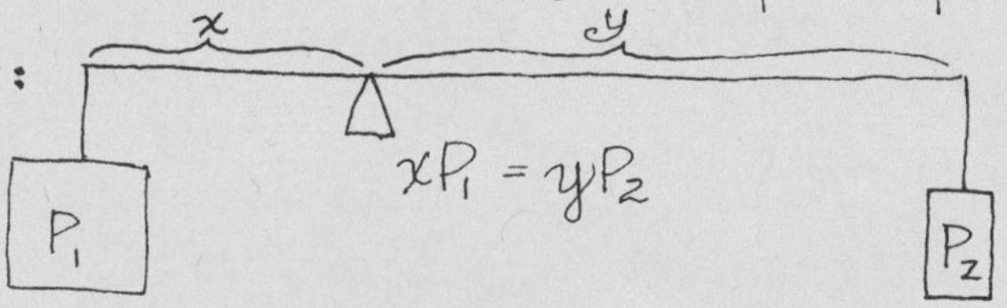

x
y
$xP_1 = yP_2$
P_1
P_2

The easiest way is to hold up the mobile and slide cord knots along the rods until balanced. Dab a bit of glue at each knot; white glue for porous materials, and epoxy for non-porous materials.

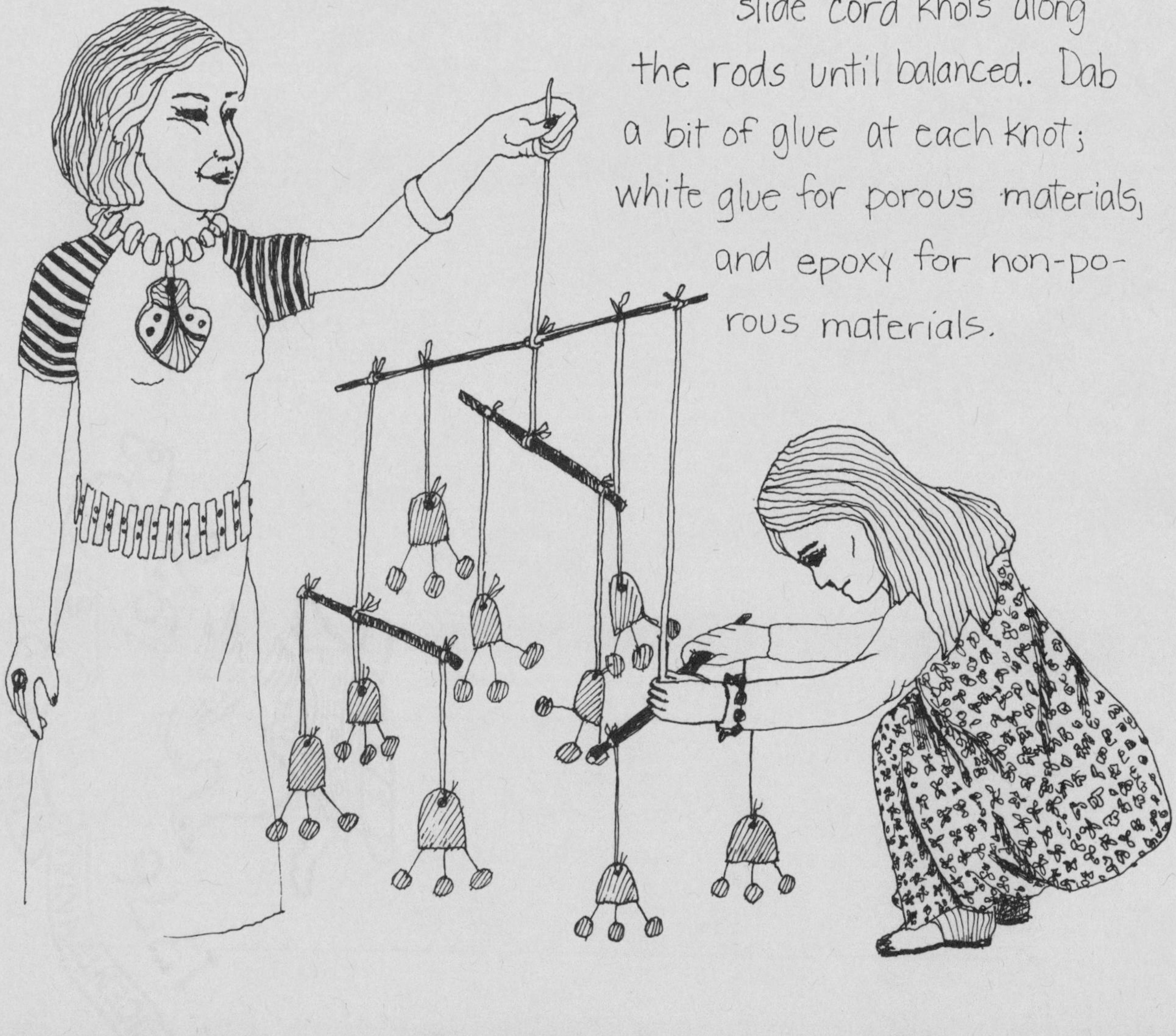

NATURAL CLAY

In many areas across the country, there is natural clay to be found. It's color ranges from grays to oranges to reds. Clay cakes on shoes after a rain and easily holds together when rolled into a ball. The clay contains stones, leaves, and other impurities which need to be removed in the following manner:

NOTE: IF LEFT UNGLAZED, THE CLAY SHOULD NOT BE USED FOR EATING OR DRINKING UTENSILS OR DISHES.

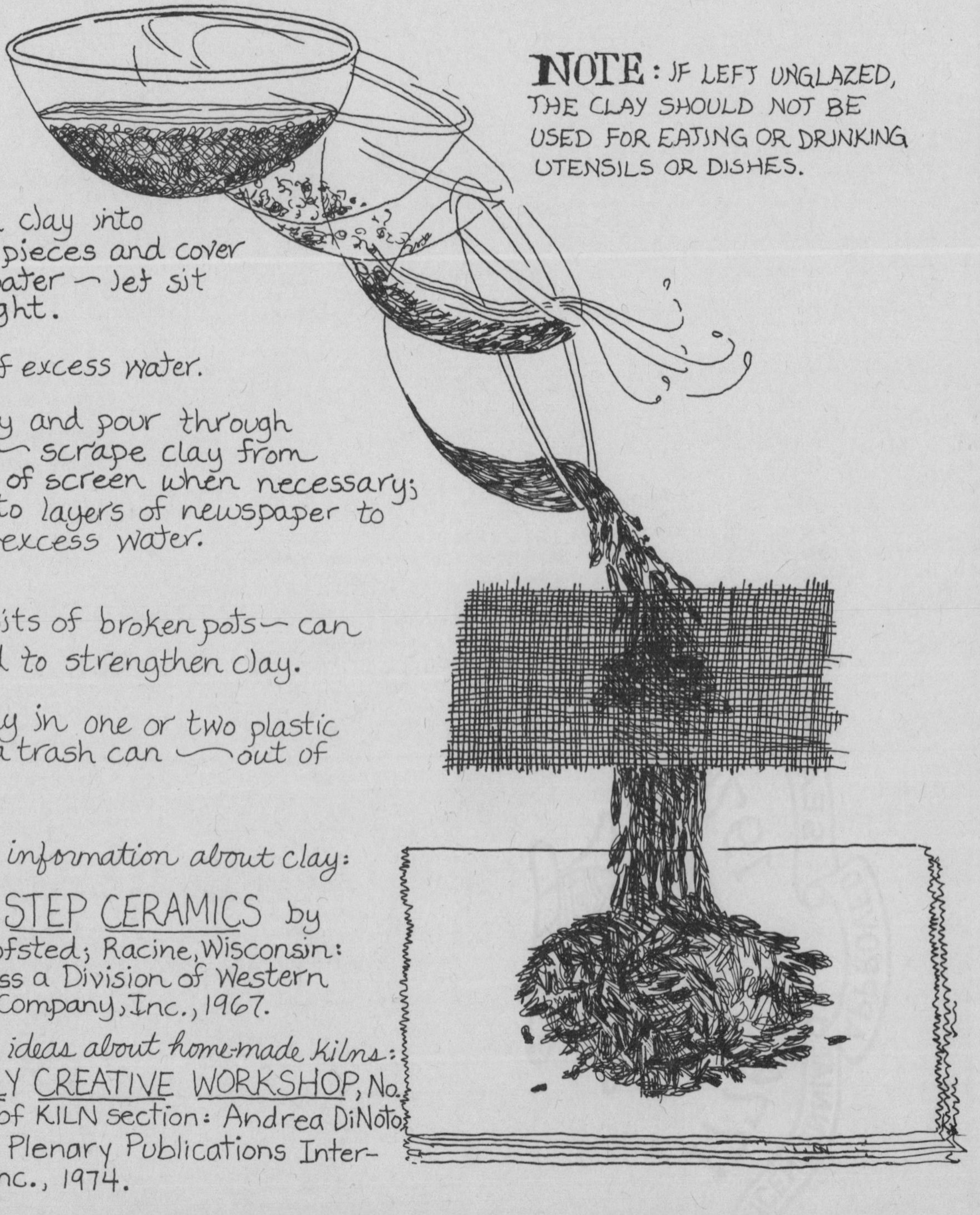

1. Break clay into small pieces and cover with water — let sit overnight.
2. Pour off excess water.
3. Stir clay and pour through screen — scrape clay from bottom of screen when necessary; pour onto layers of newspaper to absorb excess water.

Grog — bits of broken pots — can be added to strengthen clay.

Store clay in one or two plastic bags in a trash can — out of the sun.

For more information about clay:

STEP BY STEP CERAMICS by Jolyon Hofsted; Racine, Wisconsin: Golden Press a Division of Western Publishing Company, Inc., 1967.

For many ideas about home-made kilns:
THE FAMILY CREATIVE WORKSHOP, No. 8; Editor of KILN section: Andrea DiNoto; New York: Plenary Publications International, Inc., 1974.

Working with clay

SLIP is made by mixing a handful of clay with water, to a spreading consistency. Slip is used to secure sections of clay together.

CROSSHATCH joining edges of clay sections with a knife; spread both with slip and push together firmly.

Free form work is enjoyable and least restrictive; but 3 other methods of construction can also be used:

PINCH POT

Push thumb partially thru ball of clay.

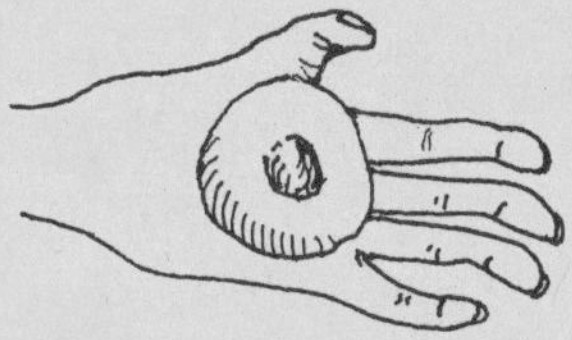

Rotate clay with fingers of one hand - enlarging the opening.

SLAB CONSTRUCTION

Roll out clay between two strips of wood, on burlap or canvas.

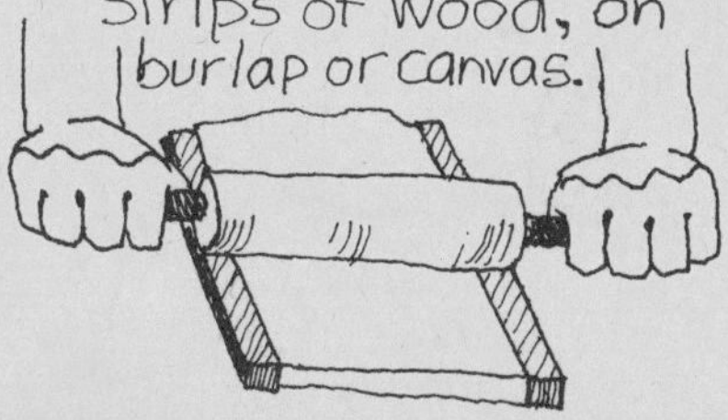

Cut edges on an angle and crosshatch.

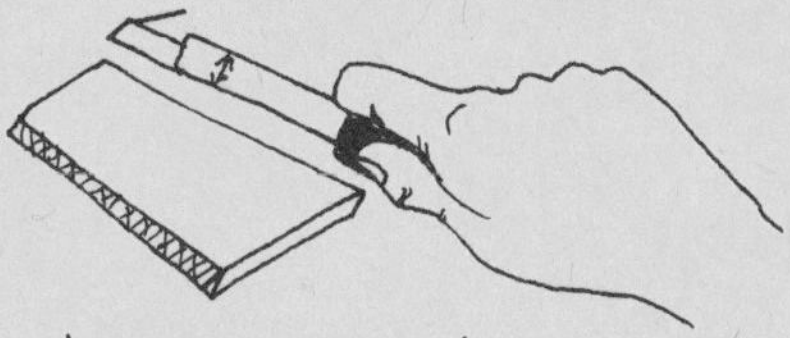

Join edges using slip. Support sides if needed.

COIL

Roll out clay and coil a base; crosshatching, applying slip, and smoothing out seams.

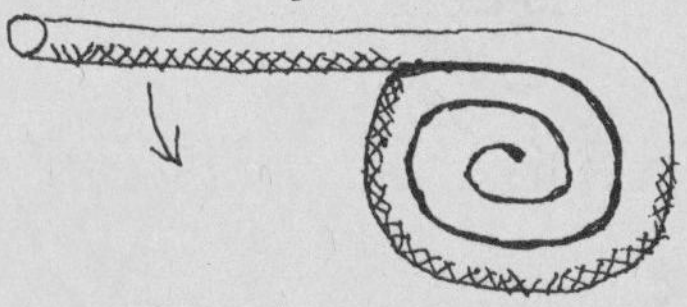

Crosshatch top edge of base, apply slip, and coil the sides of the pot. Smooth out seams inside and out.

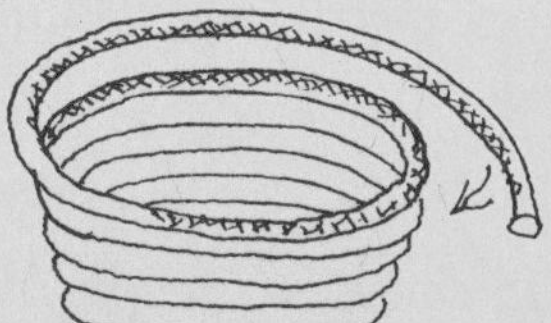

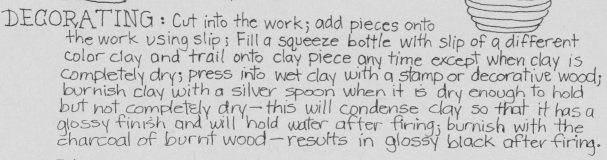

DECORATING: Cut into the work; add pieces onto the work using slip; Fill a squeeze bottle with slip of a different color clay and trail onto clay piece any time except when clay is completely dry; press into wet clay with a stamp or decorative wood; burnish clay with a silver spoon when it is dry enough to hold but not completely dry — this will condense clay so that it has a glossy finish and will hold water after firing; burnish with the charcoal of burnt wood — results in glossy black after firing.

DRYING THE CLAY: Keep finished work in a closed plastic bag, out of the sun. The first day, take the piece out of the bag for 1 hour. Each day, increase the time by 1 hour; when the piece is almost completely dry, keep it out for a few days.

FIRING: Much of the natural clay is very low-fire and can be fired in a wood stove. Use fire-brick or a metal grate to protect clay from falling wood. This makes a good winter project as you build the fire in the morning, thru evening, and the next morning remove clay pieces. Clay beads are small enough to scatter in the ashes, and dig out when the stove is emptied.

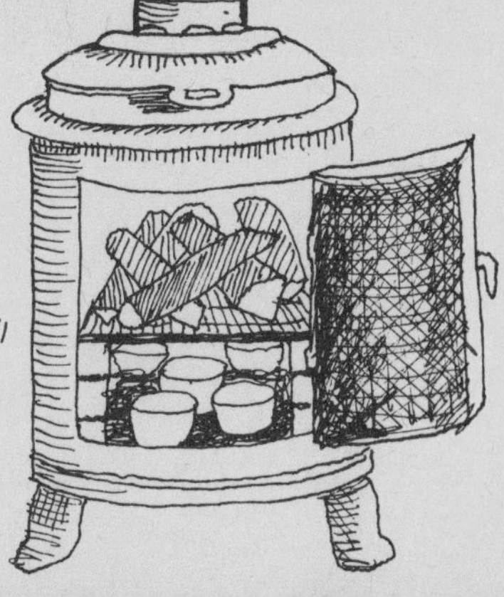

CATNIP TOYS

We have a little, gray cat named Gertrude who can be very unsociable when her friends come to visit; but give her a catnip toy and she's not only sociable but acts downright silly. Catnip can be bought in pet departments and used in the toys. But, wild catnip grows in the country, with a strong scent of mint guiding the seeker in the right direction. As for other mint teas, tie bunches together with string and hang in an airy room to dry. Run fingers along the stem to remove leaves and flowers. Sew shapes together with a blanket or slip stitch, filling with the dry catnip towards the time of the last stitches and continue the last sewing.

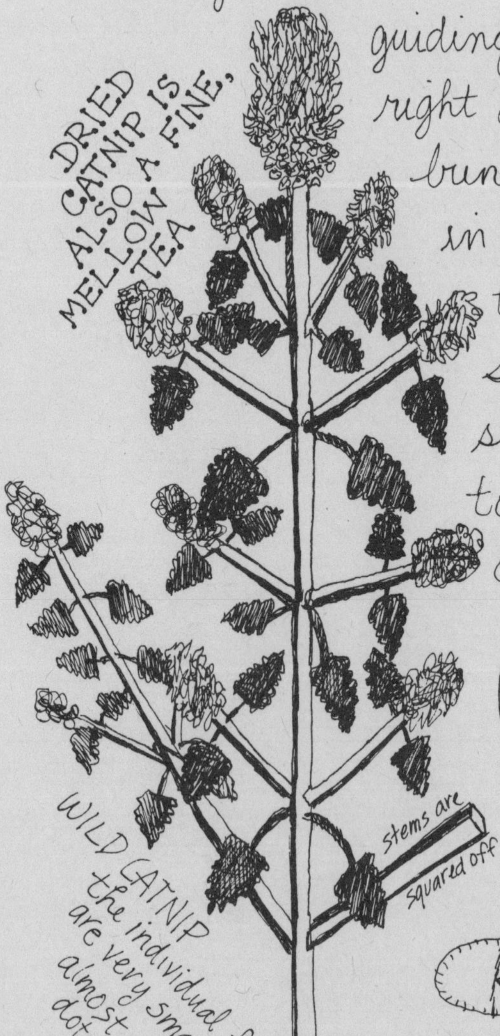
DRIED CATNIP IS ALSO A FINE, MELLOW TEA
stems are squared off
WILD CATNIP
the individual flowers are very small & white with almost unnoticeable pink dots.

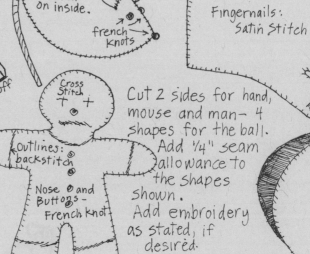

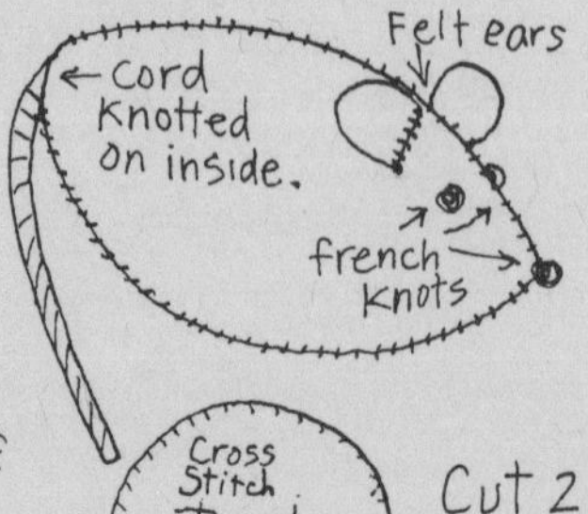
Felt ears
Cord Knotted on inside.
french Knots

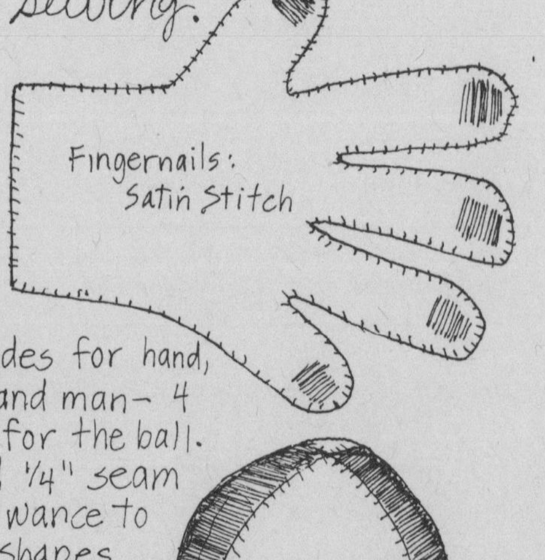
Fingernails: Satin Stitch

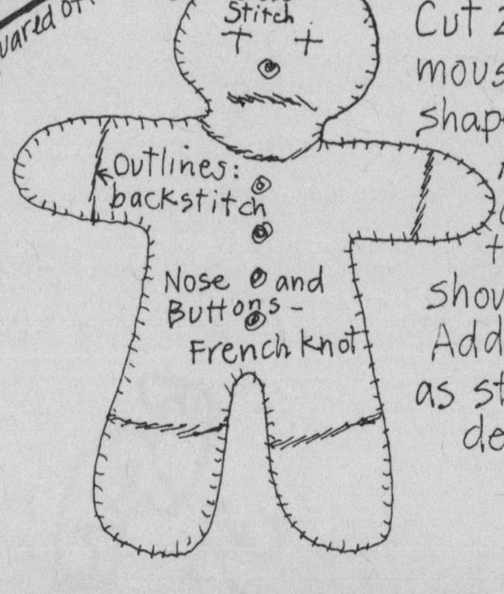
Cross Stitch
Outlines: backstitch
Nose and Buttons - French knot

Cut 2 sides for hand, mouse and man- 4 shapes for the ball. Add 1/4" seam allowance to the shapes shown. Add embroidery as stated, if desired.

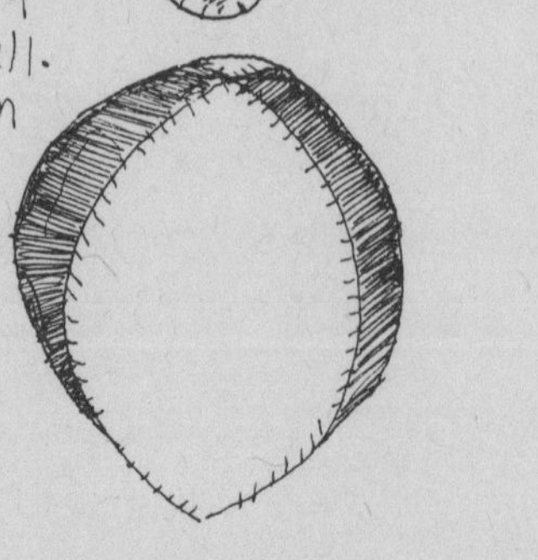

Milkweed Pod Wreath

SIDE AND FRONT VIEW OF DANGLING FLOWERS
MILKWEED SHOWN HERE AT LATE SUMMER STAGE; PODS BEGIN TO FORM
PODS

Milkweed grows during the warm months, but in late October walk through the country and enjoy the mellow colors of the winter flowers. During winter, the milkweed has mouse-color pods filled with fluffy white shoots. Collect the pods to create a unique Christmas wreath.... you just may decide to leave it up all year!

Remove the white shoots (less messy if done outside); and separate the already opened halves of the pods. Using a needle & carpet thread, sew the pod halves onto a metal wreath frame (found at florists)

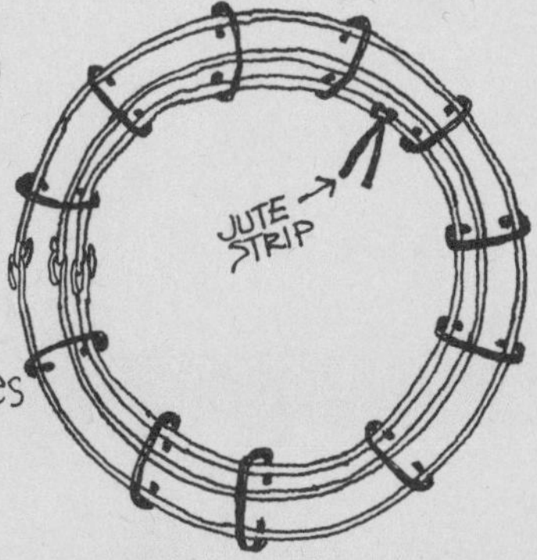
JUTE STRIP

OR make a frame, using coat hangers. Cut with metal cutters and bend 3 circles and connecting wires - as shown. Curve ends  and join, using thin wire wrapped around intersections to further secure. Sew thread through pod ends, looping thread around frame. Cut 4-inch strips of jute and tie to inside circle of frame. Trim with a ribbon bow.

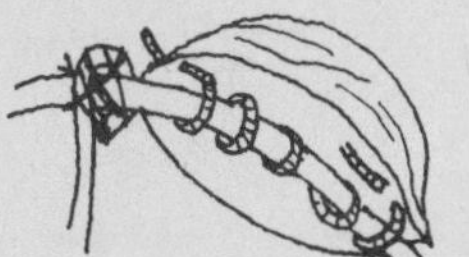

Blank Page Book

We all experience pensive, philosophical moments ~ the degree of thoughtfulness forming so much of our essence of existence. Often in periods of extremes, whether joyful, perplexing, depressing, whimsical ...., writing down passages or themes is a meaningful outlet. For this purpose a blank page book is quite perfect. The book is also useful for any type of notes, comments, recipes, or other information as well as drawings. There is something special about having a bound book that can become whatever one desires. Years ago, a friend gave me one with a beautiful, printed fabric cover. I enjoyed many happy hours, filling the pages with color theory; and from the day I received the blank page book and henceforth, it is one of my most cherished possessions. And so, as a gift, it is excellent because the receiver has such freedom to transform the pages.

The blank page books are sold in many bookstores or art departments, (they generally have a solid black cover.) Cover the book with any cotton fabric that has been embroidered, batiked, printed with oil-or-water-base ink, or naturally dyed; (See other sections in this book). OR, cover with rice paper; printed with oil·or·waterbase ink, painted with any type of paint, or decorated with pen and ink or crayons. Cut out the paper or fabric for the size of the book, as shown. Add 5 parts of

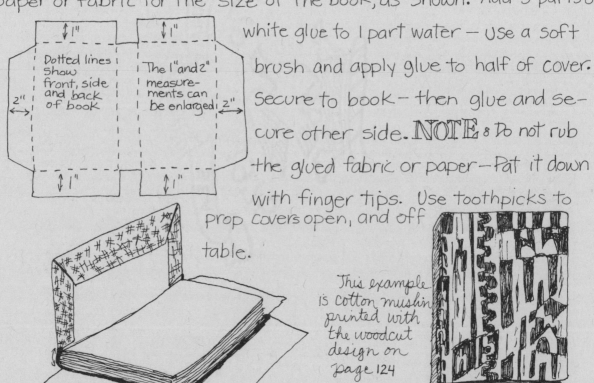

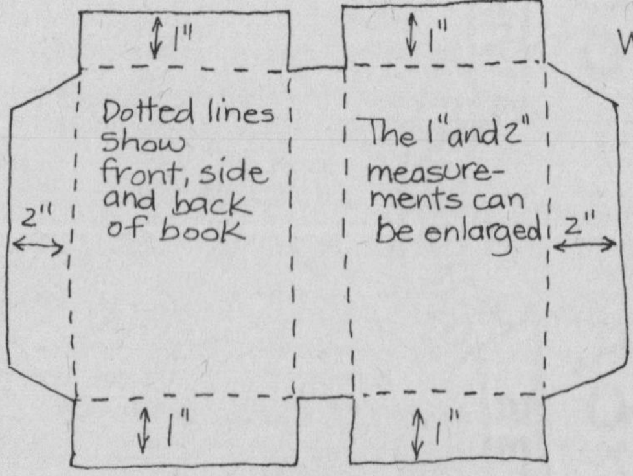
1"
1"
Dotted lines show front, side and back of book
The 1" and 2" measurements can be enlarged
2"
2"
1"
1"

white glue to 1 part water — Use a soft brush and apply glue to half of cover. Secure to book — then glue and secure other side. **NOTE**: Do not rub the glued fabric or paper — Pat it down with finger tips. Use toothpicks to prop covers open, and off table.

This example is cotton muslin printed with the woodcut design on page 124

The Avocado

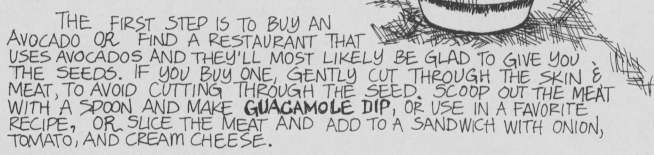

FOR YEARS I TRIED STARTING AVOCADOS; FOLLOWING SO MUCH ADVICE, THAT ROWS OF SEEDS IN GLASSES INEVITABLY ROTTED ON THE KITCHEN SINK. FINALLY, MY KITCHEN IS DONNED WITH ROWS OF AVOCADO SEEDS WITH HEALTHY ROOTS AND GORGEOUS AVOCADO "TREES" WHICH ARE OCCASIONALLY GIVEN AS GIFTS.

THE FIRST STEP IS TO BUY AN AVOCADO OR FIND A RESTAURANT THAT USES AVOCADOS AND THEY'LL MOST LIKELY BE GLAD TO GIVE YOU THE SEEDS. IF YOU BUY ONE, GENTLY CUT THROUGH THE SKIN & MEAT, TO AVOID CUTTING THROUGH THE SEED. SCOOP OUT THE MEAT WITH A SPOON AND MAKE **GUACAMOLE DIP**, OR USE IN A FAVORITE RECIPE, OR SLICE THE MEAT AND ADD TO A SANDWICH WITH ONION, TOMATO, AND CREAM CHEESE.

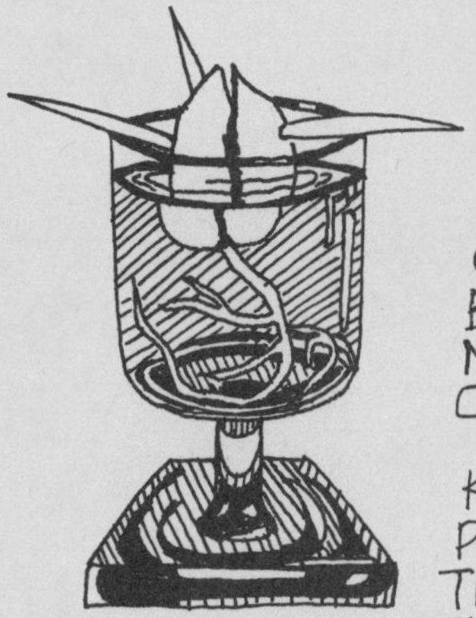

THE AVOCADO SEED HAS A BROWN SKIN WHICH IS PULLED OFF (THE SKIN IS REMOVED MOST EASILY SOON AFTER THE AVOCADO HAS BEEN CUT OPEN).

PLACE 3 TOOTHPICKS AROUND THE NARROW HALF OF THE SEED. SOME SEEDS ARE ALMOST ROUND, BUT ONE END WILL APPEAR AT LEAST SLIGHTLY NARROWER. PLACE IN WATER, WITH WIDER HALF COVERED WITH WATER — REFILL AS NEEDED.

KEEP THE GLASS WITH SEED, IN A POORLY LIT PLACE, SUCH AS THE BACK OF A SHELF. THE TIME IT TAKES FOR ROOTS TO DEVELOP VARIES ...... FROM A FEW WEEKS TO A FEW MONTHS. THE SEED WILL ALSO ROOT IN SAND; PLACING THE SEED'S WIDER HALF DOWN IN A POT OF WATERED SAND ~~~ BUT IT'S NICE TO WATCH THE ROOTS GROW IN WATER. ONCE ROOTS HAVE APPEARED, A STEM AND SMALL LEAVES WILL FOLLOW.

TRANSPLANT THE SEED TO A POT OF REGULAR POTTING SOIL, (A BIT OF SAND & VERMICULITE — *OPTIONAL*) WITH THE BOTTOM LINED WITH STONES FOR DRAINAGE. PINCH OFF THE FIRST LEAVES SO THAT THE STEM WILL THICKEN AND BRANCH OUT. WHEN NEW LEAVES DEVELOP AND GROW LARGER, PINCH OFF THE SMALL, CENTER LEAVES. CONTINUE TO PINCH THE AVOCADO AS IT GROWS, IN THE SAME MANNER. TRANSPLANT TO LARGER POTS WHEN ROOTS OUTGROW THE PRESENT POT. IN SUMMER, PUT AVOCADOS OUTSIDE, RECEIVING **MORNING** SUNLIGHT **ONLY** AND THEY WILL GROW RAPIDLY.

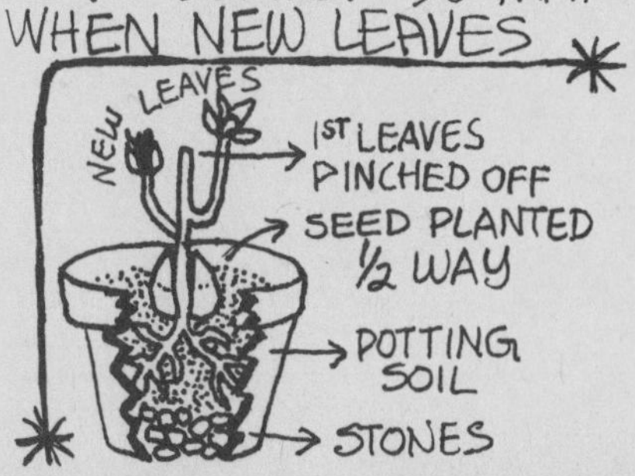
NEW LEAVES
1ST LEAVES PINCHED OFF
SEED PLANTED ½ WAY
POTTING SOIL
STONES

Rooting Plants

IMPATIENS

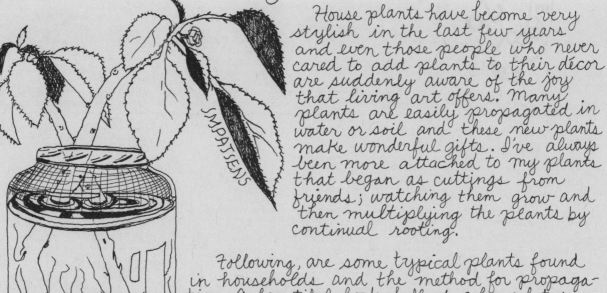

House plants have become very stylish in the last few years and even those people who never cared to add plants to their décor are suddenly aware of the joy that living art offers. Many plants are easily propagated in water or soil and these new plants make wonderful gifts. I've always been more attached to my plants that began as cuttings from friends; watching them grow and then multiplying the plants by continual rooting.

Following, are some typical plants found in households and the method for propagation. A beautiful book full of color photos and identifiable drawings of plants:

<u>FOLIAGE</u> <u>HOUSE</u> <u>PLANTS</u> by James Underwood Crockett and the Editors of TIME-LIFE BOOKS, New York: Time, Inc., 1972.

contains further information about propagation and plants.

THE TIME IT TAKES FOR A PLANT TO ROOT IS 1-4 WEEKS.

IMPATIENS ~ Cut off a stem 5 to 6 inches long; root in water, then transplant into potting soil.

PLANT OF LIFE ~ Also appropriately called: Mother of Millions and Pregnant Plant because tiny new plants hang from the leaves and fall onto the soil. After a while, the tiny plants begin to grow where they fall, or transplant them to a new pot.

SWEDISH IVY ~ (See illustration; page 152). Cut off at least 12 inches of stem. Root in water or place 2 inches into potting soil - Keep soil moist. Pull off any leaves that extend into water or soil.

SPIDER PLANT - (See illustration; page 149). The mobile-like shoots show the beginnings of roots. Cut off the shoot and plant in potting soil - Keep the soil watered.

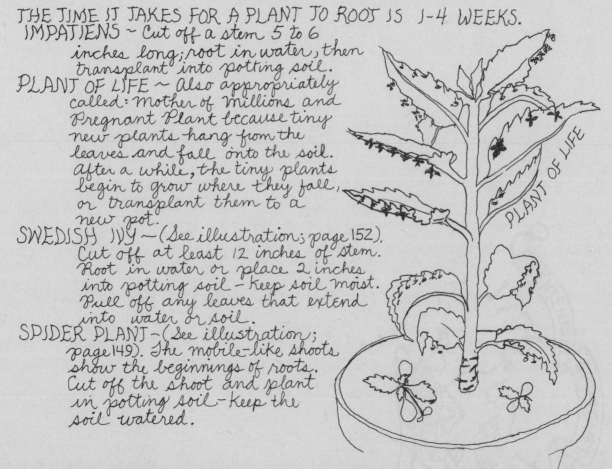

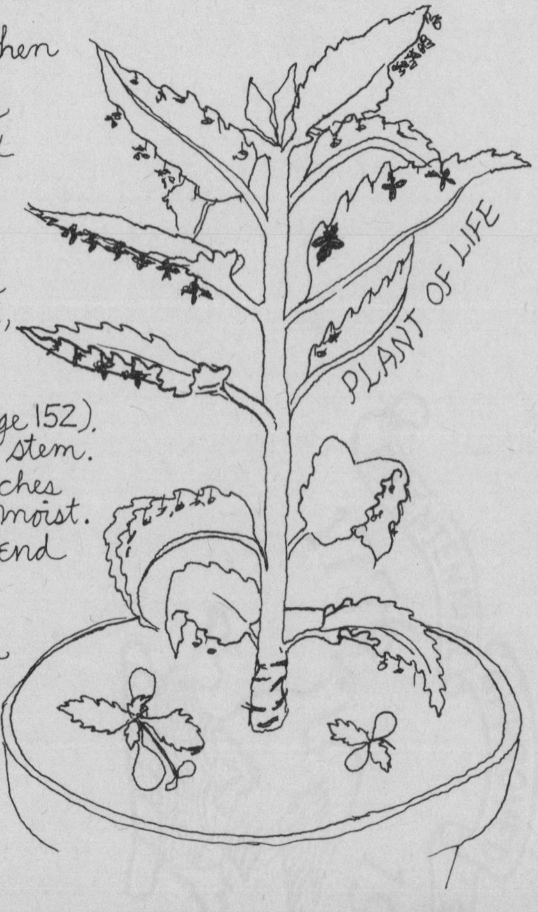
PLANT OF LIFE

WANDERING JEW ~ (See below and another variety on page 154). Cut off stem at least 12 inches long. Roots will form from small nobs opposite leaves. Root in water or soil ~ Keep soil moist. Pull off any leaves that extend into water or soil.

ARROWHEAD VINE ~ Cut stem with a nobby, root beginning (opposite leaves). Transplant to potting soil and keep moist.

LIPSTICK PLANT ~ (See illustration; page 146). The name is derived from the bright red, tubular flower of the plant. I have rooted this one in water, but it took months. Instead cut off a length of stem at least 12 inches long and plant in potting soil (Note the small root beginnings). Pull off any leaves that extend into soil. Keep soil moist.

PHILODENDRON ~ The philodendron not only roots in water but some people prefer to grow them in water rather than soil. Note the rather long nobs which will root. Cut any length of stem and place the nob ends in water or soil, kept moist.

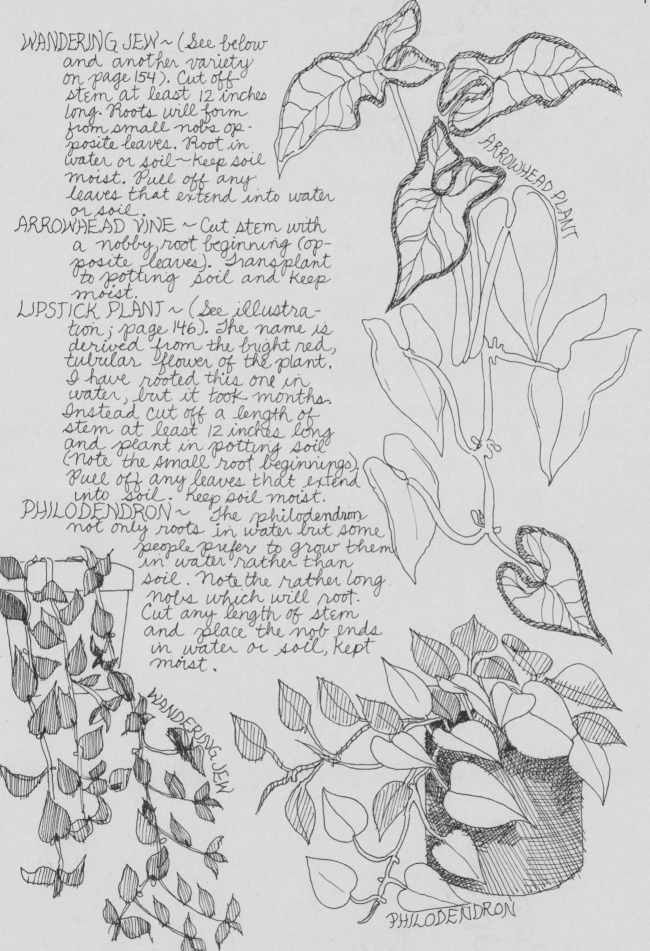

ARROWHEAD PLANT

WANDERING JEW

PHILODENDRON

Hanging Pots

The following pages illustrate and explain specific directions for hanging pot designs, although when you become familiar with the macramé knots and variations (See pages 85-93), creating new designs will not be difficult. The pot is used as a form to knot around — starting at the open end with a main starting cord wrapped around and tied, as in design #2, OR starting at the bottom of the pot with a knotted group of strands, as seen in the other designs. Just remember to incorporate a multiple of 4 strands.

Pot Plate ~ I have never known such frustration as watering a plant in a hanging pot and hearing the familiar steady stream of water exiting from the drainage hole onto my toes, or the dogs, or the chair.... I've heard various remedies: watering plants by placing ice cubes on the soil, wrapping the lower half of the pot with tin foil, placing a plastic circle inside the pot over the drainage hole, and many more. I found them all to be less than adequate, if not garish, as compared to working the design of the macramé to include a pot plate.

Materials ~ Any of the cords listed on page 85 are appropriate for the hanging pots (fabric strands are a particularly nice change from typical cording). Baling twine is used for #3; it's very inexpensive but is unpleasant to work with indoors. Work outside if using baling twine, to enable the hemp-like particles to escape through the air. The completed macramé holder can also be dyed with cold or hot water dyes according to package instructions for fabric. The type of cord used is included in the hanging pot directions; using a much thinner or thicker cord will alter the number of knots it takes to reach a certain length so use the illustrations and your own discretion.

Pot Size ~ The size of the pot used in the following designs is specified; using a pot with a slight dimensional difference doesn't matter. But, to enlarge or decrease the macramé for a totally different size pot, add or delete groups of 4 strands (∩∩). The only exception is #2, add a new group of the jute and contrasting color strands.

Cord Length ~ The symbols, ↕∩↕ ↕∩↕, used throughout the instructions refer to the length of the single strands extending from the fold of the cord. Whenever possible, the irregular folding is used in order to conserve cord.

Pot design by Ed Kindness

The design to the right holds the pot (or a glass dome) with a minimum of strands and overhand knots. The decorative bottom is made using the pot or dome as a form, winding rope around, secured in place by clove hitches of cord. In this example, some areas are made by wrapping cords around cords. The macramé holds its 3-dimensional shape because of the technique of wrapping cord around rope. In this example, the rope end below the pot is inserted through the center of the wrapped coils. I have not included specific instructions for this style because the bottom offers all the freedom of design that wallhangings have. Refer to the various pages where wrapping is discussed.

Design 1

POT SIZE:

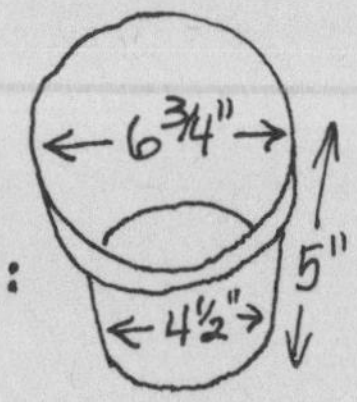

6 3/4"
4 1/2"
5"

USES 3-PLY JUTE
USES APPROXIMATELY
280 FEET OF CORD

1. JOIN 8 STRANDS OF 70 INCHES [35" ∩ 35"]; TOGETHER BY USING ONE OF THE STRANDS TO TIE AN OVERHAND KNOT AT CENTER.

Tighten Knot

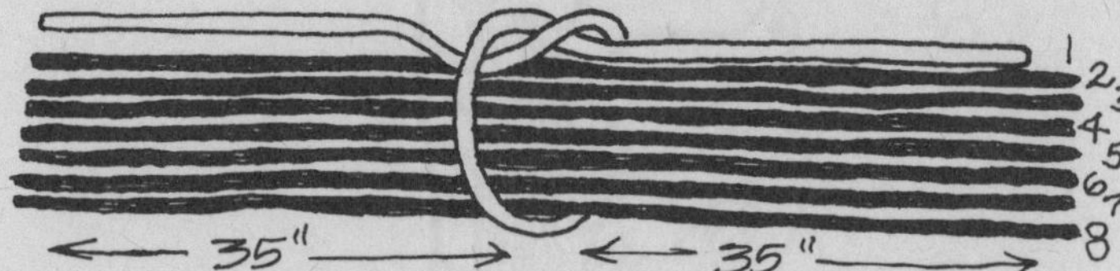

1
2
3
4
5
6
7
8
35"
35"

2. WITH KNOT AT DRAINAGE HOLE OF POT, ATTACH THE STRANDS TO POT WITH A PAPER CLIP.

A. Unfold paper clip.
B. Bend clip in half.
C. Slip over center knot and thru drainage hole.

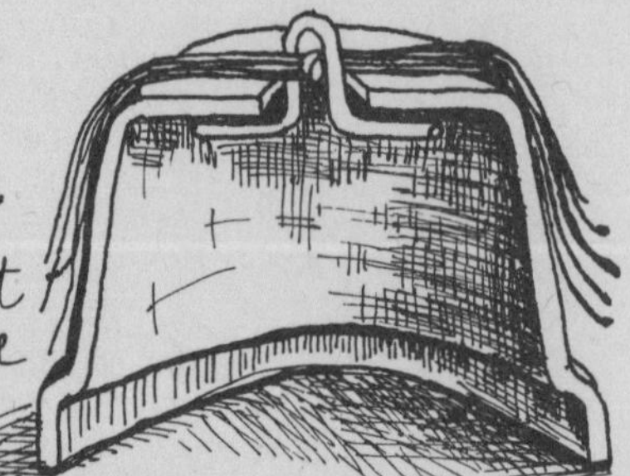

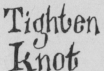

*THE CLIP ENABLES EASY HANDLING FOR MACRAME ON POTS.

D. Open clip inside the pot ~ securing strands.

3. SQUARE KNOT AROUND WITH 4 STRANDS IN EACH KNOT, FOR **2** ROWS.
4. SQUARE KNOT AROUND, WITH **3** ROWS OF EVENLY SPACED KNOTS ... ON THE 3RD ROW, ADD TO EACH KNOT, 2 STRANDS OF 60 INCHES [30" ∩ 30"].
5. ADD 2 SQUARE KNOTS, INDIVIDUALLY TO THE 4 GROUPS OF 8 STRANDS; (USE 4 STRANDS TO KNOT — WITH THE OTHER 4 AS CENTER CORDS.)

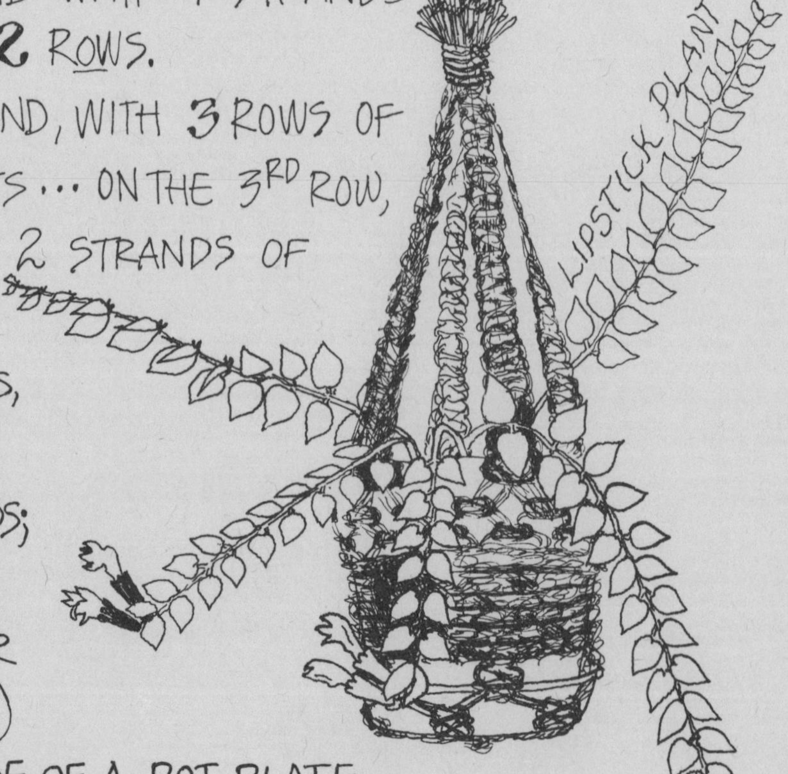

LIPSTICK PLANT

THIS WILL ENABLE USE OF A POT PLATE.

6. MACRAMÉ A ROW OF SQUARE KNOTS AROUND THE POT, WITH 4 STRANDS IN EACH KNOT **AND** ADDING TO EACH 2 STRANDS OF 48 INCHES [24" ∩ 24"].
7. ADD 1 SQUARE KNOT TO EACH KNOT (FROM STEP 6), USING 4 STRANDS TO KNOT—WITH 4 AS CENTER CORDS.
8. MACRAMÉ 6 ROWS OF SQUARE KNOTS AROUND THE POT, WITH 4 STRANDS IN EACH KNOT.
9. DOUBLE UP 2 GROUPS OF 4 CORDS EACH AND MACRAMÉ 2 ROWS OF SQUARE KNOTS (USING 4 STRANDS TO KNOT—WITH 4 AS CENTER CORDS).

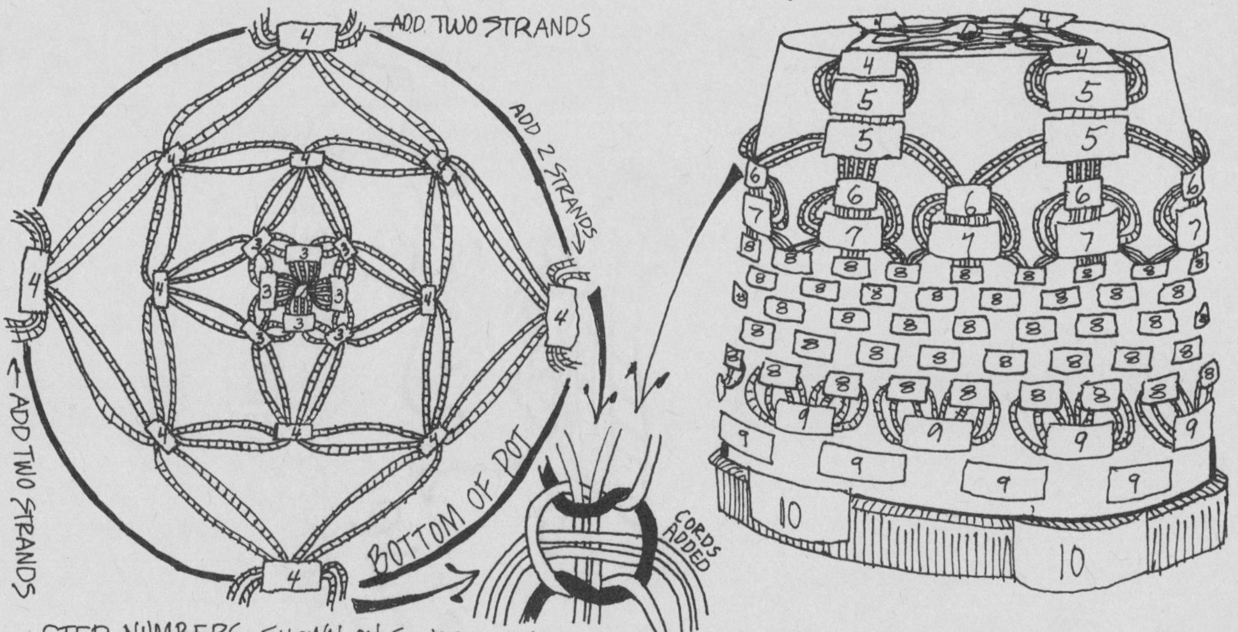

ADD TWO STRANDS
ADD 2 STRANDS
ADD TWO STRANDS
BOTTOM OF POT
CORDS ADDED

STEP NUMBERS SHOWN ON SQUARE KNOT SYMBOL → ▭

10. DOUBLE UP NEW GROUPS FROM STEP 9, AND SQUARE KNOT ONCE WITH 16 STRANDS (KNOT WITH 4—WITH 12 STRANDS AS CENTER CORDS)
11. ADD 4 STRANDS TO EACH OF the GROUPS (FROM STEP 10):
    - 2 STRANDS OF 48 INCHES [24" ∩ 24"]
    - 2 STRANDS OF 144 INCHES [72" ∩ 72"]

USE THE LONGER STRANDS TO KNOT 18 SQUARE KNOTS—THE FOUR RESULTING LENGTHS ARE FOR HANGING. **NOTE:** THE LENGTHS WILL BECOME PROGRESSIVELY THINNER AS

AS THE CENTER CORDS (STRANDS FROM STEPS 1–10) REACH THEIR ENDS.

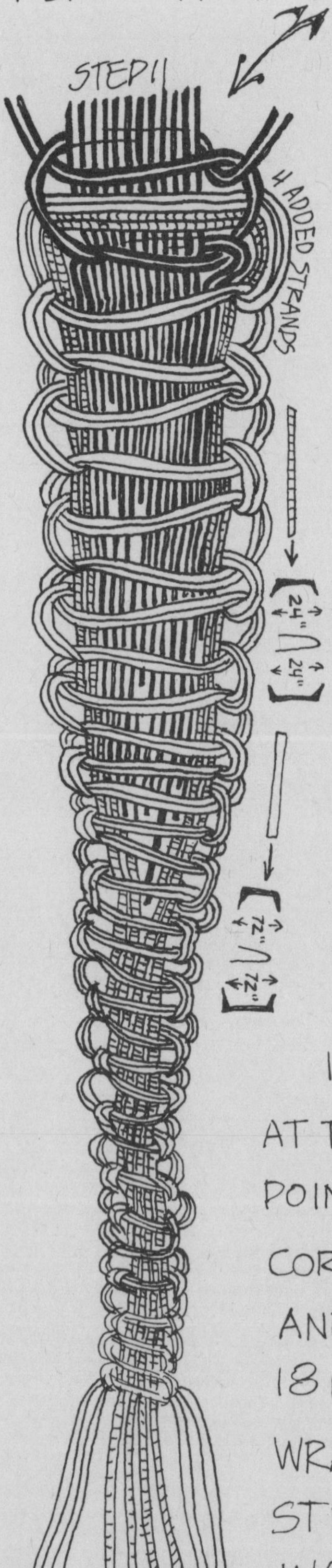

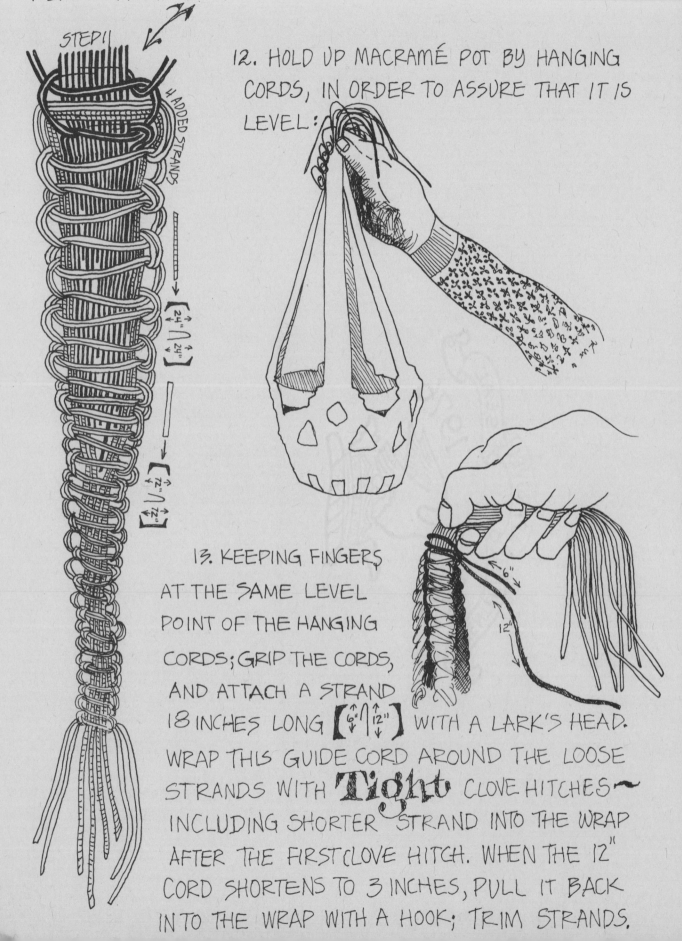

STEP 11
4 ADDED STRANDS
24"
24"
12"
12"

12. HOLD UP MACRAMÉ POT BY HANGING CORDS, IN ORDER TO ASSURE THAT IT IS LEVEL:

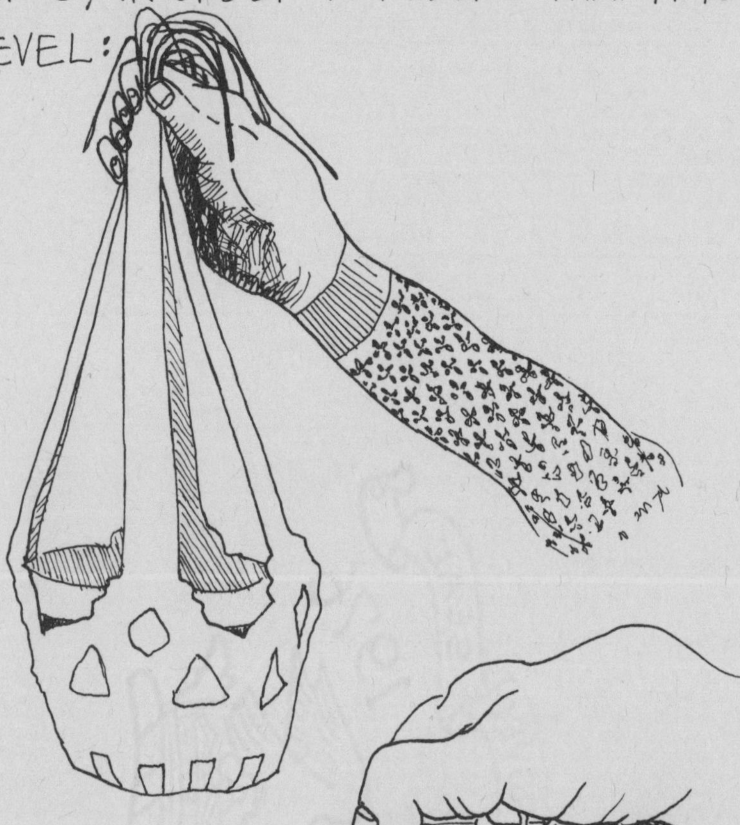

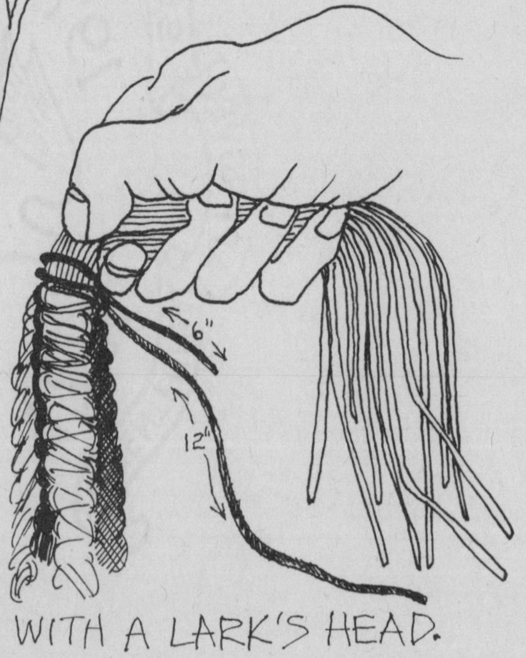

6"
12"

13. KEEPING FINGERS AT THE SAME LEVEL POINT OF THE HANGING CORDS; GRIP THE CORDS, AND ATTACH A STRAND 18 INCHES LONG [6" ⋂ 12"] WITH A LARK'S HEAD. WRAP THIS GUIDE CORD AROUND THE LOOSE STRANDS WITH **Tight** CLOVE HITCHES~ INCLUDING SHORTER STRAND INTO THE WRAP AFTER THE FIRST CLOVE HITCH. WHEN THE 12" CORD SHORTENS TO 3 INCHES, PULL IT BACK INTO THE WRAP WITH A HOOK; TRIM STRANDS.

Design 2

POT SIZE

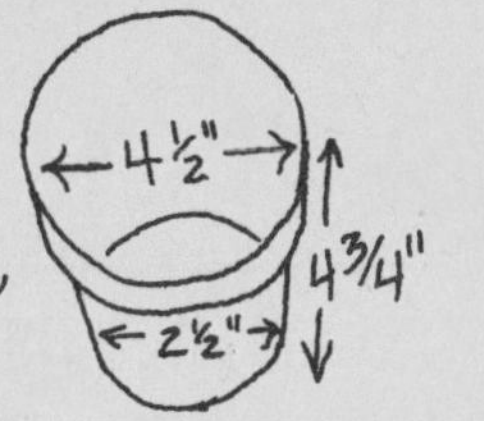
4½"
4¾"
2½"

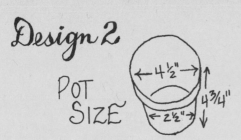

Uses 3-ply jute and rug yarn
This design is macramed from pot opening to bottom.

Uses approximately 240 feet of jute and 53 feet contrasting color rug yarn.

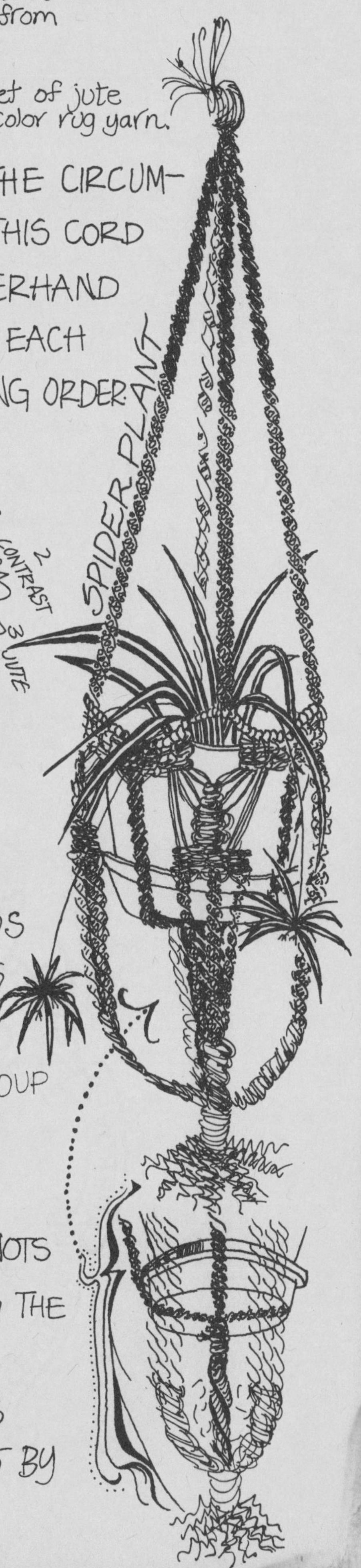
SPIDER PLANT

1. BEGIN WITH A STRAND 72 INCHES LONG PLUS THE CIRCUMFERENCE OF THE TOP OF THE POT. PLACE THIS CORD AROUND THE TOP, EVENLY; JOIN WITH AN OVERHAND KNOT. ATTACH 39 STRANDS OF 72 INCHES LONG EACH (36" ∩ 36") WITH A LARK'S HEAD; IN THE FOLLOWING ORDER.

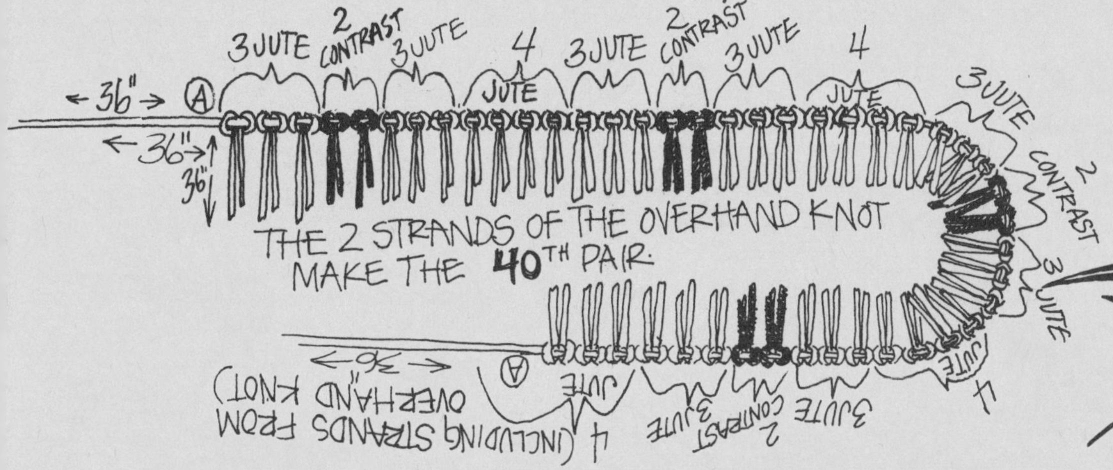
3 JUTE
2 CONTRAST
3 JUTE
4 JUTE
3 JUTE
2 CONTRAST
3 JUTE
4 JUTE
3 JUTE
2 CONTRAST
3 JUTE
4
36"
36"
36"
A
THE 2 STRANDS OF THE OVERHAND KNOT MAKE THE 40TH PAIR.
36"
A
4 JUTE (INCLUDING STRANDS FROM OVERHAND KNOT)
3 JUTE
2 CONTRAST
3 JUTE

2. PUT THE CORDS LABELED: 4 JUTE INSIDE THE POT.

3. MACRAMÉ THE 4 REMAINING GROUPS OF CORDS [3 JUTE 2 CONTRAST 3 JUTE] INDIVIDUALLY WITH 4 ROWS OF SQUARE KNOTS

4. JOIN THE LEFT AND RIGHT PAIRS OF EACH GROUP (FROM STEP 3.) WITH 3 SQUARE KNOTS.

5. JOIN THE NEXT LEFT AND RIGHT PAIRS OF EACH GROUP AND MACRAMÉ 2 SQUARE KNOTS WITH THE STRANDS OF STEP 4 — RETAINING THE SAME CENTER CORDS.

6. JOIN THE NEXT LEFT AND RIGHT PAIRS BENEATH THE SQUARE KNOTS OF STEP 5 BY

KNOTTING 2 ROWS OF SQUARE KNOTS (EACH KNOT HAVING 4 CORDS)

7. WORKING WITH EACH GROUP (FROM STEP 6) INDIVIDUALLY, TWIRL THE 3 SUBGROUPS OF 4 STRANDS SEPARATELY WITH 20 HALF KNOTS.

8. JOIN THE 3 TWIRL LENGTH WITH 7 LARGE SQUARE KNOTS — USING THE CENTER PAIR OF GUIDE CORDS OF THE LEFT & RIGHT TWIRL LENGTHS TO KNOT (AS THEY ARE LONGER.)

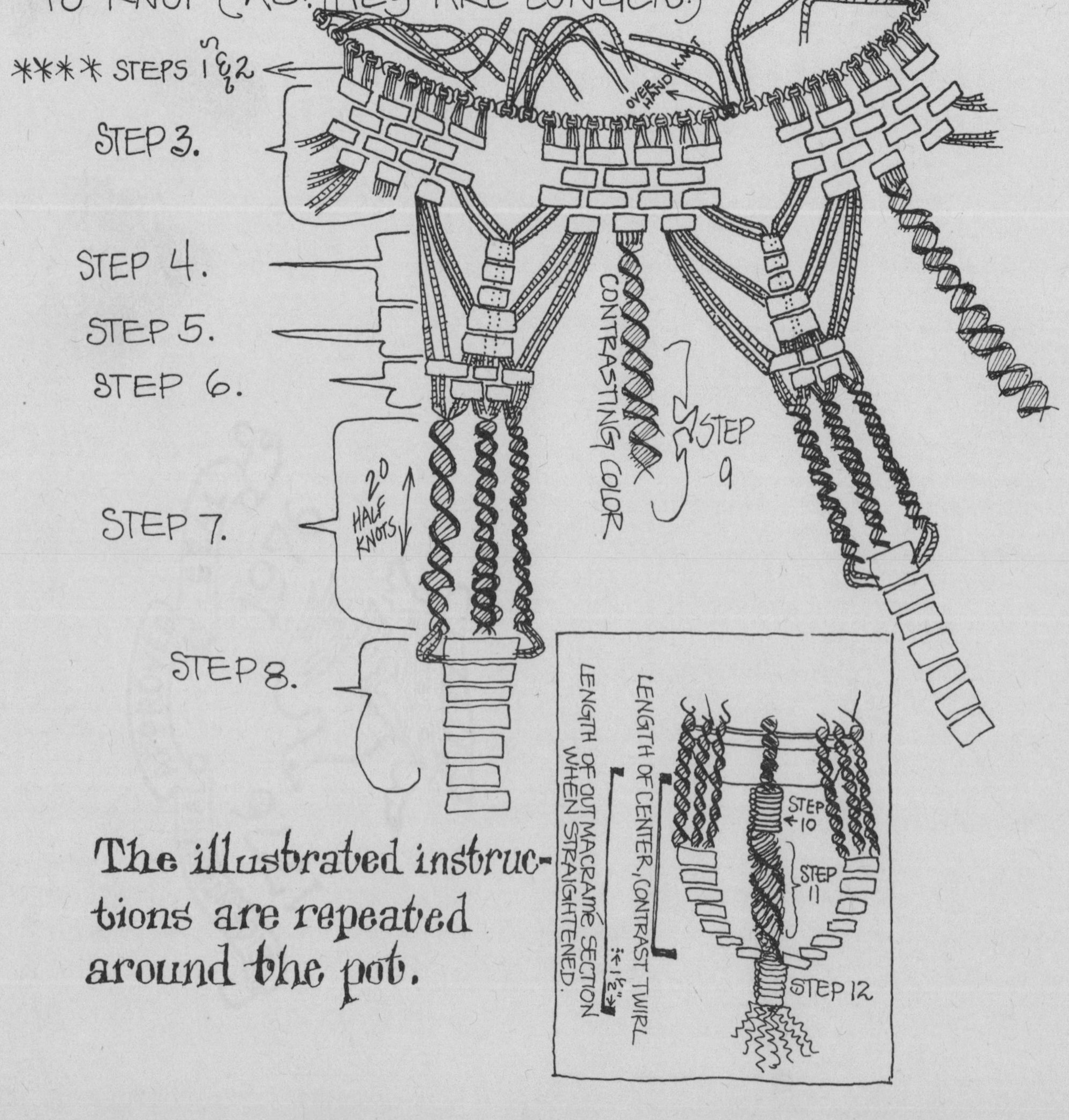
*** STEPS 1 & 2
STEP 3.
OVERHAND KNOT
STEP 4.
STEP 5.
STEP 6.
CONTRASTING COLOR
STEP 9
STEP 7.
20 HALF KNOTS
STEP 8.
LENGTH OF CENTER, CONTRAST TWIRL
LENGTH OF OUT MACRAMÉ SECTION WHEN STRAIGHTENED.
≈ 1½"
STEP 10
STEP 11
STEP 12

The illustrated instructions are repeated around the pot.

9. TWIRL THE REMAINING 4 GROUPS OF CONTRASTING COLOR STRANDS WITH ENOUGH HALF KNOTS TO FORM A LENGTH EXTENDING ^ THE SIDE OF POT & PLATE, & CENTER OF PLATE BOTTOM.

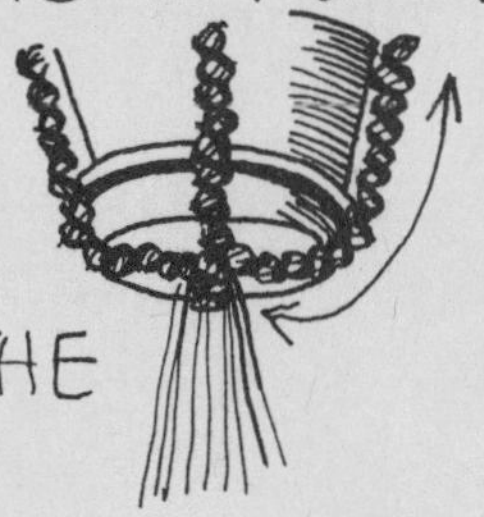

10. GATHER THE CONTRASTING CORDS AT THE CENTER BOTTOM AND ATTACH A 30 INCH LONG STRAND FOLDED: 6" 24" AROUND THE CORDS WITH A LARK'S HEAD. (with contrasting color)

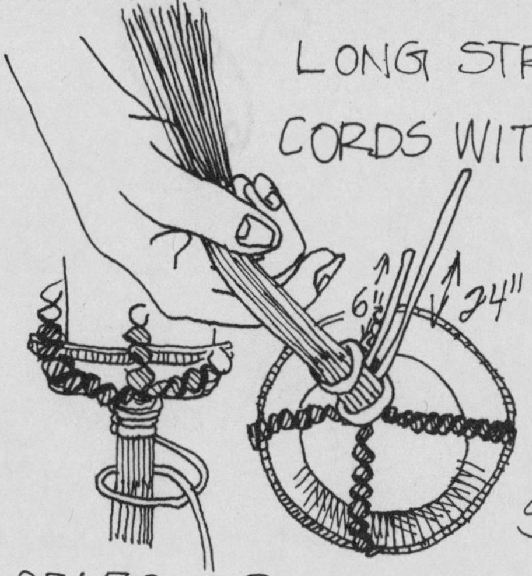
6"
24"

CLOVE HITCH THIS NEW STRAND (INCLUDING THE 6 IN. LENGTH IN WITH THE CONTRAST BUNCH) UNTIL THE STRAND IS ABOUT 3 INCHES SHORT.

11. SELECT 2 PAIRS OF LONGER CONTRASTING COLOR STRANDS AND TWIRL THE BUNCH OF CORDS WITH HALF KNOTS, ABOUT 3 INCHES. **NOTE:** LENGTH OF THIS SHOULD BE ABOUT 1½ INCHES SHORTER THAN THE OUTER 4 MACRAMÉ GROUPS)

12. BRING **ALL** STRANDS TOGETHER (OUTER MACRAMÉ SHOULD CURVE OUT A BIT.) ATTACH A STRAND 6" 24" WITH A LARKS HEAD, AS IN STEP 10... CLOVE HITCH & PULL THE LAST 3 INCHES BACK INTO THE WRAPPING. TRIM ENDS & UNRAVEL.

13. TWIRL THE 4 REMAINING GROUPS OF 4 STRANDS EACH, INDIVIDUALLY, WITH HALF KNOTS TO THE DESIRED HANGING LENGTH; ADD ON STRANDS OF CONTRASTING COLOR WHEN NEEDED.

14. JOIN THE STRANDS OF STEP 13. WITH AN OVERHAND KNOT (SEE PAGE 148).

Design 3

POT SIZE:

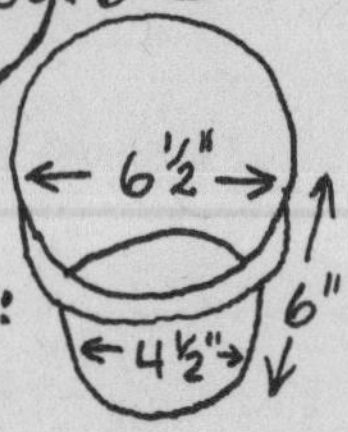
6½"
4½"
6"

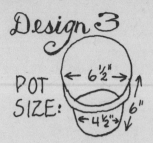

Uses baling twine — hanging pot macramé placed in dye bath (hot or cold type) and soaked for 1 hour; rinse, air dry.

Uses approximately 205 feet of cord.

SWEDISH IVY

1. JOIN 12 STRANDS OF 14 FEET (7' ∩ 7'), BY USING ONE OF THE STRANDS TO TIE AN OVERHAND KNOT AT CENTER ... AND SECURE KNOT TO DRAINAGE HOLE OF POT WITH A PAPER CLIP (FOR BOTH DIRECTIONS, SEE PAGE 146.)
2. SEPARATE CORDS INTO 6 GROUPS OF 4 STRANDS EACH. SQUARE KNOT EACH GROUP AT THE BOTTOM EDGE OF POT, ALLOWING LEFT AND RIGHT STRANDS TO CURVE →

3. SQUARE KNOT AROUND THE POT, 2 ROWS. LEAVE ENOUGH EXTRA SPACE BETWEEN SQUARE KNOTS TO ALLOW FOR USE OF A POT PLATE.

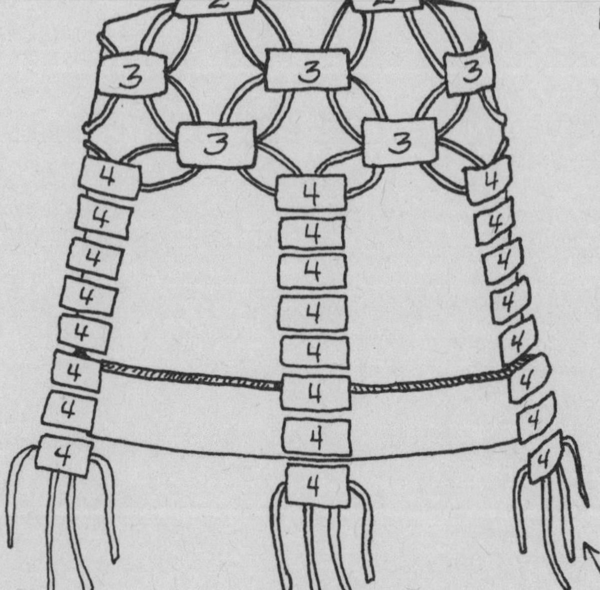

4. TIE 8 SQUARE KNOTS USING 4 STRANDS, TO EACH OF THE 6 GROUPS... THESE LENGTHS WILL BE USED TO FORM A VARIATION OF THE SQUARE KNOT BUTTON.

STEP NUMBERS ON SQUARE KNOT SYMBOL ▭.

5. WITH EACH SQUARE KNOT LENGTH, BRING THE 2 LEFT CORDS THRU THE OPENING TO THE LEFT & THE 2 RIGHT CORDS THRU THE OPENING TO THE RIGHT, AS SHOWN:

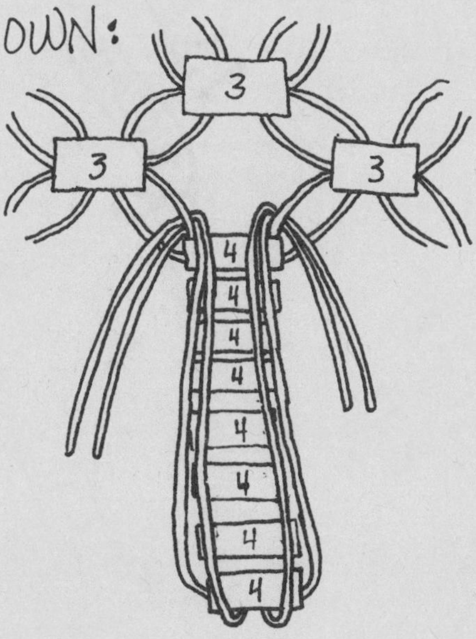
3
3
3
4
4
4
4
4
4
4
4

PULL STRANDS TO FORM A LOOP:

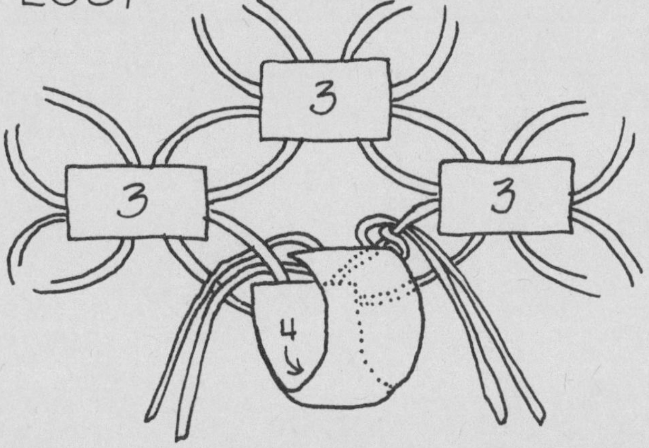
3
3
3
4

6. SECURE EACH SQUARE KNOT BUTTON-LOOP WITH A SQUARE KNOT UNDER THE LOOP, (USE LONGER CORDS TO KNOT).

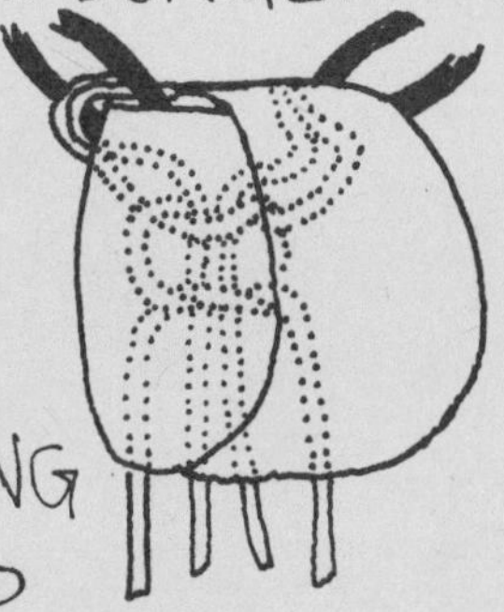

7. MAKE ANOTHER ROW OF LOOPS, REPEATING STEPS 4 & 5 & 6.

8. ON THIS ROW, REPEAT LOOP-MAKING (STEPS 4 & 5 & 6), **BUT** LOOP EVERY OTHER GROUP OF 4 STRANDS (THERE WILL BE 3 LOOPS).

9. JOIN THE 2 STRANDS TO THE LEFT & 2 STRANDS TO THE RIGHT OF EACH LOOP WITH THE LOOP'S STRANDS, BY ADDING A CORD OF 150 INCHES (6" | 144") WITH A LARK'S HEAD. CLOVE HITCH THE 3 GROUPS TO DESIRED HANGING LENGTH. WITH 1 OF THE CORDS, CLOVE HITCH GROUPS TOGETHER AT TOP; INSERT CORD BACK INTO WRAP; TRIM.

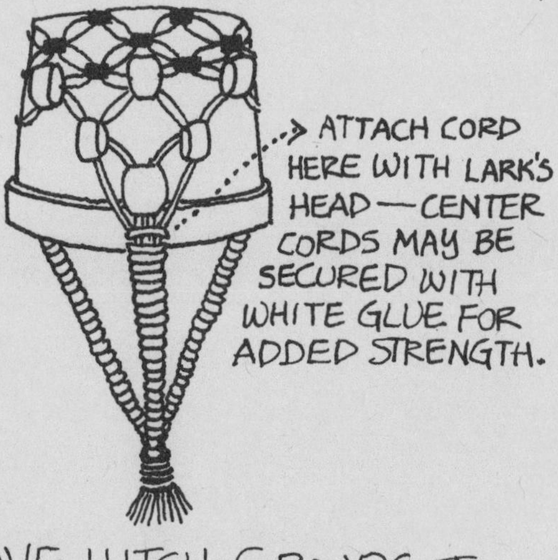
ATTACH CORD HERE WITH LARK'S HEAD — CENTER CORDS MAY BE SECURED WITH WHITE GLUE FOR ADDED STRENGTH.

Design 4

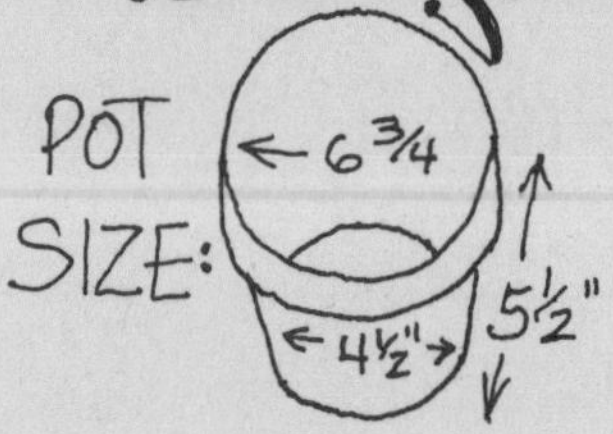
POT
SIZE:
6 3/4
4 1/2"
5 1/2"

USES 3-PLY JUTE
USES APPROXIMATELY
347 FEET OF CORD

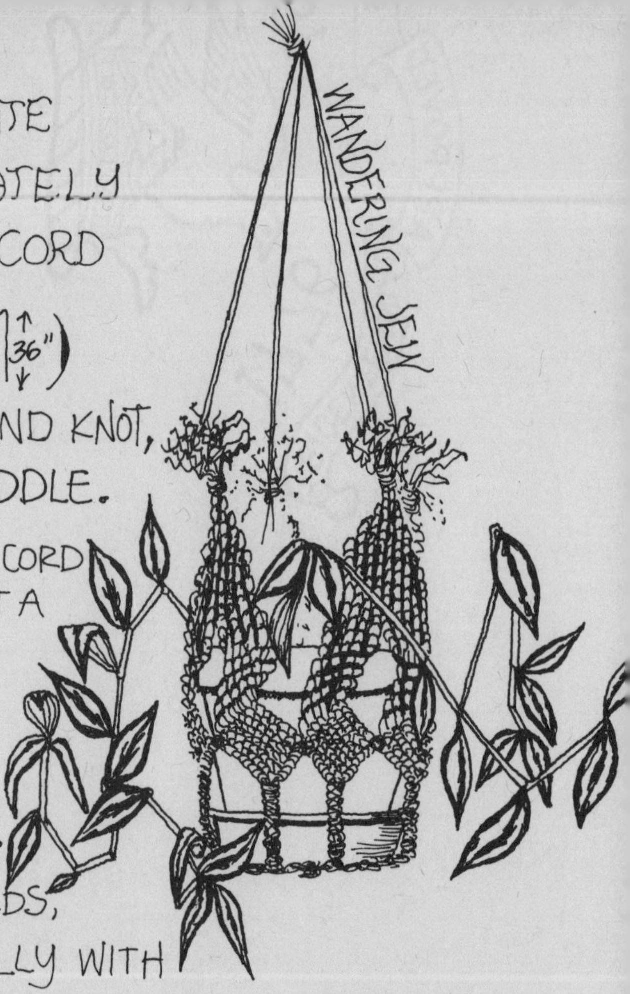
WANDERING JEW

1. TIE 16 CORDS OF 72 INCHES (36" | 36") TOGETHER WITH A SINGLE OVERHAND KNOT, AT MIDDLE.

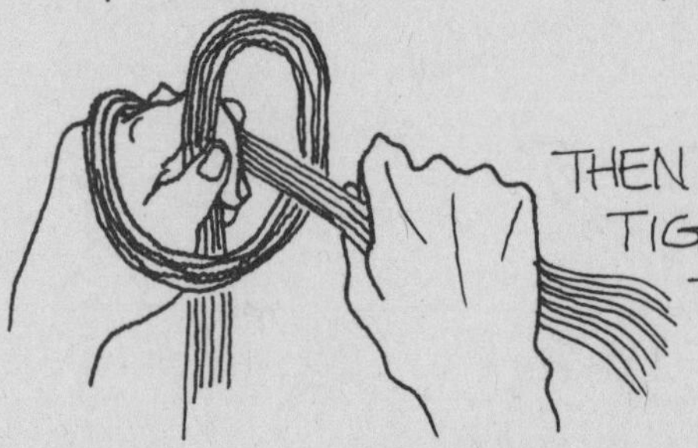

THEN PULL EACH CORD TIGHT, ONE AT A TIME.

ATTACH THIS CENTER KNOT TO THE DRAINAGE HOLE OF POT AS ON PG. 146.

2. WORKING WITH GROUPS OF 4 CORDS, MACRAMÉ EACH GROUP INDIVIDUALLY WITH 11 SQUARE KNOTS (THIS WILL ENABLE USE OF A POT PLATE.)
3. KEEPING THE SQUARE KNOT LENGTHS EVENLY SPACED AROUND THE POT, TIE THE LEFT 2 CORDS TO THE RIGHT 2 CORDS OF THE LENGTH (TO ITS LEFT), AS SHOWN, WITH AN OVERHAND KNOT.

4. ADD 4 CORDS OF 48 INCHES EACH (24" | 24") WITH THE LARK'S HEAD TO EACH LEFT 2 CORDS ABOVE KNOT (FROM STEP 3).
5. ADD 1 CORD OF 52 INCHES (26" | 26") WITH A LARK'S HEAD TO THE RIGHT 2 CORDS, BENEATH THE LAST SQUARE KNOT (FROM STEP 2). CLOVE HITCH THIS GUIDE CORD TO THE LEFT, RIGHT, & LEFT, WRAPPING THE 4 STRANDS OF THE OVERHAND KNOT TO THE LEFT, ALSO... (A TOTAL OF 7 WRAPPED LINES PER SECTION)

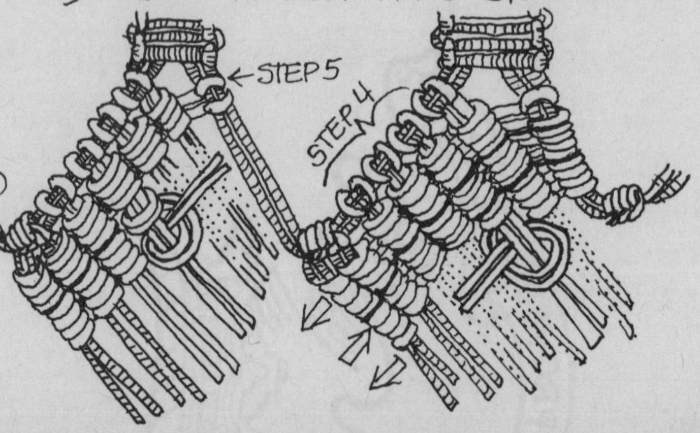
STEP 5
STEP 4

6. USING THE 6 PAIRS OF LOOSE STRANDS OF EACH MACRAMÉ SECTION, TIE 4 ROWS OF CONSECUTIVE CLOVE HITCH. INCLUDE THE SHORT ENDS OF THE GUIDE CORD (FROM STEP 5) IN WITH THE GUIDE CORD ON THE LAST WRAP OF EACH CONSECUTIVE CLOVE HITCH.

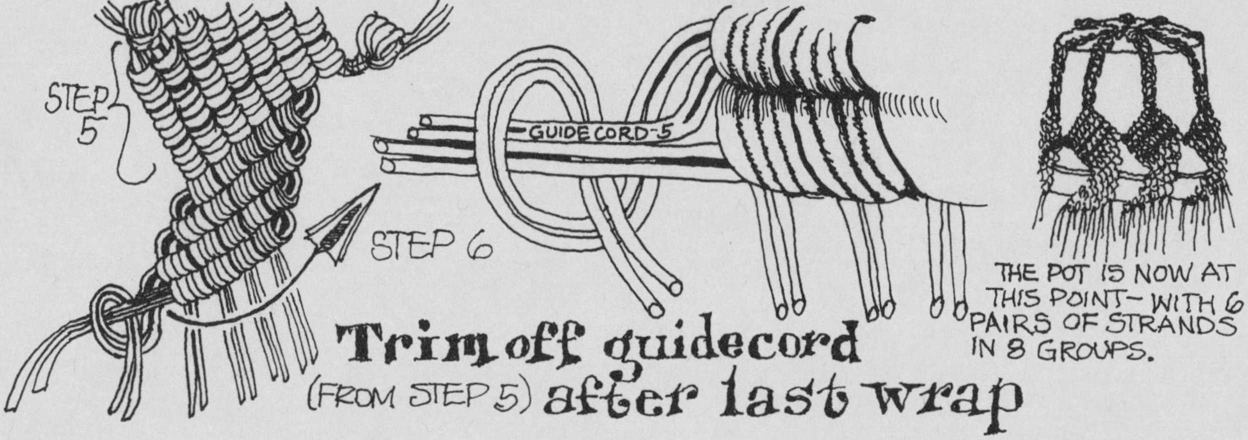
STEP 5
STEP 6
GUIDE CORD-5
Trim off guidecord
(FROM STEP 5) after last wrap
THE POT IS NOW AT THIS POINT– WITH 6 PAIRS OF STRANDS IN 8 GROUPS.

7. THE 8 GROUPS OF MACRAMÉ WILL NOW BE PAIRED OFF AND AND CLOVE HITCHED FORMING 4 MACRAMÉ SECTIONS. ADD A GUIDE CORD OF 28 FEET (14' ∩ 14') WITH A LARK'S HEAD TO THE FAR LEFT PAIR OF STRANDS OF THE 4 MACRAMÉ SECTIONS.

NOTE: *In the actual macramé, the clove hitches are close together.*

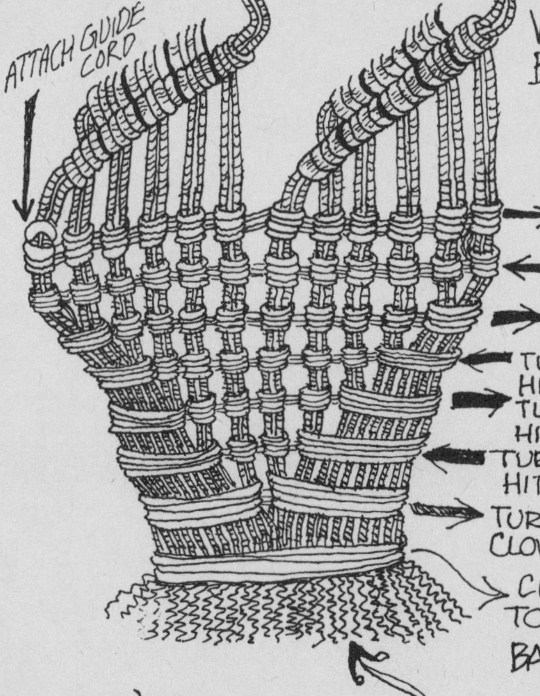
ATTACH GUIDE CORD

WIND UP THE GUIDE CORD IN A RUBBER BAND FOR EASIER HANDLING.*

BENEATH THE LARK'S HEAD OF THE GUIDE CORD, KNOT A HALFHITCH.

→ CLOVE HITCH TO THE RIGHT.
TURN GUIDE CORD UNDER AND TO LEFT.

← CLOVE HITCH RIGHT PAIR OF STRANDS AGAIN & CLOVE HITCH TO LEFT.

→ TURN GUIDE CORD UNDER AND TO RIGHT; CLOVE HITCH 2 PAIRS ON LEFT AND RIGHT.

← TURN GUIDE CORD UNDER AND TO LEFT; CLOVE HITCH 3 PAIRS ON LEFT AND RIGHT.

→ TURN GUIDE CORD UNDER AND TO RIGHT; CLOVE HITCH 4 PAIRS ON LEFT AND RIGHT.

← TURN GUIDE CORD UNDER AND TO LEFT; CLOVE HITCH 5 PAIRS ON LEFT AND RIGHT.

→ TURN GUIDE CORD UNDER AND TO RIGHT; CLOVE HITCH 6 PAIRS ON LEFT AND RIGHT.

→ CLOVE HITCH ALL 12 PAIRS OF STRANDS TOGETHER — PULL GUIDE CORD TO CENTER BACK AND SECURE WITH AN OVERHAND KNOT.

8. TRIM & UNRAVEL ENDS. USING GUIDE CORDS AS HANGING CORDS, OVERHAND KNOT AT DESIRED LENGTH.

VERY MISCELLANEOUS

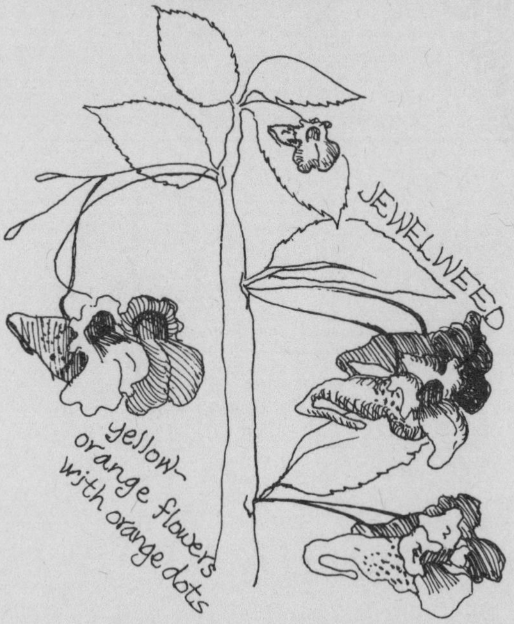
JEWELWEED
yellow-orange flowers with orange dots

Jewelweed's juice (from leaves and stem) is a good remedy for poison ivy — they often grow near each other.

1. Press flowers or leaves of fall between the pages of a book. Small flowers such as jewelweed will dry flat in a few days.

Larger flowers can be sprinkled with cornmeal to aid in proper drying.

Paste the pressed flowers or leaves with white glue onto notepaper, cards or porous material objects such as wooden boxes (objects should be spray shellacked for permanency.)

2. My friend, David, made me a shelf for for my last birthday. He took a length of rough-cut oak, planed it down, sanded and varnished it. The beauty of his thought, the process, and the wood makes it one of my most memorable gifts — it's unique and utilitarian.

3. As I sit here at the kitchen table and look up to my left and past the hanging plants to see five golden, shrivelling apples hanging from strings, I can not resist mentioning apple-head dolls. I find such great fascination in watching the heads shrink and wrinkle with humorous realism.

Wild apples should be used rather than paying the outrageous supermarket prices. Peel apples and cut out simple facial forms - at least eyes and nose. Sew string through to hang. The drying time varies alot, but when the outside is very dry and the head has shrunken noticeably, remove the string and replace with a ══ - shape of sturdy wire (for body + legs) and wind another length of wire around the first (for the arms.) Make clothes for the doll, padding around the wire with cotton. Add small beads for eyes or other added details.

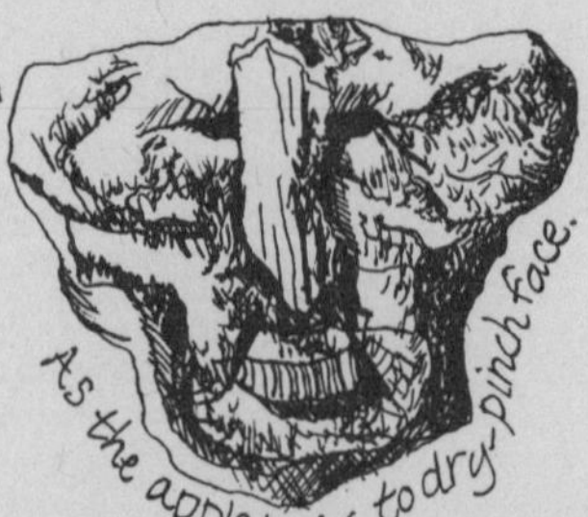

As the apple begins to dry - pinch face.

4. Make hot plates using the directions for the base of macramé baskets (page 119).

5. Cut a 2"x 2" length of pine to 2" for making baby blocks. Stain the wood (with your homemade black walnut stain!) and découpage cut-outs or drawings — burn edges of paper slightly if desired, paste onto wood with white glue, then varnish. I made one a few years ago for a dear young man named Kenneth, with personal, just-between-you & me drawings on the cube. The cube is still around - in our living room.

6. A lovely lady named Debbie makes crochet baskets with lids - gluing an unshelled walnut on the top of the lid. She completely cleans her black walnut shells, using steel wool, and fills the basket. The beauty of jute & walnut is soothing.

Lettering

The following pages of lettering for use with arts & crafts processes and much of the lettering used for titles in this book utilize the SPEEDBALL TEXTBOOK (Edited by Charles Stoner and Henry Frankenfield; Phila., Pa.: Huntmanufacturing Co., 1972.) as a guide. The Speedball Textbook is an excellent source for pen & brush lettering, although it is applicable for use with other drawing tools, as well as embroidery, appliqué, and other media.

ABCDE
FGHIJK
LMNOP
QRSTU
VWXYZ

GOTHIC

To ENLARGE lettering or any designs in this book, make a grid on tracing paper or other thin paper and trace lines onto the grid. The make a larger grid of desired size and repeat the line segments of each square on the larger scale. When lettering free-hand, always lightly pencil in the letters first; OR, when possible, measure lines and sketch letters on paper with a dark pen and trace onto the 'final' paper with the desired media.

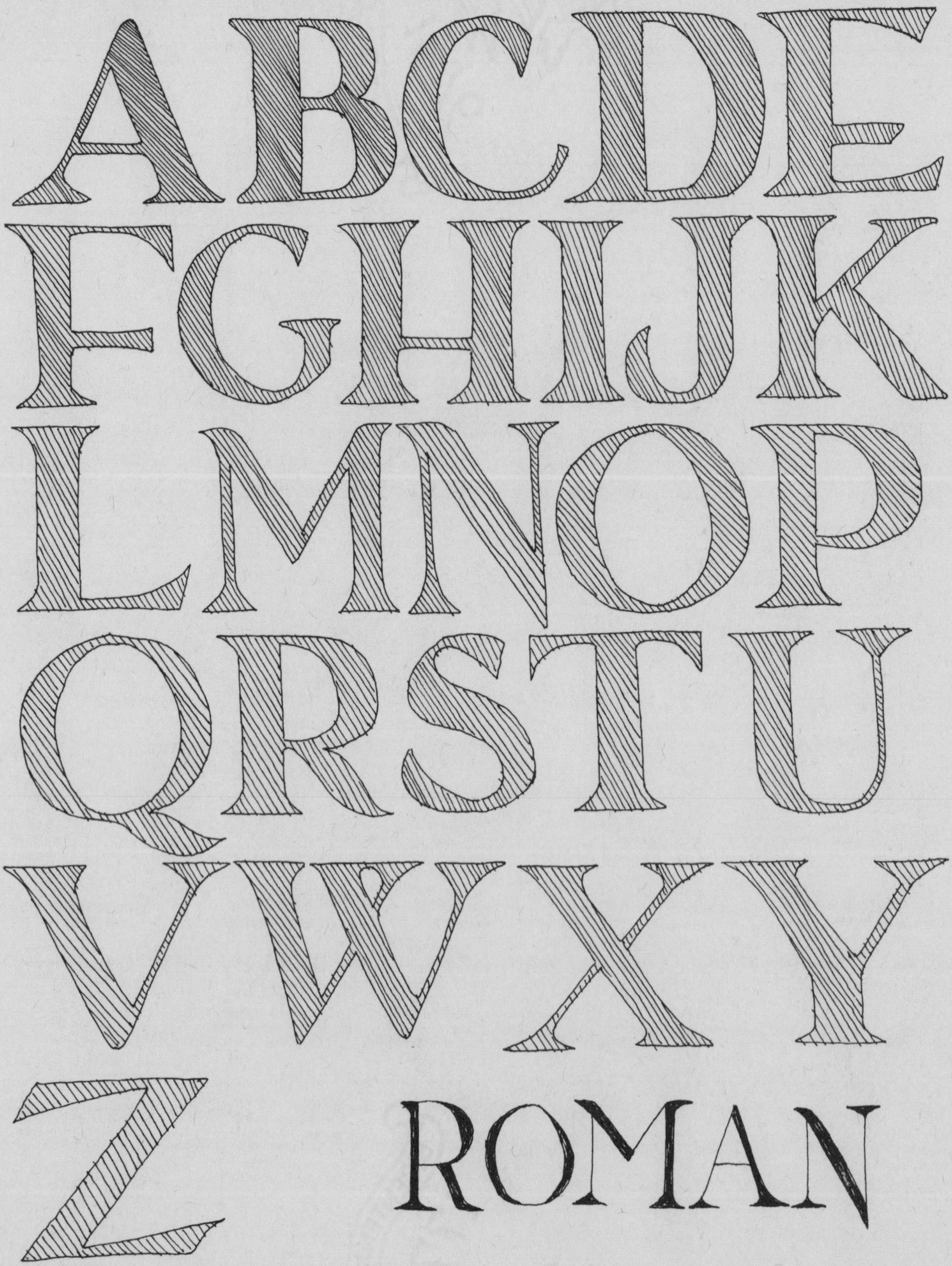
ABCDE
FGHIJK
LMNOP
QRSTU
VWXY
Z

ROMAN

A B C D E F G

H I J K L M N

O P Q R S T U

V W X Y Z

a b c d e f g h i j k

l m n o p q r s t u

v w x y z

Old English

Bibliography

Adrosko, Rita J. Natural Dyes and Home Dyeing. New York: Dover Publications, Inc., 1971.

Becker, Marion Rombauer, and Irma S. Rombauer. Joy of Cooking (paperback edition). Indianapolis: The Bobbs-Merrill Company, Inc., 1964.

Crockett, James Underwood, and the Editors of Time-Life Books. Foliage House Plants. New York: Time, Inc., 1972.

Crowhurst, Adrienne. The Weed Cookbook. New York: Lancer Books, Inc., 1972.

DiNoto, Andrea (ed. of KILN section). The Family Creative Workshop, No. 8. New York: Plenary Publications, Inc., 1974.

Dylon International Limited. Dylon Cold Dyes. London.

Frankenfield, Henry, and Charles Stoner (eds.). Speedball Textbook for pen and brush lettering. Philadelphia: Hunt Manufacturing Co., 1972.

Gibbons, Euell. Stalking the Healthful Herbs. New York: David McKay and Company, Inc., 1966.

Guinness, Jim, and Sandy Guinness. Homemade Granola (Natural Recipes Series). Jamaica Plain, MA.: Natural Recipes, 1973.

Hardwick, Homer. Winemaking at Home (paperback addition). New York: Cornerstone Library, 1972.

Hires Division, Crush International. Hires Rootbeer Extract Recipe (in partial form). Evanston, Illinois.

H.J. Heinz Company. Quick Pickling. Pittsburgh, Penna., 1972.

Jagendorf, M.A. Folk Wines, Cordials, and Brandies. New York: The Vanguard Press, Inc., 1963.

Kramer, Jack. Natural Dyes, Plants, and Processes. New York: Charles Scribner's Sons, 1972.

Lust, John. The Herb Book (paperback edition). New York: Bantam Books, Inc., 1974.

Mann, Gladys. Home Wine and Beer Making. London: Octopus Books, Limited, 1974.

McKenny, Margaret, and Roger Tory Peterson. A Field Guide to Wildflowers. Boston: Houghton Mifflin Company, 1968.

Meilach, Dona Z. Macramé - Creative Design in Knotting. New York: Crown Publishers, Inc., 1972.

Meyer, Joseph E. The Herbalist. (9th printing). Hammond, Indiana: Publication of the Indiana Botanic Garden, 1972.

Nu-Flex Company. How to Braid a Rug in One Day. St. Petersburg, Florida.

Rit Consumer Service Laboratory, Best Foods Division, CPC International. The Art of Easy Batik. Indianapolis.

Stoner, Carol (ed.) and the Editors of Organic Gardening and Farming. Stocking Up - How to Preserve the Foods You Grow, Naturally. Emmaus, Penna.: Rodale Press, Inc., Book Division, 1975.

Urdang, Laurence (editor-in-chief). The Random House College Dictionary. New York: Random House, Inc., 1973.

U.S. Dept. of Agriculture. The Complete Guide to Home Canning, Preserving, and Freezing. New York: Dover Publications, Inc., 1973.

Wilson, Erica. Crewel Embroidery Stitch Chart (Hiawatha pamphlet, No. 4). New York: Heirloom Needlework Guild, Inc., n.d.

ACKNOWLEDGMENTS

I wish to give a special thanks to the following people who shared their knowledge and enthusiasm.

Kenneth Abeles
Mary Fox
Edward Kindness
Kōsai Kobari
Al Jenkins
Deborah Valentour
Fran Schoemaker
Cindy Thorpe

INDEX

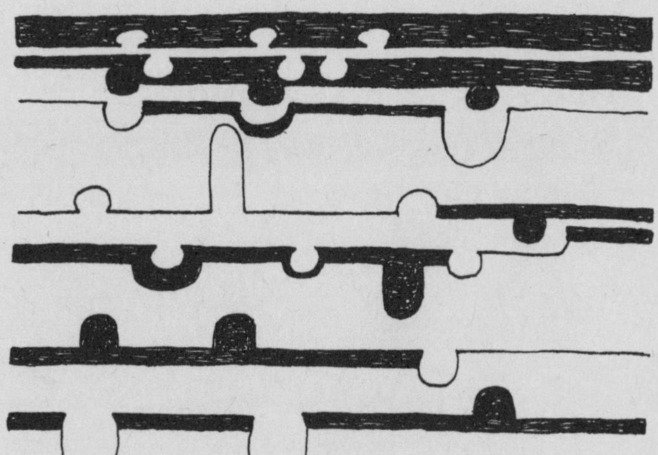

Crafts, Cookery, and Country Living is a handbook of scores of art, craft, and culinary projects you can make for yourself, your home, or your friends. Nature and the gifts of the countryside are blended here with the creative experience. Those who live on the land are encouraged to use natural supplies, but whether you use natural or manufactured materials, this guide will introduce you to activities of the senses and new experiences to stimulate further involvement in artistic and living endeavors. These are activities which Ms. Abeles has learned and experimented and fused with her life, and collected together because of a desire to express and share a bit of beauty and knowledge.

Kim Victoria Abeles graduated from Ohio University with a BFA in painting in 1974. She and her husband, Ken, live in a converted three-story concrete grain silo near Athens, Ohio, partaking in the delights of country living and learning. The silo is consistently flowing with creative gestures of wide assortment. Stitchery, macramé, woodcut prints, poetry, cookery, reading, painting, and experimentation with new media form the thread of Ms. Abeles' lifestyle. As a professional painter, she is a member of the Associated artists of Pittsburgh, and her work has been recognized in various exhibitions in Ohio and Pennsylvania.

Kim Victoria Abeles 76